Layers of Learning Language Arts

Writer's Workshop
A Family-Style Writing Program

Michelle Copher and Karen Loutzenhiser

Published by HooDoo Publishing
United States of America
© 2020 Layers of Learning

ISBN 978-1-7360624-0-1

Guidebook: How to Create a Writer's Workshop

Learn the philosophy behind Writer's Workshop, the writing process, and how to evaluate writing.

Also, find tips for setting up student notebooks and journals, learn about which writing supplies to have on hand, and understand your role as a parent or mentor within your Writer's Workshop.

Word Work

This spelling, vocabulary, and root word program is for kids of all ages up through high school. This program utilizes hands-on learning techniques, games, and lots of printables to make spelling fun and effective. It includes all of the lists and activities you need to become word whizzes together as a family.

Research Paper

This is a unit dedicated to writing a five to eight page research paper. Research Paper will help high school kids prepare for college writing and is intended for teens, ages fifteen years and up. This is a self-guided book the teen uses in a semester-long writing project.

How To Use This Guide

Writer's Workshop is a family-style program, which means your whole family, from ages six to eighteen and beyond, can use the program together. The activities are meant to be a family affair, with individual expectations being tailored to the ages and abilities of each child. We also encourage you to share completed individual work, like reports, posters, stories, and other writing projects, with one another in share-and-clap sessions.

Like all of Layers of Learning, Writer's Workshop is a pick-and-choose curriculum; you don't need to complete everything in the book. Instead, browse through and choose the Mini-Lessons and Exercises that appeal to you and are appropriate for your kids. For a more detailed look at Writer's Workshop, we invite you to read *Guidebook: How to Create a Writer's Workshop*, which you can find at Layers-of-Learning.com.

Scheduling

In general, each unit within this book is designed to last about a month and then be repeated in subsequent years, but the exact schedule and timing are completely up to you. If your kids are engaged and enthusiastic about a topic, feel free to carry on for a little while longer.

Writer's Workshop should be a daily part of your homeschool. In Writer's Workshop, each Exercise is one complete lesson plan. The exact length of each one varies and depends on your needs, the ages of the students, and how absorbed in a lesson you get. However, you can generally plan on one hour per lesson. Lessons can stretch over multiple days as needed.

Sidebars

You will find sidebars throughout Writer's Workshop. The sidebars are short Mini-Lessons about grammar, mechanics, writing skills, or a genre skill. The Mini-Lesson should be taught to all ages and abilities of students at once, as a group. Insert a Mini-Lesson before each Exercise at the beginning of your Writer's Workshop session.

Printable Packs

This curriculum includes printables. For printing convenience and to keep your costs down, the printables are found in digital Printable Packs that you can retrieve from the Layers of Learning catalog.

The Printable Packs are free with coupon code: FREEPACK.

Resources

Every unit comes with its own YouTube playlist of videos to use as enrichment or as video lectures to supplement lessons. The videos can be played at the beginning of a lesson as an introduction or as a Mini-Lesson.

On the Layers of Learning website, you can also find links to websites and resources that are especially useful when teaching each unit. The web links are located in the catalog on each guide's product page.

At Layers of Learning, we believe learning is about exploring and we invite you to joyfully explore with us. In the words of Robert Louis Stevenson: "The world is so full of a number of things, I'm sure we should all be as happy as kings."

What's In This Guide?

Key Concepts

By the end of this unit your kids should be familiar with these concepts and ideas:

Writer's Notebooks

Journals

Fiction versus nonfiction

The parts of speech (nouns, verbs, pronouns, adjectives, adverbs, prepositions, conjunctions, interjections)

Steps of the writing process (prewriting, drafting, revising, editing, and publishing)

The six traits of writing (ideas and content, organization, word choice, sentence fluency, conventions, and voice)

Authors and illustrators

More Mini-Lesson Ideas

Along with the sidebars, try these mini-lesson ideas:

- Writer's Workshop links found in Layers of Learning catalog
- Lessons from any grammar workbook
- Every-Day Edits from Education World website
- Sentence diagramming
- Copying great sentences from master writers
- Mad Libs
- Correcting a repeated error from your writing
- Practicing expanding sentences by adding details
- Combining sentences by making two or three into a single sentence

The mini-lesson sidebars in this unit have check boxes so you can keep track of which ones you have completed.

Writer's Workshop Jump Start

Use this unit at the beginning of each school year to help get your creative juices flowing, practice the writing process, settle into your Writer's Notebook, and orient yourself with Writer's Workshop. Keep the exercises and any writing you do in your Writer's Notebook so you can look back over them when you need ideas or inspiration for writing.

Much like an artist's sketchbook, your Writer's Notebook, and especially the Journal section within it, is a place for you to capture ideas, be creative, and express yourself. Your journal entries and the exercises do not all need to be polished, perfected work. They will help you generate ideas and learn writing concepts. If there is one that strikes your interest, you may want to take it through the writing process and make a polished, published piece of writing.

Within this unit, you'll be making lots of lists of things that interest you. Many of these could be terrific topics for you to write about later since they are things that matter to you. Most of your writing will go in the Journal section of your Writer's Notebook. Add any of the idea lists you create to the Ideas section of your Writer's Notebook. When you are looking for ideas, you can always look back through the Journal and Ideas sections of your Writer's Notebook.

Step 1: Mini-Lesson

After handwriting or typing practice has concluded, begin each day of Writer's Workshop with a mini-lesson. You will find some within the sidebars of this unit. You can also use a worksheet from a grammar workbook or practice editing, copying, or diagramming sentences. During writing time, watch for weak areas or mistakes being made and present a mini-lesson the next day to help correct those and improve writing skills in small, continuous ways.

The mini-lesson should take five to ten minutes and always have a positive, happy spin, free from criticism. Not every mini-lesson needs to be kept in your Writer's Notebook. Most are merely for practice.

Step 2: Writing

Now it's time to really begin writing. Most of your time during Writer's Workshop should be spent writing. Practicing is the key to improving. You can use your writing time to free write your own ideas in your Journal anytime, or use the exercises below to practice writing skills and find inspiration for things to write about. Select as many exercises as you would like to do over the month, making sure you leave

time to complete at least one writing project that will go all of the way through the writing process before the month is over. The exercises will also go in your Journal section of your Writer's Notebook. If you decide to take something from your Journal through the writing process and turn it into your writing project, move it from your Journal to the Writing section of your Writer's Notebook.

A few tips and reminders:

- You can repeat the units and the exercises in subsequent years, so don't ever feel pressured to get to all of them, and feel free to repeat ones you enjoy.
- Often a single exercise can be presented to all of your children, no matter their ages or abilities. They will naturally write at the level they are at and, as they practice, will grow as writers.
- As you progress through the exercises, watch for something that sparks interest and could become the writing project. Feel free to jump to the idea bank at the end of the unit anytime as well. If there's spare time after the project is published, return to more exercises.
- Your family may all be in different places in the writing process. That's perfectly fine. Remember, your Writer's Workshop is a garden and everyone is growing their own patch. You can all lend a hand to help each gardener's patch thrive, but you won't all grow the same crop.

It's time to write! Choose some exercises and jump right in!

Jump Starts

EXERCISE: My Goals

Draw a picture of yourself holding a piece of paper. Write down at least three school goals you have this year. They might be goals you have as a writer, things you hope to learn about, or things that can help you to be a stronger student.

Add the page to the Journal section of your Writer's Notebook. The pages you add to your Writer's Notebook can give you ideas for things you would like to write

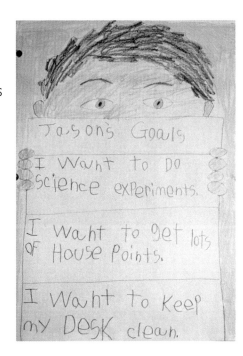

☐ Mini-Lesson

If you write every day, you'll get better at writing every day. The activities in Writer's Workshop are called exercises because, like exercise builds endurance and muscles, daily writing builds writing stamina and skills. Use your writing time well. Wasting time creates waste, but writing creates writers.

Set a timer for one minute and write as much as you can without stopping. Increase this exercise by one additional minute each day you successfully complete it until you can write in spurts of at least five minutes without stopping. Five-minute non-stop writing sessions are called quick writes.

Five-minute quick writes are excellent prewriting tools for generating ideas, getting drafts started, and overcoming writer's block.

☐ Mini-Lesson

If something seems boring to you, it is boring to your reader too. You should write about things you care about as often as you can. As a prewriting activity, make a list of things you care about. When you're looking for ideas, go back to your list. Many of these exercises are actually idea generators. You are writing about things that matter to you. If something interests you, chances are, others will be interested too.

☐ Mini-Lesson

Take a tour of your Writer's Notebook and its sections - Journal, Writing, Word Work, Writing Helps, and Ideas. Talk about what belongs in each section.

See "Guidebook: How to Create a Writer's Workshop" at Layers-of-Learning.com for information on how to set up Writer's Notebooks.

☐ Mini-Lesson

Design a custom cover for your Writer's Notebook. Let your personality shine through in everything you write. Be YOU.

☐ Mini-Lesson

The Journal section of your Writer's Notebook is for your eyes only, unless you ask someone to read it.

Grammar and spelling don't matter in your Journal. It's a place for you to write freely without worries. The entries can be exercises, story ideas, thoughts, experiences, or anything else.

If you haven't added anything to your Journal section yet, do a quick write. A quick write is when you set a timer and write for five minutes without stopping.

☐ Mini-Lesson

The Ideas section of your notebook is there as a resource. You can make as many idea lists as you want. You will also add printable idea banks as you learn new writing genres.

about in the future. For example, you might like to revisit this page later and write a journal entry about how well you did at accomplishing your goals. If you struggled, you might write a plan for how you can keep working on them.

EXERCISE: In My Head or In My Heart

On a piece of card stock, draw either a big outline of a head or a big outline of a heart that fills the page. Thumb through magazines to look for things that are either in your head (things you think about) or in your heart (things you care about). Cut them out and paste them to your card stock outlines, collage-style. Add the page to your Journal. You might want to use one of those ideas to write about later.

EXERCISE: Things I Love

Make a list of things you love. Draw a heart in the center of your page and write "Things I Love" within it.

Use a ruler to make lines extending from the heart to the page border. Write things you love in each section. Younger kids can create fewer sections and write three to ten items while older kids can create more sections to fill with things they love. Include everything from your favorite sports and movies to your top ice cream flavors, colors, holidays, people, and books.

EXERCISE: 15 Things
Use the "15 Things" printable from the Printable Pack to make a list of 15 things you would like to write about or know more about. When you're looking for a topic, you can come back to your list for inspiration. Put this in the Lists section of your Writer's Notebook.

EXERCISE: I Am
Use the "I Am" printable from the Printable Pack. Fill in the letter "I" with descriptions of yourself. Come up with as many ideas as you can that show who you are, what you enjoy, who you are associated with, places you love, personality traits, experiences you have had or hope to have, dreams and goals, and anything else that defines you as a person.

Put it in your Journal. You can use the ideas to help you come up with writing topics later. If you are a football fan, perhaps you'll write a story about a football player.

EXERCISE: Bucket List
Make a bucket list of things you'd like to do before you "kick the bucket." When I was young I made a bucket list that I kept. It's been over twenty years since then and I've accomplished everything on my list aside from one thing - scuba diving on the Great Barrier Reef in Australia. Make a bucket list now and maybe, just maybe, you'll also fill your life with the things you want to do. You can start with filling your writing with the things you want to do. Put your bucket list in your Journal.

EXERCISE: If I Could Go Anywhere
Write a journal entry about a place you would go if you could go anywhere at all. Use the "If I Could Go Anywhere" printable from the Printable Pack.

Describe things you would do and see in your dream destination. Tell about what you might eat, where you might stay, and the activities you would do. In the box, draw a head shot of yourself wearing sunglasses. Draw your destination in the reflection on the lenses.

☐ **Mini-Lesson**

Pronouns take the place of nouns and must match the noun they represent in gender and number.

For example:

"Janet" becomes *she* or *her*. "Miles" becomes *he* or *him*.

"Janet and Miles" becomes *they* or *them*.

Write some sentences that include nouns, then rewrite them using the proper pronouns.

☐ **Mini-Lesson**

Sketching pictures is a good prewriting activity to generate ideas. If you're ever feeling stuck and you aren't sure what you want to write about, try drawing something. Often a picture will spark an idea. Maybe you can draw a character, a setting, something you like, or something you want to research and learn more about.

☐ **Mini-Lesson**

What are your favorite books or stories? What is it that makes them so interesting to you? Do you have a favorite genre? A favorite character?

Try making a list as a prewriting activity. Make a list of at least three to ten things that you like about the books or stories you chose. Add your list to the Journal section of your notebook. Your Journal section can hold any writing that you aren't taking through the writing process right now.

Writer's Workshop

When you are writing about things that belong to someone, use an apostrophe and an s to show possession.

The possessive of a singular noun is formed by adding an apostrophe and an s.

Karla's candy bar

Derek's shirt

The doctor's medicine

The possessive of a plural noun is formed in two ways:

1. By adding only an apostrophe when the noun ends in s

The teachers' notebooks

2. By adding both an apostrophe and an s when it ends in a letter other than s.

Children's toys

Write sentences that include possessives by choosing a subject, stating what he or she owns, then telling about it.

Rover's bone was buried.

☐ **Mini-Lesson**

If more than one person shares possession, use a single apostrophe.

John and Jane's ball

If more than one person each own something, they each get an apostrophe.

France's and Italy's flags

Practice writing some of each of these.

EXERCISE: Your Perfect Day

Make an hour by hour account of your perfect day from the time you wake up in the morning until the time you go to bed each night. Include a specific activity or event that you will do each hour of the day. This doesn't have to be realistic. You can ride the Matterhorn at Disneyland at 9:00 A.M. and see Niagara Falls at 10:00 A.M. on this perfect day, even though that wouldn't be possible in the real world. Put your perfect day in your Journal.

EXERCISE: Yesterday, Today, & Tomorrow

Write one thing you want to always remember about yesterday, one thing you plan to do today, and one thing that you are looking forward to doing tomorrow. Put this in your Journal.

EXERCISE: When I Grow Up

Imagine what you'll be doing in five, ten, fifteen, or twenty years. Write about what you think your life will be like in one or more of these areas:

- Your education
- Your family
- Your job
- Your home
- Your contribution to the world
- Your beliefs
- Your friends
- Your travels
- Your hobbies
- Your car

Put your ideas in your Journal.

EXERCISE: Journaling

No matter what you are working on in Writer's Workshop, you are always free to journal. Journaling is writing down anything that matters to you or anything you're thinking about. You can tell about something that happened to you or just a thought you've been having lately. They can be personal, but they don't have to be. Put your journal entries in your Journal section. They won't be read or evaluated or graded unless you ask for them to be.

Try journaling. Write about anything you would like. Don't worry about making mistakes because your Journal is just for you. Along with the Jump Start Idea Bank at the end of this unit, you'll also find a "Journaling Idea Bank" printable to add to the Ideas section of your Writer's Notebook. In addition, there are more journaling ideas on the "Journal

Jar 1" and "Journal Jar 2" printable strips from the Printable Pack. Add them to your journal jar. Decorate your jar. If you want to journal but can't think of a topic, you can always pull a prompt out of the jar to give you ideas. Set it near your writing area.

EXERCISE: Topic Links

Think of any topic that interests you. Write it down on a paper link that you staple or glue into a circle. Think of another topic that is somehow connected with the first one and write it down on a second link, attaching it to the first. Now, think of a third topic that is related to the last one you added. Keep in mind that it does not directly need to be related to the first topic. Continue adding links to your chain.

Any time you need a topic, you can take a link from your chain and start writing about it.

EXERCISE: Lightning Round

Use the "Lightning Round" printable from the Printable Pack. Circle your choices. At the bottom, create some of your own lightning round options. Put the printable in your Journal.

EXERCISE: Sounds Around the World

Did you know that the sound a dog makes changes depending on what country you're in? Well, the truth is that the dogs sound the same, but we write their sounds differently.

Here are just a few ways a dog's sound can be described in languages around the world:

- English: woof-woof
- Arabic: hau-hau
- Balinese: kong-kong
- Bulgarian: jaff-jaff
- Catalan: bub-bub
- Mandarin Chinese: wang-wang

- German: vow-vow
- Hindi: bow-bow
- Spanish: guau-guau

What sounds have you heard dogs make? Can you write about a dog park and describe what the dogs are saying in a variety of ways?

You can repeat this exercise using other sound effects. Look up some of the ways people around the world describe snoring, sneezing, kissing, eating, drinking, pain sounds (like ouch!), applause, and telling someone to be quiet (shh!). You can also look up other animal sounds from around the world.

Write about situations where these sound effects might be happening and use your own unique sound effect words as you do. Put your ideas in your Journal.

EXERCISE: Ten Word Challenge
Together, brainstorm ten unusual or unique words. Write them where everyone can see them. Try to create a short piece of writing that includes all ten of the words in a cohesive way. If you're up for a tougher challenge, you can do this same activity, except include ten nouns, ten adjectives, ten verbs, and ten adverbs that must all be used in your one piece of writing. Put this in your Journal.

EXERCISE: Authors
Authors are people who write things they share with others. Some authors write as a hobby and others write full-time as a job. Authors write about all kinds of things. Some write comic books while others write stories and still others write cookbooks. Choose a book that you enjoy and find out more about the author who wrote it. Some authors have websites where they share information about themselves, the books they've written, and projects they are working on. If he or she is still living, see if the author you chose has a website.

Most books have a description that tells a little bit about the author. Read a few of them from books you have read, then make your own "About the Author" page using the printable from the Printable Pack. You will be taking writing projects through the writing process throughout this course, and that means you will become an author. The last step of the writing process is publishing, or sharing what you've written, and that will make you an author. As you publish pieces, keep in mind that you can include an "About the Author" page or a short description of yourself. Keep your "About the Author" page in your Journal.

EXERCISE: Illustrations
Read your kids a picture book that has wonderful illustrations, but hide them as you read, not allowing your kids to see the pictures. This works best if it's a book they've never seen before. Mercer Mayer's *Litter Critter* books are great for this exercise, because a lot of the story is told through his illustrations. After you read the story, read it again while showing the pictures this time. Was it any different? What things were revealed through the pictures that the words never said? Talk about what illustrations can do for a story. Write a single sentence on a blank sheet of paper, then add an illustration that tells more of the story. Put this in your Journal.

EXERCISE: Wordless Books
"Read" a wordless book together. Some great options are *A Flying Saucer Full of Spaghetti* by Fernando Krahn, *The Snowman* by Raymond Briggs, and *A Boy, A Dog, and a Frog* by Mercer Mayer. Talk about what is happening in the story as you look at the book; discuss how the illustrations tell the story.

Have your kids create their own wordless book using only illustrations. Before they begin, make sure they tell their story idea out loud so you can help their illustrations stay on track, if needed. Making a storyboard with a beginning/middle/end or a progression of events can help. You will find a "Wordless Book Storyboard" printable in the Printable Pack. Put your ideas in your Journal.

EXERCISE: Growing & Shrinking
Read Maurice Sendak's *Where the Wild Things Are*, paying special attention to his illustrations. Do you notice how as the boy enters into the realm of imagination, the illustrations grow bigger, filling more and more of the page? Write your own story that follows the same format. Begin with a kid who gets in trouble and is sent to his or her bedroom as a punishment. Tell the tale of an imaginary adventure that happens in an imaginary world, all within that very bedroom. As the story goes on, make your pictures fill more and more of the page. When the main character comes back to the reality of his or her bedroom, have the illustrations shrink on the page. Put this in your Journal.

EXERCISE: Fun Words
Words are awesome. They are often funny or just cool. I really love words like *marshmallow* and *flabbergasted* and *superfluous* because they are fun to say. I also really like words that sound smart, like *hypothetical* and *equestrian*

☐ **Mini-Lesson**
Nouns name people, places, and things. Can you find the nouns in this sentence?

***Cliff** eagerly ran up the steep, spiral-shaped **stairs** of the **tower**.*

Make a nouns word bank for the Writing Helps section of your Writer's Notebook.

☐ **Mini-Lesson**
Verbs are words that express action or a state of being. Can you find the verbs in this sentence?

*I **am** a tiny girl, but I can **run** fast like a cheetah.*

Make a verbs word bank to put in your Writing Helps.

☐ **Mini-Lesson**
Pronouns are words that take the place of a noun. He, she, them, her, we, you, us, mine, theirs, yours, it - these are all examples of pronouns. Say ten things you did this morning without using any pronouns.

Make a pronouns word bank to put in your Writing Helps.

☐ **Mini-Lesson**
Adjectives describe nouns or pronouns. Think of any noun, then list three adjectives that describe it. Take turns sharing your nouns and descriptive adjectives.

Monster - fluffy, red, huge

Make an adjectives word bank to put in your Writing Helps section.

Writer's Workshop

☐ **Mini-Lesson**

Adverbs are words that describe verbs. Think of any verb and then list three adverbs that describe it. Take turns sharing your verbs and adverbs.

Ran - swiftly, smoothly, silently.

How is an adverb different from an adjective?

Adjectives describe nouns and adverbs describe verbs.

☐ **Mini-Lesson**

Prepositions show relationships, usually in terms of location. Imagine yourself near a table. You can be under it, over it, near it, on it, behind it, with it, and so many more. Play Preposition Follow the Leader. As you go over something, everyone calls out, "OVER!" and so on.

☐ **Mini-Lesson**

Conjunctions link phrases and clauses. The most common ones are and, but, or, nor, yet, so, because, and neither.

Make a conjunction word bank and write some sentences with conjunctions.

☐ **Mini-Lesson**

Interjections usually stand alone as their own sentence and are followed by an exclamation point.

Ouch! Phew! Oops!

Make an interjection word bank for your Writing Helps section of your Writer's Notebook.

and *judicial*. Make a list of words that you like. If you need ideas, you can ask others some of their favorite words, look in books, or start reading from a dictionary.

Keep the word list in the Writing Helps section of your Writer's Notebook so you can always look to the list for words you might want to include in your writing.

EXERCISE: What If?
Use your imagination to answer one or more of these hypothetical questions. Do a few out loud together so you can start brainstorming some ideas, then choose at least one to write about.

- What if everybody grew to be the same height?
- What if you woke up alone and you couldn't find your family?
- What if mammals stopped making milk?
- What if candy became illegal?
- What if you found a million dollars on your porch?
- What if all the oceans dried up?
- What if no one could hear sounds anymore?
- What if no one needed sleep anymore?
- What if you were offered the chance to go to space?
- What if you were shipwrecked on an island?
- What if you were invited on a cruise around the world?
- What if 300 mice had just gotten out of their cages in a pet shop where you worked?
- What if you were locked inside your favorite department store overnight?
- What if you woke up one morning to find yourself invisible?
- What if you were able to communicate with animals?
- What if you could travel into the future?
- What if you could travel into the past?
- What if someone just gave you $1 million?
- What if all the electricity in the world just stopped?
- What if you could travel anywhere in the world for free?
- What if the dinner served to you in a fancy restaurant came with a fly in the mashed potatoes?
- What if you had a pet alligator?
- What if you could make magic potions?
- What if you lived under the sea?
- What if you could control the weather?
- What if you met an alien?
- What if it was your birthday every single day?
- What if your favorite stuffed animal could talk?
- What if you were the best _____ in the world? (dancer, singer, athlete, writer, detective. . . you fill in the blank!)

For even more fun, make a "What If" jar. Have everyone write a few "What If" questions on slips of paper and place them in the jar. Have each person draw one out to write about.

Keep the "What if" jar near your writing area and add your story to the Journal section of your Writer's Notebook.

EXERCISE: Double Take
Write a paragraph that includes as many words with double vowels as you can. Freedom, thirteen, moon, cookie, teen, seen, good, and roof are a few. Can you think of lots more and dovetail them into a paragraph that makes sense? Add your double vowels paragraph to your Journal.

EXERCISE: Superhero Switch
Imagine that you could flip a switch and select a super power. Which one would you choose? Would you want to fly? Turn things to gold? Disappear and reappear wherever you wanted? What is the most amazing super power you can imagine? Write about your choice, why you want that power, and what you would do with it. Put your ideas in your Journal.

EXERCISE: Pop
You have just been hired by a soda pop company to write a story for a magazine. They will pay you $10 for every time you use "pop" in your story. Think of a variety of ways you can use it and incorporate as many as you can. How much did you earn?

Pop drank a soda pop while popping popcorn when, all of a sudden, a huge helium balloon popped right above his head...

Keep your ideas in your Journal.

EXERCISE: Dreamer
Some authors keep dream journals. When they awaken in the morning, they write down what they dreamed about. Write in your Journal about a recent dream you have had.

EXERCISE: Fiction Versus Nonfiction
Fiction is writing that is not true, as in imaginary stories and make-believe. If something is made up. Nonfiction is writing that is true. It is based on facts and accurate information. Some of the writing you do will be fictional and some will be nonfictional. The format of your writing will change depending on if it's based on facts or not. Both kinds are important, but you have different responsibilities depending

---

☐ **Mini-Lesson**

Mad Libs are a perfect mini-lesson and a wonderful way to provide a constant review of the parts of speech.

☐ **Mini-Lesson**

Use the "Fiction and Nonfiction" anchor chart from the Printable Pack to discuss the differences between the two.

You may want to have a few books from each category on hand to thumb through. Look for elements of fiction within the fictional stories and elements of nonfiction within the true books. Discuss their similarities and differences.

☐ **Mini-Lesson**

Pair a fictional book from the library with a nonfictional book on the same topic. As you read each one over the course of the week, discuss the differences between fiction and nonfiction.

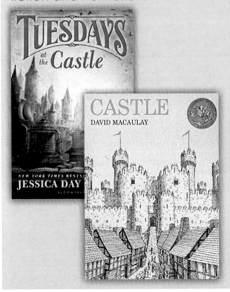

☐ Mini-Lesson

Use the "Writing Process" anchor chart from the Printable Pack to learn the writing process. Great stories, poems, songs, books, essays, and articles are never written in just one take. Writers make changes, scratch things out, get input from other people, revise, and constantly improve their writing. Great writing is crafted. It doesn't just happen.

Discuss this quote by American author, Robert Cormier:

> "The beautiful part of writing is that you don't have to get it right the first time, unlike say, a brain surgeon."

☐ Mini-Lesson

The prewriting activity you choose will depend on both your own preference and also on the kind of writing you are doing. If you are planning an essay, then an outline is a great choice. If you are writing a short story, perhaps a story mountain or character sketch are better suited to it.

Your prewrite is a tool to help you as you begin drafting, so think about what would be the most helpful to you as a writer. Look at each prewriting activity on the "Prewriting" anchor chart printable from the Printable Pack and discuss the kinds of writing that would suit each one.

on which one you're writing. Look over the "Fiction & Nonfiction" anchor charts from the Printable Pack and discuss some differences you notice. How do you think your responsibilities as a writer change depending on whether or not you are writing fiction or nonfiction?

Write a true paragraph about a frog. Now write a quick story about a frog. How are the two writings related? How are they different from each other? Keep these both in your Journal.

EXERCISE: Fiction & Nonfiction Sort

Gather a pile of books. Some should be fictional and some should be nonfictional. Sort them into two piles. Explain why each one belongs in either the fictional pile or the nonfictional pile.

EXERCISE: Parts of Speech Flip Book

One by one, learn about each of the parts of speech - nouns, pronouns, verbs, adjective, adverbs, prepositions, conjunctions, and interjections. Add the "Parts of Speech" anchor chart from the Printable Pack to the Writing Helps section of your Writer's Notebook.

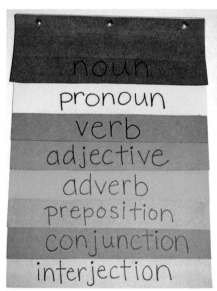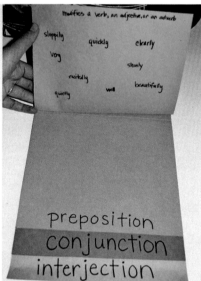

Make a flip book that will become a word bank for you to use as ideas and a review. You can do just one or two parts of speech each day and add to your flip book slowly. You'll find coordinating mini-lessons within the sidebars of this unit.

EXERCISE: Audience & Purpose

Depending on who your audience is and what your purpose is, you will need to adapt your writing style. Let's say that I'm adding a comment on my friend's social media

post, do you think I will go into the sensory details and vivid descriptions of a novelist? Of course not! No one would bother to take the time to read what I wrote in that format, no matter how eloquent I was.

I'm much more likely to just post an emoji than a paragraph. Along those same lines, it wouldn't be appropriate to post an emoji instead of detailed evidence and logic within a persuasive essay. Writer's Workshop is preparing you for written communication beyond simple online interactions. It takes more effort than emojis, but the lasting impact is greater too.

Imagine this scenario, in which a man is writing to two different audiences with two different purposes: Mr. Tom Jinks is writing two notes. One is a note to his boss, Mr. Mike Murphy, asking for time off of work so he can surprise his wife with an anniversary trip. The other is a note that he will deliver to his wife, June, on the day of the trip, inviting her to pack a bag and be ready for him to pick her up in an hour.

In what ways will Mr. Jinks change his writing for each note? What details or facts will he choose to include in each? In which note will he express emotion? How will he sign the two notes? Which note will show more excitement? Brainstorm some ways that each note will be different from the other.

Write the two notes, making sure to consider the audience and purpose as you write. Put your notes in your Journal.

EXERCISE: Formal & Informal

Just like speaking, not all writing is the same when it comes to formality. When you write a fairy tale it will sound very different than when you write a report about one of the countries in the world.

Write two paragraphs detailing much more about the story of Jack and Jill who went up a hill to fetch a pail of water. Jack fell down and broke his crown and Jill came tumbling after.

In your first paragraph, write from the point of view of Jack, who is telling his doctor in the emergency room what happened. Include the pertinent details, but keep your tone formal. In the second paragraph, Jack and Jill have arrived home and recovered. They are relating the story to their best friends. This time your tone will be less formal. You might even add some humor. Put your ideas in your Journal.

☐ Mini-Lesson

Pre- means before. Prewrites are activities that help you generate ideas before you start writing so that the writing comes more easily later.

Many of the exercises within Writer's Workshop could become prewrites. If you decide to take a piece through the writing process, move that exercise from your Journal to your Writing section within your Writer's Notebook.

☐ Mini-Lesson

Drafting is the process of beginning to write the ideas that you have come up with. Your draft is a rough draft, a sloppy copy, a messy version of your writing. Skip lines, leave extra space, and even leave large margins. You are creating space so you can make corrections, jot down ideas, or draw arrows as you revise and edit later.

Read through the "Drafting Write It Down" printable from the Printable Pack. Then, use a lined sheet of paper and a highlighter pen to make notes on your page. Which direction does the paper go? Where does your heading belong? Cross out every other line so you remember to skip lines. Draw an X in the margins. Write "Title" where the title should go.

Add your "Drafting Write it Down" printable to the Writing Helps section of your Writer's Notebook.

There are three keys to effective drafting.

1. Use your prewrite to help your writing stay organized and on track.
2. Write quickly. Since you aren't worried about mistakes, it's best to get your ideas down on the page before you forget them.
3. Leave lots of space. Skip lines. Leave big margins.

☐ Mini-Lesson

Revising means adding, subtracting, moving, and improving the parts of your writing. You can scratch things out, draw arrows to move sections, adhere sticky notes with extra things written on them, and write in between the lines of your draft. You can even cut apart your writing and glue it back together in a different order. Don't be afraid to make drastic changes. Ernest Hemingway, a famous author, said, "There is no rule on how to write. Sometimes it comes easily and perfectly; sometimes it's like drilling rock and then blasting it out with charges."

☐ Mini-Lesson

When you are asked to help someone revise their writing, it's as easy as 3-2-1. Tell them three things you like, two questions you have, and one thing you think they should improve.

The Writing Process

The writing process is a series of steps that help a piece of writing go from a vague idea to publication. Often young writers struggle because they are not taught the writing process. They believe they have to go straight from nothing to perfect writing. Teach the writing process here and then use this process through every piece of writing you take to publication in your Writer's Workshop.

EXERCISE: Prewriting

Prewriting is the first and often most important step of the writing process. Before you start writing, you must decide what you want to say. There are lots of ways to prewrite. To see some of them, look over the "Prewriting" anchor chart from the Printable Pack. Put the anchor chart within your Writing Helps section of your Writer's Notebook so you can refer to it when you need ideas.

Choose one of the prewriting activities from the anchor chart as you begin to write about this topic: What is a gift you can give that doesn't cost any money?

You may draw a picture of the gift, brainstorm a list of ideas, do a quick write, draw a cartoon, or choose another prewrite. Perhaps you'll just talk it out. Here are some questions to guide you as you talk about the topic:

- How did you come up with that idea?
- Have you ever given that gift before?
- Does it have any special meaning to you?
- What do you think the differences are between expensive gifts and those that cost nothing?
- What is the best gift you've ever been given?

After you complete your prewriting activity, decide if this is a piece you want to continue to take through the writing process. If so, add it to the Writing section of your Writer's Notebook, the place where you take pieces of writing from prewrites to published works. If not, add it to your Journal.

Is it easier to get started writing after you've done a prewriting activity?

EXERCISE: Drafting

The second step in the writing process is drafting. With your prewriting activity nearby, you will begin to make a rough draft, also called a sloppy copy. Drafting means quickly getting your thoughts on paper without worrying too much about mistakes. Take a look at the "Drafting" anchor chart from the Printable Pack to help you as you begin to create a draft. Add the anchor chart to the Writing Helps section

of your Writer's Notebook.

Choose a topic to write about and complete a prewrite and then a draft. You can continue with an exercise you've already completed during this unit, including the Prewriting exercise, or you can begin from scratch with a new prewrite. Another exercise from this unit could also serve as your inspiration.

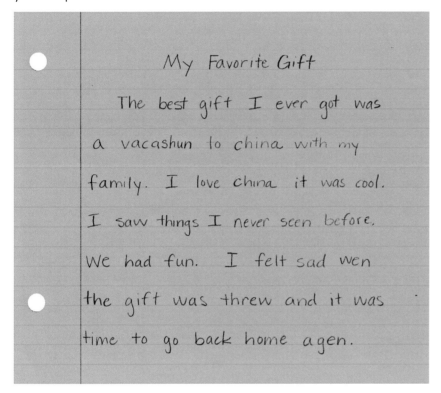

My Favorite Gift

The best gift I ever got was a vacashun to china with my family. I love china it was cool. I saw things I never seen before. We had fun. I felt sad wen the gift was threw and it was time to go back home agen.

As you draft, make sure to skip lines and leave plenty of room in the margins. You will be making changes to your draft later, so leave room to write on it. If you like typing on a word processor, you may choose to complete your draft on a computer.

EXERCISE: Revising

Revising is the third step of the writing process. Refer to the "Revising Checklist" printable from the Printable Pack and add it to the Writing Helps section of your Writer's Notebook. Use the printable to learn what the acronym ARMS stands for.

Revising is making your writing stronger. You rearrange, organize, add details, exchange boring words for better ones, check for good transitions, and make changes. Often it helps if you ask someone else to read it and offer you ideas for how you can make it better.

You can write all over your paper, add sticky notes, cross things out, change the order, and improve your message.

☐ **Mini-Lesson**

Editing marks can help you to edit someone's paper quickly. Each little symbol means something. Begin with a sentence that has a lot of mistakes in it and practice using editing marks to find the mistakes. Look at the "Editing Marks" anchor chart from the Printable Pack to help you learn the editing symbols while you work.

☐ **Mini-Lesson**

Peers are friends or people you know. Once you've written a draft, ask your peers to read it and give you feedback and suggestions. It helps to have fresh eyes when you're looking at something you've written. Peers can give overall feedback, ask questions, and help you make corrections.

☐ **Mini-Lesson**

Publishing includes sharing what you've written. At least once a month you'll be taking a piece of writing all of the way through the writing process and then publishing it. You might share it out loud with your family at dinnertime, read your story to younger siblings, gift it to a grandparent, or send a letter that you wrote in the mail. Brainstorm fun ways to share the things you've written so you can all share in the writing fun together.

☐ Mini-Lesson

Not everything you write will go all of the way through the writing process. Often you will just jot down notes, make a journal entry, or begin a story idea. Some writing needs to be finished and polished, but an awful lot of the writing we do is just for us. I've never revised and edited my shopping list. It's just for me. Discuss which things need to be perfected and which things don't.

☐ Mini-Lesson

Articles are words used with a noun. *A* and *an* are two examples of articles. *A* is used if the following noun begins with a consonant. *An* is used if the following noun begins with a vowel.

A crocodile

An acrobat

Write nouns on index cards. When you pick up the card, say an appropriate article to go with it.

☐ Mini-Lesson

Determiners are words that are used in front of nouns. *My, those, many, several, much, few, hers,* and *his* are all examples of determiners. Articles are also determiners.

Write some sentences with determiners and highlight each determiner within the sentence.

Revise the draft you've written and make it better than before. Have at least one other person give you suggestions.

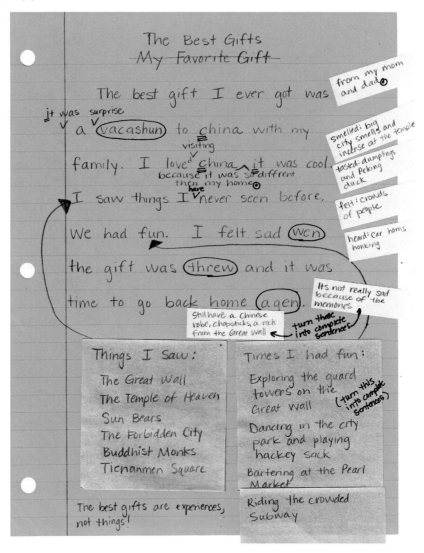

EXERCISE: Editing

Editing is the fourth step in the writing process. Editing involves fixing errors. Do your best to find all of your own mistakes first, then have someone else help you find mistakes. This can be done either on your rough draft so that when you make your final copy it is all correct, or after you have revised your draft, especially if you are using a computer. No matter when you choose to edit, make sure you give it one final check after you have written your final draft.

Take a look at the "Editing Checklist" anchor chart from the Printable Pack and at the "Basic Editing Marks" printable. Add both of those to the Writing Helps section of your Writer's Notebook.

Sit with someone and, together, add editing marks to your

draft as you spot any mistakes you made. Editing marks are little symbols that point out your mistakes so you can correct them. Correct the mistakes.

EXERCISE: Publishing

Publishing means making a polished version of your writing and sharing it. This can take a lot of different forms. If you wrote a story, perhaps you'll make it into a booklet with illustrations and read it to someone in your family. If you wrote a letter, you'll probably address the envelope, put a stamp on it, and mail it. You might read what you wrote out loud to someone, add it to your own library, or publish it online. Read through the "Steps To Publishing" anchor chart from the Printable Pack and add it to the Writing Helps section of your Writer's Notebook.

Decide the form you want your draft to take, then make a final published version of it and share it with someone.

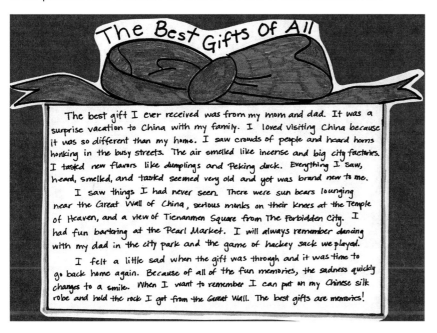

EXERCISE: A Tour of the Writing Process

This exercise was about using interesting, unfamiliar characters and describing them well so readers can picture them. Tyler was a young writer who liked creating unusual superheros, so his prewrite began with a character sketch of an unusual superhero he created named Fish Boy. Watch the writing process unfold.

Step #1: Prewriting

Tyler began by sketching a character he had been thinking about. To finish the character sketch, he surrounded the picture with adjectives that described his character, Fish Boy. Tyler keeps an entire sketchbook of unlikely

---

☐ **Mini-Lesson**

Label each of the words in this sentence with its proper part of speech:

The girl quickly twirled her sparkly baton near the crowd, but in her haste, she dropped it.

The (article) girl (noun) quickly (adverb) twirled (verb) her (determiner) sparkly (adjecive) baton (noun) near (preposition) the (article) crowd (noun), but (conjunction) in (preposition) her (determiner) haste (noun), she (pronoun) dropped (verb) it (pronoun).

☐ **Mini-Lesson**

Use the sentence in the mini-lesson above as an example and create your own sentence using sentence imitation. Craft a sentence in this order:

Article, noun, adverb, verb, determiner, adjective, noun, preposition, article, noun, conjunction, preposition, determiner, noun, pronoun, verb, pronoun.

☐ **Mini-Lesson**

Being a good audience is an important part of the publishing stage. When others are sharing their writing, the audience should quietly listen. To show you're listening your body is still, your eyes are looking at the person who is sharing, and you are actively paying attention.

☐ **Mini-Lesson**

When someone is revising you can offer suggestions, but when someone is sharing, you should only clap, congratulate, and give positive feedback.

☐ **Mini-Lesson**

You can improve ideas and content by:

- Choosing topics that are not too broad or too narrow
- Sharing important details
- Staying focused and on topic
- Painting a picture for your readers with detailed descriptions
- Including who, what, where, when, why, and how information

☐ **Mini-Lesson**

You can improve organization by:

- Planning your writing
- Including a strong topic sentence, lead, or hook
- Researching and gathering information ahead of time
- Linking ideas together and using transition words
- Guiding your reader through the topic or story in an organized order
- Ending with a good summary or conclusion

superheroes in his Writer's Notebook, and Fish Boy is one he's been thinking about using in a story.

Step #2: Drafting

After Tyler's character sketch was complete, he began drafting. He looked back at a few other stories he had written in his Journal. His villain, Mr. Shark, was actually taken from a quick write he once wrote about a shark who wanted to become king of the sea. Tyler wrote most of his draft in one day. He focused on the story and didn't worry too much about perfect spelling or punctuation. He skipped lines so he would have room to go back and add notes later.

Step #3: Revising

The next day he read it to me. I asked him all kinds of questions, which he then used to revise and add to his story. *What did Fish Boy think about being part fish? Tell me more about the fight between Fish Boy and Mr. Shark. What did the other sharks do when Fish Boy killed Mr. Shark?*

He made sure to answer the questions by adding to his story. He also crossed out a line that didn't make sense and wasn't important to the story. This step was done by adding sentences on some of the skipped lines and writing in margins. He didn't rewrite the whole thing, and he didn't worry about having a messy paper. He just jotted down his ideas and additions.

Step #4: Editing

Next, we edited it for capitalization, usage, punctuation,

and spelling. He fixed all of the mistakes he could on his own, and I sat with him and helped him spot mistakes he missed. He also showed me his dialog and we reviewed quotation marks because we've been practicing those lately. We sat together and fixed all of the mistakes right on his draft.

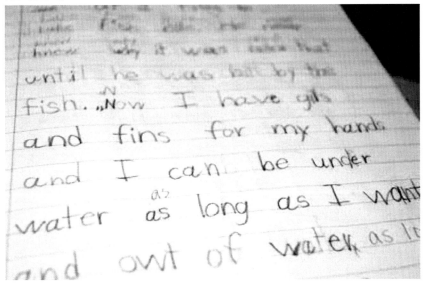

When we were finished, the draft looked pretty messy, but Tyler felt ready to finish his story.

Step #5: Publishing

The last step of the writing process is publishing. Tyler often creates illustrated booklets for our family library, but this time he wanted his story to be typed out. Here is nine-year-old Tyler's final draft:

Fish Boy

Once there was a boy – Fish Boy. He didn't look like you or I. He had sharkish fins and could breathe both in and out of the water. His feet were close together, almost like a fin. He also had two extra fins on his feet to help him go twice as fast. He was super skinny and could zoom through the water like a rocket! But Fish Boy wasn't always this way. This is his story in his own words.

I began life as a normal baby boy. When I was five years old I was bit by a fish the size of a frog in Lake Fish Bite. I never knew why the lake was called that until the day that changed my life, the day the fish bit me. I completely changed in an instant! I grew fins and soon discovered that I could breathe under the water. I had become part boy and part fish. At first, I wasn't sure about my transformation into part fish and part boy, but as I swam and played in the water, I began to love it. "Now I have gills and fins for my hands, and I can be underwater as long as I want. I can

---

☐ Mini-Lesson

Find a nonfiction picture book that has a four or five sentence paragraph within it. Write each sentence on a separate note card. Scramble the note cards, trade sets with someone, and try to put their set in order. Can you spot the organization of the paragraph?

☐ Mini-Lesson

You can improve word choice by:

- Using clear and colorful language.
- Being precise, economic, and novel with words.
- Choosing powerful verbs.
- Not repeating the same words over and over - use a thesaurus to find alternative words with a similar meaning if needed.

☐ Mini-Lesson

You can improve sentence fluency by:

- Varying the lengths of sentences, with some short, some medium, and some long sentences.
- Making sure the first word of your sentences is not repetitive.
- Changing the structure by combining sentences or swapping the subject and predicate parts.
- Utilizing a variety of sentence structures - simple, compound, and complex.

Mini-Lesson

Conventions are things we all choose to do in common so that everyone understands. What are the conventions of attending a birthday party? Going to a movie? Celebrating on Christmas morning? Navigating through traffic on the roads? The conventions, or rules we share in common, help things go more smoothly.

Try something. Take a sentence or two of your writing and apply some new conventions:

1. Misspell every third word

2. Add commas every five words

3. Capitalize everything

4. Never use the words "a" or "the"

Now read through it. Is it easy to understand? We have conventions in common so that everyone understands what is being written. Without conventions, there is chaos!

Mini-Lesson

You can improve conventions by:

- Proofreading for errors.
- Asking someone to help you edit.
- Checking capitalization, punctuation, and spelling.
- Using paragraph breaks.
- Following grammar rules.

also be out of the water as long as I want to!" I said.

But life wasn't always the way I thought it would be. One day I went out, and Mr. Shark and his shark army were there, trying to kill all of the fish in Lake Fish Bite. Mr. Shark wanted to be king of the lake. "Right now I am trying to defeat Mr. Shark and his shark army," I thought aloud to myself, "If I don't, every fish will get eaten and the scuba divers won't have any more fish to see."

Mr. Shark started his attack. He started swatting me back and forth, attacking with his sharp teeth and hitting me with his head. A head bump from a shark really hurts! I swam in circles and got him all dizzy! I charged at him! I bit him! Mr. Shark died, and all of his sharks were so afraid they swam away.

This was the end of my first mission as Fish Boy, protector of Lake Fish Bite.

The End

That's what the writing process looks like. It's easy to see what Tyler is doing well. He has a clear beginning, middle, and end. He included some vivid descriptions. His handwriting is pretty tidy and his spelling is improving. It's also very easy to see what he can work on in future Writer's Workshop sessions. In future mini-lessons we'll talk about incorporating the description throughout the story and not just focusing on our main character's description. We'll also discuss making the dialogue more meaningful by having someone to converse with. Tyler also had a few issues with his narrative mode in his early draft, mixing up the first person narrative with the third person at times. We'll have a mini-lesson on that soon too.

That's the beauty of the writing process - bit by bit kids develop as thoughtful writers. We can take things in stride, celebrate what's done well, and find areas to grow.

Memorize the steps of the writing process. Can you write them all down? This is the process you'll use again and again in Writer's Workshop, whether you're writing a story, an essay, a poem, or anything else.

Analyzing Writing

Analyzing writing is both for the writer to analyze his or her own work and for the parent to aid in grading writing. The purpose is to constructively interpret what is great and what needs work for the writer so the writer can constantly improve in small ways.

EXERCISE: The Six Traits of Writing

The six traits of writing can help you identify the ways writers effectively use words. Each time you complete a writing project you will be given a score based on the six traits of writing, so it's important that you understand each trait and what it means.

Create a six traits of writing hex-book to keep as a tool to use while you write. Use colorful card stock to print the corresponding pages from the Printable Pack. Cut out the hex-book and the tip page. Glue the tips into the book under each coordinating section.

As you learn about each of the six traits, read the tips under each flap. Write some of your own notes on the door flap about each trait as well. Keep the hex-book in the Writing Helps section of your Writer's Notebook to remind yourself of ways you can improve in each of the six traits as you write.

Ideas and content is the first trait of writing. The symbol is a light bulb. Just like a light bulb can light up a room, your writing should shed light on your subject. Your reader should come away knowing something more or seeing something in a new way. What you write should be interesting, detailed, clear, and focused. Your readers should feel involved and interested. Sensory details and pertinent information should be included.

Organization is the second trait of writing. A train represents organization. Can you imagine a train that had its cars all mixed up? If the engine was somewhere in the middle, the coal car was at the back, and the caboose was at the front, the train wouldn't be effective. Just like a train, your writing needs to be organized and orderly. Organized writing is easy to follow because it is composed in a logical order with a strong beginning and a satisfying ending. In nonfiction writing, there should be organized paragraphs with topic sentences, details, and concluding sentences. Transition words should guide your reader through the topic and link ideas together, just like the couplings that hold train

☐ **Mini-Lesson**

You can improve voice by:

- Being yourself.
- Using your own words and not copying others.
- Connecting with your readers.
- Having energy and excitement for your topics or stories.
- Giving different voices to your various characters by imagining what it's like to be them.

☐ **Mini-Lesson**

Use the "What's My Voice?" printable from the Printable Pack to practice writing things characters might say in a story. Cut apart each of the cards and turn them over so they are facing downward on the table. One at a time, draw a card and state how the character you drew would say these lines:

- I'm hungry.
- I need to go shopping.
- What's that noise?
- Can you help me?
- I'm lost.

For example, a toddler might say, "Hungee! Want cookie! Now!!"

A professor might say, "Oh my! Is it 2:00 already? I was so absorbed in my experiment I nearly forgot to eat lunch!"

A cowgirl might say, "Time to start the campfire! My belly's rumblin'."

☐ Mini-Lesson

Look at a picture in a magazine and write sentences about it. Identify which parts of speech you used in your sentences. Which nouns did you use? Which verbs? Use each part of speech at least once in your sentences.

☐ Mini-Lesson

To make a noun plural we normally just add an s to it.

book - books

cup - cups

pencil - pencils

If a noun ends with an s, x, ch, or sh, then we add an es.

class - classes

fox - foxes

peach - peaches

wish - wishes

Take turns naming nouns and then making them plural by writing them correctly with either an s or an es.

☐ Mini-Lesson

Every complete sentence must include at least one noun or pronoun. The noun helps the reader to know what the sentence is about. Have someone call out a noun and then everyone else has to come up with a complete sentence about that noun. Take turns calling out nouns and creating sentences.

cars together. In fictional writing, there should be a clear beginning, middle, and ending.

The third trait of writing is word choice. Word choice is represented by a bullseye on a target. There are millions of words to choose from, but you want to use the best words you can to share your message. You want your words to be right on target. Choose words that allow your readers to experience what you are describing. Use sensory details and precise language. Try to create a mood or a tone and write from a clear perspective. Show, don't tell.

The fourth trait is sentence fluency, and this trait is represented by a lovely stream flowing from the mountains. Just like a stream meanders back and forth gently, you want your writing to be full of gentle twists and turns that provide lovely viewpoints. Imagine a straight, concrete, man-made stream that is surrounded by concrete walls with nothing to see. If you write in a predictable and repetitive way, it is much like the concrete stream. To create sentence fluency, you need to vary your sentence structures and lengths. Your writing should flow and feel easy to read aloud. It should include smooth transitions and not jump around. Your writing should be flowing and connected, but also have variety and interest.

The fifth writing trait is the toughest for a lot of writers to master. It is conventions. It is represented by a pencil and an eraser because even the strongest writers do a lot of erasing and rewriting to make sure they get the conventions just right. Conventions are all of the rules of writing. There are lots of spelling, punctuation, and grammar conventions you are expected to follow. It will take you many years to learn all of the conventions, but in the meantime, there are things you can do. Using a dictionary and a thesaurus are really helpful. You can also ask someone to help you edit. A great tool is a computer. If you type your writing, you can use spelling and grammar checkers to help you spot mistakes.

Voice is the sixth and final writing trait. It is represented by a face because it is the personality within your writing. The only real trick to having a strong voice as you write is being yourself. You have a chance to connect with your reader by sharing your stories or your knowledge in your own voice. You might need to have the voice of an expert if you're writing an essay or report. Regardless of what you're writing, don't try to sound like someone else. You may take on a more formal or informal tone just as you would if you were having a conversation with your boss or your best friend, but in either case, you should still be yourself. A second aspect of voice enters in when you tell stories or write from

the perspective of another person. For example, each of the characters in your stories should sound different from each other. You must learn to put yourself inside of them and write from their perspective, communicating the way that character would.

Did you take some notes in your hex-book about each of the six traits of writing? Try writing a paragraph that uses each of the six traits well. Put your paragraph in your Journal.

EXERCISE: Evaluating Writing Using the Six Traits

Use the "Evaluating Writing" printable from the Printable Pack to practice evaluating two paragraphs about butterflies.

Read the first paragraph and give it a score of one through five in ideas and content. Read the paragraph again, this time evaluating its organization. Continue to read and evaluate the paragraph with each specific trait in mind. As you go, discuss your scores and make suggestions about what could be improved on.

Repeat the process with the second paragraph. Read and evaluate it based on each of the six traits of writing. Discuss each trait as you go.

Step 3: Writing Project

During this unit, you should complete at least one writing project, taking a piece of writing through the entire writing process. By the final week of the unit, if you haven't completed the project already, you should turn your attention to creating one polished piece of writing that uses the things you've practiced along the way.

Choose one topic to write about that you will take all of the way through the writing process. This piece of writing belongs in the Writing section of your Writer's Notebook. You can use something you've already started during this unit, your own idea, or something from the following idea banks. Make sure that you follow each step of the writing process and keep all of your steps to turn in with your finished writing.

- Step #1: Prewrite
- Step #2: Draft
- Step #3: Revise
- Step #4: Edit
- Step #5: Publish

Begin with a prewriting activity, then compose a draft, revise it, edit it with help from someone else, and then

---

☐ **Mini-Lesson**

Some nouns are proper. That means they are names of specific nouns. For example, your name is proper, because it is specifically talking about one special noun - YOU! We always begin proper nouns with capital letters.

Make three lists of proper nouns - names of people, names of places, and titles (books, movies, TV shows, games). Make sure to capitalize all of the items in your lists because they are all proper nouns. Use your own name as the first item on your list of people.

☐ **Mini-Lesson**

Use this list of nouns and come up with some specific examples that are proper. Make sure to capitalize the proper nouns.

- Park - **Central Park**
- Girl - **Rita**
- Movie theater -
- Pizza -
- State -
- Athlete -
- City -
- Store -
- Street -
- Country -
- Book -
- Planet -
- Song -
- State -
- Holiday -

☐ Mini-Lesson

Interjections are emotional words or phrases that stand alone. They can be punctuated using a comma or an exclamation point if the emotion is strong. They are common in everyday speaking, but not as common in writing. Can you write ten different interjections?

Ouch!

Oops,

Yuck!

☐ Mini-Lesson

When you ask a question, you always use a question mark at the end of the sentence.

Where did Luther go?
How are you feeling today?
Do I look tired?

Write down some questions and end each of them with a question mark. Trade papers with someone and answer each other's questions in writing.

☐ Mini-Lesson

When you get to the editing stage of the writing process, you are looking for mistakes in conventions. Conventions are spelling, punctuation, and grammar mistakes. We correct these to make sure our reader understands what we wrote. Can you find three mistakes to correct in this short sentence?

i luv dogs?

Answer: I love dogs.

publish it. Publishing it could include making a polished final copy, sharing it with someone, creating a book, or creating some form of finished project that is neat and done well. You'll turn in all of your work, from prewrite to publish.

Your project will be evaluated based on the six traits of writing, so make sure you look at your composition through each of those lenses - ideas and content, organization, word choice, sentence fluency, conventions, and voice. Try to incorporate things you learned from the mini-lessons and the exercises you worked on as well. Do your best work.

Jump Start Idea Bank

Use these ideas for more exercises to go with this unit or as your project. This list is also found in the Printable Pack and can be placed in the Ideas section of your Writer's Notebook. Jump Starts are short, high-interest topics to help get you started writing.

- Make a list of ways to say "no" without using the word no.
- A painting that is plain black may be entitled, "A Gnat on a Bat with an Unlucky Cat at Midnight." Come up with names of paintings that are painted in other solid colors. Create a gallery of your named art.
- What life advice do you think your pet would give you?
- Liam walks into a room and immediately the people in the room respond. Write about how each person responded and then tell what their reactions revealed about Liam.
- Imagine yourself in a different century and describe an average day in your life.
- Make a list of the most fun things to do at your house or in your neighborhood, town, or city.
- What presents do you wish you could give to someone? What presents do you wish to receive? Write about the gifts you would most like to give and receive.
- Where would you fly to today if you could fly?
- Write about what you didn't do this weekend.
- If you were ruler of the world, what things would you banish absolutely for all time (rain on weekends, Brussels sprouts, and rug burns)? Make a list.
- What commercial on TV/internet do you dislike beyond all others? What about it is particularly annoying to you?
- Imagine that you are an animal in the zoo. What type of animal are you? How do you feel about being caged? How do you feel about people that visit and watch you?
- If you had to escort a visitor from outer space for a 30-minute tour of your community, where would you begin and end?

- What would you pack in your suitcase if you could not go home again?
- What would it be like if everyone lived under the ocean?
- Describe the very best lunch in the whole entire world.
- Have you ever wished you were either older or younger? What would you consider to be the benefits? The problems?
- How do you know someone loves you, even if he or she doesn't say it?
- What do you think makes a happy family?
- If animals could talk, what would you ask them?
- Imagine that everyone in the world suddenly grew a foot taller overnight. What problems would this create?
- If you could change one thing about the world, what would it be? Why would you make this change?
- If you had to choose between having a TV, a computer, or a cell phone, which one would you choose? Why?
- Make a list of animals you might see in a zoo and describe each one.
- If you had $100,000, how would you spend it?
- Make a list of things to do at a park or playground and rank them in order, beginning with the least fun and building up to the most fun.
- If you could become a cartoon character, who would you be and why?
- Make a list of things you would never, ever do.
- If you could go somewhere where you've never gone before, where would you go and why?
- If you could be a character in any book, TV show, or movie, who would you be and why?
- If you had to work in any store at your favorite mall, which store would it be and why?
- Is there a machine you feel you could not live without? Explain.
- How do each of the colors make you feel? Write about each basic color and what you think of it.
- If a natural disaster struck and you had to leave your home right away, never to return again, what items would you grab at the last moment?
- If you could be an expert in any field, which one would you choose?
- What are the most important qualities of a friend?

Journaling Idea Bank

Here are ideas for journaling during this unit or any time. This list is also found in the Printable Pack and can be placed in the Ideas section of your Writer's Notebook. This idea bank focuses on journal entries that are related to the writer personally.

☐ **Mini-Lesson**

Combine the information from these two simple sentences into one compound sentence by adding a conjunction between them.

Kara loves dolls.

She really wants a dollhouse for Christmas.

Possible answer:

Kara loves dolls and really wants a dollhouse for Christmas.

☐ **Mini-Lesson**

Parenthesis are used when you interrupt a sentence, usually to give more information.

I exercised for three hours yesterday (jogging, biking, and swimming) because I'm getting ready to run a triathlon.

Can you imitate this sentence by writing your own example that uses parenthesis to give more information?

☐ **Mini-Lesson**

Adverbs are words that describe verbs. Think of a verb (an action word) and then come up with three ways you could describe it.

jump - high, far, quickly

High, far, and quickly are all adverbs that describe the verb *jump*. Can you come up with some of your own examples of adverbs by listing a verb and then writing adverbs that describe it?

Reminders About Your Writer's Notebook

Besides just the writing project, there should be many small writing samples that are being compiled in the Writer's Notebook from the exercises you worked on over the course of this unit. The Writer's Notebook is a tool for helping writers to grow. Explore it frequently and refer to idea lists and helps as you write.

At least once a week, it would be beneficial for you, the writer, to glance back through the exercises, lists, and mini-lessons to review and make sure that you are on track even though most of this work isn't graded.

Specifically, as you are working on the writing project, utilize your Writer's Notebook. You have anchor charts, exercises, and entries in your Journal - all of these can help you as you complete your project. Take time to review some of the concepts you've been working on during the unit so they can be incorporated into the final writing project. The things you've learned should SHOW in your writing project.

Remember that most of the work in the Writer's Notebook will never be graded, but it is still important. Use what you learned to make your project, which will be graded, the best that you can make it.

- Journal about what you did yesterday.
- Finish this thought - If I could change one thing about myself . . . (If you can't think of anything, you might want to consider telling how you got to be perfect!)
- Make a "100 Things" list. It will include 100 things you love. Use ten sports or activities, ten restaurants or stores, ten people, ten foods, ten games, ten drinks, ten desserts, ten books, ten movies, and ten places.
- Have you ever had a great fort or hideaway? Maybe you've played in a cemetery, near the railroad tracks, at a construction site, near a stream, or in a field. Write about one of these experiences.
- When your parents go out, what do you do?
- Where are some places you wish you could go on a school field trip?
- If you could be famous for anything at all, what would you like to be known for?
- Choose a holiday and write about the traditions you have and how you celebrate.
- What are you most proud of?
- What's your favorite TV show? Would you star in it if you were given the chance?
- What will you do first when you graduate from high school?
- Describe your favorite foods. What do you love to eat most?
- Think of something you absolutely can't imagine living without. What would it be?
- If you could buy anyone in the world one gift, who would you purchase it for and what would it be?
- What gift do you want most in the world?
- What is the best birthday you've ever had?
- If you could choose one season to get rid of forever, which one would it be?
- What would you do if you saw a mouse in your house?
- What animal are you most afraid of?
- What do you do when you get money? Do you save it? Spend it all? Gift it?
- Imagine the perfect party. Describe what it would be like.
- On an average day at home, how do you spend your free time?
- What makes you scream?
- Write about some things that make you feel good about yourself.
- If you could build a robot that did most of your jobs for you, what things would the robot need to be able to do?
- Are there things you worry about?
- Write about your favorite kinds of music and your favorite songs.
- What is the best book you've ever read?

- What is the best compliment you've ever received?
- What are your favorite things in nature?
- Write about your very favorite smells and what they make you think of.
- What are the ten things you are most grateful for?
- Have you learned any important life lessons that have made an impact on you?
- What's the biggest lie you've ever told?
- Have you ever done anything outrageous or surprising?
- Nobody knows that I . . .
- What are your favorite things about your mom?
- What are your favorite things about your dad?
- If you could live anywhere you wanted, where would you live?
- Write about a time you performed. It could be in an athletic event, on a stage, or in front of any audience.
- Who made you feel good this week?
- Write about someone you need to forgive.
- What did you learn this week?
- How do you stand out from the crowd?

Step 4: Evaluating Writing

The purpose of this unit is three-fold.

1. *To practice the writing process.*

2. *To become acquainted with Writer's Notebooks and Writer's Workshop procedures.*

3. *To start writing!*

As you evaluate the writing project, you will be using the "6 Traits of Writing Rubric" from the Printable Pack. In addition, you will be looking for each step of the entire writing process. For example, your child will turn in a prewriting activity, a draft that shows both revisions and edits, as well as a finished, published piece. The publishing step should involve sharing the project in some way - reading it aloud to family, presenting it at dinner time, video chatting to show it off to grandparents, or sharing a video presentation on the internet of the writer sharing his or her writing. Sharing is a time for positive feedback and celebration.

Creating a positive buzz about the published piece will create a motivating, growth atmosphere in your Writer's Workshop. As you evaluate, remember that the process is just as important as the product, so watch for successes in the process as well. The final score will be out of 50 points - 20 for the process and 30 for the final project. You can write rubric scores as well as comments down on the "Writing Report Card" printable from the Printable Pack.

Breakdown of Possible Points

- 5 points for a complete prewriting activity
- 5 points for a completed draft
- 5 points for revisions
- 5 points for edits
- 30 points for the finished writing project

The 30 points for the finished project is further broken down into each of the six traits of writing as shown on the "6 Traits of Writing Rubric" from the Printable Pack.

6 Traits of Writing Rubric

Your comments should be specifically focused on the purposes of this unit and the skills you were working on throughout the unit.

What was done well? Is the writer understanding the writing process? What should be improved on? Are there any repeated mistakes to address?

Point out a clear strength.

Comments mean more than scores, so make sure to give clear feedback.

Key Concepts

By the end of this unit your kids should be familiar with these ideas:

- Subjects and predicates
- Writing complete sentences
- The four types of sentences
- How to write compound sentences using conjunctions
- Building paragraphs with topic sentences, supporting details, and a concluding sentence
- Reasons to begin a new paragraph
- How to write a narration or short answer essay

More Mini-Lesson Ideas

Along with the sidebars, try these mini-lesson ideas:

- Writer's Workshop links found in Layers of Learning catalog
- Lessons from any grammar workbook
- Every-Day Edits from Education World website
- Sentence diagramming
- Copying great sentences from master writers
- Mad Libs
- Correcting a repeated error from your writing
- Practicing expanding sentences by adding details
- Combining sentences by making two or three into a single sentence

The mini-lesson sidebars in this unit have check boxes so you can keep track of which ones you have completed.

Sentences, Paragraphs, & Narrations

Sentences are the building blocks of writing. A sentence is a group of words that expresses one complete idea. Every single sentence must include a subject and a predicate. The subject tells what or who the sentence is about and the predicate tells what the subject does or what the subject is. We show that a sentence has come to an end by adding an end mark. All sentences end with a period, an exclamation point, or a question mark. In order to communicate our ideas clearly, we write in complete sentences so our readers can understand our messages.

If all of your sentences are bland and boring, you can bet your stories and reports will be bland and boring too. In this unit you will practice crafting sentences that will keep your readers interested. You will learn how to get the ideas in your head on to the page and help others see what you see in your mind through your words.

A paragraph is a group of sentences that goes together. Paragraphs have different formats depending on what you are writing. In a story, you change paragraphs each time you change locations or move through time. In addition, you change paragraphs each time a new person speaks. In reports and essays, paragraphs are more formal and are comprised of one topic. They begin with a topic sentence that tells what the paragraph will be about, include several supporting sentences, and then close with a concluding sentence that sums up what the paragraph discussed.

Narrations are short summaries, usually one to three paragraphs long, that involve recalling something you have learned about, read, or heard. You are the narrator and you get to tell what you know about the subject. There are two kinds of narrations - oral and written.

During this unit we will practice writing sentences, paragraphs, and narrations so that we can use them well in all of our future writing.

Step 1: Mini-Lesson

After handwriting or typing practice has concluded, begin each day of Writer's Workshop with a mini-lesson. You will find some within the sidebars of this unit. You can also use a worksheet from a grammar workbook or practice editing, copying, or diagramming sentences. During writing time, watch for weak areas or mistakes being made and present a mini-lesson the next day to help correct those and improve writing skills in small, continuous ways.

The mini-lesson should take five to ten minutes and always have a positive, happy spin, free from criticism. Not every mini-lesson needs to be kept in your Writer's Notebook. Most are merely for practice.

Step 2: Writing

Now it's time to really begin writing. Most of your time during Writer's Workshop should be spent writing. Practicing is the key to improving. You can use your writing time to free write your own ideas in your Journal anytime, or use the exercises below to practice writing skills and find inspiration for things to write about. Select as many exercises as you would like to do over the month, making sure you leave time to complete at least one writing project that will go all of the way through the writing process before the month is over. The exercises will also go in your Journal section of your Writer's Notebook. If you decide to take something from your Journal through the writing process and turn it into your writing project, move it from your Journal to the Writing section of your Writer's Notebook.

A few tips and reminders:

- You can repeat the units and the exercises in subsequent years, so don't ever feel pressured to get to all of them, and feel free to repeat ones you enjoy.
- Often a single exercise can be presented to all of your children, no matter their ages or abilities. They will naturally write at the level they are at and, as they practice, will grow as writers.
- As you progress through the exercises, watch for something that sparks interest and could become the writing project. Feel free to jump to the idea bank at the end of the unit anytime as well. If there's spare time after the project is published, return to more exercises.
- Your family may all be in different places in the writing process. That's perfectly fine. Remember, your Writer's Workshop is a garden and everyone is growing their own patch. You can all lend a hand to help each gardener's patch thrive, but you won't all grow the same crop.

It's time to write! Choose some exercises and jump right in!

Sentences

EXERCISE: Phrases

Before we can begin writing sentences we need to learn some of the parts that make up sentences. Phrases are groups of words that make up parts of sentences. They don't make sentences on their own because they only

---

☐ **Mini-Lesson**

A sentence tells what someone or something did or does. Practice creating simple sentences together by thinking of a person or thing, then telling what the person or thing did or does.

☐ **Mini-Lesson**

Like a phrase, a clause is just a part of a sentence. An independent clause contains a subject and a verb. Independent clauses can be sentence all on their own.

The bat flew.

The rat ran.

The girl jumped.

Create some of your own independent clauses that are also simple sentences.

☐ **Mini-Lesson**

Sentences can, and often do, have more than one subject and/or more than one predicate. We call parts of sentences that have at least one subject and one verb a clause. A sentence can have one or more clauses.

I like pandas, but I hate snakes.

Can you spot two clauses in that sentence? Try writing some of your own sentences that have two clauses.

☐ Mini-Lesson

Dependent clauses contain a subject and a predicate, but they can't stand on their own as a sentence.

because she was home

although the owl was gone

since he was shivering

which was unbelievable

Can you add an independent clause to each of these clauses to make a complete sentence?

☐ Mini-Lesson

Play "Is It A Sentence?" Write some sentences and fragments on note cards and post them around the room. Have everyone find and gather as many cards as they can. If you found a sentence and identified it as one, you get to keep the card. If you find a fragment, you must identify it as incomplete and then turn it into a complete sentence out loud in order to win the card. See how many cards you can get. Here are some ideas:

Sleeps on a log.

The barn is red.

Into the woods.

Frogs ribbit.

The clouds drift away.

Cows in the pasture.

Kids play in the field.

The green tractor's bucket.

contain one part of the sentence. They aren't complete ideas. There are five kinds of phrases.

- Verb phrases contain a verb, but no subject: *towered mightily*
- Adjective phrases describe nouns or pronouns: *extremely tall*
- Noun phrases are made of nouns and any words that are describing or modifying the noun: *the skyscraper*
- Adverbial phrases describe verbs, adjectives, and adverbs. They answer these questions about the sentence: How? How often? When? Where?: *mightily in the skyline*
- Prepositional phrases use prepositions, words that tell you where or when something is located: *in the skyline*

These four kinds of phrases often overlap with each other in a sentence. Can you spot the kinds of phrases in this sentence?

The skyscraper, extremely tall and foreboding, towered mightily in the skyline.

As you learn to build sentences, you'll add verb, adjective, noun, adverbial, and prepositional phrases to build sentences. Use some Legos or wooden blocks and write words on them with permanent markers Make blocks with verbs, nouns, adjectives, adverbs, and prepositions on them. You might also want to add blocks with articles (a, the) and conjunctions (and, but, or). Build simple phrases and then put the phrases together to build sentences.

EXERCISE: Subjects and Predicates

Just like food needs salt and pepper, sentences need subjects and predicates in order to be complete. You can use the S from "salt" and the P from "pepper" to help you remember the two parts that every sentence needs - the subject and the predicate.

Sometimes we call the subject of the sentence the "naming part" because it names who or what the sentence is about. It is the noun or pronoun in the sentence. The predicate is sometimes called the "action part" because it tells what the subject does or is.

Can you identify the subject and the predicate of each of these sentences?

The fish swims.

A dolphin jumps.

My family relaxes.

The waves tumble.

Below, the bold words are the simple subjects and the underlined words are the simple predicates.

The **fish** <u>swims</u>.

A **dolphin** <u>jumps</u>.

My **family** <u>relaxes</u>.

The **waves** <u>tumble</u>.

Some sentences aren't quite so simple. Try finding the simple subject and simple predicate in each sentence below.

The fish swims over the coral reef.

A dolphin jumps so high that she looks like she's flying.

My family relaxes on the beach all day long.

The waves tumble and my boat bobs up and down.

The **fish** <u>swims</u> over the coral reef.

A **dolphin** <u>jumps</u> so high that she looks like she's flying.

My **family** <u>relaxes</u> on the beach all day long.

The **waves** <u>tumble</u> and my **boat** <u>bobs</u> up and down.

Use a set of salt and pepper shakers to help you remember how to build your own complete sentences with subjects and predicates. Think of a subject first, and shake your salt shaker while you say your subject. Then think of a predicate that the subject can do or be. Shake your pepper shaker while you say the predicate. Each time you build a sentence, make sure you have added both "salt" and "pepper" to make it complete.

Practice subjects and predicates using the "Salt & Pepper Sentences" printable from the Printable Pack in two different ways. First, you can write down sentences from books and then try to find the subjects and predicates. Second, you can come up with your own subjects and predicates and then use them to write your very own sentences.

EXERCISE: Independent & Dependent Clause Match-Up

A clause is a group of words that has both a subject and a verb. A clause can be a complete simple sentence or it can function as just part of a sentence if you add another clause to it. The main clause of a sentence is called an independent clause because it can stand on its own.

☐ **Mini-Lesson**

Every sentence begins with a capital letter. That capital letter is your signal to your readers that you are starting a new idea.

Write three sentences about yourself that begin with three different letters. Make sure to capitalize each of the sentences.

☐ **Mini-Lesson**

The only difference between an independent clause and a sentence is that a sentence always begins with a capital letter and ends with an end mark - a period, question mark, or exclamation point. Turn these independent clauses into sentences:

my ball popped

the man ran away

her bike tipped over

☐ **Mini-Lesson**

We typically construct sentences in subject-verb-object order. We begin by saying who or what the sentence is about (the subject). Then we tell what the subject does (verb). Finally, we tell any related objects that are involved. Rearrange these mixed up sentences to put them in the correct subject, verb, object order.

Howling the dog is.

Over the river jumped the boy.

Into the woods she leapt.

☐ Mini-Lesson

Write each of these sentences. Underline the subject once and the predicate twice.

We saw a scary movie.

Three mice ran away.

My favorite candy is chocolate.

Johnny has a red tulip.

☐ Mini-Lesson

Write each of these sentences and then circle the subject. Make sure not to circle the object in the sentence. Both are nouns, but the subject tells who or what the sentence is about.

Miss Lily has a parrot.

Jim fell off his scooter.

Amy fetched the slippers.

Luke walks his dog, Bo, every single day.

Seashells dot the beach.

Subjects: Miss Lily, Jim, Amy, Luke, Seashells

☐ Mini-Lesson

Sentences that are missing either a subject or a predicate are incomplete and are called fragments. If you see "frag" written next to one of your sentences by your editor, that means you wrote a fragment. Add the missing subject or predicate to fix it.

frag

Dependent clauses also have a subject and a verb, but they don't make sense on their own. Try to identify the independent and dependent clauses in the following sentence:

John woke up early every morning because his cat didn't stop meowing until he got fed.

"John woke up early every morning" could stand on its own as a sentence. It is a complete thought and is the independent clause. "Because his cat didn't stop meowing until he got fed" can't stand on its own. It is the dependent clause.

Use the "Independent and Dependent Clause Match-Up" from the Printable Pack to play a matching game. As you flip each card, identify whether it's a dependent or an independent clause. If you get two independent clauses or two dependent clauses, you didn't get a match. Flip them back over. If you turn over one of each, combine them into a sentence. There are many combinations in the game that can work. Note that if you place the dependent clause first, you set it apart with a comma between the two clauses.

Benny is giving his cat a bath while the babies sleep.

While no one else is around, Benny is giving his cat a bath.

Better than anyone else can, Suzy jumps on the trampoline.

Joey is popping popcorn and everyone is cheering.

Make sure you have kids add capital letters at the beginning of each sentence, capitalize all of the proper nouns, add commas when the dependent clause is listed first, and include a period at the end of each sentence.

Keep taking turns, making matches, and writing sentences until all of the cards are matched.

(The top six on the printable are independent while the bottom six are dependent.)

EXERCISE: From Fragment to Sentence

Fragments are incomplete sentences. Write some simple fragments up on the board or on a sheet of paper. Here are a few to get you started:

Amy saw

went to the gym

ate spaghetti

The two giraffes

Are these complete sentences? What is wrong with them? How can we fix them? Some are missing the subject, some are missing the predicate, and some are just missing end marks. Take turns calling out ways to complete the sentences. Finally, choose one of the fragments and write a really excellent sentence using it. Share the sentences you came up with.

EXERCISE: What Makes a Sentence?
A sentence is made up of at least one subject and at least one predicate. Choose two different colors of craft sticks. On one color, come up with subjects together and write each one on a stick. On the other color, come up with predicates together and write each one on a stick. Draw out one subject and one predicate from each pile and use them to write your own complete sentence. Can you add anything to your sentences to help them tell even more?

EXERCISE: Silly Sentences
Practice building sentences by rolling the "Silly Sentence Dice" from the Printable Pack. Roll one subject die and one predicate die. Write the sentences down as you roll them. Can you write some of your own silly sentences that include the subject and predicate you rolled? Put your sentences in the Journal section of your Writer's Notebook.

EXERCISE: Who, What, Where, When, Why
Gather some 3" x 5" index cards. At the top of each card, write one of these words: who, what, where, when, why.

Make several sets. Write in a variety of people, events, places, times, and reasons on the cards. Rearrange them in silly or interesting ways to craft sentences that include all of these details.

☐ **Mini-Lesson**

Copy great sentences and talk about what makes them great. Here are a few great sentences that you could copy. What makes the sentence a stand-out?

"Sometimes I can feel my bones straining under the weight of all the lives I'm not living."
— Jonathan Safran Foer, *Extremely Loud and Incredibly Close*

"In spite of everything, I still believe people are really good at heart."
— Anne Frank, *The Diary of Anne Frank*

"Let the wild rumpus start!"
— Maurice Sendak, *Where the Wild Things Are*

"Tomorrow is always fresh, with no mistakes in it yet."
— L.M. Montgomery, *Anne of Green Gables*

"You can have a wonky nose and a crooked mouth and a double chin and stick-out teeth, but if you have good thoughts it will shine out of your face like sunbeams and you will always look lovely."
— Roald Dahl, *The Twits*

"Unless someone like you cares a whole lot, nothing is going to get better. It's not."
— Dr. Seuss, *The Lorax*

"You don't have to live forever, you just have to live."
— Natalie Babbit, *Tuck Everlasting*

Writer's Workshop

☐ Mini-Lesson

Practice punctuating.

Write a series of sentences up on the board or on a sheet of paper that don't have any end marks. Add the appropriate end marks to match the sentence.

☐ Mini-Lesson

Exclamation points should be used sparingly. In particular, if you are writing nonfiction (true) pieces, like essays or true stories, you should avoid over-using exclamatory sentences. Even in fictional stories, exclamation points should be used sparingly.

☐ Mini-Lesson

Run-on sentences are two sentences that are incorrectly joined together. Correct this run-on sentence by making two shorter sentences.

Dad looks up he sees fireworks.

☐ Mini-Lesson

Does your sentence have SWAG? Use the letters from SWAG to make sure to include these things:

Starts with a capital

Written neatly

A space between each word

Given punctuation

At first, stick to this order: who, what, where, when, why. Then, see if you can rearrange the order and still create sentences that make sense. You might have to add a few words here and there to make sentences that flow. As you build sentences, write down your best ones on a sheet of paper to add to the Journal in your Writer's Notebook. When you're creating sentences, always consider adding the who, what, where, when, and why details.

EXERCISE: Simple Sentence Mix and Match

Create your own simple sentences using the "Simple Sentence Mix and Match" printable from the Printable Pack. You will draw lines from one column to the other to build a sentence. See if you can write a little story using the sentences you create. If you need to add some sentences to make your story flow, go ahead. Just make sure each of your sentences includes a subject and a predicate. Keep this in your Journal.

EXERCISE: End Marks

All sentences end with an end mark. An end mark is a punctuation mark that tells you the sentence is finished. There are three marks to choose from that you place at the end of a sentence: periods, question marks, or exclamation points. Periods follow statements. Question marks follow questions. Exclamation points follow sentences that express emotion or excitement.

Players will perform actions to go with each end mark as you play Punctuation Red Light Green Light. Using three sheets of paper, draw a period, a question mark, and an exclamation point really large to fill up the sheet.

To play, stand across the yard or park from the kids. Call out "green light" to start the game. This allows everyone to begin walking toward you. Take turns holding up one sign at a time. If you hold up the period, they must stop. If you hold up the exclamation point, they must hop in place, and if you hold up the question mark, they must stop, tilt their head to the side, and shrug their shoulders. Between each one, you let them begin walking toward you again by saying, "Green light!" The first kid to get to you wins. If they make a mistake, they return to the starting line.

Talk about how we use traffic lights to communicate at intersections. Without them, we would crash into each other and there would be chaos. Punctuation also allows us to communicate with each other and prevents chaos in what we write.

Practice writing sentences that include each of the three

kinds of end marks. Put your sentences in the Journal section of your Writer's Notebook.

EXERCISE: How To Read Using End Marks

Did you know that punctuation helps us read? Our voices change pitch depending on the punctuation at the end of a sentence. When you come to a period, you drop your voice a little. When you come to a question mark, you raise the pitch of your voice a little. When you come to an exclamation point, you read the sentence a little louder or with more feeling.

Pull out some books you love and practice reading using the punctuation marks as clues. Then write some of your own sentences with each of the marks. Highlight each end mark with a highlighter pen and then read your sentences aloud to someone, taking cues from your end marks.

EXERCISE: Fill in the End Mark

Use the "Young Crab and His Mother" printable from the Printable Pack to practice filling in the end marks in the classic Aesop's Fable. You can repeat this exercise using any text for practice. Just copy and paste the text, remove the end marks, and have kids practice filling them in.

EXERCISE: 4 Types of Sentences

There are four types of sentences you can use as you write.

Declarative sentences are statements. They end with a period. Most of the sentences we write are declarative. Can you hear how the word declarative sounds similar to the word declaration? A declaration is just a statement, and that's exactly what a declarative sentences is.

> *I am going to the store.*
>
> *There's a big dog near the tree.*
>
> *That house is getting painted.*

Interrogative sentences are questions. When a detective interrogates a suspect, he or she asks the suspect many questions to try to find out what happened. Interrogative sentences end with question marks.

> *What is your name?*
>
> *Where is your dog?*
>
> *How did you get to be so tall?*

Imperative sentences are commands. The word imperative means important and the word is usually used when the command is coming from an authority. When we

---

☐ **Mini-Lesson**

Practice writing declarative sentences about each of these topics:

- Balloons
- Camera
- Cat
- Bicycle

☐ **Mini-Lesson**

Practice writing exclamatory sentences that express excitement or emotion about each of these subjects:

- Pizza
- Car
- Tiger
- Dog

☐ **Mini-Lesson**

Practice writing interrogative sentences that ask questions about each of these subjects:

- Trampoline
- Robber
- Flood
- Storm

☐ **Mini-Lesson**

Practice writing imperative sentences about each of these subjects:

- Boat
- Accident
- Vegetable
- Museum

Writer's Workshop

☐ **Mini-Lesson**

Interrogative sentences end with a question mark. Play "Ask Me Anything." Try to have a conversation using only questions. Alternate between two people, seeing who can go longer using only interrogative sentences within the conversation.

What's your name?

Why do you ask?

Don't you know your name?

Don't YOU know my name?

Are you trying to get on my nerves?

Are you ever going to tell me your name?

Have you ever heard people call me Violet?

Is that your name?

Continue the questions until one player is stumped!

☐ **Mini-Lesson**

Play Imperative Simon Says. Simon Says is a game of commands. The leader speaks for Simon and gives off commands. He or she says, "Simon says pat your head." "Simon says hop on one foot. " Each time the leader begins with the words "Simon says" the players are obliged to follow the command. If the leader gives a command without using the phrase "Simon says," they must not follow. If you fail to follow Simon's commands or do something when Simon doesn't say "Simon says," you are out.

command people to do something, it is an imperative sentence and often begins with a verb or a verb phrase. They can end with a period or an exclamation point, depending on the emotion and tone.

Go to your room!

Please walk on the sidewalk.

Don't forget to pick up the milk.

Exclamatory sentences are emotion-packed or forceful. They are just like declarative sentences except that they convey excitement or emotion.

You are crazy!

That was the best show I've ever been to!

I love the rain!

Use the "4 Types of Sentences" flip book printable from the Printable Pack to practice writing sentences of each type. Cut between each kind of sentence along the lines. Glue the printable to another sheet of paper, adhering the glue only in the area under the "4 Types of Sentences" heading. Lift each of the flaps and write sentences of each kind under each flap. Younger students can write one of each kind while older students can practice writing many well-crafted sentences of each kind.

EXERCISE: Declarative Sentence ABCs
Write declarative sentences until you have managed to use every single letter in the alphabet at least one time. Use the "Alphabet Sentences" printable from the Printable Pack and cross out each letter as you use it. You can try this activity again using a variety of kinds of sentences. Try it with interrogative, imperative, or exclamatory sentences.

EXERCISE: Interrogative Conversation
Write a conversation between two people that is entirely made up of interrogative sentences, or questions. How long can you stretch the conversation and still have it make sense while only conversing in questions?

EXERCISE: Imperative Warnings
You might encounter imperative warning labels. There are warning labels on all kinds of things, and many of them are really obvious. "Warning: Do not use in tub," reads the label on a hair dryer. "Be careful. Hot chocolate is hot," reads the label on the hot chocolate cup. Write some imperative sentences that could be found on warning labels, the more obvious the better.

EXERCISE: Interjections

Interjections are short phrases that express emotion or excitement. They aren't common in formal writing, but if you are writing dialogue, you'll probably use them since people tend to speak less formally than they write. If the emotions they express are strong, then you set them apart in their own exclamatory sentence and end it with an exclamation point.

Ouch! Hooray! Uh oh! Shh! Phew!

If they are milder emotions, you can include them within your sentence and set them apart using a comma.

Hmm, I'm not sure where to go.

Yuck, I hate cauliflower.

Ow, I just pinched my finger.

Have a conversation with a partner in which you take turns speaking using interjections. If it's a mild emotion, trace a comma in the air with your finger as you speak it. If it's a strong emotion, trace an exclamation point in the air with your finger as you speak it. As you write, you should use interjections sparingly, and usually only when someone is speaking them inside quotation marks.

EXERCISE: Describe the Picture

Look at some pictures from a book or the internet. Write a sentence about the picture you see. Make sure to include a capital letter at the beginning, a subject, a predicate, and an end mark. Here's a picture to get you started.

EXERCISE: This Sentence Has Five Words

Sentences often have five words. Listen to several of them. Five words are fine sometimes. Five words are pretty easy.

☐ **Mini-Lesson**

As you craft sentences, it can be helpful to start with a word cloud as a prewrite. Write your topic in the center, then surround it with as many related words and phrases as you can come up with that describe your topic. As you're writing, your word cloud can serve as an inspiration board.

☐ **Mini-Lesson**

We use adjectives to help us describe things. Adjectives can tell us the size, color, shape, texture, and even smell of something. Play "I Spy." Have someone choose an object in the room that they spy. The others must try to guess the object by asking only yes or no questions. Any time an adjective is spoken during the game, write it on a piece of paper. See how many adjectives you come up with while you play.

☐ **Mini-Lesson**

Sentence fluency is one of the six traits of writing. When we create sentences of different formats and lengths, we improve our sentence fluency. Open a book you're reading and count the words or syllables in each sentence within a paragraph or two. How did the author do on varying sentence length?

☐ Mini-Lesson

As you build sentences, one trick is to join two action parts together. In the following sentences you can see two actions: going to the aviary and holding an owl.

We went to the aviary.

We held an owl.

You can join those two actions together into one sentence because the subject (we) is the same.

We went to the aviary and held an owl.

Can you write two simple action sentences that share the same subject and then combine them into one sentence?

☐ Mini-Lesson

You can also combine two describing parts of sentences if they tell about the same subject.

The alligator is large.

It has sharp teeth.

Those two sentences are both describing the same subject, the alligator, so we can combine them together.

The alligator is large and has sharp teeth.

Try combining these describing sentences into just one sentence:

Manatees are friendly.

They are sometimes called sea cows.

Then they take a turn. Five word sentences get boring. They become monotonous when read. Listen to what is happening. It is a similar rhythm. Your ear craves more variety. Please add or remove words. Five words drive me crazy!

Now listen as I create a new rhythm. Listen. There is a lilt, a sing-song rhythm that sounds in my ear. Short sentences, medium sentences, and long sentences all come together to create a symphony of sound. It's like music to my ears. Sometimes, every so often, I will even throw in a sentence that keeps on going, drawing my reader in deeper and deeper as I build up to the big moment that sounds off, signaling that this sentence, this one building sentence, is important.

Practice writing a series of sentences that include sentences of different lengths. Choose something you would like to write about and compose several sentences of varying lengths, some short, some medium, and at least one long sentence.

EXERCISE: Stretch-A-Sentence

To stretch a sentence, begin by asking...

Who?

My playful puppy

Did what?

My playful puppy barked and played.

When?

My playful puppy barked and played in the afternoon sunshine.

Where?

My playful puppy barked and played in the afternoon sunshine in the grassy meadow.

Why?

My playful puppy barked and played in the afternoon sunshine in the grassy meadow, just waiting for the rabbits to pop out of their holes and play too.

Can you stretch some sentences?

EXERCISE: Digging Deeper

As we practice writing sentences we can start with an idea, then keep expanding it to give even more details. Think of your idea like a pit you are digging. It takes some effort to come up with an idea. It takes even more effort to dig deep and tell more details about the idea you began with.

The deeper you go, the more effort it takes, but your big ideas will have a much bigger impact on your readers and how much they understand your idea.

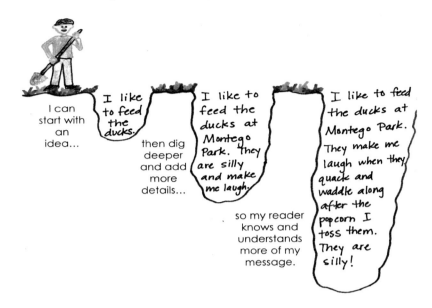

Use the "Digging Deeper" printable from the Printable Pack to practice taking an idea and digging deep with details.

EXERCISE: Compound Sentences

If we only write using simple sentences, our writing begins to feel dry and mundane. To make our sentences more varied and interesting, we can combine them and create sentences with a variety of formats and lengths. Begin with two related sentences and then see if you can join them into one compound sentence by adding a conjunction in between. Can you combine these two simple sentences and create one compound sentence?

> I want to go to the park.
>
> I need to clean my room.

I want to go to the park, but I need to clean my room.

Think of a train with cars. The conjunction goes in between to link up the cars of the train, or the clauses of the sentence.

Use the "Conjunctions and Compound Sentences" printable from the Printable Pack to craft several of your own compound sentences.

☐ **Mini-Lesson**

Conjunctions are words that link simple sentences and clauses together. Memorize the seven most common conjunctions using the FANBOYS acronym:

For

And

Nor

But

Or

Yet

So

☐ **Mini-Lesson**

There are two ways to fix a run-on sentence. One way is to create two shorter sentences. Another way is to join the sentences by adding a conjunction and a comma. This creates a compound sentence. Transform these run-on sentences in each way.

Juniper ran in the thick fog she couldn't find her way home.

The stars shone brightly they made pictures in the sky.

Desmond couldn't believe his luck he found money in his mailbox.

The circus was coming to town everyone was buying tickets and making plans.

☐ Mini-Lesson

☐ Mini-Lesson

Just because you see the word "and" or another conjunction does not mean you have a compound sentence. Compound sentences are formed with two independent clauses. That means each part could stand on its own as one sentence.

In the middle of the night I heard a noise and got out of bed.

Because *got out of bed* is not a complete sentence on its own, the sentence is not a compound sentence and does not need a comma after the *and*.

Can you imitate the sentence above and craft some of your own sentences that include the word *and* without requiring a comma?

☐ Mini-Lesson

Play a game called "Just One Word." Go around the room and tell a story with each person adding just one word at a time. Keep going around the room adding one word at a time in turn. The only rule is that the story must continue to make sense. See where the story takes you as you build it just one word at a time. It will end when someone says "The" and the next person says "End."

EXERCISE: Famous Quote Conjunctions

Combine these sentences by famous authors. Add a conjunction between the two or three written sentences to join them into one single sentence. As you combine several simple sentences you are forming one compound sentence.

> *"Some journeys take us far from home. Some adventures lead us to our destiny."*
> — C.S. Lewis, The Lion, The Witch, and the Wardrobe

> *"You have been my friend. That in itself is a tremendous thing."*
> — E.B. White, Charlotte's Web

> *"She smelled something wonderful. It smelled like candy and lemons and cloves. It smelled like sleeping in the sun and staying up late for a party."*
> — Dashka Slater, Dangerously Ever After

Now try taking apart these compound sentences by removing the conjunction and breaking the sentence apart into two sentences.

> *"Grown-ups never understand anything by themselves, and it is tiresome for children to be always and forever explaining things to them."*
> — Antoine de Saint-Exupéry, The Little Prince

> *"Her heart grew tired and sore, but she was too proud to make trouble."*
> — Frances Hodgson Burnett, A Little Princess

> *"What she really wanted was a nice plate of lima beans, but she had been laughed at enough for one day."*
> — David Shannon, A Bad Case of Stripes

EXERCISE: Sentence Links

Create compound sentences by making sentence links.

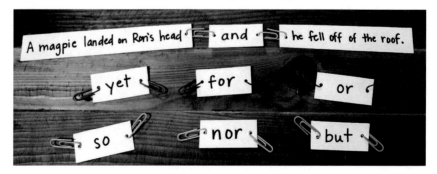

Cut out one-inch strips of card stock. Gather some pens, paper clips, and a hole punch. Begin by writing the seven most common coordinating conjunctions (for, and, nor,

but, or, yet, so) on the strips and hole punching each end. Connect a paper clip to each side, then write your own sentence parts on the paper strips, hole punch the appropriate end, and connect your links.

Using the conjunctions helps you to craft compound sentences. Create at least one compound sentence for each coordinating conjunction.

EXERCISE: Rearrange the Sentence

Rearranging the words within sentences can also help you create better sentence fluency and rhythm within your writing. Sometimes we can change the order of the words within our sentences to make them more interesting and varied. We craft sentences thoughtfully by deciding not only the words we should say, but also how we should say them. Just like varying the sentence length, varying the sentence structure will help keep the interest of your readers. There's not one perfect format for sentences. The truth is, always writing in just one format would be boring. We want to write with variety.

Here are a few examples of ways you can rearrange sentences:

> *The lion raised its regal head and roared.*
>
> *The lion roared, raising its regal head.*
>
> *Shane is the best chess player I know, so I've never dared to play with him.*
>
> *I've never dared to play with Shane because he's the best chess player I know.*
>
> *She barely escaped, but she was running as fast as she could.*
>
> *Running as fast as she could, she barely escaped.*

Sometimes, rather than simply rearranging, you can even combine the information from several sentences to condense what you're saying into one detailed thought.

> *I made a delicious pie for Thanksgiving.*
>
> *It has peanut butter and bananas in it.*
>
> *The delicious pie I made for Thanksgiving has peanut butter and bananas in it.*

Practice writing and rearranging your own sentences. Begin by writing some sentences that include several details. If your sentences are too short they will be difficult to rearrange. Make at least two or three versions of each sentence you wrote. Try having the verb come first sometimes. If your sentence is a compound sentence,

☐ Mini-Lesson

As we rearrange sentences we need to be careful to always craft sentences that still make sense. If you read the sentences aloud as you write, your ear can help you know if you put them in the proper order.

Rearrange these sentences so they are in the right order. Keep in mind that we use Subject-Verb-Object order. Also, make sure to add a capital letter at the beginning and a proper end mark at the end.

> *drinks milk my brother*
>
> *a fish Lisa caught*
>
> *her shares Penelope lunch*
>
> *grew green beans Ralph*
>
> *peanut butter Kim likes and jam*

☐ Mini-Lesson

Sentence fluency includes beginning sentences in a variety of ways. Try to avoid using the same word to begin every one of your sentences. Can you rewrite these sentences so they can start in a variety of ways instead of always using *The* at the beginning?

> *The ants were coming to the picnic. The ants could see the food! The food looked so good. The girls had packed sandwiches, grapes, crackers, and cookies. The ants were coming for it all. The picnic was just too tasty and the ants couldn't resist!*

☐ Mini-Lesson

Often prepositions are used to connect two nouns and show their relationship. For example, take the nouns "cupcake" and "baby." I could keep the cupcake away from the baby. Or maybe I will give the cupcake to the baby. Perhaps the baby will crawl toward the cupcake. The words that show their relationship to each other are prepositions.

Play Preposition Simon Says. It's the same as normal Simon Says, except the leader must include a preposition in his or her command.

Simon says touch under your nose.

Simon says rub near your ears.

☐ Mini-Lesson

Memorize the prepositions of time:

in

on

at

since

for

ago

before

to

past

from/to

till/until

by

think about how you can rearrange the two halves. Try combining the details of several sentences into one idea. Play with your sentences and see how many ways you can arrange them. In your writing, strive to have a variety of formats to improve your sentence fluency.

EXERCISE: Adding Prepositions

We've practiced writing basic sentences, but with practice, you can begin to write sentences that are more and more complex. One simple way to add on to your sentences is by adding a prepositional phrase. Prepositions are words that tell more about the location or status of your sentence's subject. For example, you could tell where your subject is.

*My doll is smiling **in** her cradle.*

*Janice is swimming **at** the neighborhood pool.*

*She breezed **through** her driver's test with ease.*

*Monkeys played **near** the banana tree.*

Prepositions tell us about the relationships and locations of the things we're writing about. If you are trying to identify prepositions, you can think of a cloud. Anything a plane can do to a cloud is a preposition. You can go **through** it, sit **near** it, go **over** it, go **under** it, look **at** it, be **with** it. Can you think of any more?

Use the "Prepositions Anchor Chart" from the Printable Pack. Look at the cloud and think of the ways you could interact with it. Write down all the prepositions you can think of on the cloud - through, into, over, near, towards, between, across, behind, beyond, by, around, under, off, on, with, along, in, above, below.

Besides prepositions of place, there are also prepositions of time. For example, before, after, since, during, and throughout are all prepositions.

For every preposition you come up with, write a sentence that includes a preposition. Add your "Prepositions Anchor Chart" to the Writing Helps section of your Writer's Notebook.

EXERCISE: Imagine A...

As you write sentences, strive to create images. Your readers are using their imaginations to fill in the blanks of what you write. They are trying to picture in their minds what your words are telling them. Great writing makes it easy for

us to imagine. It gives just enough information to paint a picture in our minds.

Imagine a scene in your mind. It could be a person, an animal, or a place. Take a minute to close your eyes and look around your mind's eye at all the things you see, hear, smell, and experience in the scene. In a few sentences, write about the scene. Start out with the words "Imagine a" and then create an image using words.

> *Imagine an old woman, apron strings tied tightly around her pressed, blue, striped dress, her face wrinkled from years of smiling. She's at her farmhouse sink, looking out the window at her garden of red tulips.*

Two simple sentences can create a complete picture in your imagination if you include a few details that matter.

EXERCISE: Sentence Diagramming

There are six steps to learning to diagram basic sentences.

Step #1: Write the simple subject and the verb on a horizontal line. Separate them by drawing a vertical line that intersects the horizontal line.

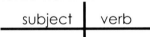

Step #2: If the verb has a direct object it's acting on, write it after the verb on the line.

Step #3: Put any adjectives on a slanted line under the noun or pronoun they modify.

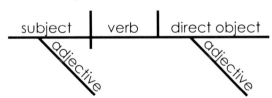

Step #4: Put any adverbs on a slanted line under the verb, adverb, or adjective they modify.

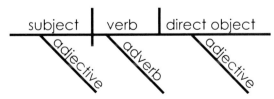

Step #5: Decide whether prepositional phrases are acting as adverbs or adjectives and put them under the words they modify.

☐ **Mini-Lesson**

Write a sentence. The first word should have one letter. The second word should have two letters. The third word should have three letters, and so on. How long can you make your sentence?

☐ **Mini-Lesson**

Semi-colons can be used to combine two sentences into one. They show a close relationship between the two ideas. The two parts could stand as sentences on their own, but the writer wants to show a close relationship, so a semi-colon separates them instead of a period.

> *The vampire was coming; Winnie screamed.*

> *I've never hurt so much; the viper's venom tore through my whole body.*

> *Bulls bolted from the area; cowboys chased them down.*

Write some of your own. Note that you don't need to use a capital letter after a semi-colon.

☐ **Mini-Lesson**

How do you come up with an idea when someone asks you to write, but doesn't assign a topic? An idea might just pop into your head. If it doesn't, you can thumb through your Journal and look at some things you've written about before or turn to your idea lists. These are all prewriting activities.

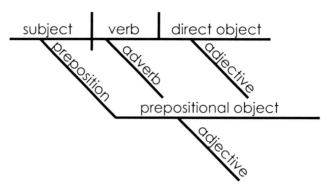

Sentence combining always makes a great mini-lesson and can be used over and over again. Look at this example, then try some of your own. Write down two or three related simple sentences. Combine the information from all of the sentences into one sentence.

The giraffe has a long neck.

He lives at the zoo.

He spends most of the day eating.

Possible answer:

The long-necked giraffe lives at the zoo and spends most of his day eating.

Step #6: Connect any compound elements with a dotted line and the conjunction.

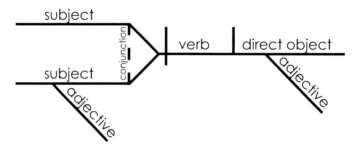

Use the "6 Steps To Diagramming Basic Sentences" anchor chart and the "Diagramming Sentences" printable from the Printable Pack to practice diagramming. You can continue to practice this skill using any sentence. Diagramming sentences helps you understand complete sentences, sentence structure, parts of speech, and punctuation rules. From time to time, use a sentence from your own writing or from a book you are reading and practice diagramming it as a mini-lesson.

Paragraphs

EXERCISE: Sweet as Ice Cream Details

Imagine for a moment that I offer you an ice cream cone. Just when you're licking your lips and getting anxious, I put an empty ice cream cone in your hand without any ice cream at all. Do you feel disappointed? That's how writing is when it doesn't include details. It's disappointing.

Think of a topic that interests you. Write the topic on the cone of the "Sweet as Ice Cream Details" printable from the Printable Pack. Add a detail about your topic on each scoop. If you don't know any details about your topic, you might need to look some up online or in a book. Make sure you use your own words if you look at another source for help. As you write paragraphs, picture an ice cream cone. Every important detail about the topic is like another sweet scoop of ice cream getting piled on top.

Commas separate dependent clauses, the part of a sentence that can't stand on its own, from independent clauses. The simplest sentences have only an independent clause and don't need a comma. Often the dependent clause provides a little more information. Here's an independent clause:

My grandpa is taking me to the zoo.

If we add a dependent clause, we set it apart with commas.

My grandpa, who rides in a wheelchair, is taking me to the zoo.

EXERCISE: A Paragraph Sandwich

Strong paragraphs have a very straightforward format. If you learn to follow the format well, you'll create clear ideas for your reader. You will build a paragraph much like you build a sandwich. Everything in the sandwich should go together. You wouldn't put mayonnaise on your peanut butter and jelly sandwich, would you? Everything in your paragraph sandwich should belong together.

The first sentence of a paragraph is like the bread, and it's called the topic sentence. Its job is to tell your reader what the entire paragraph is about.

The next several sentences share details about the topic. They are your sandwich toppings. They are the details that directly go with the bread. Everything in your paragraph should belong, just as everything on your sandwich should belong.

The final sentence is the other piece of bread. It is really similar to the first slice. Its job in the paragraph is to summarize what the paragraph was about. It might feel like you're repeating yourself, but actually you are restating your topic, not repeating it. Repeating would mean using the exact same words again, and that would be boring. Restating, on the other hand, is telling about your topic in a new way. You'll choose different words to solidify the same message. It helps hold the whole paragraph together, just like the two slices of bread on your sandwich.

Practice this format using the "Sandwich Organizer" from the Printable Pack. Choose a topic you are interested in and fill out the chart to help you plan your paragraph. Then write your paragraph on a sheet of paper.

EXERCISE: Building A Strong Paragraph House

Use the "Paragraph House" printable from the Printable Pack to practice writing strong paragraphs. Each paragraph is like a house that you build. The foundation is the main idea, or the topic of your paragraph, told in a complete sentence. Make it an interesting sentence by asking a question, sharing a great quote, or offering an interesting fact. The supporting ideas are the pillars that

☐ Mini-Lesson

A paragraph is a group of sentences that are all about one subject. They are built in three main parts: a topic sentence that tells what the paragraph is about, supporting details that give information about the topic, and a concluding sentence that sums up the information.

Share the pen, and as a group, create a paragraph about a vacation or outing you've been on.

☐ Mini-Lesson

At the beginning of a new paragraph we indent, or leave about half an inch space, before beginning the topic sentence. You can use the width of two fingers to estimate how much space you should leave.

☐ Mini-Lesson

Five seems like a magic number in writing. We use five sentences in paragraphs and five paragraphs in essays when we are learning to write. This isn't as magic as it seems though. It's perfectly okay to have a paragraph that is four sentences or six sentences (or more!). If you want to add more details to your paragraph, just add a slice of cheese to your paragraph sandwich.

☐ Mini-Lesson

Here are some reasons To start a new paragraph:

- A new idea is introduced
- The setting changes
- A new character comes along
- A new event happens
- A new person is speaking
- Time jumps forward (or backward)
- The "camera" or point of view moves.

Open a book and look at where a new paragraph begins. Can you tell why the author used a new paragraph in that spot?

☐ Mini-Lesson

Sometimes it's easier for writers to speak their sentences or paragraphs out loud before writing them down. Speaking can help you to gather your thoughts before you put your pencil to your paper. Think, speak, then write.

Practice speaking several topic sentences. Choose one of those to write down. Then practice speaking some sentences with supporting details. Write them down. Finally, practice speaking a concluding sentence that sums up your paragraph in a new way. Write down your conclusion.

Speaking out loud is a good prewriting activity that prepares you for drafting.

provide support for what you are saying. Make sure you have enough details so no one can knock down your paragraph house. Finally, the closing sentence is like a roof that protects the ideas you just shared.

EXERCISE: Highlighting Paragraph Parts

Use the "Highlighting Paragraph Parts" printable from the Printable Pack to practice identifying the parts of a paragraph. Highlight the topic sentence in one color, the supporting details in a second color, and the concluding sentence in a third color. You can practice this more using a nonfiction paragraph from a magazine. Find an interesting article from a children's magazine and read one or more of the paragraphs, highlighting as you go.

EXERCISE: Paragraph Booklet

Make a booklet to help you write a paragraph. Print the "Paragraph Booklet" from the Printable Pack. Cut apart the boxes and stack them, smallest to largest, with the biggest one at the back. Staple the top. On each page, write a sentence to accompany the label. Begin by choosing a topic you would like to write about. Write it on your first page. On the next page, add a topic sentence explaining your topic. On the following three pages, write sentences that describe the details of your topic. Add your concluding sentence on the final page.

A paragraph has a very clear and repetitive structure on purpose. This helps the reader to understand the topic clearly. Practice writing paragraphs until the structure becomes natural for you. As you develop your paragraph skills, make sure to also apply the lessons you learned about descriptive, well-crafted sentences in your booklet.

EXERCISE: Illustrated Paragraph

Choose something specific you are learning about in history, geography, science, or art. It may be a famous person or event, a landmark, an animal, or a painting. Make sure your topic is narrow enough that you can fit the information you want to share about it into one paragraph. Make an illustration or diagram and write one paragraph to accompany it.

The Sun

The sun helps the earth. The sun helps our plants to grow. It also gives us warmth. The sun also helps us to grow fruits and vegetables, plants to make our clothes, and wood to build our houses. There are so many things that the sun gives us. I love the sun.

EXERCISE: Quadrama

Make a quadrama. Begin with four pieces of card stock, some glue, and a pair of scissors. Create four perfect squares with your four pieces of card stock. Fold each square along each diagonal, then cut along one of the diagonal lines up until the midpoint of the line.

Apply glue to the bottom of one flap adjacent to the cut, then stick it down to the opposite adjacent side. Repeat that process with the other squares, then glue each one together. On each side, draw pictures about your topic.

Write a paragraph about your topic, then attach it to the bottom of your quadrama. You can write about a book you've read, a science or history topic, a place that's interesting to you, or a person. You can even make your own simple story and draw a scene in each section.

EXERCISE: Story Paragraphs

We use paragraphs when we write stories too, but the paragraphs serve a different purpose. In a story, you don't focus on a topic sentence and supporting details, but rather the order of the events. Make sure you tell what happens in the right order so your reader can follow the story. If there's a change of time, setting, or character, you show that change by beginning a new paragraph. For now, we'll focus on single paragraph short stories. We'll practice more story paragraphs in the Fanciful Stories and the True Stories units.

Make up a short story about a duck who gets lost. Make sure your story has a clear beginning, middle, and ending, all in one paragraph. Plan your events before writing each one so they are told in the right order. Write your one-paragraph story and then add an illustration.

☐ **Mini-Lesson**

The most important sentences to craft well are the opening and closing ones. The topic sentences and concluding sentences of a paragraph or a narration drive your writing and stick with your reader. Take extra time to really think about what you're writing and make these two sentences as clear and well-composed as you can.

☐ **Mini-Lesson**

A literature professor once told me, "You should never read an ugly book. There are too many beautiful books out there to waste your time on the ugly ones." Discuss how this could apply to the publishing stage of your writing.

☐ **Mini-Lesson**

Organization is one of the six traits of writing. Your organization score relies a lot on whether you use paragraphs properly.

Using transition words will boost your organization. Use transition words like first, second, third, last, then, next, therefore, finally, and similarly.

Write a paragraph that describes how to make a peanut butter and jelly sandwich. Make sure to use transition words within your paragraph to create an organized framework.

☐ Mini-Lesson

Narrating is telling about something you know. Communicating information that we've learned helps us solidify the knowledge and commit it to memory. It's a simple way to show what we know. The neat part about narrations is that you also get to combine your own ideas with what you learned. You aren't just going to relate a bunch of facts. Instead, you'll share the facts and tell what you think of them, offering your own ideas and experiences with the information you learned. Try to think about why your topic matters to you.

☐ Mini-Lesson

Listen to a familiar story and then tell it back out loud. Picture the events of the story in your mind as you listen so you will be able to recall them in order when you tell the story. Putting stories in the right order creates organized writing.

Familiar fairy tales are an excellent place to start. Picture books you've read many times work well too. Think of the important details of the story and make sure you relate them back in order as you give your retelling. As you practice, you can progress to retelling stories that are new to you that you've only heard once before.

Narrations

EXERCISE: Oral Narration

To narrate means to explain or tell about something. The word "oral" means out loud. When you do an oral narration you simply speak out loud about a topic. You tell what you know or remember about your topic, and then tell why it matters to you. Often before we write, it helps to speak our ideas out loud in this pattern.

Choose a topic you've learned about lately in history, geography, science, art, or from a book you've read. Answer one or more of these questions out loud about your topic:

- What were the big ideas you learned about?
- What was the most impressive thing to you?
- Were there any important people that stood out to you?
- Does anything about your topic relate to you and your life?
- What was your favorite thing you learned?
- Was there anything that surprised you?

EXERCISE: Illustrated Note Sheets

Illustrated note sheets include a variety of sketches along with written descriptions. You can write a short caption near each one, or be more detailed and include a paragraph or so about each picture. You'll begin by choosing a topic and deciding on at least three or four things you learned about the topic. For each thing you learned, include an illustration and then create a descriptive caption to go with it. You will end up with a page of illustrations and captions that has lots of information about your topic all on one page. Make it colorful, tidy, and descriptive.

EXERCISE: Written Narration

A written narration is just like an oral narration, except instead of speaking it out loud, you write down what you know. Written ideas, articulated, can stay with us. When you learn about something new, you can write a narration to show the things you learned. Usually, narrations are between one and three paragraphs. For young kids, they might be just one to three sentences.

Sentences, Paragraphs, & Narrations

Just like in oral narrations, you will tell the most important ideas, the details you remember, and your own thoughts about the topic.

Choose a topic you've been learning about and write a narration about it. Remember the things you've learned about crafting interesting sentences and building strong paragraphs as you write your narration. You'll find six different narration templates to choose from (blank pages with lines to write on) in the Printable Pack. You may want to keep a variety of them near your writing area to use often.

EXERCISE: Illustrated Narration

An illustrated narration is just like any other written narration, except you include at least one picture. It can be a simple drawing, a series of drawings, printed clip art or photographs, a diagram, a chart, or any other picture that goes along with your writing. The picture should add to what you have written, and be neat and colorful. Use a book you are reading currently and make an illustrated narration about the book, the author, or one of the characters.

EXERCISE: Short Answer Questions

Short answer questions are really common on tests, so it's important to practice writing them. They are a lot like narrations except that you aren't choosing your own topic. The test will ask you to write about something specific.

There are a few things you need to include in every short answer response. First, you write a topic sentence by restating the question as a declarative sentence and completing the thought. Second, you include evidence that supports your idea. Third, you write clearly and concisely. It is a short answer, not a complete essay. You are being asked to give as much information as you can about a topic using very few words.

Normally a single paragraph is the appropriate length. Some short answers allow you to write between one and three paragraphs. Your goal is to pack that paragraph with as much pertinent information as you can to show what you know clearly. Lastly, end with a concluding sentence that restates the topic of your paragraph in a new way.

☐ **Mini-Lesson**

Narrations are a way of summarizing. When asked to summarize something you've read, include

- Who it was about
- Where it happened
- What took place
- The lesson you learned from it

Practice by reading a short magazine article or a short story and then summarizing out loud.

☐ **Mini-Lesson**

Besides just telling what we know, written narrations also force us to think. Writing is about taking what we have learned and adding our own ideas to it. Use your thoughts, experiences, and stories to expand on what you learned. Put something of yourself into every narration you write. Ideas and content, one of the six traits of writing, relies on good information and your own ideas being included.

☐ **Mini-Lesson**

Narrations should be shared in the publishing step. When you share, you can either read what you wrote or tell it in your own words without reading it. Always stand up, smile, speak clearly, and make eye contact. When you're finished, always ask if anyone has any questions. If you don't know the answers, offer to try to find out. Conclude a presentation by simply saying thank you and giving a little nod.

Writer's Workshop

Some tips for short answer test questions:

- If you don't know the answer, you should still make an educated guess. Even if you don't get full credit, you may get a point or two just by responding in a thoughtful way.
- On a test, it's good to answer the questions you know first. You can waste a lot of time thinking and not finish the test if you are worrying over things you don't know. If you skip a question, make a little mark in the margin to remind you to come back to it after you've finished answering the ones you know.
- Answer every part. Often short answer questions will have multiple parts. For example, in the following question you would need to list both the struggles AND the triumphs.

What struggles and triumphs did Thomas Edison face as he invented the light bulb?

- After you've answered, go back and reread the question to make sure you answered it completely.
- Use your time wisely. If you have to answer ten questions, don't spend half of your time on the first one.

Here's an example question:

What are the important things we learn about the character of Joey in the story?

First, restate the question as a declarative sentence and complete the thought. Add evidence. Be concise. End with a concluding sentence that restates your idea.

The important things we learn about Joey's character are that he is brave, he is selfless, and he is caring. He shows he is brave when he stands up to the bully without even hesitating. His selflessness shows through as he forgets about his own troubles when he gets the phone call from his friend and drops everything to come and help. Finally, when the poor family is going without food and clothing, he shows how caring he is as he provides for them even though he doesn't have a lot of money for himself. Although the text never once used the words brave, selfless, or caring, these qualities showed through in Joey's actions.

Practice writing your own by answering some questions you create for each other about a topic you've been studying.

Here are some example questions to get you started:

- What are some contributions of the ancient Egyptians?
- Describe the life cycle of a butterfly.
- Explain the reasons exercise is good for your body.
- In what ways can a person show that he or she is a true friend?
- Tell about a species of animal that is endangered and what must be done in order to save it from extinction.
- Describe your favorite book and why it is your favorite.
- What elements of art did Van Gogh use in his famous painting, *Starry Night*?

EXERCISE: Types of Short Answer Questions

Short answer questions are usually in these common forms:

- Definition questions ask you to define a concept.
- Explanation questions have you explain details about a topic or how something works.
- Example questions ask you to give specific examples.
- Relationship questions expect you to show how two or more things are related. Specifically, they may require you to compare, or state the similarities, and contrast, or state the differences, between several items.

Practice answering each of these types of short answer questions. Begin by reading "Learning More About Fungus" from the Printable Pack. Study it and memorize the important material. Put the article away, then answer each

of these short answer questions on a sheet of paper. The questions correspond with the four types of questions listed above. Make sure to include a topic sentence, supporting details, and a concluding sentence regardless of what type of short answer question you are responding to.

1. Define photosynthesis, a feeding feature that makes fungus unlike plants.

2. Explain the things all fungi have in common.

3. Give examples of useful benefits humans get from fungus.

4. Compare and contrast the feeding of fungi and animals.

EXERCISE: Putting On The Teacher's Hat
Find some online articles for kids to read. The National Geographic Kids website has some excellent ones. Read an article, then practice writing short answer questions based on the article you read.

You can answer your own questions, or you can trade papers with someone, read each others' articles, then answer each others' questions. When you are finished, trade papers again and grade your partner's short answers. Is there a topic sentence that restates the question? Are there supporting details? Were all of the major points covered? Is there a concluding sentence? Finally, check to make sure all of the sentences are complete and include a capital letter and a proper end mark. Score your partner and then talk about the reasons behind the grades you gave.

Step 3: Writing Project

During this unit, you should complete at least one writing project, taking a piece of writing through the entire writing process. By the final week of the unit, if you haven't completed the project already, you should turn your attention to creating one polished piece of writing that uses the things you've practiced along the way.

Choose one topic to write about that you will take all of the way through the writing process. This piece of writing belongs in the Writing section of your Writer's Notebook. You can use something you've already started during this unit, your own idea, or something from the following idea banks. Make sure that you follow each step of the writing process and keep all of your steps to turn in with your finished writing.

• Step #1: Prewrite

☐ **Mini-Lesson**

The acronym ACE can help you as you answer short answer questions.

Answer the question completely.

Cite examples.

Extend your thinking. Connect your own thoughts about the subject with the examples you gave.

☐ **Mini-Lesson**

There are five basic types of short answer questions.

1. Definition questions: these ask you to define a concept so you can show you understand it.

2. Explanation questions: these require that you explain how something works or why something is true or events that occurred.

3. Example questions: these ask you to provide examples of a concept.

4. Relationship questions: these expect you to show how two or more things are related to each other. Often you will compare, or show how they are the same, and contrast, or show how they are different.

5. Math questions: these require math calculations along with an explanation of what you did. Sometimes a graph or chart is needed.

Writer's Workshop

☐ **Mini-Lesson**

After the end mark, you should include a space before you begin the next sentence. You probably naturally do this as you write, but you'll need to pay special attention to it as you type. In some academic writing and with certain fonts you will be asked to include two spaces after each period, but typically you can use just one.

☐ **Mini-Lesson**

For most of your typed school assignments you will be expected to use a standard font like Times New Roman or Arial. You should always use either 11 or 12-point font size and standard 1" margins. Your text should be double spaced.

☐ **Mini-Lesson**

Ellipses are sets of three dots (or periods) that are placed either at the end of a sentence to show that the sentence does not end or in the middle of a sentence to show that something was omitted.

I opened the door and then...

You can also use it to show hesitation.

Uh...never mind.

Whether you put spaces in between the periods is a style choice. Some people say you should include spaces while others say you should not. Whichever you choose, be consistent.

- Step #2: Draft
- Step #3: Revise
- Step #4: Edit
- Step #5: Publish

Begin with a prewriting activity, then compose a draft, revise it, edit it with help from someone else, and then publish it. Publishing it could include making a polished final copy, sharing it with someone, creating a book, or creating some form of finished project that is neat and done well. You'll turn in all of your work, from prewrite to publish.

Your project will be evaluated based on the six traits of writing, so make sure you look at your composition through each of those lenses - ideas and content, organization, word choice, sentence fluency, conventions, and voice. Try to incorporate things you learned from the mini-lessons and the exercises you worked on as well. Do your best work.

Sentences, Paragraphs, & Narrations Idea Bank

- Compose a paragraph about the most interesting thing you ever learned.
- Begin with the phrase "I didn't know that . . ." and continue to tell about something you learned that somehow changed your life or your perspective.
- Fill in the blank: I wonder why _____. Go on to describe what you are wondering and how you will find out in complete paragraph form.
- Write a paragraph about the biggest surprise you've ever gotten.
- Imagine that you are magically transported back to a specific historical event and tell how it would have been different if you were there.
- Begin by making a top ten list of places you'd like to visit and then transform the list into paragraph form.
- Compare two leaders, one from your studies and one who leads your nation today. Which one would you rather live under and why?
- Choose someone you know to interview. Discover new and interesting things about the person, then write a paragraph about the person and his or her life and experiences.
- Compare a real-life person to a character you've read about in a book. How are the two alike? How are they different?
- Choose a famous artist, scientist, explorer, or inventor. Write a paragraph about what the person should be remembered for.
- Describe a problem you've experienced and how you solved it.

- Look up an article online. Read and study it. Close the article and write about it in your own words.
- Look at a famous painting and study it closely. Describe details about the picture in a paragraph.
- Write a short answer quiz about something you're studying, complete with an answer key.
- Think of your favorite movie. Write a paragraph about what you would change in the movie.
- Read an article from the opinion page of a newspaper. What viewpoint was presented? Compare and contrast two ways to look at the issue.
- What famous person, living or dead, do you wish you could be friends with? What would you like to talk about or do together? What do you have in common?
- Draw a diagram and label or describe it in complete and descriptive sentences.
- Make a list of twenty-five interesting things. Choose one to research and write a paragraph about it.
- Natural disasters like earthquakes, floods, fires, and tornadoes can hit unexpectedly. Choose one or more of these and write about what you can do to be prepared for it.
- Have you ever moved? Do you wish you could move or would you rather stay in the same place? Write about what might make people either want to move frequently or set down roots and stay in the same place. Also include which you would prefer.
- Compose one to three paragraphs about how you can be healthy. Each paragraph should have its own focus. For example, you could write one about sleep, one about eating well, and another about exercise.
- Are you competitive? Do you think being competitive is a positive trait or a negative one? Include examples and evidence to support your ideas.
- Write a paragraph about the qualities you appreciate and admire in your friends. Are there traits that you think are particularly important in a friendship?
- Write about a childhood memory you have that has somehow shaped you or that helped you understand who you are. Perhaps there's something specific that helped you develop a certain trait or talent.
- Explain why good parents provide a mixture of love and discipline. What happens if this gets out of balance?
- What things do you need to do to be safe in your home? Write at least one paragraph about the steps you should take to be safe in your particular location. What are the potential hazards? How can you guard against them?
- Write a descriptive paragraph about what it would be like to be in a spooky, abandoned house. Describe the scene.
- Expound on some ideas you have for small, everyday

☐ **Mini-Lesson**

I am.

That is the shortest complete sentence in the English language. It has a subject (I) and a predicate (am). Can you write some more short sentences?

☐ **Mini-Lesson**

Besides punctuation, capitalization, and spelling, there are writing conventions about how to format your page when you are using notebook paper. The holes should always be on the left side. Your heading goes on the right and includes your name, your class, the assignment, and the date. A capitalized title is centered on the top line. Each new paragraph should begin on a new line and be indented.

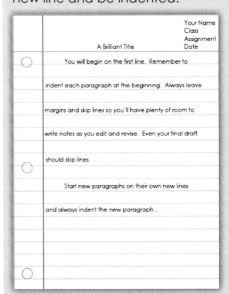

Remember to leave margins and plenty of space for revising and editing. It will make those stages of the writing process much easier later on.

Reminders About Your Writer's Notebook

Besides just the writing project, there should be many small writing samples that are being compiled in the Writer's Notebook from the exercises you worked on over the course of this unit. The Writer's Notebook is a tool for helping writers to grow. Explore it frequently and refer to idea lists and helps as you write.

At least once a week, it would be beneficial for you, the writer, to glance back through the exercises, lists, and mini-lessons to review and make sure that you are on track even though most of this work isn't graded.

Specifically, as you are working on the writing project, utilize your Writer's Notebook. You have anchor charts, exercises, and entries in your Journal - all of these can help you as you complete your project. Take time to review some of the concepts you've been working on during the unit so they can be incorporated into the final writing project. The things you've learned should SHOW in your writing project.

Remember that most of the work in the Writer's Notebook will never be graded, but it is still important. Use what you learned to make your project, which will be graded, the best that you can make it.

things that can be done to change the world.

- Have you ever won anything? Explain what it was like to win, what you experienced, and how you felt.
- Describe a costume you've worn before. Perhaps it was for a play you performed in, a Halloween costume, or just when you played dress-up for fun.
- Describe some responsibilities you have. Is there anything or anyone that you take care of? Do you have tasks that are just yours to accomplish? What do you think if means to be responsible?
- Describe how you clean your room. What steps do you take? How often do you clean it? How long does it take you? How do you feel as you clean and when you're done?
- Have you ever fixed something? Describe what you fixed and how you learned how to fix it.
- Write about what you wish you could be famous for. Is there anything you wish you could say you accomplished that you would always be known for?
- Describe the biggest thing you've ever seen with your two eyes.
- Describe the smallest thing you've ever seen.
- Write about your proudest moment.
- If you could magically appear in a television show and live there forever, which show would you choose and why?
- What does your morning look like? What do you do when you first wake up? How do you feel in the morning? How do you act?
- Write about something fun you do in your family. Do you have any neat traditions or fun activities you enjoy doing together?
- What things can you do on a computer? What skills and capabilities do you have? In a second paragraph, write about the things you still hope to be able to learn to do on a computer.
- Explain several things you would never want to live without.
- Describe your favorite holiday and tell about the things you do that make it your favorite.
- Write about three specific things you would do if you were invisible.
- Would you want to travel to space? Why or why not?
- Choose one of these weather phenomena to write about: snow, rain, lightning, thunder, wind, hurricanes, tornadoes, or hail. Do a little research and share what you discovered.
- Discuss some things you would never, ever eat. Are there any foods that you consider 100% off limits in your mouth?
- What would you do if you saw a wild critter in your

house? Perhaps a mouse, a raccoon, a snake, a rat, or a bat got into your house. What would you do?

- What do you think it would be like to live in a tree house? What things would you need in your tree house to live a happy and comfortable life?
- Are you better at spending money or saving money? Which do you think is more important and why?
- Use this sentence starter and complete the paragraph: I scream whenever I see . . .
- Describe some things you have accomplished that make you feel good about yourself.
- If you could go back in time to some part of your life, would you? What event or time would you want to return to? Are you returning because you loved that time so much, or is it because there's something you wish you could change?
- Tell about your ideal vacation, where you would go, and what you would do.

Step 4: Evaluating Writing

The purpose of this unit is to learn to write in complete sentences and to practice putting those sentences into meaningful, organized paragraphs. As you evaluate the project, look for complete sentences that contain subjects, predicates, capital letters at the beginning, and proper end marks. Also look for paragraphs that have topic sentences, supporting details, and concluding sentences.

As you evaluate the writing project, you will be using the "6 Traits of Writing Rubric" from the Printable Pack. In addition, you will be looking for each step of the entire writing process. For example, your child will turn in a prewriting activity, a draft that shows both revisions and edits, as well as a finished, published piece. The publishing step should involve sharing the project in some way - reading it aloud to family, presenting it at dinner time, video chatting to show it off to grandparents, or sharing a video presentation on the internet of the writer sharing his or her writing. Sharing is a time for positive feedback and celebration.

Creating a positive buzz about the published piece will create a motivating, growth atmosphere in your Writer's Workshop. As you evaluate, remember that the process is just as important as the product, so watch for successes in the process as well. The final score will be out of 50 points - 20 for the process and 30 for the final project. You can write rubric scores as well as comments down on the "Writing Report Card" printable from the Printable Pack.

Breakdown of Possible Points

- 5 points for a complete prewriting activity
- 5 points for a completed draft
- 5 points for revisions
- 5 points for edits
- 30 points for the finished writing project

The 30 points for the finished project is further broken down into each of the six traits of writing as shown on the "6 Traits of Writing Rubric" from the Printable Pack.

Your comments should be specifically focused on the purposes of this unit and the skills you were working on throughout the unit.

What was done well? Is the writer understanding the writing process? What should be improved on? Are there any repeated mistakes to address?

Point out a clear strength.

Comments mean more than scores, so make sure to give clear feedback.

Key Concepts

By the end of this unit your kids should be familiar with these ideas:

Writing descriptively

Using precise language

Sprinkling in figurative language (similes, metaphors, personification, idioms, hyperboles, alliterations, onomatopoeias, allusions, oxymorons)

The difference between denotation and connotation

Using adjectives and adverbs

Using a dictionary and a thesaurus

Showing instead of just telling

More Mini-Lesson Ideas

Along with the sidebars, try these mini-lesson ideas:

- Writer's Workshop links found in Layers of Learning catalog
- Lessons from any grammar workbook
- Every-Day Edits from Education World website
- Sentence diagramming
- Copying great sentences from master writers
- Mad Libs
- Correcting a repeated error from your writing
- Practicing expanding sentences by adding details
- Combining sentences by making two or three into a single sentence

The mini-lesson sidebars in this unit have check boxes so you can keep track of which ones you have completed.

Descriptions & Instructions

Descriptions and instructions both involve precise language. Writers often play with words much like chefs play with ingredients. They arrange them in unique ways and use literary devices to make the descriptions varied and interesting. Descriptive writing describes people, places, and events in great detail. Its aim is to make readers experience what is being described and be able to visualize it. In the case of instructions, the aim is to enable your readers to duplicate the process. We will focus on all of the six traits of writing, but word choice will be of particular importance in this unit as we will play with words and practice using both precise and figurative language.

Step 1: Mini-Lesson

After handwriting or typing practice has concluded, begin each day of Writer's Workshop with a mini-lesson. You will find some within the sidebars of this unit. You can also use a worksheet from a grammar workbook or practice editing, copying, or diagramming sentences. During writing time, watch for weak areas or mistakes being made and present a mini-lesson the next day to help correct those and improve writing skills in small, continuous ways.

The mini-lesson should take five to ten minutes and always have a positive, happy spin, free from criticism. Not every mini-lesson needs to be kept in your Writer's Notebook. Most are merely for practice.

Step 2: Writing

Now it's time to really begin writing. Most of your time during Writer's Workshop should be spent writing. Practicing is the key to improving. You can use your writing time to free write your own ideas in your Journal anytime, or use the exercises below to practice writing skills and find inspiration for things to write about. Select as many exercises as you would like to do over the month, making sure you leave time to complete at least one writing project that will go all of the way through the writing process before the month is over. The exercises will also go in your Journal section of your Writer's Notebook. If you decide to take something from your Journal through the writing process and turn it into your writing project, move it from your Journal to the Writing section of your Writer's Notebook.

A few tips and reminders:

- You can repeat the units and the exercises in subsequent years, so don't ever feel pressured to get to all of them, and feel free to repeat ones you enjoy.

- Often a single exercise can be presented to all of your children, no matter their ages or abilities. They will naturally write at the level they are at and, as they practice, will grow as writers.
- As you progress through the exercises, watch for something that sparks interest and could become the writing project. Feel free to jump to the idea bank at the end of the unit anytime as well. If there's spare time after the project is published, return to more exercises.
- Your family may all be in different places in the writing process. That's perfectly fine. Remember, your Writer's Workshop is a garden and everyone is growing their own patch. You can all lend a hand to help each gardener's patch thrive, but you won't all grow the same crop.

It's time to write! Choose some exercises and jump right in!

Descriptions

EXERCISE: Juicy Sentences

Adding details to writing can drastically improve its quality.

The dog sat.

I wore a hat.

The cat was soft.

Yawn. Boring, same old sentences. Boring, same old stories.

Instead, write sentences you can really sink your teeth into – juicy sentences. Writing with description is an important and practiced skill, not one that naturally comes with time. Use the "Juicy Sentences" printable from the Printable Pack and start with one of the sentences above. Write "The" in the article box. Write "dog" in the noun box. Write "ran" in the verb box.

Close your eyes and picture the dog exactly, then describe what is in your mind. It might be a large, honey colored dog with a blue collar running through the park near your house. It could be a tiny white toy poodle wearing a pink and black collar with a little bell on it, running through a shopping mall. See how the same sentence can yield two very different pictures? As writers, it is our job to paint a picture for our readers.

Use the "Juicy Sentences" printable and fill in the other boxes. Your final sentence might look like this:

The fuzzy, blue dog ran sideways through the forest in my dream last night.

Not every sentence needs to follow this precise format to

☐ **Mini-Lesson**

Word choice is the most important of the six traits of writing when it comes to writing descriptions and instructions. By using exact language we can get our message across. Without it, our writing is either bland or confusing. I can picture in my mind exactly what I mean as I write, but my reader can't read my mind. Writers must use words to paint the pictures they have in their minds.

Let's say I'm telling a story and my main character says, "Please help me." What do you think is wrong? What help is needed? It's hard to tell from that simple phrase.

"Please help me," she whispered raspingly, collapsing on the ground and clutching her chest.

What kind of help does she need?

"Please help me," Mom growled, "the table isn't going to set itself and we have company coming for dinner."

Now what kind of help does she need?

☐ **Mini-Lesson**

Mark Twain said, "The difference between the right word and the almost right word is the difference between lightning and the lightning bug." What do you think he meant? How does it relate to word choice?

Mini-Lesson

As we write descriptions, sometimes we want to utilize one perfectly descriptive word, but other times a longer description is a better word choice. If you need help writing a longer description, open a dictionary to give you inspiration.

Find the definition of *cold* in the dictionary. Use the definition to help you write a longer description rather than a single word.

Cold: Having the sensation of cold; chill; shivering.

Change this simple sentence:

I was cold.

Here's how mine changed after I read the dictionary entry:

Feeling chilled, I shivered.

Mini-Lesson

Word economy is an important component of strong writing. It means that you shouldn't use twenty words if ten words will say the very same thing. Considering word economy will keep you from rambling and being too wordy in your writing. Watch for times when you say the same things over and over, even if you say them in new ways. Eliminate the extra words, phrases, and sentences. Choose something you've written and see how much you can cut out while still saying the same thing. Word economy is as important in word choice as vivid descriptions.

be juicy. When you think of juicy sentences, think about adding details in a variety of orders and ways. Practice writing some juicy sentences in your Writer's Notebook. Add them to your Journal.

EXERCISE: 5 Senses

Using our five senses, we are able to take in all of the information in the world. Imagine the world if you were unable to see, smell, taste, touch, or hear anything. What would it be like to lose your senses one by one? Writing without sensory language creates a bland experience, just as living in the world without senses would be bland.

When you write using your senses, you can help your reader to experience what you're describing. Here are a few everyday scenes to describe using your senses:

- Yourself at bedtime
- Enjoying your favorite meal
- Running away during a game of tag
- Jumping on a trampoline
- Helping your mom or dad cook
- Deciding what you will wear in the morning
- Riding your bike
- Going to the grocery store
- Falling asleep

Use the "Writing With All 5 Senses" printable from the Printable Pack to practice writing sensory details about at least one of the scenes listed above. Add them to the Journal section of your Writer's Notebook.

EXERCISE: Describe It

Write the following words or others you come up with on slips of paper and draw them out one at a time, taking turns describing each one aloud while everyone else guesses. Use as many descriptive words as you can.

Words: sunshine, ice cubes, ivy, rose, elephant, pond, globe, grass, library book, marshmallow, pencil, gasoline, pretzels, glitter, button, sugar cookie, scooter, campfire, lipstick, pizza, ice cream cone, baby, bumper sticker

While writing, you can use this same exercise in your mind. Ask yourself, how would I describe this to someone who doesn't know what it is? What small details can be added that will help readers to picture what you are describing in their minds? Thinking and speaking are prewriting

techniques that don't involve writing, but help a lot in the writing process.

EXERCISE: Tiger on the Prowl

Write a paragraph about a tiger attacking someone, but don't use the words tiger, pounce, prowl, stalk, or scratch. Add your paragraph to the Journal section of your Writer's Notebook. You can try it using other animals too. Think of any animal and then list five words that describe it. Try to describe it using any words aside from the five you listed. Put your descriptions in your Journal.

EXERCISE: Sell It

Pretend you are a writer for a catalog. Choose an item from your bedroom; you could choose a toy, an item of clothing, or your blanket. Write a description of the item that would help it sell. Catalog writers use words like periwinkle or ruby red to describe colors. They also include adjectives that help the potential buyer feel what it will be like to own it - luxurious, playful, or buttery soft.

When you are finished writing your ad, you can try writing another one just for fun. Describe the very same item, but this time tell the absolute truth about it. Put your descriptions in the Journal section of your Writer's Notebook.

EXERCISE: Dreamer

Think for awhile about one of your dreams. Dream settings can be fantastic and unique. Describe the ground, water, sky, and everything you see in your dream in great detail so your reader can see it too. It can be hard to remember the exact details of dreams, so feel free to use your imagination too. If you'd like, you can use the "Dreams" printable from the Printable Pack and write about your dream in the dream bubble on it. Put it in your Journal.

EXERCISE: Mr. Dirty's Beard

Your neighbor, Mr. Dirty, has been growing his beard for twenty years. He's never washed it in all those years, and a lot of things have built up in his long, tangled beard. Imagine some of the things that may have gotten caught in his beard and write a description of what's inside. You can draw a picture of his beard and some of the things that got caught in it too. Add it to your Journal.

☐ Mini-Lesson

Good and bad are overused words in descriptions. Instead of saying good or bad, think about how good or bad the thing is.

Is it just slightly better or worse? Is it amazing? Is it decent? Is it worthy? Is it awful? Is it the best you've ever seen? Is it sub par?

Expand on the words good and bad so you aren't overusing them. Out loud, say a description of several things that are either good or bad, but use more specific language. Don't use the words good or bad in your description at all.

☐ Mini-Lesson

The words good and well often get misused. Good is an adjective; it is used to describe a noun. *Well is an adverb; it is used to describe a verb. Something is good. You do something well.

Strawberry jam is so good.

He played the piano well.

Write your own sentences using good and well. Make sure to use good to describe nouns and well to describe verbs.

*Well is also an adjective sometimes, but only when using it to mean healthy.

After a long bout with pneumonia, Tom is well again.

☐ Mini-Lesson

The entry words in dictionaries are in bold print and are in ABC order. To use a dictionary, you must know how ABC order works. Brainstorm a list of words and put them in alphabetical order, with A first and Z last. If two or more words begin with the same letter, look at the second letter. If the first and second are the same, go to the third letter (and so on). If two words are spelled the same way at the beginning, but one stops and the other continues, the shorter word comes first.

abacus, bake, bakes, cake, cookies, fun, maybe, mom, sunshine

☐ Mini-Lesson

Compare several different dictionaries and see if the word definitions are different. If possible, compare an older dictionary and a newer one. Look up the same words in each dictionary and spot differences.

☐ Mini-Lesson

Practice looking up words in the dictionary. Identify their definition or definitions. Find out the part of speech that the word is. Does it show how the word should be pronounced? How many syllables does it have? What else does the entry show about the word?

EXERCISE: Up High or Down Low

We spend a lot of time on land, but much less time high in the air or down below the waves. Choose between flying high in the sky or swimming deep in the ocean. Describe what you experience. You can be in an airplane, hang gliding, or using your flying superpowers. You could be wearing a scuba tank, magically able to breathe underwater, or be an ocean animal. Put your description in your Journal.

EXERCISE: P.E.N.

P.E.N. is an acronym writers use to remind themselves to avoid being overly wordy.

P stands for precision. Precise words will help you get your meaning across efficiently. They are exact words. For example, I could use the word smiled, but if I say beamed, grinned, or smirked, that's even more precise.

E stands for economy. Using words economically means using them sparingly. Use the right words instead of a lot of words.

N stands for novelty. Novel sentences are those that contribute new information somehow. There's a fine line between including interesting descriptions and using so many words that you bore your readers before you ever get to the point. Make sure that each thing you add to your writing is there for a reason.

Use the "P.E.N." printable from the Printable Pack and rewrite the passage on it using more precise, economical, and novel words. Shorten the story without losing any of the message. Add this activity to your Writing Helps section.

EXERCISE: Dictionary

A dictionary is a book of words. The words are listed in alphabetical order and are defined. You can also see information about each word, such as what part of speech it is, how many syllables it has, and other possible suffixes it can utilize.

Word choice is one of the six traits of writing and having a big vocabulary is important if you want to write well. A dictionary can help your vocabulary to grow. Dictionaries aren't books we usually read cover to cover, but you can certainly read a page or two. Find several words that are new to you that you can incorporate into your writing today. Make sure you pay attention to which part of speech the word is. For example, if you use the word *subterranean*, you should note that it is an adjective, not

a verb or a noun. Therefore, your sentence should use it to describe a noun.

The subterranean fort was hidden away and stocked with food and supplies to last a year.

Become familiar with your dictionary by going on a scavenger hunt. Use the "Dictionary Scavenger Hunt" printable from the Printable Pack. During the activity, look for words you can incorporate into a quick write or journal entry you write today.

EXERCISE: Dictionary Dig

Everyone needs a dictionary to play this game. Take turns giving clues while the remaining players search for words that satisfy the clues.

Here's an example of a clue: Find a word that begins with the letter D, is three syllables long, and is a noun.

Each clue will follow that format: Find a word that begins with the letter ____, is ____ syllables long and is a ____ (noun, verb, adverb, or adjective). There will be many possible answers, but each person should write down the answer they found that satisfies each clue. After you've played several rounds you will have a list of your answers. Use your list as a word bank and try to write a journal entry that includes every word you found while you played "Dictionary Dig."

EXERCISE: Thesaurus

Be careful not to repeat the same word over and over again as you write. It becomes boring and predictable instead of fresh and interesting. Are you short? Kind? Stubborn? Then perhaps you could also describe yourself as petite, affectionate, and determined. These are synonyms, or words with similar meanings.

Write down ten words that describe you. Include things that describe both your appearance and your personality. Next, use a thesaurus to find synonyms for each of your ten words. You can repeat this activity using lists of words that describe your friend, your town, your family members, and your pet.

As you write, remember that you can use a thesaurus as a tool to help you find the right word. Rather than use a weak word or repeat the same word again and again, take a minute and find a new way to describe things to keep your descriptions fresh and exact and improve your word choices. Add your descriptions to the Journal section of your Writer's Notebook.

☐ **Mini-Lesson**

Take care when you use a thesaurus to help you find replacement words. Words may be similar, but have their own unique uses. For example, the word "capture" can mean a variety of things.

Synonyms for capture: abduct, seize, hook, snatch, catch, trap, pinch, take into custody, arrest, grasp

If you capture a butterfly in a net, you can substitute words like *catch* or *trap*, but you probably wouldn't want to use *arrest* or *take into custody*.

Know the full meanings of words you replace.

☐ **Mini-Lesson**

Word choice is one of the six traits of writing. Consider the emotional responses your word choices create. If you want your reader to cringe, use the word vomit and other ugly words. If you want your reader to feel good, use the word cozy and other warm words. Make lists of ugly and warm words to keep in the Writing Helps section of your Writer's Notebook.

☐ **Mini-Lesson**

Review some parts of speech. Look at a picture in a magazine. Write a list of nouns you see in the picture. Add at least two adjectives to describe each noun you see. Are there any verbs in the picture? Modify the verbs with at least one adverb.

Writer's Workshop

Mini-Lesson

Practice expanding sentences by adding details. Here are some simple sentences to expand.

This parrot talks.

The tank holds fish.

The kitten needs a hug.

The cricket chirps.

Frogs are in the pond.

My puppy is lonely.

Turtles are slow.

Where is the goose?

Have you seen my hamster?

Mini-Lesson

When you list several adjectives to describe one thing, you use a comma to separate the adjectives.

The lonely, sad, old man decided to put on his red shoes and go to the dance. His monotonous, solitary days were about to end forever.

Mini-Lesson

People misuse the word "literally" often. You'll hear someone say, "I literally just died laughing." If they had LITERALLY died, they wouldn't be alive right now to tell you the story. A literal definition is a true and exact one, not an exaggeration.

Write a literal and a figurative description of someone laughing.

EXERCISE: More Synonyms

Synonyms are words that have the same or a similar meaning. For example, fast, quick, swift, rapid, breakneck, speedy, and turbo are all synonyms.

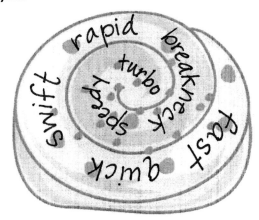

Use the "Synonym Roll" printable from the Printable Pack. Write words that are synonyms on each roll. You can use a thesaurus to help you come up with ideas of words to add to each of your "synonym rolls." Put the synonyms in the Writing Helps section of your notebook to remind you to use synonyms instead of repeating the same words again and again.

EXERCISE: Word Choice Flip Book

Although synonyms are different words that mean the same thing, there are slight differences in their definitions. Think of the words "small" and "tiny." They both mean the same thing, and yet, there is a bit of a difference. If I use the word "tiny" I am suggesting that it is even smaller than "small."

Gather long paint chips from a paint counter that have at least four shades of a color. On each of the colorful squares on a chip, write words that are synonyms to

each other. Hole punch the top corner and make a little booklet of words you can flip through as you write. Practice writing some sentences with the various words substituted for each other and discuss how it affects the meaning. Just as the colors on the paint chip are all the same, but are different shades, the words are synonyms, but have slightly different meanings. Keep your flip book handy as you write whenever you need ideas for other ways to say common words. Put the flip book in a pocket in your Writer's Notebook.

EXERCISE: Antonyms

Antonyms are words that are opposites of each other. For example, the words hot and cold are antonyms. Brainstorm some antonyms and write them in the bodies of the ants on the "Antonyms" printable from the Printable Pack. Add it to your Writing Helps section of your Writer's Notebook.

EXERCISE: Connotation/Denotation - Moody Words

The denotation of a word is the dictionary definition. The connotation of a word is packed with even more meaning. It includes emotional responses we have to words. When I read the word "snake" I have an immediate emotional response. It makes me shudder a little. When I looked up snake in the dictionary it said: "a long limbless reptile that has no eyelids, a short tail, and jaws that are capable of considerable extension." Denotations and connotations coexist and are both true assessments of the word. It's important to understand both when writing because it helps us choose our words carefully.

Sometimes words have the same definition, but give a different feeling or mood to the reader. For example, house and home mean the same thing, but when we say "house" we think mostly of the building. When we say "home" we imagine the coziness of a family and the smell of good food and the feeling of being loved.

Use the "Moody Words" printable from the Printable Pack to figure out the moods that some of our words communicate through their connotations. As you write descriptions, consider carefully your word choice to make sure they carry the mood and meaning you intend.

Practice writing the same sentence several times with only one word changed each time. See if you can create a different mood or meaning by choosing words with the same denotation but differing connotations. Pay special attention to words that give either a negative or positive emotion to the reader.

☐ **Mini-Lesson**

Verbs can be used in two voices: active voice and passive voice. In active voice the subject performs an action.

The chipmunk bit the nut.

In passive voice, the word order is reversed so the subject receives the action and the object performs it.

The nut was bit by the chipmunk.

Turn these passive sentences into active sentences.

The girls were taught algebra by Mr. Norse.

The photos of Julie were taken by the photographer.

John was driven to the restaurant by Jake.

☐ **Mini-Lesson**

Very is an overused word. How can you change these phrases so they exclude the word very?

Some possible answers are in parenthesis.

- Very scared **(petrified)**
- Very old **(ancient)**
- Very loud **(deafening)**
- Very pretty **(beautiful)**
- Very poor **(destitute)**
- Very often **(frequently)**
- Very quick **(rapid)**
- Very rainy **(pouring)**
- Very sad **(sorrowful)**
- Very serious **(grave)**
- Very shiny **(gleaming)**

Writer's Workshop

Mini-Lesson

You can add -er to most single-syllable adjectives and adverbs if you want to compare two things. This is the comparison form.

This boat is bigger than that one.

McKayla is smarter than her friends.

You can add -est to compare more than two things.

Sirius is the brightest star.

The giant sequoia is the widest of all the trees.

Write your own comparison sentences using -er and -est.

Mini-Lesson

Many multi-syllable words cannot be modified with -er or -est. Instead, use the words more or most. We don't say her shirt was yellower. We say it was more yellow.

The suit was more expensive than the tie.

Jackie's car is the most terrific on the lot.

Write some of your own.

Mini-Lesson

When you are showing (not just telling), it's helpful to think about body language. What might your body do if you are bored? Thirsty? Irritated? Write descriptions of the body language that may be happening in each of these scenarios.

Write sentences using these pairs to get you started, then come up with some of your own to add in to your Writing Helps section of your Writer's Notebook.

- Smart/know-it-all
- Scrawny/slender
- Strong-willed/stubborn
- Smirk/smile
- Cheap/frugal
- Cabin/hut

EXERCISE: Antique

Gather at least one item that isn't used often anymore. You can usually find something like a coffee grinder, a hand beater, a meat grinder, a rotary phone, or an old record at a thrift store. You can also use a picture of an item from  the internet if you need to. It should be something your child is not familiar with. Without revealing what the item is used for, have your child write a description of it based on its appearance. The child should focus both on the appearance and the function and go into as much detail as possible. Add the description to the Journal section.

EXERCISE: Accordion Sentences

Every description, story, sentence, or paragraph can be a little like an accordion. You can have the short, compressed version or the longer, more spread out version. The real trick is to balance specific details with length. Have you ever read a description that went on and on and on? You probably wished the author would just get to the story already! It's important to have specific details so you can paint a picture in your reader's mind, but it's equally important not to bore your reader with too much detail. I once put down a book because I got to chapter 4 and I still didn't know what color of hair the main character had. It was driving me crazy! I have also put down a book that spent over four chapters describing the setting before ever beginning the story. Balance is the key.

Write three versions of a sentence. Begin with one that is short and lacking details, like a compressed accordion. Next, rewrite the same sentence like a stretched out accordion, with far too many details that enter into the realm of boring. Finally, write a just right sentence that includes vivid details without being overly wordy. Put your accordion sentences in your Writing Helps section to remind you to use sentences that balance details with length while you are revising things you write.

EXERCISE: Abstract to Concrete

One technique writers use is taking abstract concepts and putting them into a familiar, concrete form. Begin with an abstract concept like love, kindness, joy, sadness, wealth, or loneliness. Then describe that concept using concrete, real life examples. Doing this allows you tap into experiences people have had so they feel the emotion you're describing from some of their own memories.

Here's one to get you started:

> *Loneliness is a rainy day with nothing to do, a single cloud in the blue sky, a party without friends, a lost child in a crowded store.*

Put your descriptions in your Journal.

EXERCISE: Strong Verbs

Strong verbs can take boring sentences and give them life. Use the "Strong Verbs" printable from the Printable Pack to practice turning weak sentences into strong ones by changing the verbs. Keep a list of strong verbs in your Writing Helps section of your Writer's Notebook.

EXERCISE: Show, Don't Tell

Often writers are told, "Show, don't tell." This means to show the actions and emotions people are experiencing instead of just telling about them. I could simply tell you I'm cold, or I could say, "Every hair on my arms stood on end, my teeth chattering, as I tried to get deeper inside the quilt." You know I'm cold from that sentence because I showed you; I never even said the word *cold*.

Any time you see weak verbs in your descriptions, pause and ask yourself if you could make them stronger to <u>show</u> your readers instead of just <u>telling</u> them. Look back in your Journal and find a description or a story you've written. Search for weak verbs and make them stronger. Weak verbs are being verbs rather than action verbs. Here are some weak verbs to look for: is, are, am, was, were.

In your Journal, rewrite these telling sentences and transform them into showing sentences by thinking about the things that happen actively in these situations:

- He is hot.
- You are tired.
- I am hungry.
- Eleanor was scared.
- Timothy and Jerry were angry.
- My family was leaving the house late.

☐ Mini-Lesson

Adjectives describe nouns. Make an adjectives anchor chart to put in your Writing Helps section of your Writer's Notebook that can remind you of words you can use to describe the things you write about. You can make your own or color the one from the Printable Pack. Use it as you brainstorm adjectives.

☐ Mini-Lesson

Contractions are formed when you shorten two words by creating one word from the two. You insert an apostrophe where the missing letters are.

are not = aren't

were not = weren't

it is = it's

she is = she's

I am = I'm

you are = you're

we are = we're

I have = I've

Draw apples on a page, each one with two leaves. Write the two words on the leaves and the combined word on the apple. Add it to your Writing Helps.

Writer's Workshop

☐ Mini-Lesson

Most verbs are action words, but some are linking verbs. Linking verbs link the subject to a word or phrase that describes it. Am is the verb in this sentence:

I am in love.

I is the subject and *am* links the subject to the phrase that describes it: *in love*.

Linking verbs include verbs related to the senses and states of existence: feel, taste, smell, look, hear, be, become, appear, remain. Note that these verbs can be in other tenses and forms. For example, some forms of the verb "be" are: is, am, are, was, and were.

Divide your paper in half. Write sentences with action verbs on the top half and sentences with linking verbs on the bottom half.

☐ Mini-Lesson

Sometimes a verb is identified as a linking verb by how it is used.

The squirrel looked for nuts and seeds in the forest.

The squirrel looked cute with its bushy tail.

Can you tell which sentence used looked as an action and which used it as a link?

Write your own sets of action and linking verb sentences using these verbs: smelled, felt, tastes, appears.

The first example uses looked at an action and the second example uses it as a linking verb.

EXERCISE: Adjective Adventure

Write a descriptive paragraph about an adventure in your Journal. Use at least 25 adjectives within the paragraph. An adjective is any word that describes a noun. You can begin by making a list of some of the nouns (people, places, and things) in your story and then brainstorming together some adjectives that could describe those nouns. Write your adjective-packed adventure in just one paragraph.

EXERCISE: Describing Hands

Hands tell a lot about a person. Think about the difference between a baby's tiny, smooth hands and the leathery, wrinkled hands of an eighty-year-old man who has been a carpenter his whole life. Picture a person in your mind and then describe that person's hands. If it's an actress who is nervous to go on stage they may be shaky and clammy. If it's a sailor who is tying up her boat to a dock they might be dexterous and slender. If it's a little boy climbing trees, they might be calloused and suntanned. Write a description of your person's hands. Include strong adjectives, precise language, and at least one element of figurative language, like a simile, hyperbole, or personification. Add the description to your Journal.

EXERCISE: Describing Eyes

Sometimes eyes are just described using their physical characteristics. Someone could have round eyes or almond eyes or big eyes. Eyes can also be described by what they are doing, like watering eyes or squinting eyes. Beyond that, they can be used to describe what we're feeling. Someone could have brave eyes, tired eyes, or determined eyes. They say that eyes are the windows to our souls. Write a description in your Journal of a pair of eyes that reveals something about the person.

EXERCISE: Mysterious 5 Ws and 1 H

Use the "Mysterious 5 Ws and 1 H" printable from the Printable Pack to help you write a spooky mystery story for your Journal. Make sure to choose spooky characters, places, times, and events as you fill out your chart. When you've finished your chart, write a descriptive spooky mystery story following this format:

- Paragraph 1: Describe the spooky setting (when and where)
- Paragraph 2: Describe the spooky characters (who)
- Paragraph 3: Explain the mysterious problem (what)
- Paragraph 4: Explain how the mystery will be solved

(how), but then leave your reader hanging and don't solve it entirely. End in a mysterious cliffhanger.

EXERCISE: Other Ways To Say It

Use the "Other Ways To Say It" printable from the Printable Pack for this exercise. You will begin by reading this passage aloud.

> The _nice_ man felt _good_ as he _walked_ along in the sunshine on the way to the store. It was a _pretty_ day and he _liked_ how the _bad_ weather of yesterday had changed into clear skies and a _big_ sun shining down. As he _looked_ up he _said_, "I am happy. Who could be _sad_ on a day like this?" Then, in an instant, everything changed. A _little_ snake came out of the grass near the sidewalk. _Scared_, the man _ran_ all the way home, slammed the door, and didn't dare come out the rest of the day.

Use the printable to write replacement words for each underlined word. Choose the word that you think best describes the situation. Rewrite the passage in your Journal with the new words. Keep the "Other Ways To Say It" printable in the Writing Helps section of your Writer's Notebook so you can refer to it when you need ideas for other ways to say these commonly used words.

EXERCISE: A Century Away

Do you know the story of Rip Van Winkle? He wandered into the woods, drank a magic potion, and fell asleep for twenty years! When he awakened, the world was a very different place. His beard was long and many of the people he loved were gone. He completely missed the entire American Revolution during his long nap!

Imagine that you fell asleep today and didn't wake up for one hundred years. What do you think the world would be like when you awakened? In your Journal description, include these details:

- When you awaken, what do you see?
- What new inventions are there?
- What did you miss while you were sleeping?
- How are people different?

EXERCISE: Mystery Noun

Think of a person, place, or thing that you would like to describe, but don't tell anyone what you are describing. Try describing it in writing without revealing what noun you chose. See if someone can read your description and guess accurately what your noun is.

Mini-Lesson

Create a notebooking sheet over the course of this unit. Make a chart that includes the definition of each kind of figurative language and an example. Add one each day during a mini-lesson on that type of figurative language.

Simile: A comparison of two things using _like_ or _as_

Metaphor: a direct comparison of two things (doesn't use _like_ or _as_)

Personification: giving human qualities to things that aren't human

Idiom: a phrase that has a meaning that is not literal

Hyperbole: an exaggeration

Alliteration: the repetition of the same sound

Onomatopoeia: Sound effects words

Allusion: a reference to a famous event, person, or place

Oxymoron: A phrase whose words contradict each other.

Mini-Lesson

Sarcasm, puns, irony, understatement, imagery, anaphora, assonance, consonance, metonymy, and synecdoche are more kinds of figurative language. Older students can look up these terms and create a notebooking page with descriptions and examples.

☐ Mini-Lesson

Part of sentence fluency is creating sentences with varying lengths. If you need to insert a longer sentence in a description, you can often combine two or more sentences together into one. Can you combine these sentences into one?

A barn that stood on the edge of the field was red. It looked like it was about to fall over.

A barn that stood on the edge of the field was red and looked like it was about to fall over.

☐ Mini-Lesson

Your Journal is like a holding tank for ideas that you've begun writing about. Whenever you write during an exercise you can add it to your Journal.

At any point in time you can take something from your Journal, move it to the Writing section of your Writer's Notebook, and then begin to take it through the writing process. If something you write sparks your interest, go ahead and move it to your Writing section. You aren't committed at this point. You can move things back and forth if you change your mind. You're the writer, and that makes you the boss of your own ideas. Take a few minutes to peruse your Journal.

EXERCISE: Choosing The Right Details

As you write descriptions, you might feel tempted to tell your reader every last detail. Don't. Writing that shares details without mood is bland.

> *The castle was longer than it was wide and the grass lawn surrounding it seemed to fill the valley where it was situated. The giant wooden doors at the end of the front walk measured 15 feet wide by 10 feet tall and were ornamented with a black metal knocker and giant hinges. The staircase in the entryway had twenty steps leading up to the second story. All around the foyer were sets of tables - 12 of them to be exact - with four chairs at each table. Besides that, the foyer was deserted.*

That's very descriptive, informative even. The problem is that with all of that description, I still don't know if it's a light, airy, joyful castle or whether it's scary and foreboding. Physical details are important, but emotional details are even more important. Readers want to feel like they are a part of the story. I would rather know how the castle feels than the dimensions of the door and number of tables in the foyer.

In your Journal, write your own short description of a setting. It might be a castle or something else that interests you. Include some physical details, but not at the expense of sharing the mood.

Figurative Language for Descriptions

EXERCISE: Similes

Similes are comparisons you make between two things using the words like or as. They can be short and direct or more descriptive and lengthy.

> *His shirt was as colorful as a box of crayons.*

> *Suzie's smile beamed like sunshine that reached into your darkest places.*

> *The polo star moved like a shark in the water, quick and exact.*

> *The toddlers played in the sandbox as quiet as two kittens, cooing and whispering.*

Practice writing some of your own similes using the "Similes Make Me Smile" printable from the Printable Pack. Put this in your Writing Helps for future reference. As you revise your writing, you can often improve your word choice by adding similes.

Descriptions & Instructions

EXERCISE: A Zoo of Similes

Practice writing similes that compare things to animals. Write these phrases on a piece of paper and then choose an animal that could fill in the blank to complete the simile. Make them accurate. If you don't swim well, you might swim like a kitten who is afraid of the water. Add these to the Writing Helps section of your Writer's Notebook.

- I run like a _____.
- I see like a _____.
- I swim like a _____.
- I jump like a _____.
- I sit like a _____.
- I talk like a _____.
- I climb like a _____.
- I sleep like a _____.

EXERCISE: Simile Monster

Use the "Simile Monster" printable from the Printable Pack for this exercise. Have fun creating your own similes that describe a monster out of your own imagination. In the center, draw the monster you described. Add this to your Journal section. Your monster might even become a character in a story you will write someday.

EXERCISE: Clever Similes

Bruce Lansky wrote a poem about similes called "Predictable." Look it up online and read it aloud. You can transform his poem into one called "Clever: A Simile Poem" with the corresponding printable from the Printable Pack. Put it in your Journal.

For an extra challenge, try to fill in as many of the blanks in the poem as you can by only using historical people or famous characters. For example, "As thin as Gandhi." "As strong as Samson." "As neat as "Mary Poppins." You could also try only using your own friends and family.

EXERCISE: Tired Clichés

Clichés are descriptive phrases that have been used so many times they are predictable and tired.

Cliché: It's raining cats and dogs.

Meaning	Details	Senses
It's raining really, really hard.	<ul><li>Clouds seem to fall to the ground</li><li>dark and dreary</li><li>I'm instantly soaked.</li><li>Car tires whoosh</li><li>Worms on sidewalks</li><li>People take cover... empty streets</li></ul>	Looks: downpour of water, darkness, ground flooding. Feels: like being petted by tiny pinpricks Sounds: plink, plunk, whoosh, faster than a drummer could play Smells: sweet, fresh, ozone Tastes: I don't taste it, but I feel less thirsty!

Fresh, new description: Dark clouds seem to fall to the ground all at once and I'm instantly soaked. People take cover to avoid the pinpricks of thousands of determined drops. Just as people disappear from the streets, earthworms emerge.

☐ **Mini-Lesson**

Come up with one creative simile and illustrate it. Begin by filling in one of the following phrases.

As ugly as _____.

As calm as _____.

As surprising as _____.

☐ **Mini-Lesson**

Overusing figurative language can be just as problematic as not using any at all. If all of your sentences have similes, alliteration, and allusions, it will be overwhelming to your reader. We practice using figurative language so we can sprinkle it in, not drown our stories in it. Read something you've written from your Writer's Notebook. Did you use any figurative language? If not, try sprinkling a few in.

☐ **Mini-Lesson**

Place a piece of fruit in front of you and observe it for one minute. Describe it out loud. How many ways can you describe it? Is there anything unusual about it? What specific adjectives, verbs, and adverbs can you associate with it?

☐ **Mini-Lesson**

Look at a picture. Write as many adjectives as you can that describe the picture.

☐ Mini-Lesson

This poem by Emily Dickinson is full of personification. Read it together and spot the areas where she uses personification.

The Sky is Low

By Emily Dickinson

The sky is low, the clouds are mean,

A traveling flake of snow

Across a barn or through a rut

Debates if it will go.

A narrow wind complains all day

How some one treated him;

Nature, like us, is sometimes caught

Without her diadem.

☐ Mini-Lesson

Many is an overused word. Can you use the actual number? If not, you can often still be more specific. Perhaps you could say dozens, hundreds, or thousands. Handful and numerous are other substitutes.

Describe each of these groups of things without using the word many.

- A flock of birds
- Kids at a playground
- A soccer team
- Drummers in a parade
- A crowd of people at a concert

Instead of using repetitive phrases, create fresh and unexpected descriptions. Begin by reading the "Tired Clichés" printable from the Printable Pack so you can know the cliché phrases you should be avoiding. You can discuss the meanings of each phrase.

Practice writing fresh descriptions by choosing one of the clichés from the list. Write it down. Fill in the meaning of the phrase. Now, think of some specific details about the actual meaning and write those down. Write at least one sensory detail for each of the senses. Feel free to make other comparisons, brainstorm, and jot down ideas. Then, write a fresh new description. Put this in your Journal.

EXERCISE: Metaphors

A metaphor is a direct comparison. It is similar to a simile except that it does not use "like" or "as" in its description. In general, the comparison made in a metaphor is between two things that do not seem to be alike but compares them directly.

Example of a simile: Love is like a red rose.

Example of a metaphor: Love is a red rose.

You can easily describe yourself using metaphors because you know yourself better than anyone else. In your Journal, write metaphors comparing yourself to an animal, a food, a landmark, a vehicle, a color, and a place.

I am a bird because I see the big picture, travel the blue skies, and always return to my home to be with the people I love most.

EXERCISE: Colorful Metaphors

In your Journal, write a basic description of something you found outdoors. Make sure to describe what it looks like as well as what it is used for. If I described our trampoline, I might use the words "black" as well as "bouncy" and "round" and "flat." Make sure to include the color of the item in your description. Write that color down and then make a list of things that are that color. Since our trampoline is black, I might list licorice, bats, the night sky, a burned log, and an ant.

Within the description you already wrote, substitute one or

two of the items you listed for the color.

My trampoline is a flat, round, bouncy patch of the night sky in our grass.

EXERCISE: Personification

Personification is giving human characteristics to something that isn't human.

The field of grass danced in the wind.

Hmm, grass doesn't really dance. People do. When I say it is dancing I'm giving a human characteristic to the field of grass. Here are a few more:

The tree invited us to come play.

Ben's old car chugged gasoline.

Banjo, my old dog, smiled mysteriously like he knew all my secrets.

The park sang with the happy sounds of children.

The snow knelt down across the whole cemetery.

In your Journal, make a list of nouns that aren't human. They can be places, things, or animals: *my house, my pet goldfish, the roller skates, loneliness, a board game, pride, our campsite, the desert, a map, my cell phone, clouds.*

The angry cloud threw a tantrum in the sky.

Then think of some verbs that describe things people have done: *yawned, played, sang, jumped, ached, swung,*

□ **Mini-Lesson**

A dangling modifier describes something in a sentence without including the subject it modifies.

Hoping to become their favorite child, my parents were impressed with their gift.

The sentence is missing the subject so it's unclear. It should say:

Hoping to become their favorite child, I gave my parents a gift that impressed them.

Avoid dangling modifiers.

□ **Mini-Lesson**

The phrase "like looking for a needle in a haystack" means something is nearly impossible to find. Write at least three descriptive phrases that mean the same thing but don't reference needles or haystacks.

□ **Mini-Lesson**

Your Writer's Notebook is a tool to help you become a better writer. Any time you feel like an exercise could help you in lots of kinds of writing, you can add it to your Writing Helps section of your Writer's Notebook instead of your Journal. For example, personification, idioms, hyperboles, and other figurative language can be used in essays, stories, letters, and more.

☐ **Mini-Lesson**

Animal sounds are common onomatopoeias. Brainstorm animals and their sounds to create a word bank of animal onomatopoeias you can use in your writing. Add your list to the Writing Helps section of your Writer's Notebook.

Continue your list tomorrow by adding non-animal sound effects on the back side of your page.

☐ **Mini-Lesson**

A lot of people wonder if onomatopoeias should be in quotation marks or italicized. The answer is no. Unless someone is actually saying it, you don't need any special punctuation for sound effects.

The camel's feet went plunk, plod, thud across the sand.

The bees swarmed in a cloud of buzzing.

If someone is saying the word, you would punctuate it with quotation marks as you would any dialogue. That punctuation follows the dialogue rule and has nothing to do with the onomatopoeia.

"Achoo!" she sneezed, spraying germs all over me.

Practice writing sentences with onomatopoeias using proper punctuation.

shouted, stood up, relaxed, moaned, whispered, ate, threw a tantrum, clapped.

Choose noun/verb pairs from your list to write your own examples of personification. Draw a picture to go along with the sentence you wrote.

My roller skates whispered from the corner of the garage that they felt forgotten.

After I dropped it on the ground, my cell phone moaned every time I tried to turn it on.

My pet goldfish relaxed day after day.

EXERCISE: A Pencil Is A Person Too

You can use personification in an extended way when you think of an object and then assign several human characteristics to it. To try it, just write from the point of view of the object. Do your writing in your Journal.

Imagine you are a pencil. These are some things you might say:

You use me all the time and I never hear a single word of thanks. My sharp tip is so perfect until you go and scribble away, dulling and ruining it. Oh, man! Stop making mistakes. My pink eraser gets darker and dingier every time you mess up. Ouch! Stop grinding me down in that metal sharpener of death.

You try it. Choose an item and imagine what it might say if it could talk - your backpack, shoes, your pet, your favorite shirt, a mailbox, your family car, your iPad, the clouds, the sun, a Christmas tree, a cupcake, your dinner, your toothbrush, a clock, the slide at the park, or your bowl of cereal.

EXERCISE: Playing With Idioms

Before you start this exercise, read an *Amelia Bedelia* picture book out loud. Talk about the difference between figurative meanings and literal meanings. Figurative language uses similes, metaphors, personification, idioms, and hyperbole. Literal language uses exact definitions.

In *Amelia Bedelia*, the author utilizes common idioms, or phrases that native speakers of a language understand to mean something other than their literal meaning. When you use the literal definitions of the phrases, it creates humorous misunderstandings. If I tell you I'm like a fish out of water, what I mean is that I'm uncomfortable because I'm in an unfamiliar situation. It doesn't mean that I'm actually a fish that isn't in her fish bowl.

a
fish out
of water

Talk about what these idioms mean and then draw a picture of the literal definition of some of these idioms. Next, in your Journal, write a story that uses at least one idiom in a humorous way.

- Driving me up the wall
- Every cloud has a sliver lining
- Flighting like cats and dogs
- A penny for your thoughts
- Back to the drawing board
- The ball is in your court
- Don't bite off more than you can chew
- Don't let the cat out of the bag
- Don't put all your eggs in one basket
- Costs an arm and a leg
- A broken heart
- Don't cry over spilled milk

EXERCISE: Hyperbole
Hyperboles are exaggerations. If you wanted to make a point that the king had a big nose, you might say that the king's nose was ten feet long. It isn't really ten feet, but everyone can deduce that the king's nose is really big because of your hyperbole. Turn each of these phrases into a hyperbole. Make sure your exaggeration is so extreme that it is clear that you are exaggerating and not being literal. Add your hyperboles to your Writing Helps section so you can review hyperboles again.

- That's expensive.
- I'm hungry.
- She really wants to go to the mall.
- Grandpa is old.
- Jake runs fast.
- Millie walked really far.
- The kitten was sick.
- The chickens smelled bad.

☐ **Mini-Lesson**

Prepositional phrases can be used as modifiers. They should be placed closest to what they are modifying. Compare:

Pam went to the vet with her cat in her new sweater.

In her new sweater, Pam went to the vet with her cat.

In the first sentence, the cat is wearing the sweater. In the second sentence, Pam is. Place the modifiers nearby to what they are describing.

Write sentences that are modified with these prepositional phrases and place each one close to the thing it is modifying:

In his new car

Around the block

Near the door

☐ **Mini-Lesson**

Most allusions refer to Greek or Roman mythology, the Bible, or famous literature like fairy tales, folk tales, or works of Shakespeare. Sometimes they also refer to more modern people or events - current politicians, stars, or famous news items. Make a list of famous people, places, events, or stories that you could allude to as you write. Put it in the Writing Helps section of your Writer's Notebook.

☐ Mini-Lesson

A modifier is a word, phrase, or clause that describes another word, phrase, or clause. If they aren't placed well, we might be describing the wrong thing.

Only, almost, just, and nearly are four common adverb modifiers that should be placed directly before the word they modify.

I just asked Matilda on a date. (This means I asked her recently. Just modifies asked.)

I asked just Matilda on a date. (This means I asked her and no one else. Just modifies Matilda.)

Use the words only, almost, just, and nearly to practice writing modifying sentences.

☐ Mini-Lesson

Adjective modifiers should be placed close to the adjective so readers know what you are modifying.

Bernice saw a blue man's bag on the bench.

Because the word blue is nearer to man than to bag, this sentences mistakenly says the man is blue, not the bag. Can you fix the sentence?

Write three more sentences that have well-placed modifiers. Tell how you could have placed them to mean something else.

EXERCISE: Alliteration Allie

Alliteration is a technique that repeats the same beginning sound of words. Start by writing a letter at the top of a sheet of paper in your Journal and setting one minute on a timer. Write down as many words as you can on your page that begin with that letter, including nouns, verbs, articles, adverbs, adjectives – anything! This is a brainstorm, so nothing should be rejected. Do this several times with various letters.

Now, meet Alliteration Allie. She is a giggly girl who loves letters. She writes the names of people using alliterations. Use your letter pages as word banks and help Alliteration Allie make name alliterations. Use the "Alliteration Allie" printable from the Printable Pack to make name alliterations for the people you know. Put it in your Journal.

EXERCISE: Alliteration Tongue Twisters

You can extend the use of alliteration by repeating a letter sound throughout a sentence or paragraph.

> *Amanda almost always attached abstract art to her awfully awkward airmail.*

> *Harry hardly huffed while hiking the high hills of Hampton.*

> *Wild Willy waited woefully while Wilma wailed and wailed.*

Because of the repeated sounds, alliterative sentences can be really hard to say, especially if you say them three times fast! Write some alliteration tongue twisters. Try creating at least one using your own name and five or more words that begin with the same sound your name begins with.

EXERCISE: Onomatopoeia

Onomatopoeias, or sound effect words, are a fun element of writing because they bring language to life in the reader's imagination.

Plop, whack, chug, puff, ding-dong, buzz, pow, snort, bang, clunk, boing, honk, splash, poof, zoom, slam, kapow, squeak, slurp, crunch, hiss, boom, quack, swish, tick-tock, vroom, zip

In your Journal, write a paragraph about someone who jumps out of an airplane with a parachute and describe what the person experiences using at least five onomatopoeia words.

EXERCISE: Allusion

Allusions are figures of speech that refer to a famous person, place, or event. They generally don't go into detail about the famous reference, but instead, rely on the reader to be familiar with the famous thing.

> *Jen is Einstein when it comes to algebra.*
>
> *Cheesecake is my Achilles' heel.*
>
> *I want those Legos so much. I need a magic lamp.*
>
> *He lied again? Did his nose grow?*
>
> *She picked up the car off her child like she was Hercules.*

Can you recognize the famous people, places, or things those sentences are alluding to? Albert Einstein was the famous scientist who developed the theory of relativity. Achilles was an ancient Greek hero who had just one weak spot on his entire body, his heel. A magic lamp is from the story of Aladdin where a magic lamp holds a genie that will grant wishes. The growing nose is an allusion to Pinocchio, a wooden puppet who is enchanted so that his nose grows a little bit each time he tells a lie. Hercules was a Greek hero who was known for his incredible strength.

Can you allude of any famous people, places, or events that you know? Try it in your Journal.

EXERCISE: Oxymoron

Oxymorons are phrases that contradict each other. Write these words, each one on its own note card, using blue ink: silently, clearly, exact, small, act, fully, original, only, jumbo, seriously, pretty. Write these words on note cards using green ink: copies, ugly, crowd, misunderstood, screaming, estimate, naturally, funny, empty, choice, shrimp. Try to match each blue card with a green card that completes the phrase as an oxymoron.

Answers: silently screaming, clearly misunderstood, exact estimate, small crowd, act naturally, fully empty, original copies, only choice, jumbo shrimp, seriously funny, pretty ugly.

Instructions

EXERCISE: Instructions

In your Journal, write out instructions for how to build a snowman. Before you begin, make a list of the supplies you will need and think about the order of the steps. Make sure your instructions include the supplies and the logical sequence in the proper order.

☐ Mini-Lesson

Commas can be used to set aside extra information in a sentence that could be removed and have the sentence still make sense. Modifying information can often be set apart by commas. Begin with this simple sentence:

> *My suitcase came down the airport conveyor belt toward me.*

Now I will describe the suitcase by adding a modifier after the word suitcase that is set apart by commas.

> *My suitcase, battered and worn from years of travels, came down the airport conveyor belt toward me.*

Can you describe the word fire engine by following it up with a modifier in this sentence?

> *A fire engine from Station 22 rushed toward the burning building.*

☐ Mini-Lesson

Memorize common measurement abbreviations used in recipes. Note which abbreviations include a period.

☐ Mini-Lesson

If your procedures involve any measurements, make sure to be clear about how to measure them and what units you are using. For example, "add 3 level cups," "stir in 9 milligrams," or "use a 4-inch piece of twine."

Writer's Workshop

Action verbs are key when you're writing procedures and instructions. You will use words like cut, mix, glue, nail, stir, pour, sift, or combine. Recipes also use precise action verbs. For example, grilling chicken is different than sautéing it. The verb matters, so choose your verbs carefully when writing procedures and instructions.

To make your strong verbs more clear, add precise adverbs. "Whisk vigorously" is more clear than just "whisk." Each time you include a verb, ask yourself if you should clarify by adding an adverb. What adverbs could you add to these verbs?

knead, run, combine, stir

Transition words connect your sentences to each other. Written instructions often include sequence transitions like first, next, and last. When placed at the beginning of the sentence, they are set apart from the sentence by a comma. Make an anchor chart of sequence transition words to add to the Writing Helps section of your Writer's Notebook. You'll find one in the Printable Pack.

EXERCISE: First, Next, Last
Use the "First, Next, Last" printable from the Printable Pack to describe a three-step process. Draw the steps in order, then write a clear sentence to describe each step. Some topics you might use are: getting ready for your day, making an ice cream sundae, making a pizza, getting dressed, making hot chocolate, putting on your shoes, riding a bike, sharpening a pencil, feeding fish, mailing a letter, or taking a picture. Put this in your Journal.

EXERCISE: Giving Directions
Giving people directions for how to get from place to place can be tricky. The best directions involve exact street names, landmarks, and cardinal directions (north, south, east, west). Use the "Zoo Map" printable from the Printable Pack and practice giving directions out loud. Your task is to describe where each animal pen is located so that another person can cut out and then paste each animal from the bottom of the page into the correct pen. There are no right answers; the person giving directions gets to decide where each animal's pen is.

For example, I might say, "From the entrance, head north on Safari Street and then turn east on Forest Trail. The elephants live off to the left, across from the duck pond." The other person would have to find that spot and glue the elephant into the proper pen. Put this in your Journal.

Older kids can practice giving directions using a city map from their own city. Google Maps is a good resource.

EXERCISE: Writing A Recipe
Much like science experiments, recipes are written very exactly so they can be duplicated by anyone who is trying to make them. Choose a recipe you will cook or bake from scratch. Cookies work well for this exercise, but you can use any recipe you would like.

Here's an example of a recipe for blueberry muffins:

- 2 cups all-purpose flour
- 3 teaspoons baking powder
- 1/2 teaspoon salt
- 3/4 cups sugar
- 1 egg
- 1 cup milk
- 1/4 cup vegetable oil
- 1 cup blueberries

1. Preheat oven to 400 degrees F (205 degrees C).
2. Stir together the flour, baking powder, salt and sugar

in a large bowl until they are thoroughly combined. Make a well in the center.

3. In a small bowl, beat the egg with a fork. Stir in the milk and oil, combining all three. Pour all at once into the well in the flour mixture. Mix quickly and lightly with a fork until moistened, but do not beat. The batter will be lumpy.

4. Add 1 cup fresh blueberries and fold in carefully.

5. Pour the batter into paper-lined muffin pan cups.

6. Bake for 25 minutes or until golden brown and cooked through.

Write three simple recipes on the "Recipe Cards" printable from the Printable Pack. You can use recipes your family makes, look online or in a cookbook, or make up your own. Highlight words that use exact language on your recipe cards. Put this in the Journal section of your Writer's Notebook.

EXERCISE: Procedures Checklist

A procedures checklist is a to-do list. When I worked at a hotel we had a list of things we needed to do before we closed our office each night. We had a cash register that needed to be balanced and locked up, paperwork that needed to be filed, cleaning tasks that had to be completed, supplies we needed to stock, and a memo log that had to be filled out with information for the person who was responsible for opening in the morning. All of the procedures were written on a checklist that we initialed each night, indicating that we had completed each task. Procedures checklists are common in workplaces and you should understand how to both write and use one.

Do you have any responsibilities in your life that you are expected to complete regularly? Perhaps before bed you are supposed to take a bath, brush your teeth, put on your pajamas, tidy your bedroom, and read your book. You might have chore responsibilities, morning tasks, or school assignments that you are expected to complete. Procedures checklists can help you stay accountable and remember all the things you need to do. Write yourself an organized procedures checklist and check the things off each day for at least a week. When you're finished keep it in your Journal.

☐ Mini-Lesson

Drawing a picture is an excellent prewriting activity. Drawing can stir up ideas. While you draw, think of describing words - adjectives and adverbs. Describe both the physical characteristics of your picture as well as the mood or emotion behind it. Your picture might even become an illustration for your final project.

☐ Mini-Lesson

There are some guidelines to follow when you write numbers. In general, you should spell out any number words up to one hundred (eight, not 8). Above one hundred, you'll use the numerals (116, 290, and 563). If you begin a sentence with a number, you should always write out the word instead of using a numeral.

There are exceptions to this rule, and you may encounter them as you're writing instructions. If you are numbering the steps in a process, you typically write them using a numeral followed by a period, with each step beginning on a new line. You will also use numerals for writing dates, measurements, time, money, decimals, and years.

The most important thing is consistency. Choose numerals or spelled out numbers and be consistent.

Take turns giving examples of sentences with numbers and having others say whether to use numerals or not in the sentence.

☐ Mini-Lesson

When you write about living people or things, it's just as important to describe their attitudes as it is to tell about their appearance.

If I ask you to describe your Mom, you might say she has brown hair and she's short. Although that's good to know, I'm much more interested in her insides. What does she feel? What is her demeanor?

Brainstorm a list of adjectives and adverbs that describe living things and add your list to the Writing Helps section of your Writer's Notebook so you can look through it for ideas when you're describing people, animals, or other living things.

Here are a few to get you started:

- Smiley
- Sweet
- Angry
- Lazy
- Tired
- Curt
- Cynical
- Feeble
- Forceful
- Hesitant
- Grave
- Lively
- Graceful
- Intense
- Sarcastic
- Sharp
- Stiff
- Unkind
- Unpredictable
- Full of life
- Silly
- Loud
- Vivacious
- Shy
- Sullen
- Charismatic

EXERCISE: Written Procedures

There is a specific format to use when you write procedures. You've probably seen it if you've ever done a science experiment.

First, you state the goal. What do you want to have happen in the end?

Second, you list all of the materials you will need.

Third, you outline the steps to take to reach the goal in clear language so that anyone could easily duplicate your steps.

Finally, you can include extras if they will be helpful. Some common extras are charts, definitions, illustrations, safety notes or warnings, comments about the process, and an explanation of why something worked.

Think back on an experiment you've done and make a written procedure for the experiment to put in your Journal. Include the three steps above. If needed, you can also add on any of the extras.

EXERCISE: Game Rules

People who invent games have to write the rules very clearly so that anyone who picks up the game can read the rules and then understand how to play the game.

Make your own game, either from scratch or using dice, cards, or a game you already own. Write your own rule book that explains the rules and procedures for playing the game.

Have someone try your game, rewrite any unclear rules, and then play your game some more for fun.

EXERCISE: Peanut Butter and Jelly Sandwich

Making a peanut butter and jelly sandwich seems pretty simple, but giving precise instructions can be a bit harder. Set out all of the supplies you need for making a peanut butter and jelly sandwich on the counter (bread, jar of peanut butter, jar of jelly, knife, plate). Take turns having someone give directions for making the peanut butter and jelly sandwich. If PB&J isn't available in your culture, choose a food equally familiar and simple for your kids.

Meanwhile, Mom or Dad will follow the directions precisely, but badly. For example, when kiddo says to put peanut butter on the bread, you will set the entire jar of peanut butter on top of the entire loaf of bread. If asked to spread peanut butter on a slice of bread, use your hands to smear it on or just put it on the narrow browned edge only. When

told to put it on the plate, make sure the plate is upside down. When instructed to add jelly, dump the entire jar out right on top. Along the way, your kids will catch on that they need to be more exact with their words.

When we give instructions, we can't assume prior knowledge. We need to think carefully about the meaning words have and be precise. Keep practicing until a sandwich can be made properly because of the accurately given directions.

Choose something else to write instructions for and use the peanut butter and jelly lesson as inspiration for choosing words wisely. Keep your instructions in your Journal.

EXERCISE: Brushing Your Teeth

As you write instructions, you must remember to write concisely. This means you want to use short sentences that are clear and direct. You will say only one thing in each sentence. You will be using imperative sentences (commands). Short, clear sentences make instructions that are easy to follow, one step at a time.

Try writing instructions for how to brush your teeth. Use short sentences. Make sure you arrange your sentences in the proper order. Be specific and clear. Begin with the materials you need to gather. Clearly write every step to take along the way. End by making sure the toothpaste and toothbrush are put away. You can put your written instructions in your Journal.

Step 3: Writing Project

During this unit, you should complete at least one writing project, taking a piece of writing through the entire writing process. By the final week of the unit, if you haven't completed the project already, you should turn your attention to creating one polished piece of writing that uses the things you've practiced along the way.

Choose one topic to write about that you will take all of the way through the writing process. This piece of writing belongs in the Writing section of your Writer's Notebook. You can use something you've already started during this unit, your own idea, or something from the following idea banks. Make sure that you follow each step of the writing process and keep all of your steps to turn in with your

---

☐ **Mini-Lesson**

It would be sad to write a beautifully descriptive passage and then make a bland presentation for it. Make sure that you add color, illustrations, or other visually interesting elements to your project so it is appealing in every way.

What are some things you can do to make your project attractive to the eye in the publishing step of the writing process?

☐ **Mini-Lesson**

When you write abbreviations, you generally use a period at the end.

Dr.   St.   Mrs.

tsp.   Mr.   Tbsp.

Brainstorm a list of abbreviations to add to the Writing Helps section of your Writer's Notebook.

☐ **Mini-Lesson**

That and *which* are two words that are often misused when used to describe things. Use *that* for clauses that include essential information. Use *which* if the additional information isn't essential. Because it could be omitted, you'll also set the clause aside with commas. The word you choose can show your intent - whether or not you believe it's essential.

The puppies that are tired can't go outside today.

The puppies, which are tired, can't go outside today.

☐ Mini-Lesson

The word adverb means "to add to a verb." Adverbs just add extra information to verbs. Brainstorm a list of verbs together. Then make adverb webs about each verb that shows how, when, where, or how often the verb is happening.

☐ Mini-Lesson

You can make adjective webs that are similar to your adverb webs. Begin with a noun in the center, then surround the noun with words that describe it.

You can keep your webs in the Writing Helps section of your Writer's Notebook.

finished writing.

- Step #1: Prewrite
- Step #2: Draft
- Step #3: Revise
- Step #4: Edit
- Step #5: Publish

Begin with a prewriting activity, then compose a draft, revise it, edit it with help from someone else, and then publish it. Publishing it could include making a polished final copy, sharing it with someone, creating a book, or creating some form of finished project that is neat and done well. You'll turn in all of your work, from prewrite to publish.

Your project will be evaluated based on the six traits of writing, so make sure you look at your composition through each of those lenses - ideas and content, organization, word choice, sentence fluency, conventions, and voice. Try to incorporate things you learned from the mini-lessons and the exercises you worked on as well. Do your best work.

Descriptions Idea Bank

Use these ideas for more exercises to go with this unit or as your project. These lists are also found in the Printable Pack and can be placed in the Ideas section of your Writer's Notebook.

- Imagine riding on a roller coaster in your mind. Think about what it's like from the moment you step into line until you are getting off at the end. Describe what you see, think, feel, and experience.
- Think about the last time you attended a special event such as a concert, a fair, or a sports event. Describe what it was like to be there and include sights, sounds, and smells that will make the reader feel he or she is there with you.
- Think of a favorite object you own. Write a description using sensory details—words that tell how something looks, feels, tastes, smells, and sounds.
- Describe your favorite game.
- Describe your favorite food.
- Describe your favorite season.
- Describe a vegetable you truly dislike.
- Describe a real or made-up dream or nightmare.
- Describe a typical day in your life.
- Describe your perfect meal.
- Describe the best way to honor a hero.
- Describe your pet.
- Draw a picture of yourself in an awesome costume and then describe the costume.

Descriptions & Instructions

- Describe your favorite sport. Choose a specific scene or moment to tell about.
- Describe yourself when you're angry.
- Invent and describe a new food.
- Describe in great detail what you would wish for if you could be granted three wishes.
- Vividly describe what you're wearing today.
- Write a detailed description of a rainy day. Include the things you like to do when it's raining.
- Describe a squirrel and what he's doing.
- Describe your design for a perfect pair of socks.
- Design the perfect car and describe it.
- Invent a new toy and describe it.
- Invent new technology and describe it.
- Describe your perfect park, playground, or amusement park.
- Describe four things you would take with you if you were trapped on an island. None of the things can be people.
- Compile a list of inanimate or animate objects to which you might compare yourself metaphorically. (I am a windmill. I change direction with passing breezes, always looking for a new path to walk along . . .)
- Find objects that are the colors of the rainbow and use the items you found as descriptors as you tell about an actual rainbow.
- Describe an event that changed your life forever, or make up and describe an event that would change your life forever.
- Describe someone who is a hero to you and explain why.
- Compile a list of words that describe you as a very young child. Compile a second list that describes you as you are now. How are these lists the same? How are they different? Use the lists to pen a description of how you've grown.
- Invent a monster and describe it. Tell where it lives, what it eats, and what it does.
- Be a building you know well. Talk about your life and memories.
- Describe an outdoor game you play during the summer.
- Be a grape that becomes a raisin: describe how it feels to shrink, to shrivel, to become dry and wrinkled.
- Be an icicle that becomes water. Describe how it feels to be cold and firm and full of beautiful crystals but only to melt and lose your shape.
- Write a physical description of one of your parents, siblings, or grandparents. Write as if you were looking at a movie rather than a photograph.
- Describe your dream house.
- Tell about what you see when you take a long look in the mirror. This can be physical characteristics as well as the

☐ **Mini-Lesson**

Review the parts of speech and then craft a sentence in this order:

Article, noun, adverb, verb, determiner, adjective, noun, preposition, article, noun, conjunction, preposition, determiner, noun, pronoun, verb, pronoun.

☐ **Mini-Lesson**

As you begin to write longer, more descriptive sentences, you need to think about the best order to write in. There are lots of ways to rearrange sentences, but there are a few guidelines you should follow:

- Verbs follow the noun or pronoun that is doing the action.
- Adverbs come before the verb they describe.
- Adjectives usually go before the noun they describe.
- Articles go before the noun they accompany.

Use the guidelines above to help you correct this mixed up sentence:

Ran quickly Jane little all over house the.

Answer: Little Jane ran quickly all over the house.

☐ **Mini-Lesson**

Collective nouns are names given to groups of people, places, or things. Your family is a collection of people, so family is a collective noun. Can you think of other groups we give names to? Brainstorm some together.

☐ Mini-Lesson

Here are eight basic comma rules to help you know when you need to use commas within your sentences. You can break this mini-lesson down over several days and write example sentences with proper comma usage in each sentence.

Rule #1: Use commas to separate independent clauses when they are joined by any of these seven coordinating conjunctions: and, but, for, or, nor, so, yet.

Rule #2: Use commas after introductory clauses or phrases.

Rule #3: Use a pair of commas in the middle of a sentence to set off clauses, phrases, and words that are not essential to the meaning of the sentence.

Rule #4: Use commas to separate three or more words, phrases, or clauses written in a series.

Rule #5: Use commas to separate two or more coordinate adjectives that describe the same noun.

Rule #6: Use commas to set off phrases at the end of the sentence that refer back to the beginning or middle of the sentence.

Rule #7: Use commas to set off all geographical names, items in dates (except the month and day), addresses (except the street number and name), and titles in names.

Rule #8: Use a comma to shift between the main discourse and a quotation.

things you see on the inside.

- Describe what it was like to learn something new. Choose an actual event and describe the learning process.
- Describe the very same scene and what that place is like in all four seasons - winter, spring, summer, and autumn.
- Detail the physical, emotional, spiritual, and mental descriptions of someone you know well.
- Describe the worst storm you've ever been in.
- Discuss your scariest moment ever.
- Write a description of your favorite place that you like to go.
- Describe an imaginary setting that could never happen on earth because it is too fantastical.
- Write descriptions of each of the members of your family. You know them well, so be thorough.
- Describe a scene that involves a terrible smell.
- Describe a scene in which someone is following or chasing you.
- Choose a wildlife habitat and describe what you see, hear, touch, taste, and smell.
- Write descriptions for three people: a hero, a villain, and an unlikely victim.
- Describe a time you were lost.
- Describe a superhero our world needs. What is s/he like and what will s/he accomplish?
- Tell about someone who is happy without using the word happy at all in your description.
- Describe the best part of you. It might be something physical, a character trait, or something you've done that has made you who you are.
- Choose a place in the world that you've always wanted to go. Write about what it's like descriptively. It could be a city, a landmark, or a country.
- Think of something humorous that might happen at a bus stop in a rainstorm. Write about the scene and what enfolds.
- Tell a spooky story in vivid detail.
- Describe what it's like to be pulled over by a police officer when you've broken the law.
- Give an account of an ice cream man's trip around the neighborhood on a hot summer day.
- Recount one of your firsts in vivid detail - the first time you went to the ocean, to a concert, to a parade, or on a road trip.
- Describe the worst pain you've ever experienced.
- Write a description that uses one or more imaginary words so richly that your reader can tell what you're talking about by your description. For example, you might make up a word for the way it smells after it rains or the name of a person who has never ridden a horse or

a word for the look on a surprised person's face.
- Write about your favorite place in the whole world. Remember to set the mood while you share the physical details and let your reader in on why you love the place.
- Choose a school supply or household object and imagine that it has come to life and can talk, move, think, and feel. Describe what it's like to be that object.
- Write an underwater description from the perspective of an ocean animal.

Instructions Idea Bank

- Write a composition in which you explain how to make something. You might write about a food item, a handcrafted item, or anything else that you know how to make. Be sure to clearly explain each step in the process so that a reader could make the item the way you do.
- Think about one favorite activity that you enjoy. For example, it could be playing a favorite sport or participating in a hobby. Write a composition in which you tell a friend how to do your favorite activity. Be sure to include all the details your friend will need to do the activity.
- Tell how to pack for a camping trip.
- Tell how to make a new friend.
- Describe how to prepare for an important job interview.
- You want to buy a new computer. Detail the steps in making a wise purchase.
- Describe how to build a perfect sandwich.
- Tell how to set the table.
- Write instructions for how people can become more involved citizens. This might include things like random acts of kindness, service organizations, attending events, or voting.
- Choose a hobby you have and offer directions for how someone can get started on that hobby. It could be anything from building model rockets to painting.
- Explain how to write a great resume.
- Describe how to build a birdhouse.
- Every recipe is a how-to essay of sorts. Write your own original recipe.
- Explain how to choose the right college.
- Write instructions for how to blow the perfect bubble with bubble gum.
- Write the instructions for creating a science fair project. Choose one project to focus on and create a written set of instructions anyone could follow.
- Explain how to build the perfect pizza.
- You've been asked to plan your best friend's surprise birthday party. Write out step by step instructions of how

Review of the Six Traits of Writing

Ideas and content focuses on your message. For descriptions and instructions, you should make sure your writing is clear and complete without being overly wordy.

Organization varies depending on the form you chose. Indent paragraphs and include topic sentences. Use transition words. Write instructions in a logical order.

Word choice involves using active verbs and vivid adjectives and adverbs. You should incorporate figurative language thoughtfully.

Sentence fluency involves rearranging sentence structure and including sentences of various lengths. As you write descriptively, you can begin to include longer sentences.

Conventions includes proper spelling, grammar, and punctuation. Edit carefully and ask someone else to help you edit and spot mistakes as well.

Voice involves sounding like a real person, you, instead of like an encyclopedia article. Write in a friendly tone and use words that you understand and that convey meaning and emotion that is genuine to you.

Writer's Workshop

Reminders About Your Writer's Notebook

Besides just the writing project, there should be many small writing samples that are being compiled in the Writer's Notebook from the exercises you worked on over the course of this unit. The Writer's Notebook is a tool for helping writers to grow. Explore it frequently and refer to idea lists and helps as you write.

At least once a week, it would be beneficial for you, the writer, to glance back through the exercises, lists, and mini-lessons to review and make sure that you are on track even though most of this work isn't graded.

Specifically, as you are working on the writing project, utilize your Writer's Notebook. You have anchor charts, exercises, and entries in your Journal - all of these can help you as you complete your project. Take time to review some of the concepts you've been working on during the unit so they can be incorporated into the final writing project. The things you've learned should SHOW in your writing project.

Remember that most of the work in the Writer's Notebook will never be graded, but it is still important. Use what you learned to make your project, which will be graded, the best that you can make it.

you will pull it off. You can describe a theme, a menu, activities, decor, and any other important details.

- List instructions for building something. It could be a wood project, a Lego creation, or something else that interests you.
- Write about how to make a garden. Include everything from preparing the soil and selecting seeds to harvesting.
- Create a set of instructions for an animal. For example, write to a honeybee telling it how to do its job or to a bear, offering instructions on how to hibernate.
- Write directions for how to get from your home to somewhere else you go to frequently. Include landmarks and descriptions as well as precise directions that could help anyone find the place.
- Your grandpa lives far away, but he asked you to write to him and explain how to turn on his new computer that is just like yours and check his e-mail. Write out a set of specific instructions for him, including obvious things like where the power switch is located and making sure it is plugged in.
- Write instructions for how to build a delicious banana split and include sensory details along the way.
- Write a guide to health, complete with all of the instructions you need for having a healthy life. You could also just choose one element of this. You might write a guide to sleep, a guide to vitamins, or a guide to germs, for example.
- Create a brochure with instructions for how to successfully travel to a place that you have visited. For example, if your family visited Yellowstone National Park, your brochure will include instructions for places to stay, things to do, and directions for getting to the park.
- Write instructions for someone who is beginning to homeschool. Give steps they can take to have a happy, successful homeschool.
- Explain how to take care of a specific pet. Include descriptions of the proper habitat and steps for the actual care you must give.
- Make a set of instructions for someone who is deciding what they want to be when they grow up.
- Create a procedure list for someone else to accomplish what you do every day. Imagine a stranger must slip into your shoes and become you for a whole day. What must they know and do to fill your shoes and live in your skin for a single day?
- Make a set of instructions for someone younger than you about how to be successful at your age. It might be called: "A Guide To Being Thirteen Years Old."
- Write a guide to developing a certain personality trait or quality. It could be how to be an honest person, or how to develop compassion, or how to become a hard

worker. Include examples and specific steps.

- Create a set of written instructions for a simple task like skipping or jumping rope. Sometimes simple actions can be difficult to describe.
- Write instructions about how to make the perfect salad.
- Make a list of procedures for carving a pumpkin.
- Write directions for how to catch a fish.

Step 4: Evaluating Writing

The purpose of this unit is to write descriptions and instructions using precise words that help readers see and feel what is happening. As you evaluate the monthly project, look for strong verbs, descriptive adjectives, and sensory details. You should also see at least one instance of figurative language, such as a simile, onomatopoeia, or allusion. Did the writer show instead of just telling? The details or procedures should also be in a logical order that guides the reader, with transition words to help clarify the message.

As you evaluate the writing project, you will be using the "6 Traits of Writing Rubric" from the Printable Pack. In addition, you will be looking for each step of the entire writing process. For example, your child will turn in a prewriting activity, a draft that shows both revisions and edits, as well as a finished, published piece. The publishing step should involve sharing the project in some way - reading it aloud to family, presenting it at dinner time, video chatting to show it off to grandparents, or sharing a video presentation on the internet of the writer sharing his or her writing. Sharing is a time for positive feedback and celebration.

Creating a positive buzz about the published piece will create a motivating, growth atmosphere in your Writer's Workshop. As you evaluate, remember that the process is just as important as the product, so watch for successes in the process as well. The final score will be out of 50 points - 20 for the process and 30 for the final project. You can write rubric scores as well as comments down on the "Writing Report Card" printable from the Printable Pack.

Breakdown of Possible Points

- 5 points for a complete prewriting activity
- 5 points for a completed draft
- 5 points for revisions
- 5 points for edits
- 30 points for the finished writing project

The 30 points for the finished project is further broken down into each of the six traits of writing as shown on the "6 Traits of Writing Rubric" from the Printable Pack.

Your comments should be specifically focused on the purposes of this unit and the skills you were working on throughout the unit.

What was done well? Is the writer understanding the writing process? What should be improved on? Are there any repeated mistakes to address?

Point out a clear strength.

Comments mean more than scores, so make sure to give clear feedback.

Fanciful Stories

Fanciful stories include any stories that stem from imagination rather than reality. Many of the great stories of all time are fanciful stories. There is great value in stories, even made up ones. Besides being merely entertaining, they also teach us things, allow us to examine human nature, communicate about values, and make us think and experience things we otherwise could not. They are not true, but that doesn't mean they don't have truths within them.

They say there are no new stories, only new ways of telling them. This means that the stories we tell are about love, kindness, beauty, hatred, jealousy, fear, and all the other things people have been experiencing throughout the history of mankind. They might come packaged in different settings or center around a new character, but the very same traits and emotions have always existed in mankind, and those are the things our stories are really about.

As you write stories, you will begin building them using simple structures. For example, all stories have a beginning, a middle, and an ending. As you progress, the structures will become more complex and varied. You will come to understand the importance of setting, characters, and conflict. You will begin to utilize dialogue, description, figurative language, and the element of surprise to give your stories even more substance.

Learning to write a compelling story is about a lot more than just saying, "Okay, let's all write a story. Do you have an idea?" Real writers consider a theme, plan out their plots, think about their characters' motivations, determine a problem and solution, create a world, and think about some unexpected elements for their readers. All of this happens before the story is ever put into words.

During this unit we'll learn about the ingredients of stories as well as some popular kinds of fanciful stories.

Step I: Mini-Lesson

After handwriting or typing practice has concluded, begin each day of Writer's Workshop with a mini-lesson. You will find some within the sidebars of this unit. You can also use a worksheet from a grammar workbook or practice editing, copying, or diagramming sentences. During writing time, watch for weak areas or mistakes being made and present a mini-lesson the next day to help correct those and improve writing skills in small, continuous ways.

The mini-lesson should take five to ten minutes and always have a positive happy spin, free from criticism. Not every mini-lesson needs to be kept in your Writer's Notebook. Most are merely for practice.

Step 2: Writing

Now it's time to really begin writing. Most of your time during Writer's Workshop should be spent writing. Practicing is the key to improving. You can use your writing time to free write your own ideas in your Journal anytime, or use the exercises below to practice writing skills and find inspiration for things to write about. Select as many exercises as you would like to do over the month, making sure you leave time to complete at least one writing project that will go all of the way through the writing process before the month is over. The exercises will also go in your Journal section of your Writer's Notebook. If you decide to take something from your Journal through the writing process and turn it into your writing project, move it from your Journal to the Writing section of your Writer's Notebook.

A few tips and reminders:

- You can repeat the units and the exercises in subsequent years, so don't ever feel pressured to get to all of them, and feel free to repeat ones you enjoy.
- Often a single exercise can be presented to all of your children, no matter their ages or abilities. They will naturally write at the level they are at and, as they practice, will grow as writers.
- As you progress through the exercises, watch for something that sparks interest and could become the writing project. Feel free to jump to the idea bank at the end of the unit anytime as well. If there's spare time after the project is published, return to more exercises.
- Your family may all be in different places in the writing process. That's perfectly fine. Remember, your Writer's Workshop is a garden and everyone is growing their own patch. You can all lend a hand to help each gardener's patch thrive, but you won't all grow the same crop.

It's time to write! Choose some exercises and jump right in!

EXERCISE: Story Elements Booklet

To learn the basic elements of a story, create a "Story Elements" booklet using the printable from the Printable Pack. Copy it on colorful card stock, then cut out the booklet around its perimeter and along the dashed lines. If you have several people making the booklet, you can use a variety of colors and then mix and match the pieces for multi-colored booklets.

☐ **Mini-Lesson**

Go back and review the "Fiction/Nonfiction" anchor chart from Writer's Workshop Jump Start Printable Pack.

Make a new anchor chart for the Writing Helps section of your Writer's Notebook by brainstorming a list of genres within the umbrella of fanciful stories that you could choose to write about during this unit.

- Fairy tale
- Folk tale
- Fable
- Tall tale
- Mystery
- Science fiction
- Thriller
- Fantasy
- Adventure
- Western
- Superhero
- Myths
- Dystopian
- Historical fiction
- Picture book

☐ **Mini-Lesson**

Put yourself into the stories you tell. Your feelings, experiences, friends, and adventures can all become part of your fanciful stories. Discuss this quote by Charles de Lint:

"Don't forget - no one else sees the world the way you do, so no one else can tell the stories that you have to tell."

☐ Mini-Lesson

Stories can be written from different points of view. Experienced authors can change point of view mid-story, but it's helpful as you're learning to write to choose a point of view and stick with it through your whole story.

1st person point of view is someone telling his or her own story. It involves using the pronouns I or we.

2nd person point of view means you are being told directly and uses the pronoun you.

3rd person point of view uses he, she, it, and they. It is a narrator or an outsider telling the events of the story.

Practice telling the story of Jack and Jill out loud in each of the three points of view.

☐ Mini-Lesson

Setting descriptions should always include three parts:

1. The time - consider the time of day, time of year, time of someone's life, or the past, present, or future.

2. The place - consider the physical location, geography, landmarks, cultural references, or fantasy elements related to the location.

3. The environment - consider the weather or climate and the current lay of the land based on conditions.

After cutting out the pieces, fold each flap, creating little doors. Glue the appropriate definition under each door. Glue the "Story Elements" title to the flap at the top.

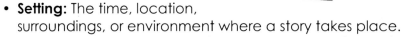

Talk about some of your favorite stories while you're working. Try to identify the settings, characters, plot points, and themes of some of your favorite stories. Also, share why the story is a favorite of yours. What do you like about it?

- **Setting:** The time, location, surroundings, or environment where a story takes place.
- **Characters:** Any people, animals, creatures, or figures in story.
- **Plot:** Events that take place in a story.
- **Theme:** The underlying message or big idea, often a universal truth or belief.

Setting

EXERCISE: My Story Setting

Use the "My Story Setting" printable from the Printable Pack. Think of a time and place that you think would make a great setting for a story - an African safari, another planet, deep underground, or maybe in your own town. Close your eyes for a minute or two and imagine that you are walking around (or swimming or driving or flying or bouncing or swinging, depending on the place in your imagination). See the details around you. Notice the sky, the wildlife, the buildings, and the landscape. Take in the smells and the sounds. How light or dark is it? Once you've explored within your mind, write down what you saw. In the first two boxes of the printable, write about where and when your story will be set. In the third box, draw the scene you saw in your imagination. Make sure to add details and color.

You can add this to your Journal so you can come back to it when you choose to write a story about it. Your setting may even spark an idea for a story that could take place there. If so, each time you work on your story, make sure to have this page out in front of you so you remember to add in details from your imagination throughout the story. Remember, your reader can't know what's in your mind unless you describe it in words.

EXERCISE: Gallery of Settings

Using the "Gallery of Settings" printable from the Printable Pack, draw a gallery of settings. Draw your ideas for fun story settings and then write a little bit about each setting below the picture. Add your gallery to your Writing Helps section of your Writer's Notebook so you can turn to it when you need a setting idea. Feel free to make several copies of the printable and create more than just four setting ideas for you to return to later.

EXERCISE: Setting Box

A story's setting is critical to the plot and the characters. If I tell you a tale from America's Wild West it will have a very different tone, hero, and storyline than a story from the Far West of China. Get a shoe box and craft a setting box. Create a diorama of a story setting you'd like to write about. Use construction paper, felt, fabric, magazine or online pictures, markers, clay, small toys, and other art supplies or household objects to create a 3-D version of your setting inside your box that showcases the time and place of your story.

You can choose any place in the universe, from a black hole in another galaxy right down to your own bedroom. It could be on a pirate ship, in the sky in a cloud city, in your home town, at the Great Pyramids of Giza, in London, or in a far-off, imaginary kingdom. Imagine any place that sounds like a fun setting for a story and craft your setting box to match your imagination.

If you have a fun idea for a story that could take place in your setting, write a few sentences about your idea down on a sheet of paper and glue the page to the back side of your setting box. You might even choose this story idea to take all of the way through the writing process for your project.

EXERCISE: Setting Switcheroo

Think of an imaginary story you like. I really love the story of *Alice in Wonderland*. Alice follows a white rabbit into a wondrous, mysterious world with talking animals and interesting people. She doesn't know how to escape from the world and return home, but she is brave enough to

☐ **Mini-Lesson**

Once you've decided on a setting, no matter how magical or fantastical it is, you should obey the rules of your world. For example, if you are in an underwater world, you don't want to have humans live within it unless you explain how they can breathe. Even in imaginary settings, readers want to understand the world. Draw an imaginary setting and write at least three rules of your world.

☐ **Mini-Lesson**

Sometimes story settings also involve the cultural or historical context of a society. In particular, organizations or governments can be a defining characteristic. For example, many dystopian stories include an oppressive government as part of the setting. Brainstorm out loud some problems that settings could create for a hero or heroine. It could be anything from natural disasters to an evil government.

☐ **Mini-Lesson**

A noun that describes one thing is singular. A noun that describes two things is a plural noun. Can you turn each of these singular nouns into plural nouns by adding an s?

lake, house, shop, friend, dog, duck, car, clock

Writer's Workshop

☐ Mini-Lesson

There are lots of ways to begin stories:

- Dialogue
- Character description
- Setting description
- A question
- A riddle
- An onomatopoeia
- An interesting fact
- Once upon a time . . .

Imagine you are writing the story of Mary from the familiar nursery rhyme *Mary Had A Little Lamb*. Craft eight different first lines, one of each of the types listed above.

☐ Mini-Lesson

Past tense verbs talk about things that already happened: I ran, she jumped, they sang, we cooked.

Present tense verbs talk about things that are happening right now: I am running, she is jumping, they are singing, we are cooking.

Future tense verbs talk about things that will happen in the future: I will run, she will jump, they will sing, we will cook.

Draw three columns and write past, present, and future tense verbs. It's important to write consistently in the same tense in a story or piece of writing.

keep exploring, meeting strange characters, and having adventures along the way.

Now I want you to imagine what would happen to Alice in another setting. Pretend for a moment that she visited Narnia (from The Chronicles of Narnia) or Gotham (from Batman). What adventures might she have in one of those settings?

Try your own setting switcheroo. Think of a story you like. Imagine that the main character were transported to a totally new setting. Can you think of an adventure he or she might have there? Write a little about the adventure and your ideas about what could happen to the character in the new setting. Add this to the Journal section of your Writer's Notebook.

EXERCISE: Setting Map

Using a piece of poster board or an oversized sheet of paper, draw a map of a setting you would like to write about. On the map, draw a picture of the main character in the location the character starts out at the beginning of the story. Add stars to your map where things happen to your character. At each star the character will have to overcome something. When characters overcome, they learn and grow. If you'd like to, you can add little notes near the stars that tell what happens to the character there.

Finally, mark the place where the problem is finally resolved with another star and make a little note telling how the story comes to a conclusion. The path your character travels can actually be drawn on the map if you'd like. You can also label any other important landmarks along the way. Use your setting map and the notes you made to draft a story.

EXERCISE: Foreshadowing With Setting

Experienced writers use settings to foreshadow events within the story. To do this, you must think of your setting almost like a character. If your character is a cheerful optimist, the setting will be full of hope, help, and possibilities. If your character is bravely embarking on a dangerous quest, the setting should be foreboding and full of potential danger. Settings are never neutral. The setting should give hints about what is to come in the plot.

J.K. Rowling describes Diagon Alley, Harry's first encounter with the wizarding world, as an exciting place with wondrous objects, magic all around, and more possibility than Harry could ever have imagined.

> *Harry wished he had about eight more eyes. He turned his head in every direction as they walked up the street, trying to look at everything at once: the shops, the things outside them, the people doing their shopping. A plump woman outside an Apothecary was shaking her head as they passed, saying, "Dragon liver, seventeen sickles an ounce, they're mad . . ."*
>
> *A low soft hooting came from a dark shop with a sign saying Eeylops Own Emporium -- Tawny, Screech, Barn, Brown, and Snowy. Several boys of about Harry's age had their noses pressed against a window with broomsticks in it. "Look," Harry heard one of them say, "the new Nimbus Two Thousand - fastest ever -" There were shops selling robes, shops selling telescopes and strange silver instruments Harry had never seen before, windows stacked with barrels of bat spleens and eels' eyes, potion bottles, globes of the moon . . ."*

Discuss things within this setting that give clues about the kinds of things that may happen to Harry within the story.

Write your own interesting setting description that includes your main character walking through it and interacting with the setting in a way that foreshadows events that could come up in the story. Use the "Foreshadowing with Setting" printable from the Printable Pack. Add it to the Journal section of your Writer's Notebook when you're finished.

Characters

EXERCISE: Character Sketch

Begin by drawing a full body picture of a character from your own imagination. It can be a person, animal, object, creature, or anything else from your imagination that has a personality. Draw it large on your paper, using pencil or

☐ Mini-Lesson

Foreshadowing is a literary device writers use. It often appears at the beginning of a story and is a hint for something that is to come. For example, in *Mary Poppins*, Mary explains early on that she'll stay until the winds change. She flew in with her umbrella and we weren't surprised later when she flew off the same way. Similarly, a murder mystery could give tiny clues as to who the murderer is. Likewise, a superhero tale might give clues as to the weakness of the villain that will create the defeat.

Often you add foreshadowing as you revise a story. Once you know the end, you can add in tiny clues. Think of a story ending and a way to foreshadow the final event.

☐ Mini-Lesson

J.R.R. Tolkien describes the setting in *The Two Towers* this way: "High mounds of crushed and powdered rock, great cones of earth fire-blasted and poison-stained . . . like an obscene graveyard." What kinds of events do you think the main characters will face in a setting like this?

Write a few sentences that vividly describe a setting and then write an event that you can imagine happening in your setting.

☐ Mini-Lesson

To write memorable characters, ponder these:

- Secrets
- Mistakes
- Sacrifices
- Emotions
- Goals
- Best moments
- Worst moments

As you create a character sketch, add these elements. They will help you write in the character's voice when you pen your story. A character sketch is one of the best prewriting activities for writing stories.

☐ Mini-Lesson

Besides simple past, present, and future tenses, verbs can also have perfect and continuous tenses.

Perfect tense is used when an action is happening over a span of time.

Maggie **has biked** every day for the past ten years.

We **have smiled** every day since the baby arrived.

You **will have jogged** 100 miles before the race.

Continuous tense is used when an action is still happening.

I **am hiding** in the cave until the dragon leaves.

I **will be waiting** a long time for the king to arrive.

Write two sentences - one in perfect tense and one in continuous tense.

colored pencils.

When you are finished sketching, use strong adjectives that could reveal exactly what your character looks like even without your audience seeing the picture. Write the adjectives about your character's appearance all around the outside of your sketch.

You just described the outside appearance, but now you have to think even harder and describe what your character is like on the inside. What does he think about? What does she feel? What does he struggle with? Who is she worrying about? What are her favorite things? Who does he love?

On the back, write ideas for at least three problems your character might have to solve. Now you have three strong story ideas and a thought out character that you can write about.

Draft a story about your character. Make sure to include the traits and descriptions you included on your character sketch. Add the draft to your Journal.

EXERCISE: Protagonist Versus Antagonist
In a story, the protagonist is most often the main character and considered to be the hero or heroine. The antagonist opposes the protagonist and creates some sort of challenge. Use the "Protagonist Antagonist" printable from the Printable Pack to plan out both characters.

Let's begin with your antagonist, or villain. Cut out a picture from a magazine or print one from the internet. Write a few sentences about your antagonist. What makes him or her villainous? Where is s/he from? What is his/her goal? Does s/he have any special powers or abilities? Does s/he have any helpers?

Now cut out a picture from a magazine or the internet of your protagonist. A protagonist is a heroine or hero, the one who will save the day. Write a few sentences about your

protagonist and give details about his or her hero traits and tendencies.

Think about a conflict that could happen between your protagonist and antagonist and write about it in the center box. Use the two characters and the conflict to draft a story. Add your character sketches and your draft to the Journal section of your Writer's Notebook. If you decide to turn it into your writing project for this unit, move these to the Writing section of your notebook instead.

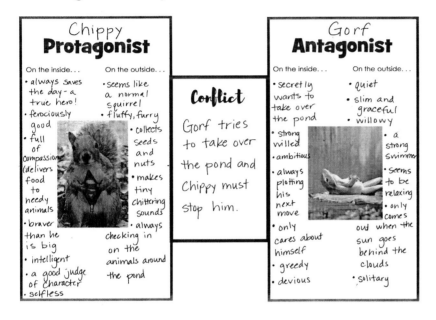

EXERCISE: Character Cards

Gather blank 3" x 5" index cards. On each card, draw (or print from the internet) several of each of these characters: a hero, a sidekick, a villain, a minion, a mentor, and a love interest. Give each character a name and write a short description on each card. Also, write on the card what the deepest desire of the person, animal, or creature is. Have everyone in your family put all of the hero character cards they created into a bowl and take turns drawing them out, with each person drawing out one hero they will write about. Repeat the process five more times, once for each of the remaining five character types.

Draft a story that includes each of the six characters you selected. Remember that each character has a role to fulfill. They each have a desire, or something that motivates them in the story. This desire is something they want more than anything else. Make sure that as you write your story you have each of the characters act according to their deepest desires. If you are unclear about what the character desires, you can ask the person who drew the character to further explain the character's motivation.

☐ **Mini-Lesson**

Proper nouns include the names of people or other characters. We always capitalize the names of characters. Think of some characters from a story you love. Write sentences about the character and make sure to capitalize his or her name in the sentences.

☐ **Mini-Lesson**

Like other names, titles for people are also considered proper nouns and should be capitalized only if they are being used as a name. Ask yourself if you could fill in the person's name where you used the title to see if it should be capitalized.

Can I go with **Mom** to the store?

Can I go with my **mom** to the store?

In the second one, you couldn't replace the word mom with her given name, so you wouldn't capitalize it.

Write your own sentences using these titles and determine whether or not each should have a capital in your sentences: mom, dad, grandma, grandpa, doctor, president, uncle.

☐ **Mini-Lesson**

A villain is often a mirror image of the hero. Together, brainstorm a list of words that could describe a hero. Across from each word, write its antonym, or opposite. These words can describe the hero's villain.

☐ **Mini-Lesson**

Brainstorm out loud together:

- Animal characters
- Monster characters
- Magical characters
- Otherworldly characters
- Mythical characters
- Heroic characters
- Villainous characters

☐ **Mini-Lesson**

Write descriptions of some stereotypical characters you might like to write about in a story. Perhaps you will have a hard-working lumberjack, a blonde woman who isn't very smart and just likes to shop, or a nerdy kid who wants to grow up to be a scientist. Once you've written your stereotypes, make some unexpected changes in them. Maybe you'll describe a blond lumberjack lady who loves science. When we create unexpected characters in stories, they can be meaningful and memorable and interesting to our readers. As you write your descriptions, include at least three evidences that show the person is more than just a stereotype.

☐ **Mini-Lesson**

Identify the hero, sidekick, villain, minion, mentor, and love interest in stories you've read.

EXERCISE: Mythical Characters

One of the fun parts of fanciful stories is that they don't have to be real. Your characters can be anything you can dream up, from a talking bowling ball to a wizard who lost his magic or an invisible monster who secretly helps people. Your imagination is the limit.

Cut pieces of card stock into fourths. Create mythical characters that have special abilities, superpowers, unusual characteristics, or otherworldly origins. Monsters, fairies, ghosts, mermaids, and elves are just the beginning. Can you create some new characters? On the front side of each card, draw your creatures. On the back sides, write about their abilities, goals, origin, and unusual traits.

Glue an envelope to a sheet of card stock. Put the character cards you created inside the envelope. They can give you ideas as you're penning a story. Add your character bank into the Writing Helps section of your Writer's Notebook.

EXERCISE: Character Archetypes

There are universal patterns woven through the stories we tell. No matter what culture, language, historical period, or group of people the story is told within, there are certain universal things we all seem to share in common. This concept was first pointed out by Carl Jung, a psychologist who recognized archetypes within literature. He noticed that the same types of characters, plots, and struggles occurred over and over again, with only the details varying slightly. Characters are just one type of archetype Jung noticed. Character archetypes are universal characters

with common characteristics. They may have unique specific details, but their overall character is the same.

Think of a hero from a story you know who was born in unusual circumstances and is raised by someone other than his two parents. He had to leave his homeland or family but would return again. Courageous and strong, he risked his life for the good of all.

You may have thought of Simba from the Lion King. Or were you thinking of Luke Skywalker? Or perhaps you pictured Hercules in your mind. Maybe you thought of Harry Potter or Beowulf. Each of these is a hero archetype.

Use the "Character Archetype" printable from the Printable Pack and read the descriptions, then write down examples of characters from stories you know that fit each description. Using universal characters like these helps your readers relate to your characters. Add the printable to the Writing Helps section of your Writer's Notebook.

EXERCISE: Flat Versus Round Characters

Round characters are complex. They are realistic because they are fully developed. For example, your hero may be good and virtuous, and yet have weaknesses or flaws. The stay-at-home mother in the story may surprise you by having a top secret spy lab in her basement. Round characters surprise us a little because they aren't predictable and boring. They might be evil but have a little speck of goodness that comes out when it really matters. They might be good through and through but also be a little annoying. They could have an evil plan but a really virtuous reason for carrying it out. Often even your hero, who seems to be nearly perfect, will have a fatal flaw that creates a greater problem within the story.

Real people are not one-dimensional. They are complex and full of contradictions. By contrast, flat characters are predictable and not thoughtfully crafted. They tend to be extreme and defined by just one or two characteristics. For example, the jealous boyfriend is ALWAYS jealous and not much else. The superhero is SO super that she never makes a mistake or loses a fight. Try to avoid flat characters. Readers don't get excited to read the rest of a story with flat characters because it is too predictable.

Use the "Round Characters" printable from the Printable Pack to practice rounding out flat characters. Choose one of these flat characters and then round him or her out, creating a character that is full of dimension.

- A noble knight

☐ Mini-Lesson

Interesting characters need flaws. As you craft characters, think of their strengths and their weaknesses. Some characters have a flaw so big it leads to their downfall. That's called a fatal flaw. Can you think of a fatal flaw a character might have?

☐ Mini-Lesson

As you write stories, remember to add in strong verbs, vivid descriptions, and fun literary devices. All of these help improve word choice, one of the six traits of writing. Look through your Writing Helps section of your Writer's Notebook for ideas.

☐ Mini-Lesson

Even magical characters need to have limitations. An all-powerful person with no limitations isn't interesting. Limited magic and power is much more interesting. Magic is more valuable when it costs something. It might take energy or life force. It might require certain ingredients. Perhaps using magic leaves your character vulnerable to other enemies. Maybe enemies can find him or her because of a trace magic leaves.

Do a 5-minute quick write about a character who has amazing magical powers and then describe the limitations or weaknesses he or she has.

☐ Mini-Lesson

Symbolism can be a fun addition to a story. Often character names are symbolic. For example, if you are writing about a strong hero, you might name him Valerius since that means "strong" in Latin. You can also add other symbols into your stories.

Black = death

White = purity

Purple = royalty

Dogs = loyalty

Snakes = evil

Lambs = innocence

Roses = romance

Butterflies= transformation

Storms = turmoil

Discuss how you can add symbols into stories to foreshadow events.

☐ Mini-Lesson

Some plural nouns are irregular. For example, most nouns that end in -f change their ending to -ves when they are plural (thief becomes thieves), but these don't.

belief	beliefs
chief	chiefs
roof	roofs
cliff	cliffs

Keep a list in your Word Work section of your Writer's Notebook of irregular word spellings you come across.

- A wandering and adventurous cowboy
- A loyal puppy dog
- A traitorous, wealthy tycoon
- A hilarious jester
- A greedy and power-hungry queen
- A curious kitty cat
- A kind caregiver
- A dishonest lawyer
- A humble guy who just wants to fit in
- A majestic eagle
- A bumbling, idiotic king
- A nerdy scientist

Add your round character to the Journal section of your Writer's Notebook.

EXERCISE: Character Growth, Static Versus Dynamic
Stories often have a combination of static and dynamic characters. Static characters do not progress or grow during the story, They are often stubborn and set in their ways. Dynamic characters show growth. They build stronger character, develop talents, or learn to rise up to challenges, becoming better people. It's helpful to think about which of your characters will grow and which will stagnate as you write stories.

Use the "Character Growth" printable from the Printable Pack to create a character that is growing. Draw your character in the flower and write about his or her overshadowing problem in the cloud. In the drops of water, list things that will happen to your character to cause him or her to grow - the challenges he or she will overcome. Write more about that growth with some before and after notes.

Remember that the protagonist often grows, but

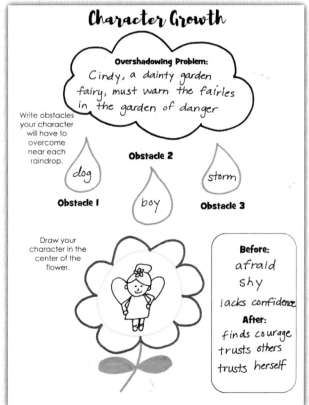

Character Growth

Overshadowing Problem:
Cindy, a dainty garden fairy, must warn the fairies in the garden of danger

Write obstacles your character will have to overcome near each raindrop.

Obstacle 1 — dog

Obstacle 2 — boy

Obstacle 3 — storm

Draw your character in the center of the flower.

Before:
afraid
shy
lacks confidence
After:
finds courage
trusts others
trusts herself

the antagonist in the story can grow too. Often part of the rising action and suspense in a story comes because the antagonist is growing stronger as the story goes on. Even the sidekick or another less important character might be growing. You may want to repeat this exercise with several characters that you plan to use within a story you want to write.

EXERCISE: Naming Characters

Create a list of character names to add to your Writing Helps section of your Writer's Notebook. As you make your list, you can add notes about the character you have in mind too. For example, you might be thinking of a good name for a frog. Her name will probably be different than if you're naming an alien from the planet Zogg.

Here are some ways to come up with names if you're feeling stuck:

- Think of people you know
- Look at a newspaper or magazine
- Flip through story books
- Read an atlas (this works well for place names as well as character names)
- Use a baby name book or website (you can also search out the meanings of names through this, which can add another dimension to your character)
- Look up the names of flowers, trees, and plants
- Use names from Greek or Roman mythology

EXERCISE: Character Quick Pick

Use the "Character Quick Pick" printable from the Printable Pack to make some quick decisions about a character. Draft a short story about the character you picked.

EXERCISE: Roll-A-Complete Character

Roll a die and answer the corresponding question from the "Roll-A-Complete Character" printable from the Printable Pack. You can either develop one main character or answer the questions for multiple characters within your story. Write down your answers and keep them nearby as you draft your story. Whether or not the information appears in your story, it's helpful to truly know your characters as you tell their story.

EXERCISE: Complete Character Map

If you want to dive really deeply into who your character is, use the "Complete Character Map" printable from the Printable Pack. Think about the details of your character

---

☐ Mini-Lesson

Dialogue is conversation in a story that uses quotation marks around the speaker's exact words. It is usually accompanied by a dialogue tag, which is an explanation of who is speaking and how they are expressing themselves.

Go over some rules for punctuating dialogue and put the "Basic Dialogue Rules" printable from the Printable Pack in the Writing Helps section of your Writer's Notebook.

Practice writing your own sentences by mimicking the sentences on the printable. You may want to repeat this mini-lesson and practice writing dialogue several days in a row.

☐ Mini-Lesson

As characters talk back and forth to each other in a story, you must begin a new paragraph each time a new character is speaking. To begin a new paragraph, go down to the next line and indent the sentence. These paragraphs help readers keep track of who is speaking.

"How are you, Mr. Fox?" Rabbit asked.

"I'm feeling rather ill," Mr. Fox replied, hanging his head low. He pulled his blanket up to his chin.

"I'm sorry to hear that, but I've brought something that might cheer you up."

☐ Mini-Lesson

Sometimes characters use inner dialogue, or dialogue between the character and his or her mind. If you're telling the story in first person, inner dialogue is often shown using italics.

I will be late to the party. Will she ever forgive me?

If the story is being told in third person, you usually use quotes.

"I will be late to the party. Will she ever forgive me?" Carlene thought.

Practice writing some examples of inner dialogue in first and third person.

☐ Mini-Lesson

The word "said" is used often in dialogue tags. It's a good word that usually disappears for your readers. Their minds skim over it, but sometimes it can feel repetitive. Use the "Put Said to Bed" printable from the Printable Pack. Write your own dialogue sentences using alternatives to *said* to improve your word choice. Add the printable to the Writing Helps section of your Writer's Notebook.

☐ Mini-Lesson

Practice writing some sentences of dialogue that are missing commas, periods, question marks, exclamation points, and quotation marks. Trade papers and fill in the missing punctuation. This is good practice for the editing phase of the writing process in which you must always check your punctuation.

so they can come out in natural ways as you draft a story about him or her.

EXERCISE: Character Wanted Poster

Often we think first of the heroic character in a story, but you can reverse that. Think of a villainous character and create a character wanted poster for him or her using the "Wanted" printable from the Printable Pack. Based on his or her crimes and sidekicks, write a story from the criminal's point of view. Describe what led to this life of crime and tell the other side of the story. Decide whether the criminal goes free or is captured in the end. Add your story to your Journal.

EXERCISE: Dialogue

Dialogue in a story means conversation. In order to make your story and your characters believable, they need to talk and interact with each other.

Use the "Dialogue Duos" printable from the Printable Pack. Cut out each of the cards and place them in a hat. One at a time, have pairs of people act out a conversation between the people on the card while everyone else tries to guess who their characters are. Don't use names or obvious clues in your dialogue. Simply pretend you are the character and imagine what you might say in the situation.

EXERCISE: Putting Words Into My Mouth

Read a wordless book together. Create dialogue for the story. This can be done out loud together or in writing. You can even make a copy of the pages and add talk bubbles to write down what each character is saying.

EXERCISE: Talk Bubbles

Look through your Writer's Notebook and find a character you've developed. Draw some talk bubbles and fill in words your character would say in response to these questions:

- What do you want most?
- What did you have for breakfast?
- Where would you go if you could go anywhere?
- What is your biggest threat?
- What do you believe in?
- Who do you wish you could meet?

Do a quick write of a scene within a story that includes at least one of the pieces of dialogue you crafted. A quick write involves setting a timer for five minutes and writing continuously until the time runs out. Continue to imagine what each character would say in situations that arise in

the story and include it as dialogue.

The key to believable dialogue isn't just in what the characters say but also in how they say it. A chatty waitress will describe a car to an inquiring police officer very differently than the old gentleman in the booth who hardly ever says a word but also witnessed the car. They may both be describing the same car, but their responses will be entirely different. Think about not just *what* your character would say, but *how* he or she would say it. Include those kinds of details in your quick write. Add it to the Journal section of your Writer's Notebook.

EXERCISE: Adding Action to Dialogue
As you practice writing dialogue within stories, make sure to incorporate action. Along with the actual words, describe what the character is doing.

> *"I lost my keys again," she muttered under her breath, frantically opening drawers.*

> *Scampering to and fro, Mouse reveled in the sweet sunshine of springtime, belting out, "Yahoo! The rain has stopped!"*

> *"Twinkle, winkle, whip!" Francesca called out hopefully, imitating the words of her fairy godmother. "Oh," she shrugged, "Nothing ever happens. I guess I just don't have magic after all."*

Create a notebooking sheet entitled "Dialogue." Write down things that some of your characters might say, adding actions that are happening as they speak. Actions, gestures, expressions, emotions, and manner of speaking can all be added into dialogue descriptions. Add your dialogue ideas to the Writing Helps section of your Writer's Notebook.

EXERCISE: Two Points of View
As you are developing characters, you must also consider the point of view you want to tell your story from. Which character is telling the story? It could be an omniscient narrator who is observing the whole thing, your hero, your villain, a friend, or just a third party character who is there observing but isn't really important to the story.

To practice writing from different points of view, choose one of these pairings and try writing the same short story twice, but from different points of view each time.

- Fisherman/fish
- Astronaut/martian
- Beekeeper/bee

☐ **Mini-Lesson**

An important part of word choice is to use vivid and exact language in your setting and character descriptions. Make sure your sentences use strong verbs and plenty of adjectives and adverbs to help paint a picture for your reader.

☐ **Mini-Lesson**

If your characters are speaking naturally, sometimes the dialogue you write won't be in complete sentences. That's okay. Write your dialogue in the style that you would speak it. Dialogue tends to be less formal than normal writing.

☐ **Mini-Lesson**

Some stories begin in medias res, which is Latin for "in the middle of things." The story may begin at an exciting moment, and then the narrator goes back and describes the back story and tells how the characters came to that point in the story.

> *She clung to the cliff wall with only her fingernails, not sure whether she could hang on until help arrived. Sally never would have imagined that she would be in such a pickle when she awakened this morning, snuggled into her cozy bed. The day had begun like any other . . .*

Writer's Workshop

Mini-Lesson

Make an illustrated note sheet about conflicts in stories. Divide a sheet of paper into six equal sections. Write one type of conflict in each section and make an illustration to show each one.

The conflicts in stories have six basic forms:

1. Character versus character, in which a problem arises between two characters. The two characters are usually called the protagonist (hero) and the antagonist (villain).

2. Character versus self, in which the character has a flaw or struggle which must be overcome.

3. Character versus supernatural, in which the character must defeat something paranormal, like a ghost, superstition, or curse.

4. Character versus society, in which the hero or heroine must change unjust laws, an unjust ruler, or an oppressive culture.

5. Character versus nature, in which animals, natural disasters, or severe weather create a problem.

6. Character versus technology, in which a robot, machine, or another form of technology create a problem that must be overcome.

- Gardener/flower
- Princess/prince
- Dragon/knight
- Farmer/cow
- Lion tamer/lion
- Hunter/deer
- Beach bum/crab

EXERCISE: Character Wheel

It's pretty easy to develop one character at a time, but to really write an interesting story you need to understand all of your characters and how they interact with each other. Create a character wheel that you can keep beside you while you draft a story. Create eight interesting characters, all featured in the same story. Draw a picture of each character and name him or her. Within the oval below each character, write a short description of who the character is or something they do within your story.

Plot

EXERCISE: Story Map

Every story has a beginning, a middle, and an ending. The beginning is a chance for you to tell about your character

and his or her life. Your character lives somewhere, knows certain people, and has something happen that triggers the story. Maybe a problem arises. Perhaps an adventure is beginning, It could be that your character had something unexpected happen that will somehow change the course of his or her life. The beginning of your story is a time to set up this background information for your reader.

Use the "Story Scroll" printable from the Printable Pack to jot down the beginning, middle, and ending of a fanciful story you know. Here are a few ideas of stories you could analyze:

- *Where the Wild Things Are* by Maurice Sendak
- *The Cat in the Hat* by Dr. Seuss
- *The Story of Ferdinand* by Munro Leaf
- *Hansel and Gretel* by Jacob and Wilhelm Grimm
- *Charlotte's Web* by E.B. White
- *James and the Giant Peach* by Roald Dahl
- *The Borrowers* by Mary Norton
- *The Chronicles of Narnia* by C.S. Lewis
- *The Giver* by Lois Lowry

You aren't examining every detail, but rather, you are stepping back and seeing the big picture of the story. Once you've practiced with familiar stories, try using the "Story Map" printable from the Printable Pack to plan out your own story idea. Add it to your Journal.

EXERCISE: Climax
The climax of a story is the most exciting part. It's the part where you aren't quite sure if the hero or heroine will overcome or not.

Play a game called "Climax Champion." One person will begin by telling a problem that a character might face in the climax of a story.

> *She's about to get chased by a bear.*

Then the next person will try to outdo the first with an even more dramatic climax.

> *His best friend is about to fall off a cliff.*

The next person will try to outdo both of the previous ones.

> *There's a fire-breathing dragon chasing the villagers who are about to perish.*

This will continue until someone fails to come up with a more exciting climax. Jot down any of the climax ideas you think you might like to write about and add the list to your Ideas section of your Writer's Notebook.

☐ **Mini-Lesson**

Cause and effect are a really important part of creating a plot in a story. With each action you write, it needs to have an effect on the characters. Your characters must change, learn, grow, or have something happen with each event within the story.

The British novelist E.M. Forster said, "'The king died and then the queen died' is a story. 'The king died, and then the queen died of grief,' is a plot."

Look through a story you are writing and try to think of effects of some of the events you have written about. If you can't spot any effects, add one to your story by writing them on sticky notes and sticking them to the event on your page as part of your revising stage of the writing process. Ask yourself what effect the event had on your character.

☐ **Mini-Lesson**

Time order is important in stories. Unless you are clearly including a flashback, tell the story in the order it happens. Writing the events in order will help your reader understand the events and the timeline. Plan out the events and put them in order before you draft your story.

Stories that are told in a logical order are clear and organized. Prewriting activities will help improve your organization as you write stories.

☐ Mini-Lesson

Published books have short book blurbs on the back cover or dust jacket. They are a quick summary of what the story is about and are there to draw people in and get them interested in reading the story. Write a book blurb for a story you have started that you are taking through the writing process to the publishing phase. The book blurb should be about 100 words long and include vivid description and a cliffhanger at the end so your reader wants to find out more.

☐ Mini-Lesson

Common story themes include:

- Love
- Death
- Good versus evil
- Coming of age
- Power and corruption
- Survival
- Courage
- Heroism
- Prejudice
- Individual versus society
- Injustice
- War
- Deception
- Circle of life
- Suffering
- Peace
- Friendship
- Family
- Fading beauty
- Technology
- Immortality
- Rebirth

Can you think of stories that have these themes?

EXERCISE: Problems and Solutions

To be complete, a story has to have a problem and a solution to the problem. Talk through stories you know and discuss the problems and solutions in those stories.

Here are a few to get you started:

- The Gingerbread Man
- The Three Little Pigs
- Goldilocks and the Three Bears
- Hansel and Gretel
- The Three Billy Goats Gruff
- Little Red Riding Hood

Do a five-minute quick write of a short story in the style of one of these tales that has at least three clear problems and a single clear solution. Add it to your Journal.

EXERCISE: Story Mountain

Great stories have a structure that builds tension as the story unfolds. A story mountain is a graphic organizer that helps you build tension into your story. Imagine climbing a mountain. Before you begin, you take in the scenery and enjoy the company of your party. Together, you begin to climb. The trail isn't always perfectly smooth and easy. It's hard to climb. The higher you go, the harder it gets, and the struggle becomes intense. Just when you think you might not make it, you reach the peak, the big moment! The way back down celebrates your accomplishment and takes you to a happy place of success.

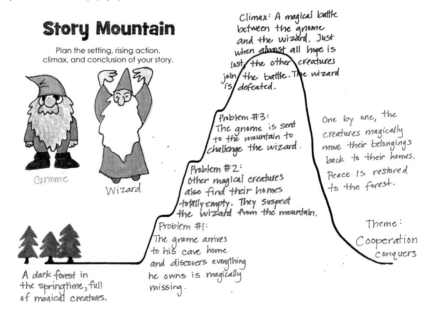

Story Mountain

Plan the setting, rising action, climax, and conclusion of your story.

Gnome

Wizard

A dark forest in the springtime, full of magical creatures.

Problem #1: The gnome arrives to his cave home and discovers everything he owns is magically missing.

Problem #2: Other magical creatures also find their homes totally empty. They suspect the wizard from the mountain.

Problem #3: The gnome is sent to the mountain to challenge the wizard.

Climax: A magical battle between the gnome and the wizard. Just when almost all hope is lost, the other creatures join the battle. The wizard is defeated.

One by one, the creatures magically move their belongings back to their homes. Peace is restored to the forest.

Theme: Cooperation conquers

Use the feelings of climbing a mountain to map your story idea out on the "Story Mountain" printable from the Printable Pack. You'll start by writing about your setting and characters. Describe events, or problems, that occur

on your way up, each one a little harder than the one before it. Right at the peak, describe the climax, or the most interesting part of the story, the part that presents the biggest challenge. Finally, map out your conclusion as you descend the mountain and celebrate your success. You can write your theme, or message, last of all.

EXERCISE: Build-A-Story

Use the "Build-A-Story" printable from the Printable Pack to help you get started drafting a story. Cut out the pieces, making sure to keep the beginning, middle, and end pieces separate from each other. Put each set into its own container. Draw out three cards, one from each set, and draft a story for your Journal using the ideas on the cards.

EXERCISE: Roll-A-Story

Use the "Roll-A-Story" printable from the Printable Pack to help you decide on the basic structure of a story. Roll the dice three times. The first roll decides your main character. The second roll decides your setting. The third roll determines what the main conflict of the story will be. Once you've got all three, begin drafting your story. Add your story to your Journal.

EXERCISE: Story Hooks

Every great story should start with a great hook. A hook is the opening sentence or paragraph of your story. If you begin a story in an interesting way, your reader will immediately be hooked and want to keep on reading.

There are lots of ways to start stories. Often stories begin right in the middle of the action. After the reader is hooked, you can back up and tell a little more of the back story that led to the action. If you begin with the problem, readers feel invested in finding out how the character will solve the problem.

The "Story Hooks" printable from the Printable Pack offers ideas for specific ways you can begin a story to help your reader get hooked right away. Fill in the chart using a story you're working on. Come up with five different beginnings on the chart, then choose the one you like best to include in your story. Here's an example of five different ways to write a story hook about a little pixie named Pim who loved to sneak into beehives and steal honey even though she was terribly allergic to bee stings.

An onomotopeia is a sound effect word.

Buzz! Owww! The bee's stinger sunk deep into Pim's shoulder. She only had minutes until her throat would

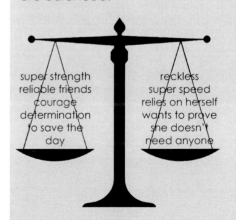

super strength
reliable friends
courage
determination
to save the
day

reckless
super speed
relies on herself
wants to prove
she doesn't
need anyone

☐ Mini-Lesson

Symbolism is another important part of stories. Discuss some of these common symbols together and brainstorm stories that include these symbols.

- Light and Darkness - light usually represents hope, intellect, or renewal while darkness represents ignorance, despair, or the unknown.
- Fire and Ice - fire represents light, life, and warmth while ice represents darkness, death, or ignorance.
- The Underworld - represents evil and fear of dying.
- Crossroads - indicate that a decision must be made.
- Maze - Symbolic of a journey or search for something that seems impossible.
- Castle - represents a stronghold, protection, and safety.
- Fog - symbolizes confusion or uncertainty.
- Whirlpool, tornado, hurricane, storm, or any other natural disaster - shows the weaknesses of mankind and civilization compared with nature, also represents mortality.
- Tower - a place of isolation and evil, is often a trap.

swell and she would stop breathing.

A fact used as a hook should be interesting.

Did you know honeybees will die if they sting you?

Vivid descriptions can draw readers in through their interesting word choice.

Pim dove in and out, clutching her fists and flying through the forest like a hummingbird, her wings fluttering faster than ever before. The tall oaks chatted around her, crawling with moss and shading the creatures below.

Questions can be interesting hooks because readers immediately answer them in their minds.

Have you ever wanted something so badly you would risk your own life for it?

Dialogue involves a conversation or statement, usually within quotation marks.

"Why, oh, why can't I resist? Po will never forgive me for breaking into the hive again! And now I've gone and gotten stung!" Pim spoke aloud, although Po was nowhere to be seen. She needed him right now, though she wasn't sure how she would explain that she had gotten stung again while try to steal honey.

EXERCISE: Plot Archetypes

Just as there are character archetypes, there are also plot archetypes. They involve the same basic plots, or stories, told again and again, with only the details differing.

Here are a few plot archetypes you may have seen:

- Quests - Usually quests involve a search for something. Finding this item or person will somehow restore peace.
- Tasks - Task-oriented stories have a protagonist who must use his or her strengths to accomplish an overwhelming challenge. He or she is uniquely able to accomplish this.
- Coming of Age - In these stories the protagonist matures from youth into adulthood, making an internal change.
- Cycles - Cycle archetypes are stories that begin and end in the same place. This includes seasons, lifespans, life cycles within nature and the concept of the circle of life. Sometimes characters become like their predecessors or order in the story is restored to its beginning. Often there is symbolism as well - springtime or morning represents beginnings, birth, or youth. Evening and winter represent endings, death, or aging.
- Good versus Evil - These stories always portray goodness

as being the conquerer of evil in the end. Despite overwhelming odds, good triumphs.

Choose one of these plot archetypes and draft your own short story. Think of the pattern outlined then add fresh characters and a specific problem within the archetype.

EXERCISE: Story Starters

Print the four "Story Starters" pages from the Printable Pack on four different colors of card stock. Cut the cards apart and flip them upside down on a table. Mix them up and then draw out one card of each color.

Set a clock for three minutes. During those three minutes, map out a basic story in your mind that incorporates each of your four cards - a character, a problem, an object, and an adjective. When the timer is finished, set the timer again, this time for five minutes. Do a five-minute quick write to begin a draft of your story.

Don't let your pencil stop no matter what. Just keep writing, jotting down any ideas that come to your mind. It's okay if the ideas are a little messy and out of order. Just keep writing until the timer sounds.

When the timer is finished this time, share what you've written out loud. Get feedback and ideas from others, then continue writing your story.

Theme

EXERCISE: What is a Theme?

The theme of a story is its message. Stories can have one simple theme or a variety of themes all within the same story. The theme can be stated directly. In Aesop's fables, for example, you always see the theme stated directly right after the story ends.

> *Never run faster than you can handle.*

> *Always tell the truth.*

> *Slow and steady wins the race.*

Often themes aren't directly stated though. They are just implied. Love is one of the obvious themes of *Romeo and Juliet* by William Shakespeare, but it is never directly stated as the theme. It is implied.

Create a theme notebooking page using the "Story Themes" printable from the Printable Pack. Cut out the flower. Fold each petal, then glue the center on to a sheet of card stock, leaving the petals unglued. Write a story

---

☐ **Mini-Lesson**

Transition words will help your stories to move forward, be organized, and show the sequence of events.

Write lists of transition words to add to the Writing Helps section of your Writer's Notebook. Here are some ideas. You can add more of your own if you'd like to.

Story Beginnings

- First
- Once
- One time
- In the beginning
- It started when
- One morning
- One afternoon
- One evening
- One night
- Long ago
- To begin

Story Middles

- Then
- Next
- Later
- Also
- Soon
- After that
- Suddenly
- Before long
- In the meantime
- Meanwhile
- As soon as

Story Endings

- Finally
- At last
- In the end
- Eventually
- Last, but not least
- As a result
- Last
- In conclusion

☐ Mini-Lesson

Interjections are commonly used in stories. They are single words or short phrases that precede a sentence. They usually express emotion and are set apart from the rest of the sentence by an exclamation point or a comma.

Ouch! That bug bit me.

Oh my, I didn't know she would be here.

Wow! Aliens landed on Earth!

Yee haw! I'm a cowboy now!

Aw, I feel just terrible about that.

Practice writing some of your own interjections. Include some that have exclamation points, indicating strong emotions, and others with commas, which show milder emotions.

☐ Mini-Lesson

The animal characters within fables are anthropomorphic. That means they have the characteristics of people instead of animals. They can walk, talk, think, and act like people.

Sketch several animal characters and make a word cloud surrounding each one that describes some human traits and abilities your animals have.

theme on each petal. Add the theme notebooking page to the Writing Helps section of your notebook so you can refer to it when you need an idea for a story you are writing.

EXERCISE: What Did the Character Learn?

Think of some stories you enjoy. Can you identify the theme or themes? One way to find the theme is to ask yourself, "What did the main character learn?

Think of a lesson you have learned in your life. Write down the lesson. Create a character who will learn the same lesson and draft a short story about how he or she learned it. It could be a similar story to the one that caused you to learn it, or it could be entirely different, as long as the same lesson is learned at the end. Add your story to your Journal.

EXERCISE: Theme

Use the "Theme" printable from the Printable Pack to help you make plans about a theme you'd like to create a story about. Write your theme in the oval. Think not only of the theme itself but also of the things the character will do or say to show the theme. Write the things your character will do that connect with the theme in the boxes and the things your character will say that connect with the theme in the talking bubbles.

Fanciful Story Styles

EXERCISE: Superhero Tale

In a superhero tale, your hero has at least one superpower. Decide specifically what powers he or she has and stick to those. If you make your character too powerful, there will be no tension in your story and it won't be believable. In the story of *The Incredibles*, there are many characters with different superpowers, but no single character has all the power. If one contained too much power there wouldn't be any challenge for the hero to overcome.

Superheros often have to overcome nearly impossible odds. Plan out your story by drawing a picture of your superhero's super suit and writing down what his or her powers are. Flip your page over and draw your super villain's suit. Write down the powers your villain has too.

Before you begin drafting your story, think about the goals of each character, what stands in the way of their goals, and what the climax of the story will be. What will stand in your hero's way at the biggest moment in the story and how will the superhero's powers be used to conquer?

Sometimes superheros are aided by friends who make them stronger than they could be on their own. If your superhero has any sidekicks, add them to the drawings you created.

EXERCISE: Gamer

Write a story about your favorite video game character. Create a quest, either within or outside of the game, that the character must complete. Begin with the end in mind. What is it that your character will have to accomplish to complete the quest? Brainstorm a list of challenges that must be overcome along the way. Will he or she have helpers or special tools? You may want to create a map of the game world to serve as a guide as you write the story.

Plan your story using the "Storyboard" printable from the Printable Pack. Within each box, show and tell about the most important events that will unfold in the quest.

EXERCISE: A New Twist On An Old Tale

Re-write a familiar story in a new way. First, choose at least one story element to change - character, setting, or plot. This has been done many times with the familiar story of *The Three Little Pigs*. There is one version called *The Three Little Fish and the Big, Bad Shark* which is set in the ocean. Another is called *The Three Little Wolves and the Big, Bad Pig*, in which the characters are reversed. In some versions the plot is changed; in *The True Story of the Three Little Pigs*, the houses were innocently blown down with a sneeze.

Choose a story that you've read before and rewrite it by changing at least one of these story elements.

Once upon a time there was a fairy named Tink. She had a green dress and green shoes with pom poms on the toes. Her hair was golden yellow.

- Main character
- Setting (time, place, environment, or all three)
- Several plot details
- Ending
- Role reversal of the bad guy/ good guy
- Conflict
- Same character on a new adventure

Once you've chosen your story and thought of your changes, do a quick write. Set the timer for five minutes and draft as much as you can of your story without stopping. Add it to the Journal section of your Writer's Notebook. If you're interested in the story, continue to draft it and take it through the writing process.

☐ **Mini-Lesson**

Brainstorm a list of pairs of animal characters and some possible weaknesses and virtues. Here's one that Aesop, the most famous fable author, used:

The tortoise was slow, steady, humble, and persistent.

The hare was quick, impatient, cocky, and boastful.

Together, the outcome of the race showed that the tortoise's qualities were superior.

☐ **Mini-Lesson**

Sometimes italics are used for emphasis. Write a sentence with an italicized word you're emphasizing.

He ate *ten* cookies.

☐ **Mini-Lesson**

Many characters within fanciful stories are archetypes, or standard characters. They may go by different names, but think of how many wicked witches you find in various tales. Likewise, there are heroes and heroines that all have similar characteristics. They typically have some kind of helper who has special abilities. Create your own version of a fairy godmother character. Describe the helper and his or her personality and special abilities.

☐ Mini-Lesson

Fairy Tales often begin with "Once upon a time" and end with "and they all lived happily ever after." These phrases have been used in hundreds of fairy tales, folk tales, and other fanciful stories for many years and have been translated from many languages across the globe.

☐ Mini-Lesson

The rule of threes is a writing principle that says a trio of events in a story is satisfying. Each of the three pigs built a house and went up against the wolf. Rumpelstiltskin offered three tries to guess his name. Snow White is visited by her evil stepmother three times. Draw a triangle surrounding a "3" on a sheet of paper. One each corner of the triangle, write an element you could include in a story to satisfy the rule of threes.

☐ Mini-Lesson

Revising a story can feel like a big job, but it's really valuable. Each time you rewrite you are not only correcting mistakes, but you are adding more details, learning more about your characters, or creating a more complete picture of the scene. Stories grow with each retelling, so never be afraid to revise.

EXERCISE: Fable

Fables were stories that were traditionally told out loud over and over again before they were written down. They have several important features:

- The characters are typically animals who have the characteristics of people. For example, you might have a lazy turtle who is looking for a home or a bright crow who wants more than anything to go to school with the fish. The characters will be animals, but they will talk and think and interact like people do.
- They are set in the natural environment - in a forest, a cave, a desert, grasslands, or another spot in nature.
- Fables include a moral, or a lesson to be learned through the story. One of the characters often has a weakness that leads to a bad outcome. In contrast, another character has a virtue that leads to a good outcome. Through their characteristics and outcomes, we can see why we want to be like the virtuous character.

Write a fable that includes two main characters - one with a weakness and the other with a corresponding virtue. Begin by planning your fable elements on the "Fable Diagram" printable from the Printable Pack. Before you begin drafting your fable, use the diagram you created to tell your story out loud to an audience. Fables were told out loud by storytellers before they were written down, so put on your storyteller hat and share your fable. Get feedback and ideas from others before you begin writing. Feel free to make any changes you would like as you draft your fable.

EXERCISE: Fairy Tale Features

Use the "Fairy Tale Features" printable from the Printable Pack to make a chart that can help you write a fairy tale. Write each of these features fairy tales have in common

on the chart (in the clouds, the trees, on parts of the castle, etc.).

- Characters that are very good and very bad
- Royalty
- Magical or imaginary characters (witches, giants, talking animals)
- A setting that is a long time ago, often near a castle and some woods
- The number three or seven (or both!)
- Magic
- A conflict between good and evil
- The good character always wins in the end
- The bad character disappears or dies in the end

Once you've learned the features of a fairy tale, try making your own tale using the features. Begin by brainstorming together between ten and twenty characters you might read about in a fairy tale and writing down each character on an index card. Here are a few to get you started: a princess, a king, a bride, a good witch, an evil wizard, a troll, a maiden, a knight, an elf, a mermaid, a magical horse, a fairy, a sorceress, a monster, a dragon, a thief, a beast, a tiny person, and a squire sidekick.

Next, brainstorm between ten and twenty settings a fairy tale could take place in and write each of those on index cards as well. For example: a kingdom, a garden, a forest, a cottage, a river, the ocean, a tiny town, a mountain, a moat, a dungeon, a castle, a faraway land, a green valley, a cave, a bridge, a tower, an ice palace, or a meadow.

Finally, brainstorm together ten to twenty fairy tale elements and write them on index cards. Here are a few: a potion, the number three, the number seven, rich versus poor, someone or something being locked up, a trick, magic, a kiss, eating or drinking, true love, a rescue, someone or something that disappears, an unexplained incident, good versus evil, a transformation, an enchanted object, a talking animal or creature.

Now, draw two to three of the cards from each pile and craft a fairy tale that involves each of the characters, settings, and elements you chose.

EXERCISE: Folk Tales
Folk tales can have either human characters or animal characters with human traits. They often include magic or other unexplained wonders. They either have a moral or explain why something happens as it does. For example, they may explain why animals have a certain look or behavior using fanciful, imaginary explanations. Rudyard

☐ Mini-Lesson
As you revise stories, it can be helpful to visualize the story in your mind. See the sidewalk and the trees and the houses in your story. Ask yourself if your words describe the same picture you see in your mind. What details or specifics can you add to help your reader see the same things you see?

Close your eyes and picture a scene. Open your eyes and write down the details. You can choose any scene from any story you're working on.

☐ Mini-Lesson
Once you've finished drafting and revising a story, put it away for a day, and then read it out loud to yourself. Try to spot mistakes and proofread as part of the editing phase. Then, ask someone else to edit for you too.

☐ Mini-Lesson
Repetition is a fun story technique. You can choose to repeat a phrase, an event, or an encounter with a character. What are some repeated elements in *Goldilocks and the Three Bears*? Look through some of the story drafts you have created and find one that you could add the element of repetition into. Write your idea on a sticky note and stick it to your draft. Sticky notes are a powerful tool for revising.

☐ Mini-Lesson

Use precise language as you write stories. Words like "stuff" and "things" are overused and too general.

Change the general words that are **bold** to more precise words.

*I bought more **stuff** for my baby dolls.*

*My monster's hair was full of **things**.*

*Grandma has lots of **stuff** on the table.*

*Trina spilled **things** on the carpet.*

*The fairy's home was full of **stuff**.*

*Dragons can fly over **things**.*

☐ Mini-Lesson

Remember to add details like a colorful cover with a title, an about the author page, a dedication page, and a book blurb to your stories when you are in the publishing phase of the writing process.

☐ Mini-Lesson

Sentence fluency is important in all writing, including stories. When you want to create suspense in a story you can use a series of short sentences in a row. This creates a feeling of tension for readers.

Growl. Crash. Rumble. Jason glanced up. Beady dinosaur eyes stared back.

Practice writing a suspenseful series of short sentences.

Kipling wrote many folk tales, including his *Just So Stories* that explain why certain animals look or act the way they do. It might be fun to read some of his before you write your own. Use your imagination to write a story that explains one of these. Why...

- Do giraffes have long necks?
- Do roosters crow?
- Do dogs bark?
- Do sharks have a fin?
- Do bees buzz?
- Do bluebirds have blue feathers?
- Do chameleons change colors?
- Do frogs have bulging eyes?
- Does the moon change?
- Do the tides rise and fall?

Talk about your ideas together, then draft your own folk tale. If you create a published version, write your story on your own homemade animal shape book. Draw your animal full-size on your page. Cut around your animal, leaving a small border. Trace the cut outline and make copies of it on additional sheets of paper; the copies will become your interior pages. Write the final draft of your story on your pages and staple them together.

EXERCISE: Time Machine

Draw a time machine. Somewhere on the time machine, show a date and time you would like to travel to, either in the past or in the future.

Surround your time machine with captions that include events you think might happen in that time period. If you go back in time, you can even look up some historical dates and incorporate real famous events. Turn your ideas into your own time travel story. Put this in your Journal.

Robots everywhere

Cities in the clouds and no more pollution

No paper or money

Vehicles that can drive, fly, and go underwater

Time Machine

July 1, 2090

A chip in my wrist with a little screen

Nutrition pills instead of food

Rocket shoes

EXERCISE: Swashbuckler Story

Most of the fanciful stories so far have been about fictitious characters, but you can also use real people as your inspiration for characters. In this swashbuckler story you'll

imagine what it would be like if you were a swashbuckler on an adventure. A swashbuckler is a daring adventurer. At some point in the story you will become deserted on an island during your voyage at sea.

Gather a small map that shows at least one island on it, a bottle with a lid for each kid, and some sort of water container. Thrift stores usually have fancy bottles, or plastic bottles will work too. We also live right by a lake, so it was a convenient water source for us, but a basin, a sink, or tub would work if you don't live near a lake or pond.

Write a one-page adventure story on the back of your map about an imaginary trip that left you stranded on a deserted island. Tell the tale of how you came to land on the island. You are pleading for anyone who finds your message to come and rescue you. Mark the location of the island on the map so your rescuer will be able to locate you. Roll up your story and put it into the bottle. Your only hope of being rescued is to tell your story and write a convincing message. Put it in a bottle and toss it out to sea

EXERCISE: Children's Picture Book
Read some of your favorite children's picture books and then write your own, including illustrations. Building stories can be particularly enjoyable to write. In a building story, you begin with one thing. On each page, something is added.

For example, you might be building a snowman and on each page one more element of the snowman is added until it is complete on the final page. Some famous building stories you might like are *The Mitten* by Jan Brett, *Five Little Monkeys* by Eileen Christelow, *Chicka Chicka Boom Boom* by Bill Martin Jr. and John Archambault, and *Bear Wants More* by Karma Wilson.

Think of a storyline that can build and build a bit more with each page. Plan out your story by drawing stair steps

☐ Mini-Lesson

Active sentences describe actions done by the subject of the sentence.

Archie won the baseball game.

Passive sentences describe an action done to the subject. In other words, the subject is acted upon.

The baseball game was won by Archie.

They both give the same information and are both acceptable in writing, but too many passive sentences can feel cumbersome. When possible, use a more active voice to sound clearer and more direct.

Practice changing these sentences from passive voice into active voice:

The party was enjoyed by the whole family.

The monster's hair was cut by the elf.

My car was stolen by a thief.

Junie was stung by a bee.

☐ Mini-Lesson

When you make a list of three or more items, you separate the items in the list by commas.

The dwarfs needed to pick up milk, eggs, bread, and cheese for dinner.

Can you write some sentences that include lists? Don't forget to include commas.

Mini-Lesson

Revise these wordy sentences to improve word choice and sentence fluency.

1. These people, who really love aquariums and fish and things, would swim every day if they could.

2. People who lived a long time ago had to learn about lots of things in the old ways before books and computers, and they just used their senses.

3. Being very curious, the little monster with lots of purple fur loved to sniff, touch, and look at everything around him every minute of every day.

☐ **Mini-Lesson**

As you begin your Fanciful Stories writing project, make sure you include these things:

- Title
- Author
- Beginning, middle, end
- Theme
- Symbols
- Literary devices (like similes, personification, or onomatopoeias)

Look over the six traits of writing together and talk about how each trait applies to fanciful stories. As you revise, edit, and publish your story, make sure you have included the story skills you have worked on during the unit.

and writing your ideas for your building elements on each step. Make your story into a book and have one building element per page. Make sure to fill the pages with colorful illustrations so it will excite the kids who read it.

EXERCISE: Rebus Story

Write a short story. It can be a familiar story you already know that you tell in your own words or a completely original story. Once it's written, type out the story. Read through it and delete words that you could fill in with pictures instead. Leave a gap in the typed story at each spot you will fill with a picture. Print the pages and then illustrate the blank spots to create your own rebus story.

EXERCISE: Tall Tale

Tall tales are stories about larger-than-life characters who solve problems in fantastical ways. Often the characters are super strong, really tall, or able to do seemingly impossible things. Details in a tall tale are also exaggerated. To write a tall tale, you can think of any regular story.

A squirrel needed to collect acorns before the big storm.

Then you will transform the story to include impressive characters and lots of exaggeration.

A squirrel with super speed collected a million acorns and fed all of the animals in the forest before the biggest storm to ever hit the land came swirling in.

Craft a tall version of your tall tale character using a sheet of card stock, cut in half the long way. Add your larger-than-life character's head and feet to the card stock. Write or type your tall tale on another long sheet of paper and attach it to your character. If you choose to type your story, you can adjust your document so it is formatted in two columns. Only fill one column with your story. You can adjust the font, size, and margins to make it fit on half of a sheet of paper perfectly.

EXERCISE: Futuristic Fun

Many of the cool technologies we have today were first dreamed up by story authors who imagined what the future would be like. Submarines, space travel, cell phones, debit cards, X-ray machines, tablets, electric cars, and lots of other technologies were all written about in stories long before they were actually invented. After all, we can't invent something if we don't come up with the idea first.

Do a quick brainstorm session. Set a timer for five minutes and write down a list of as many cool inventions and technologies as you can think of. What do you wish existed now? When the timer sounds, choose at least one of your ideas to include in a futuristic short story.

EXERCISE: Twist & Turn Shared Story

Have everyone sit around a table with a six-page booklet and a pencil in front of them. Set a timer for five minutes. Each person must begin a story on the first page (younger children may need an older helper or teammate). When the timer dings, pass the books to the left. Everyone reads what was written quietly, then the timer is set for five more minutes and the stories continue with their new authors on a new page. This pattern continues until all six pages have been written. The final author must wrap up the story into a tidy conclusion.

Take turns reading each book and seeing how the stories twist and turn.

EXERCISE: Plan A Story

No matter what kind of fanciful story you write, it can be helpful to make a plan on one single page before you begin to write.

Learn this little rhyme, then use the "Plan-A-Story" page from the Printable Pack to help you plan a story to write.

When I write a story it has more than one part.
The title and the author are places I start.
The setting, characters, and plot are parts of the story too.
I add a great theme and have a story for you.

Step 3: Writing Project

During this unit, you should complete at least one writing project, taking a piece of writing through the entire writing process. By the final week of the unit, if you haven't completed the project already, you should turn your attention to creating one polished piece of writing that uses the things you've practiced along the way.

☐ **Mini-Lesson**

Just as there are many ways to begin stories, there are also many ways to end them. Here a few to consider as you bring your stories to a close:

- Full circle - your story can come full circle and end right where you began.
- Lesson learned - the main character can learn a lesson or grow.
- Surprise twist - this unexpected ending might even leave the reader feeling a little confused or sad.
- Warm fuzzy - this is a just-right ending that is happy and emotional.
- Cliffhanger - an ending like this leaves the reader uncertain, not really knowing how it will all turn out.
- Dialogue - several characters can talk at the end, often thinking out loud about how it all turned out.
- Descriptive scene - this is a vividly described scene that is often symbolic (perhaps the sun is rising, symbolizing the hope of a new day).
- Belly laugh - you can end on a funny note, making the reader chuckle or leaving a funny thought.
- Moral of the story - end by stating the moral or theme directly.

☐ Mini-Lesson

You can create a final version of your story in a variety of formats when you are in the publishing stage of the writing process. It could be a slide show on the computer, a picture book, a document with boxes or blanks for illustrations, or you could create a poster with word and picture boxes. Decide on a format you would like for your story and create it. Your project is your final draft, so take care to do your best work.

☐ Mini-Lesson

Making stories into picture books is fun. Just write a few of the lines on each page and add illustrations. Your final project should:

1. Be tidy - Revise and edit first, then make a neat final draft for your final project.

2. Be colorful - Add color and creativity to your final project.

3. Fill each page - You want to allow enough white space to rest your eyes, but also make sure to fill the page so your words and illustrations don't look awkwardly small.

☐ Mini-Lesson

Exclamation points express emotion and excitement. Don't overuse them. You don't need to use multiple exclamation points!!!!

Choose one topic to write about that you will take all of the way through the writing process. This piece of writing belongs in the Writing section of your Writer's Notebook. You can use something you've already started during this unit, your own idea, or something from the following idea banks. Make sure that you follow each step of the writing process and keep all of your steps to turn in with your finished writing.

- Step #1: Prewrite
- Step #2: Draft
- Step #3: Revise
- Step #4: Edit
- Step #5: Publish

Begin with a prewriting activity, then compose a draft, revise it, edit it with help from someone else, and then publish it. Publishing it could include making a polished final copy, sharing it with someone, creating a book, or creating some form of finished project that is neat and done well. You'll turn in all of your work, from prewrite to publish.

Your project will be evaluated based on the six traits of writing, so make sure you look at your composition through each of those lenses - ideas and content, organization, word choice, sentence fluency, conventions, and voice. Try to incorporate things you learned from the mini-lessons and the exercises you worked on as well. Do your best work.

Fanciful Stories Idea Bank

- Draw an imaginary constellation. Write a story about the figure in the constellation the way ancient people might have.
- Think about an incident that really happened to you and exaggerate as you tell it (like a tall tale).
- Imagine that you fall asleep while reading your favorite book. Write the story that would result from your dream melding with your favorite story.
- Write a first line story, in which someone gives you an unexpected first line and you must create a story around it. You can create your own first lines for each other or choose from one of these:

1. The lake smelled red.
2. Fish were falling from the sky.
3. It was a dark and stormy night.
4. Growl. Snarl. Hiss. The creature was coming closer.
5. Grandma pulled a box down from the shelf and told me it was high time I learned my family legacy.
6. Alison had two things on her mind: bananas and magic.

7. Fairy Hollow was full of billowing, green smoke.
8. The power was out, and the streets were silent.
9. The gleaming gates opened in the balmy courtyard.
10. Her eyes clouded over. She was one of them now.

- Write a big and small story. Choose one big character, like an ogre, giant, or dragon, and one small character, like a fairy, pixie, or elf. Create an adventure story for the pair to tackle together.
- Imagine you hear something wiggling inside of an unexpected box on your porch. Tell a story about what happened when you opened the box.
- You look up into the sky and see a flying saucer careen downward and land near your house. Tell the story of what happens next.
- What if you went to sleep in your bed but awakened across the globe in a faraway land? Tell the tale of your travels home.
- Create a story that takes place in a zoo overnight after all the visitors have gone home.
- Read three fairy tales. Choose the setting from the first, the main character from the second, and the plot from the third. Write your own mix-and-match fairy tale.
- Write a story that happens in space. It can involve astronauts and real people or imaginary space creatures . . . or both.
- Write a myth about a hero with some kind of powers who overcomes a challenge.
- Write a reverse story, in which the protagonist seems like a bad guy (like a troll or monster) and the antagonist seems innocent at first (like a fairy or elf).
- Imagine that your main character opened a crate and suddenly was surrounded by magical creatures of all sorts. Tell the story of what he or she would do.
- Make up your own imaginary animal and create an adventure story for your mythical character. It can be fun to combine animal characteristics to create a new creature - the ears of an elephant, the tail of a horse, the body of a jaguar, and a dolphin fin, for example.
- Tell a story that includes these elements: a magic carpet, a talking beetle, and a mysterious storm that rolled in unexpectedly.
- Write a story set in a historical time period. You might imagine what it would be like to fight in World War I and tell the story of a soldier there. You can use whatever time period you are studying in history and create a fictional story that could have happened in that real setting.
- Make up your own imaginary world with your own imaginary creatures that you invent names for. Reading a Dr. Seuss book (like *Sneetches and Other Stories*

☐ **Mini-Lesson**

Part of the publishing stage includes sharing your story. You can read it to someone, give the book you made as a gift, or even self-publish it. There are companies that will print your book for you as a paperback or hard cover book.

☐ **Mini-Lesson**

Tips for sharing stories out loud:

- Read slowly and clearly.
- Make sure everyone has a chance to see the pictures.
- Give each character a distinct voice when you are reading the dialogue.
- Read it with feeling.
- After you're done, you can ask everyone who their favorite character was or what part they liked best.

☐ **Mini-Lesson**

Tips for listeners:

- Be attentive. The reader should have your eyes and ears.
- Keep your body still while you listen. If that's hard for you, hold something small or twiddle your thumbs quietly.
- Be positive. Tell what you liked.

Reminders About Your Writer's Notebook

Besides just the writing project, there should be many small writing samples that are being compiled in the Writer's Notebook from the exercises you worked on over the course of this unit. The Writer's Notebook is a tool for helping writers to grow. Explore it frequently and refer to idea lists and helps as you write.

At least once a week, it would be beneficial for you, the writer, to glance back through the exercises, lists, and mini-lessons to review and make sure that you are on track even though most of this work isn't graded.

Specifically, as you are working on the writing project, utilize your Writer's Notebook. You have anchor charts, exercises, and entries in your Journal - all of these can help you as you complete your project. Take time to review some of the concepts you've been working on during the unit so they can be incorporated into the final writing project. The things you've learned should SHOW in your writing project.

Remember that most of the work in the Writer's Notebook will never be graded, but it is still important. Use what you learned to make your project, which will be graded, the best that you can make it.

or *There's A Wocket in My Pocket*) can be a good inspiration.

- Write a falling from the sky story, in which something unusual is falling from the sky.
- Invent a tale in which your main character awakens as an invisible person and must solve a problem without anyone being able to see him or her.
- Tell the story of an inanimate object that comes to life. It could be a rock, a chair, a snowman, a scarecrow, a stuffed animal, or any other object that isn't normally living.
- Set up a scene with toys (Legos, Little People, a train set, Matchbox cars, dolls, or other toys). Imagine a story that could happen within your toy scene and write it.
- Use Laura Numeroff's *If You Give A Moose a Muffin* and her other similar circular stories as inspiration and fill in your own ideas in story form. If you give a _____ a _____, she'll probably _____.
- Write a spy adventure story.
- Imagine a superhero with fantastic powers that must save the city or town you live in. Include some of the familiar landmarks you visit within your story.
- Write a story with a surprise twist that reveals that the hero's sidekick is actually the villain.
- Create a storyline that begins and ends with the exact same phrase.
- Look up a famous mythical creature to find out more about. In your story, declare that the mythical creature is real, after all.
- Begin a story with someone blowing out birthday candles and making a wish, then let the story unfold about how the wish comes true.
- Make up a tale of magic that costs something drastic. Perhaps it depletes your life force or takes something valuable from you every time you use it. What problem would you be willing to use it on anyway?
- Write about a group of people who have superhuman powers and are all best friends.
- Tell a familiar tale but create some role reversals within it. Perhaps the male characters will all be female, the old characters will all be young, and the virtuous characters will all be evil (and vice versa).
- Ask your family or friends to each contribute one element you must include in a story. For example, one person could give you a character idea, another could give you a first line, and a third person could give you a setting. Incorporate all of their ideas into one story.
- Write about a town of people that, all of a sudden, find themselves invisible.
- Invent a new world that has different rules than our own. Perhaps all the plants and animals speak, things can fly,

or everything is black and white. Write a story that takes place in this new and different world.

- Imagine you found a magical object in your attic. Describe the item, its magic, and the trouble it gets you out of (or into!).
- Write a story in which the main character can make time stand still.
- Use one of these one-word writing prompts: nightmares, backwards, happiness, wander, adventure, rainstorm, stand, escape, pain, or hope.
- Write a pick-a-path story, in which the reader makes choices as the story goes on. You'll need to write several options for paths and endings as you go, then indicate which page to turn to, depending on the choices made.
- Use the Scholastic online story starter for ideas (search online for "Scholastic story starter"). It features a little machine on the screen that helps you choose elements to incorporate into a story.

Step 4: Evaluating Writing

The purpose of this unit is to write fanciful stories using an interesting setting, developed characters, a plot with a climax, and a theme. As you evaluate the project, look for each of those story elements. You can also look for interesting descriptions, figurative language, dialogue, and story elements like foreshadowing.

As you evaluate the writing project, you will be using the "6 Traits of Writing Rubric" from the Printable Pack. In addition, you will be looking for each step of the entire writing process. For example, your child will turn in a prewriting activity, a draft that shows both revisions and edits, as well as a finished, published piece. The publishing step should involve sharing the project in some way - reading it aloud to family, presenting it at dinner time, video chatting to show it off to grandparents, or sharing a video presentation on the internet of the writer sharing his or her writing. Sharing is a time for positive feedback and celebration.

Creating a positive buzz about the published piece will create a motivating, growth atmosphere in your Writer's Workshop. As you evaluate, remember that the process is just as important as the product, so watch for successes in the process as well. The final score will be out of 50 points - 20 for the process and 30 for the final project. You can write rubric scores as well as comments down on the "Writing Report Card" printable from the Printable Pack.

Breakdown of Possible Points

- 5 points for a complete prewriting activity
- 5 points for a completed draft
- 5 points for revisions
- 5 points for edits
- 30 points for the finished writing project

The 30 points for the finished project is further broken down into each of the six traits of writing as shown on the "6 Traits of Writing Rubric" from the Printable Pack.

Your comments should be specifically focused on the purposes of this unit and the skills you were working on throughout the unit.

What was done well? Is the writer understanding the writing process? What should be improved on? Are there any repeated mistakes to address?

Point out a clear strength.

Comments mean more than scores, so make sure to give clear feedback.

Poetry

Poetry is different from prose; it is writing that concisely expresses emotions and ideas. Although there are formulas for certain poems, poetry is the freest of all the forms of writing. There are no hard and fast rules because poetry is an art. Just as I would never tell an artist which colors to use within a painting, I will never tell you how you must compose your words in your poem. You can ignore comma rules. You don't have to use periods or capitalize your sentences. In fact, you don't even have to use sentences at all if you don't want to.

As you begin writing poetry, start by choosing some of the Exercises that teach you poetry skills. Whenever you are ready, move on to writing formula poems. Formula poems do have "rules," but ultimately, you are the boss of your own words and get to decide which rules to follow. After you've written some formula poems, you can branch out into free verse poems and write in any style you want. Be creative, play with words, and read and write lots of poems as you explore the world of poetry.

Step I: Mini-Lesson

After handwriting or typing practice has concluded, begin each day of Writer's Workshop with a Mini-Lesson. You will find some within the sidebars of this unit. You can also use a worksheet from a grammar workbook or practice editing, copying, or diagramming sentences. During writing time, watch for weak areas or mistakes being made and present a Mini-Lesson the next day to help correct those and improve writing skills in small, continuous ways.

The mini-lesson should take five to ten minutes and always have a positive happy spin, free from criticism. Not every mini-lesson needs to be kept in your Writer's Notebook. Most are merely for practice.

Step 2: Writing

Now it's time to really begin writing. Most of your time during Writer's Workshop should be spent writing. Practicing is the key to improving. You can use your writing time to free write your own ideas in your Journal anytime, or use the exercises below to practice writing skills and find inspiration for things to write about. Select as many exercises as you would like to do over the month, making sure you leave time to complete at least one writing project that will go all of the way through the writing process before the month is over. The exercises will also go in your Journal section of your Writer's Notebook. If you decide to take something from your Journal through the writing process and turn it into your writing project, move it from your Journal to the Writing section of your Writer's Notebook.

A few tips and reminders:

- You can repeat the units and the exercises in subsequent years, so don't ever feel pressured to get to all of them, and feel free to repeat ones you enjoy.
- Often a single exercise can be presented to all of your children, no matter their ages or abilities. They will naturally write at the level they are at and, as they practice, will grow as writers.
- As you progress through the exercises, watch for something that sparks interest and could become the writing project. Feel free to jump to the idea bank at the end of the unit anytime as well. If there's spare time after the project is published, return to more exercises.
- Your family may all be in different places in the writing process. That's perfectly fine. Remember, your Writer's Workshop is a garden and everyone is growing their own patch. You can all lend a hand to help each gardener's patch thrive, but you won't all grow the same crop.

It's time to write! Choose some exercises and jump right in!

Poetry and the Writing Process

EXERCISE: Poetry and the Writing Process
While learning to write poetry you can implement the writing process to help things go more smoothly. We'll go through each step of the writing process together so you can see how it's done.

☐ **Mini-Lesson**

Along with writing poetry, you should read lots of poetry during this unit. Go on a poetry picnic. Gather a nice picnic lunch and some books of poetry from your library. Eat as you read poems together. As you do, here are a few things you can notice and talk about in the poems.

- Why do you think the poet

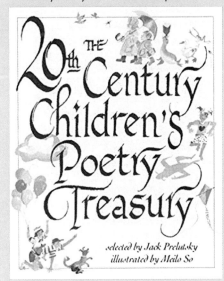

chose that title?
- What is the mood of the poem?
- How is it organized?
- Does it have any patterns? Rhymes? Repetition?
- Can you spot any similes of metaphors?
- What is the theme?
- What feelings or moods does it capture?

Reading and discussing poems will help you as you write them. Start with some children's poetry anthologies so you will have a variety of interesting poems to read together. You'll also find a list of "Wonderful Poems for Families" in the Printable Pack.

Mini-Lesson

When we write reports or stories, we worry about the rules of writing. We make sure we have complete sentences and proper punctuation. We consider commas and transition words. There are a lot of rules that help us to write in clear and organized ways.

When you are writing poetry, you get to throw all of the rules out! Although you will see common threads within poems, there really aren't any rules. You can put words together in any way you fancy. You can write in complete sentences or just use one word on a line. You can write in straight lines or go topsy turvy all over your page. You can keep your handwriting tidy and straight or write in all shapes and sizes and directions. Poetry is a place where you can choose to break the rules.

Mini-Lesson

Often we write on lined notebook paper or on a computer, but as you write poetry, begin with a blank page or a page you have illustrated. Get creative in combining words and pictures on one page. Perhaps some of your artwork will even inspire your poem.

1. Prewriting

Before beginning to write, do a prewriting activity out loud together. Let's choose a season of the year and brainstorm a word bank for the season together. As you create the word bank, talk about the season and all the things you see, hear, smell, touch, and taste during that season. Discuss some colors that make you think of the season you chose.

Autumn

acorns   leaves   apples   pie   football
squirrel   basket   windy day   wheat
scarecrow   pumpkins   piles of leaves   corn
brown   orange   yellow   red
falling leaves   rustling   blustery   apple cider
bare branches   pumpkin patch   hayrides   cinnamon

2. Drafting

Now, you'll draft a poem together. Write a line that describes the season as a color and uses at least one of your words from your word bank to expand on the idea.

> *Autumn is orange*
> *like a pumpkin.*
> *a leaf,*
> *some cider.*

3. Revising

As you add ideas to your poem, focus on vivid descriptions. Discuss literary devices like personification, figurative language, and alliteration. Revise your poem to make it even better than before.

> *Autumn is orange*
> *like a pumpkin sitting sweetly in the patch,*
> *a lacy, little, leaf drifting down from the branch,*
> *and a mug of sweet cider with cinnamon.*

4. Editing

Look through your poem together and check for spelling, capitalization, and punctuation. Remember, in poetry, even these rules are flexible. You may want to make some changes to the rules within your personal poem.

> *AUTUMN is ORANGE*
> *Like a pumpkin sitting sweetly in the patch . . .*
> *A lacy, little leaf drifting down from the branch . . .*
> *A mug of sweet cider with cinnamon.*

5. Publishing

For the final publishing step, decide on a way to present

your poem. You could write it neatly, illustrate the border, add art, or write with decorative letters.

No matter what form it takes, make sure to share it with someone. You could share it out loud or even create a greeting card to send to someone with the illustrated poem on the front.

EXERCISE: Ideas for Poems

One of the most difficult tasks for many poets is getting started. The next few exercises tackle this hardest step of prewriting by giving you a few ways to generate and keep track of your ideas for poems you might like to write. It can be helpful to make a list of ideas, a word bank, or complete another prewriting activity to help you get started. Use the "Ideas for Poems" printable from the Printable Pack.

Cut out the "Ideas for Poems" picture along the solid outline and then fold each flap along the dotted lines. Glue the center to a sheet of card stock, leaving the flaps unglued. On each flap, write an idea of something you could write about in a poem. Include people, events, and topics that interest you. Add your page to the Ideas section of your Writer's Notebook to refer to if you need any ideas.

EXERCISE: Heart Map

You'll need some colorful writing utensils and the "Heart Map" printable from the Printable Pack for this exercise. Inside each section of the heart, draw a picture of something you love that could inspire you to write a poem about it. Add the "Heart Map" to the Ideas section of your Writer's Notebook.

EXERCISE: Making Lists

Making a list is a really effective way to prewrite a poem. Choose one of these things to make a list about:

- Reasons for doing nothing at all
- Your favorite people
- Places you feel at home
- Destinations you dream of traveling to

☐ Mini-Lesson

Prewriting Ideas for Poems:

- Read some poems written by others.
- Draw or paint a picture.
- Think of a favorite memory.
- Make a word bank.
- Write a list.
- Close your eyes and think of a time you felt a strong emotion.
- Write down some silly rhymes.
- Write down descriptive words about a person, place, or event.
- Do a five-minute quick write and then cross out, rearrange, and adjust the words.
- Tell a story out loud using very few words.
- Draw a character sketch, animal, landscape, or another scene and then surround it with a cloud of descriptive words.
- Brainstorm a list of your favorite holidays, seasons, or events.
- Look up information about a topic you are learning about and write down notes about it.

☐ Mini-Lesson

As you write poetry, make sure to use the tools available to you. A poet's toolkit includes:

- A dictionary, in book form and online.
- A thesaurus, in book form and online.
- A rhyming dictionary.
- A reverse dictionary.
- Poetry generators.
- Syllable counters.
- A web browser.

☐ Mini-Lesson

Read a nonfiction book on anything that interests you, anything at all. You might want to take a few notes on the topic as you read. Then create a poem using one of the forms from this unit—either an acrostic or a list poem or a clerihew—anything you choose!

While you are learning history, geography, science, or art topics, instead of writing an essay, paragraph, or narration, compose a poem. A poem combines creativity and knowledge of the topic.

Writing an acrostic about Albert Einstein causes you not only to recall facts, but also to think critically, be creative, and push your mind beyond mere regurgitation of facts.

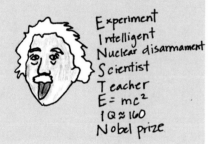

Experiment
Intelligent
Nuclear disarmament
Scientist
Teacher
$E = mc^2$
$IQ \approx 160$
Nobel prize

☐ Mini-Lesson

Find a poem from a poetry book or online and turn it into your very own Mad Lib. Delete several of the words from the poem and insert a blank. Notate the part of speech that the deleted word was - noun, verb, adjective, and so on. Have your family call out new words for the blanks and then read the new version of the poem out loud to everyone.

• Chores you are responsible for
• Things that bring a smile to your face
• Things that make you frown

Add your list to the Ideas section of your Writer's Notebook so you can look at your list for ideas as you write poems during this unit.

Poetry Elements

EXERCISE: Poet-Tree

For this exercise, you'll need the "Poet-Tree" and the "Poet-Tree Examples" printables from the Printable Pack. Before you can understand or write poetry, it's important to learn some of the common elements poets use. Each exercise within the Poetry Elements section of this unit corresponds with one of the apples on the Poet-Tree. As you learn about each element, color in the apple

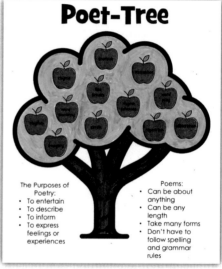

Poet-Tree

The Purposes of Poetry:
• To entertain
• To describe
• To inform
• To express feelings or experiences

Poems:
• Can be about anything
• Can be any length
• Take many forms
• Don't have to follow spelling and grammar rules

on the tree and write an example of the element on the "Poet-Tree Examples" printable.

You may want to do this activity over a number of days. You don't have to complete every accompanying exercise, nor do you need to incorporate every element into every poem you write. Color in the ones you complete so you can remember them. Keep your "Poet-Tree" handy in the Writing Helps section of your Writer's Notebook so you can refer to it often and get ideas for fun elements to add to the poems you are writing.

EXERCISE: Word Economy

In all of our writing we focus on word economy, the idea that you shouldn't use more words than you need. This falls under the sentence fluency and word choice umbrellas of the six traits of writing. If you can say the same thing in ten words, why would you use a hundred? When it comes to poetry, word economy is often taken even further. Since we don't have to follow spelling, grammar, or punctuation rules, we can cut out any words we wish - no need to worry about whether or not your sentences are complete!

Write these words on note cards with one word on each

card: *A deer is a quaint little animal with a lovely fur coat and delicate white spots. Blending into the trees, his brown coat makes him disappear in the woods.*

Now, take the cards and move them around to write your own poem about deer. Remove some of the cards to practice word economy. When you've rearranged the cards and are happy with it, write your poem on a sheet of paper to add to the Journal section of your Writer's Notebook.

> *Deer*
> *Blending*
> *Quaint*
> *Little spots in the woods*
> *Delicate and disappearing*

You can repeat this activity by writing your own description of something in complete sentences, transferring the words to cards, then rearranging them to create your own poem.

EXERCISE: Word Play

Poets play with words. Word smashing, combining parts of two words into a single word, is one example of word play. These words are also called portmanteaus.

- Chill + relax = chillax
- Stay + vacation = staycation
- Gigantic + enormous = ginormous
- Hungry + angry = hangry
- Smoke + fog = smog
- Spoon + fork = spork
- Clean + organized = clorganized

Make a list of more word smashes that you've heard or can think up all on your own. Choose one or more of them to write and illustrate a poem about.

Here is a word smash poem written by Laura Richards called *Eletelephony*.

Once there was an elephant,
Who tried to use the telephant—
No! No! I mean an elephone
Who tried to use the telephone—
(Dear me! I am not certain quite
That even now I've got it right.)
Howe'er it was, he got his trunk
Entangled in the telephunk;
The more he tried to get it free,
The louder buzzed the telephee—
(I fear I'd better drop the song of
elephop and telephong!)

Besides two, three, and four line stanzas, there are also longer stanzas that have names. Quintets are five-line stanzas and sextets have six lines. Septets have seven lines, and octaves have eight lines. Choose one of these stanzas and compose a poem together of the length you chose.

Rhyming words are words that end in the same sound as each other. Practice making rhymes by having one person call out a single syllable word, then everyone else coming up with a word that rhymes with it as fast as they can. Take turns calling out words and coming up with rhymes.

Lamb - ram, ma'am, ham, jam, tram, gram, wham

Read this little poem out loud and spot the rhyming words at the ends of some of the lines. Can you identify the stanza style? **(quatrain)** Can you tell what rhyme scheme was used to compose it?
(ABAB)

What are your hopes, your goals, your dreams?

"I just don't know," I said.

People keep saying to follow my dreams,

So I'm going back to bed,

EXERCISE: Line Breaks

Line breaks are used in poetry frequently. Line breaks are abrupt beginnings of new lines. They create unique spacing that is used frequently by poets.

> *Blowing me away*
> *A windy day*
> *Blustery*
> *Gusting*
> *Squally*
> *Flags fly and so do I*

Try writing your own poem with line breaks. Choose a weather word to inspire you—rain, snow, sunshine, storm, rainbow, or another one of your choice. Think about the line breaks and spacing and how they may cause you to read the poem with pauses and emphasis in different places.

EXERCISE: Stanzas

A stanza is a group of lines in a poem that is arranged together. Various lengths of stanzas have specific names.

A couplet is a two-line stanza. Usually the two lines rhyme.

> *Little bumblebees sat basking in the sun.*
> *Buzzing, drifting, floating, and having summer fun.*

A tercet is a three-line stanza. This example uses two tercets.

> *With a parrot on his shoulder*
> *And his peg leg on a boulder,*
> *Blackbeard looked out across the sea.*

> *He gazed over waves*
> *And searched through the caves,*
> *In search of the chest's golden key.*

A quatrain is a four-line stanza.

> *A poem is a little walk*
> *Weaving along the shore -*
> *Bobbing in and out with words*
> *And helping you explore.*

Often poems include multiple couplets, tercets, and quatrains. Use the "2, 3, 4" printable from the Printable Pack and practice writing some of your own stanzas of various lengths. Add it to the Journal section of your Writer's Notebook.

EXERCISE: Rhyme

Make a list of five rhyming words. Use them to write a poem that includes all five of your rhyming words but does NOT

rhyme at the end of each line. Here's an example:

Words: sand, hand, banned, manned, fanned

> *Believe you can write your path in the sand.*
> *Your life. Your story.*
> *Banned from nothing.*
> *You steer the ship. Manned by you and you alone.*
> *Alone*
> *But not wanting*
> *Fanned by the wind of determination,*
> *Your hand is at the helm.*

EXERCISE: Rhyme Schemes

Not all poems rhyme, but rhyme is certainly a fun element that can be a part of poetry. Rhyming words sound similar because they share the same ending sounds—*lamp, stamp, ramp, camp, damp.* Often the words that rhyme within poems are found at the ends of certain lines within the poem. A poem's rhyme scheme is its master plan of which words should rhyme in the poem, depending on their placement.

Once you become good at coming up with rhyming words, it's easy to incorporate them into the rhyme schemes in poems. Rhyme schemes are labeled using letters. Any time the letter repeats means that line must rhyme with the lines that have matching letters. Practice rhyming by finishing these poems that use various rhyme schemes:

ABCB rhyme schemes have rhymes in the 2nd and 4th lines. See how the B's match, so those are the lines that must rhyme? Fill in the blanks with appropriate rhymes.

(A)	*I dreamed I was riding a zebra*
(B)	*He had pink hair on his head*
(C)	*But when I woke up in the morning*
(B)	_____.

ABAB means the 1st and 3rd lines must rhyme as well as the 2nd and 4th.

(A)	*I like to picnic in the park.*
(B)	*I take a basket of food.*
(A)	*All around me the dogs bark.*
(B)	_____.

AAAA means every line must rhyme.

☐ Mini-Lesson

Play *Rhyme Go Fish*. Create sets of four rhyming words on index cards, one word per card. Place the cards in the "pond" and have each player take five cards. The first player asks the second, "Do you have any words that rhyme with plane? The rhyming words are surrendered. If there are none, player two says "Go Fish." Continue the game using standard *Go Fish* rules. The winner is the one who collects the most sets.

☐ Mini-Lesson

There are three ways to write the titles of poems. You can put the title in quotation marks, underline it, or use italic letters. Just like the titles of books or songs, the titles of poems are also capitalized.

☐ Mini-Lesson

Near rhymes, words that almost rhyme, are commonly used in poems too. They might have the same vowel sound or the same consonant sound, but not both. Sometimes words are adjusted a bit, like dropping the "g" from an -ing word, to make it a near rhyme to a word that ends in the "n" sound.

- *look and stood*
- *rose and lose*
- *adhere and admire*
- *confessin' and lesson*
- *want and can't*

Come up with a few of your own. Think of a common vowel or consonant sound and list words that share that sound but don't quite rhyme.

Mini-Lesson

One thing to consider when you're writing a poem is the mood you want to convey. Make a list of moods poems could have on a notebooking sheet and add it to the Writing Helps section of your Writer's Notebook. Here are a few to get you started:

- Optimistic
- Playful
- Angry
- Gloomy
- Serious

Mini-Lesson

Imagery is often created using similes and metaphors. Use a simile and a metaphor as you do a five-minute quick write that describes your favorite season or holiday of the year.

Mini-Lesson

Imagery is description that helps us see a scene in our mind's eye. There are seven kinds of imagery.

- Visual (what you see)
- Auditory (what you hear)
- Olfactory (what you smell
- Gustatory (what you taste)
- Tactile (what you touch)
- Kinesthetic (motion you feel)
- Organic (internal feelings, like hunger, tiredness, fear)

Write a sentence for each of the seven. Describe something in each of the categories in detail so your reader can experience the scene you are describing through your imagery.

(A)   *I want to go to outer space.*
(A)   *I want to get out of this place!*
(A)   *I'm going to pack my big suitcase.*
(A)   _____.

Use the "Rhyme Scheme" printable from the Printable Pack. Identify the rhyme scheme used in each of the poems by labeling it with letters. The first poem is AABB, because the first two lines rhyme (AA) and the last two lines rhyme (BB). Can you figure out the rhyme schemes of *The Cow* and *At The Seaside*? Then make up some of your own rhymes and identify and label the rhyme schemes you used in your own poems.

EXERCISE: Repetition

Poems often have words, phrases, or lines that repeat. This technique makes the reader feel that the repeated part is important and should be emphasized. Choose one of these topics: friendship, love, kindness, hope, laughter, disappointment, fear, fun, or luck. Write a quatrain, a four-line stanza, about your topic. In each line of the poem, repeat the word you chose as a topic to emphasize its importance.

> *LUCK is finding a penny in the road, or better yet, a dollar.*
> *Rubbing a rabbit's foot brings me LUCK.*
> *I have LUCK even if I don't have skill.*
> *Good LUCK, come my way. Bad LUCK, stay away,*

EXERCISE: Imagery

Something that sets poems apart from other writing is imagery. Imagery is visually descriptive language that helps us picture something in our minds, Here are some examples of imagery:

- He fell down like an old tree in a windstorm, cracking his cheek right open.
- The surface of the lake was like glass.
- Autumn had arrived; the fiery tree was ablaze with color.

Imagery uses sensory experiences to help readers see and experience a scene in their mind's eye. In this exercise you will create some color imagery to practice writing descriptively.

Close your eyes. Imagine that you are in a dark room. A color will come into the room and go right through you. As it goes through your body you will feel varying degrees of hot or cold and you will describe it out loud. You may see, taste, hear, smell, or touch something. You may experience movement. You might feel other things too - emotions like

loneliness, fear, happiness, or elation. Think about each color in these ways so you will be able to create images.

- Feel orange as it comes into the room. Your blood is turning orange. Your heart is pumping orange. Your whole body is orange. How do you feel? What do you taste or hear?
- Feel purple as it comes into the room. It is coming in like a wave and filling the whole room from top to bottom and you are smack dab in the middle. What things do you see? Are you touching anything?
- Feel yellow as it comes into the room. It's falling through the sky, soaking everything, and turning it all yellow too. Bit by bit, you and everything in the room are drowned in yellow. How do you feel inside and out?
- Feel black as it comes into the room. Blackness is everywhere all at once, and everything else disappears. You try to adjust your eyes, but the blackness has enveloped you and become you. What do you imagine is in the room with you? Can you hear anything?

Choose one or more of the colors and write down a description of the color that includes your descriptions as well as objects that are not that color. Write your description using a pen that is the color you are describing.

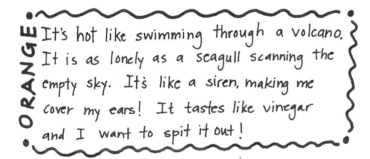

ORANGE: It's hot like swimming through a volcano. It is as lonely as a seagull scanning the empty sky. It's like a siren, making me cover my ears! It tastes like vinegar and I want to spit it out!

EXERCISE: Simile
A simile is a comparison that uses the words "like" or "as." If my friend, Alice, is noisy and energetic, I might say Alice is like a firecracker.

Practice creating similes by creating a "Like What" list. Choose an object or an emotion and then describe it using a variety of ways like color, temperature, shape, sound, taste, smell, appearance, texture, and movement.

Anger can be . . .

- Red like tomato sauce boiling over on Mom's stove.
- Gray like a mean storm cloud crashing through the sky.
- Sharp like icicles jutting off the roof.
- Cold as a friend who is acting like she hates you.

☐ **Mini-Lesson**

You can describe many things using imagery. You don't have to use colors like in the "Imagery" exercise at all. Think of a fun memory your family shares. Write about the memory vividly without directly saying what event you are describing. See if anyone can guess the shared family memory you described.

☐ **Mini-Lesson**

Use the "Simile Self-Portrait" printable from the Printable Pack. Describe each part of yourself by making comparisons using the words "like" or "as" in them, Fill in each box with a simile and then finish your self-portrait by drawing yourself into the body.

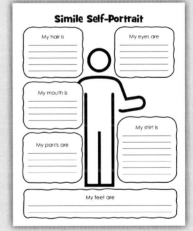

Simile Self-Portrait

My hair is / My eyes are / My mouth is / My shirt is / My pants are / My feet are

☐ **Mini-Lesson**

Similes use "like" or "as" to compare two things.

She is as bright as the sunshine. His laugh is like a hyena's.

Write some of your own examples on your "Poet-Tree Examples" printable.

Metaphors compare two things that might not seem similar at first. Play *Metaphor Match-Up*. Have everyone write a series of nouns - people, places, and things - on note cards. It can be fun to add in some familiar nouns to your family, like adding your Grandma Edna or Majestic Park, where you ride bikes on Saturdays. Put all of the noun cards into a hat. Take turns drawing out two cards at a time. Set a timer for five minutes and have each player (or team) list as many similarities as they can between the two nouns. When the timer goes off, read all of the comparisons out loud.

Print the "Metaphor Machine" printable from the Printable Pack on card stock. Cut along the dotted lines and fold the outer edges to create doors. Write a noun inside each door. Take turns opening two of the doors at a time and create a metaphor about the two nouns.

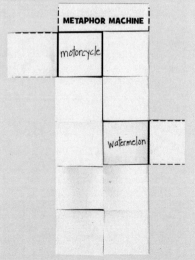

- Stinky like a skunk under the back deck.
- Gross like a rotten egg.
- Yucky like a cobra with venom coursing through my body.
- Jolting as ocean waves thrashing the shore.

Now try your own. Choose any object or emotion and describe it by making comparisons. Write down your similes and add them to the Writing Helps section of your Writer's Notebook.

EXERCISE: Metaphor

Metaphors are direct comparisons, often between things that don't seem similar at first. We'll practice writing a metaphor about someone you know. Think of a friend of yours. Start by writing your friend's name. List three characteristics about him or her on the outside (appearance), and three characteristics about him or her on the inside (personality).

> *Lyla is . . . tiny, delicate, young*
> *. . . strong-minded, courageous, determined*

Next, look only at the adjectives on each row that you wrote, and decide on an animal that has those characteristics. Lyla's outside characteristics - tiny, delicate, and young - sound like a butterfly. Her inside characteristics - strong-minded, courageous, and determined - are like a lion.

Now, I can eliminate the adjectives and make the comparison directly to create metaphors.

EXERCISE: Alliteration

Make a 26-page *Letter Round-Up* booklet using half sheets of construction paper or card stock for the pages. Write one letter of the alphabet on each page. For each letter, set the timer for one minute and write as many words as you can using that letter on its page.

Much like practicing rhyming, practicing alliteration and coming up with the same initial sounds is a great skill for

a poet. Fill out a page for each letter. Turn to one of your letter pages and write an alliterative sentence using some of the words from your page. The more you practice, the better you will get. Keep the book on hand to use as a reference while you write poetry.

Formula Poems

EXERCISE: Recycled Poems
Use a familiar poem or rhyme and then change some of the words to recycle the poem. Here's an example that is based on the popular rhyme, *Mary Had A Little Lamb*.

> *Mary had a little dog*
> *Whose fur was black as night*
> *And everywhere that Mary went*
> *She held her dog leash tight!*

Mary Had A Little Lamb; Roses Are Red, Violets Are Blue; and *Twinkle, Twinkle Little Star* are all fun poems to recycle. You can recycle poems from any poetry book you enjoy or open a book of nursery rhymes and choose one of those to recycle.

EXERCISE: I Can't Write A Poem
Together, brainstorm all the reasons writing poetry is hard. Write down everyone's ideas. At the end, turn your list of reasons into a poem entitled *I Can't Write A Poem*.

> *I Can't Write A Poem*
> *No way.*
> *I hate poetry.*

☐ **Mini-Lesson**

Alliteration is the repetition of a consonant sound at the beginnings of words. It is a technique writers use to add interest to their writing.

Casey Carson crashed his cool crimson car and caused chaos.

Write your own example of alliteration on your "Poet-Tree Examples" printable.

☐ **Mini-Lesson**

Consonance is very similar to alliteration, but the consonant sounds you repeat can be located anywhere within the words, not just at the beginnings.

Sam sat in his uncertain and sad state, rustling branches and whistling his sad song.

Write an example of consonance using the P sound.

☐ **Mini-Lesson**

Assonance is in the same family as consonance and alliteration, except it is the repetition of vowel sounds. Try writing one.

Stay at the lake, see fish take the bait, then watch waves as the sunlight fades.

☐ **Mini-Lesson**

Formula poems have specific formats. When you are a beginner, following a format is helpful. Remember though, you are the poet and there are no rules.

Writer's Workshop

☐ **Mini-Lesson**

Have a growing poem challenge. Begin writing a poem that has one word on the first line, two words on the second line, three words on the third line, and so on.

See who can create the longest poem while maintaining the pattern.

☐ **Mini-Lesson**

As you begin writing list poems, read Shel Silverstein's famous list poem entitled *Sick*. After reading it, write a list poem together as a group. Try one of these:

- All the reasons math should be canceled today
- Why you should buy ice cream
- Places you want to go on vacation
- Things that make you smile

☐ **Mini-Lesson**

Just for fun, do a list poem challenge. As a group you will write a list poem with a twist.

Each person will roll a die and add the extra element they rolled somewhere in the list poem.

1 = a rhyme

2 = alliteration

3 = simile

4 = repetition

5 = metaphor

6 = onomatopoeia

I can't rhyme.
I'm bored already.
I don't know what to say.
Just tell me what to write.
I'm not going to be a poet when I grow up.
It's too bright in here.
My head hurts.
I should have been sick today.
My hand is cramping.
Oh, no! I can't be out of time yet!
All I have is this list!
A list can be a poem?
Awesome! I'm glad you like it!

EXERCISE: Number Poem

Choose a number between one and ten and number the lines on your paper up to that number. On each line, write that many words of a poem. You don't need to worry about complete sentences. Line breaks are one of the interesting things about poems.

1 I
2 want more
3 dessert before dinner
4 cake, cookies, candy, pie
5 I want it all please
6 It tastes better than my BROCCOLI

EXERCISE: Telephone Syllables

One fun trick poets use is playing with syllables. In this kind of poem there is only one guideline: you can only use as many syllables as your phone number says.

Write your phone number vertically down the side of your paper. Now fill in each line using that number of syllables. If my phone number were 555-8073, this might be my poem:

5 *Nature is my friend.*
5 *The outdoors call me.*
5 *I ride, run, jump, swing.*
8 *Come play outside with me today*
0
7 *Trees, clouds, sunshine, flowers, grass.*
3 *Happy day!*

EXERCISE: List Poem

A list poem is simply that – a list! Think of a topic and then list things about it. Choose a person, place, hobby, animal, country, landmark, sport, book, or another topic that interests you. The topic will become the title of your poem. Underneath the title, write your list.

My Mother

She always makes me clean my room.
She expects me to practice the piano every day.
She thinks homework should come before playing.
She serves vegetables at dinner every single night.
She sends me away from the dinner table when I burp.

EXERCISE: Book Spine Poetry

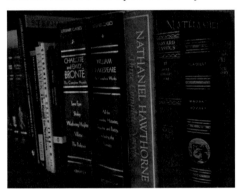

For this exercise, you'll need a variety of books, a highlighter pen, and also the "Book Spine Poetry" printable from the Printable Pack. It's okay to leave all of the books on your bookshelf as you complete this exercise. You'll write down book titles on each space within the printable. Now, highlight one word from each title and see if you can create a poem using only the words you highlighted. You can rearrange the order if you need to.

EXERCISE: Poetry Blackout

Photocopy a page of your favorite book for this exercise. Use a black pen to cross out most of the words, leaving only the words that you want to turn into a poem.

☐ Mini-Lesson

An onomatopoeia is a word that suggests the sound that it describes. They include animal noises and a variety of sound effect words.

oink, bam, buzz, klank, rip

Write a list poem called *Sounds* that includes at least one onomatopoeia on each line and describes a variety of sounds you might hear.

☐ Mini-Lesson

No matter what kind of poem you are writing, it can be helpful to make a plan. This is part of the prewriting stage in the writing process. Practice making a plan using the "Poem Planner" printable from the Printable Pack. Before you begin drafting, write some notes about the topic, type of poem, words you could incorporate, and figurative language you could include. You can also color the artist's palette in colors that relate to your poem if you'd like. Keep your notes on hand as you draft the poem.

☐ Mini-Lesson

Gather several dictionaries. Look up the same word in each dictionary and compare the definitions. Discuss the similarities and differences you find.

☐ Mini-Lesson

Words that imitate the sound they are naming are called onomatopoeias. Because they are so vivid, they are fun to add to poems.

Can you create a two-line couplet that uses one of these onomatopoeias listed below?

buzz, zap, kaboom, crash, roar, poof, gurgle, oink, hum, gasp, pow, meow, chirp, gulp, ha ha, zap, moo, chirp, bang, slap, honk, zoom

☐ Mini-Lesson

To introduce acrostic poems, compose a garbage acrostic together. Write GARBAGE vertically and then brainstorm together some bits of garbage that begin with each of those letters.

Gross leftovers
Anchovies...yuck!
Random socks
Broken dishes
Apple cores
Glue that dried up
Expired food

☐ Mini-Lesson

Read a poem together from a children's poetry book. Together, spot each noun. Next, spot each verb. Are there any prepositions? Now, spot the describing words, beginning with the adjectives and then the adverbs. As you write your own poems, think about the kinds of words you are using in your poems and what part of speech they are.

Use pencil first as you are working out the exact wording. In the end though, most of your page will be blacked out and the remaining words become your poem.

EXERCISE: A Dictionary Poem
Choose one of the words from this list:

- Joy
- Pride
- Friendship
- Hatred
- Knowledge
- Loyalty
- Jealousy
- Nature

Look up your word in the dictionary. Look for nouns and adjectives you can incorporate into your poem that you see in the dictionary definitions. Arrange your words in an interesting way, incorporating the definition, line breaks, and any other poetry ingredients you would like.

> *Prejudice*
> *Unfair*
> *Unreasonable*
> *Judgmental*
> *BIAS*
> *Deciding not to like a person*
> *Before really knowing them*

EXERCISE: Alliteration Alphabet
Choose letters in the alphabet and create alliterations by writing a description of a person whose name begins with that letter. You can use people you know or have learned about or use imaginary characters. Draw a picture of each of your characters. If you did the *Letter Round Up* exploration, use your booklet to help you with this activity.

Bossy Betty bullied big boys and broke the blokes' baseball bats before bolting.

EXERCISE: Man on the Moon
Write a man on the moon poem by completing this sentence in at least ten different ways: If we can send a man to the moon, surely we can _____.

If we can send a man to the moon, surely we can make a car fly.
If we can send a man to the moon, surely we can invent plastic wrap that doesn't stick to itself.
If we can send a man to the moon, surely we can do better than "Dad jokes."

EXERCISE: Single Word Acrostic Poem

For this exercise you will need several blank sheets of paper and coloring utensils. You will be writing a series of three single-word acrostic poems.

To write an acrostic poem, write the letters of your topic vertically on your page. Next, look at each letter you wrote vertically. Think of a word that relates the topic that begins with that letter of the alphabet.

Jokester
Artistic
Smart
Observant
Noisy

For your first acrostic, use someone's name. It can be your own, someone you know, a fictional character, or a historical person. Write the letters of the person's name vertically.

For your second acrostic, choose one of your favorites. It could be your favorite place, hobby, food, activity, or another of your favorites to compose an acrostic about.

For your third acrostic, choose a topic you've been learning about lately. Write down the topic vertically and then add related words that show some of the things you learned about the topic.

EXERCISE: Phrase Acrostics

Phrase acrostics are just like single word acrostics, except you can use more than one word per line. Choose any topic you would like and try writing a phrase acrostic that describes the topic.

Bouncing in his crib
Adorable little smile
Babbling and cooing
Yawning in the morning

EXERCISE: Sentence Acrostics

Sentence acrostics are written in complete sentences instead of single words or phrases. The sentences can run from line to line, but even though they use line breaks freely, they reflect complete thoughts. Generally, because

---

☐ **Mini-Lesson**

Dictionaries are really useful tools for poets, so let's practice our dictionary skills. Put these words in alphabetical order:

at

big

blue

eyes

little

looking

me

the

through

tiny

window

and

bright

gazed

into

night

saw

sky

stars

we

monster

☐ **Mini-Lesson**

Symbolism is when a person, place, thing, or event has meaning beyond the physical item it represents. For example, a lamb represents innocence or a dove represents peace. Make a list of five animals, five items in your home, and five natural items and what each one symbolizes to you.

☐ **Mini-Lesson**

Can you think of something that is loud and fuzzy? Write a shape poem in the shape of the item you thought of.

☐ **Mini-Lesson**

Go on a texture scavenger hunt. Try to find items that are:

- Slimy
- Scratchy
- Soft
- Prickly
- Hard
- Sharp
- Wet
- Hot
- Smooth

☐ **Mini-Lesson**

Poems tend to use a lot of adjectives. Adjectives are words that describe nouns.

Can you make a list of adjectives about smells? Think of some smelly nouns and the words that describe their smells.

Set a timer for two minutes. During the two minutes, draw a simple nose and then make a word cloud of adjectives that describe different smells surrounding it.

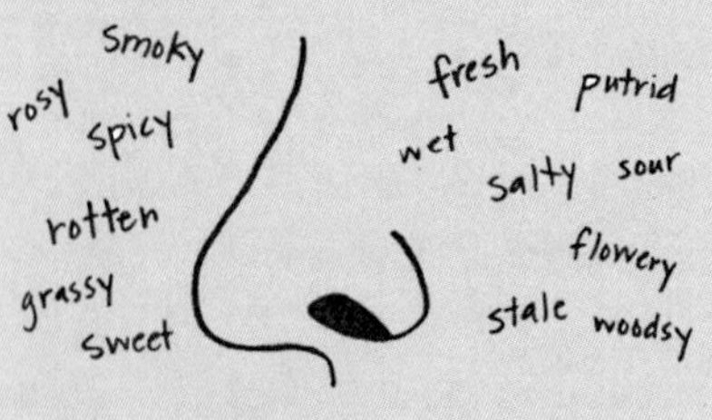
smoky
rosy
spicy
rotten
grassy
sweet
fresh
putrid
wet
salty
sour
flowery
stale
woodsy

You can repeat this with textures, tastes, and sounds.

they are in complete sentences, you will use standard punctuation and capitalization, but ultimately, you are the poet and get to decide that.

Choose any topic you would like and try writing your own sentence acrostic.

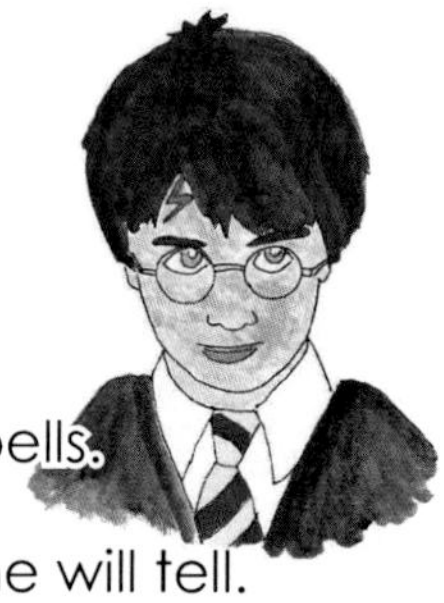

Harry Potter, the wizard boy, hardly knows

A spell when he first

Resides at Hogwarts School,

Reading about quidditch and practicing spells.

Youthful courage takes him far, but only time will tell.

EXERCISE: Diamante

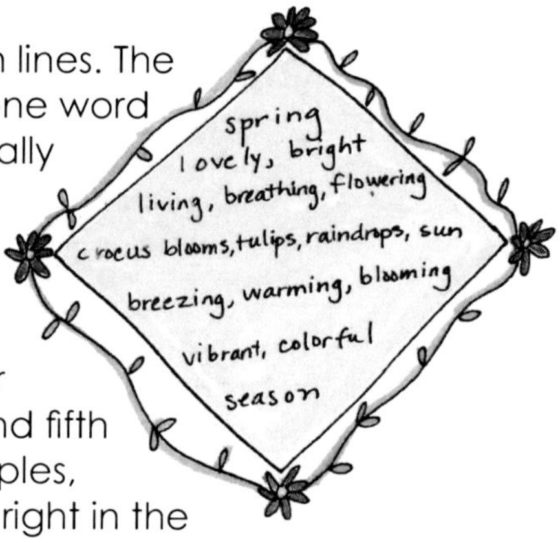
spring
lovely, bright
living, breathing, flowering
crocus blooms, tulips, raindrops, sun
breezing, warming, blooming
vibrant, colorful
season

A diamante poem has seven lines. The first and last lines only have one word in each of them and are usually nouns. The second and sixth lines each have two words that are adjectives. The adjectives you choose will describe the nouns from your first and last lines. The third and fifth lines each have three participles, or -ing words. The fourth line, right in the middle, is the longest line, with four nouns. When you put them all together, the poem creates a diamond shape.

For this exercise, you'll need the "Diamante" printable from the Printable Pack. Choose a topic to write about and fill in the poem in a diamond shape.

EXERCISE: Clerihew

There are a few rules for clerihews. (Remember, in poetry you're allowed to throw rules right out the door if you don't like them!)

- Rule #1 – They are quatrains, four lines long.
- Rule #2 – They use AABB rhyme scheme, which means the first two lines rhyme with each other and the last two lines rhyme with each other.
- Rule #3 – The first line ends with the name of the person you're writing about, which means that the second line ends with a word that rhymes with their name.
- Rule #4 – Keep it light and funny.

I have the nicest dad
But darn it, he is mad.

What made him go boo hoo?
The dog pooped in his shoe.

Here's one more for you:

Doctor Rick
Makes me sick.
His needle poke
Makes me croak.

EXERCISE: Shape Poem

A shape poem is a graphic poem whose visual appearance somehow matches the topic of the poem. In this poetry style, the visual aspect of the poem is as important as the words themselves. The words of the poem may form a shape, fill in a picture, or create an outline of what the poem describes using simply the words alone.

CLOUDS
FLUFFY AND WHITE
BRIGHT SHAPES DRIFTING OVERHEAD
PICTURES IN THE SKY
CLOUDS

I
LOVE
CHRISTMAS
BECAUSE ALL THE
ORNAMENTS ON MY TREE
REMIND ME OF SUMMER TRIPS
AND GOOD TIMES WITH MY FAMILY.
THE LIGHTS
ARE NICE TOO.

EXERCISE: Name Poem

You'll need the "Name Poem" printable from the Printable Pack for this exercise. A name poem is a poem about you, so get ready to describe yourself poetically! Fill in each blank on the printable.

Here's one I once wrote. It's more on the serious side, but reflects what I was experiencing at that time of my life.

Karen
It means patient, happy, peaceful.
It is the number 5.
It is like snow on Christmas morning.
It is camping at the ocean.
It is the memory of my baby daughter
Who taught me perseverance and strength
When she died before I was ready to say goodbye.
My name is Karen;

☐ Mini-Lesson

You can also write poems about other people besides yourself using the same basic formulas you used in the name and biography poems.

Don't limit yourself! It could be about anyone you know and want to write about.

☐ Mini-Lesson

Antonyms are words that are opposites of each other. Light and dark are antonyms. Can you name the antonyms for these words?

- Wrong
- False
- Laugh
- Rich
- Under
- Day
- Awake
- Tall
- Left
- Go
- Win

☐ Mini-Lesson

Practice looking up words in a thesaurus so you can become familiar with how one works. Sometimes when you can't think of just the right word to use, a thesaurus can help you find it. Look up each of these words:

- Search
- Chase
- Furry
- Admire
- Heavy
- Lazy
- Clear
- Tell
- Rich
- Tall

Mini-Lesson

Many poems have syllable schemes. We call the syllable patterns in poems *feet*. One foot usually has a pair or trio of syllables - either stressed or unstressed. Poets arrange their words in different ways to create feet with interesting rhythms.

Read this list of basic feet and then clap and say the example words or phrases that are in the parenthesis. The capital letters show the stressed syllables.

- Iambic - unstressed/ stressed (a-FRAID)
- Trochais - stressed/ unstressed (HEAV-en)
- Anapestic - unstressed/ unstressed/stressed (in a FLASH)
- Dactylic - stressed/ unstressed/unstressed (END-less-ly)

Name these meters:
- a-LONE
- MEM-or-ies
- in a DREAM
- ON-ly

Mini-Lesson

Poets often create rhythm with their words. Rhythm is the beat that is naturally created by the sounds of the words as you read them in a poem. Try to clap the rhythm as you read these lines. Can you hear the beat?

I must go down to the sea again.
To the lonely beach of sand.
The sun in the sky and the waves of blue
Lead me out to sea far from land.

It means living every day full of love.

Now you give it a try. If I wrote ten name poems about myself, they would all be different depending on what I'm thinking about, experiencing, and feeling. People have lots of sides and lots of layers. Add your name poem to the Journal section of your Writer's Notebook.

EXERCISE: Biography Poem

A biography poem is really similar to a name poem. They tend to be a little more generic, focusing on biographical information more than personal life experiences. Here's a basic formula to jump off from:

Line 1 - First name
Line 2 - Four adjectives to describe the person
Line 3 - Brother/Sister or Son/Daughter of...
Line 4 - Lover of...(one to three nouns)
Line 5 - Who feels...(one to three things)
Line 6 - Who needs...(one to three things)
Line 7 - Who gives...(one to three things)
Line 8 - Who fears...(one to three things)
Line 9 - Who would like to...(one to three things)
Line 10 - Resident of...(the location the person lives)
Line 11 - Last name

Here's an example:

Thomas
Curious, creative, persistent, famous
Son of Nancy and Sam
Lover of science, discovery, and learning
Who feels you should never give up
Who needs a laboratory, supplies, and experiments
Who gives light to the world
Who fears giving up, but not failing
Who would like to bring light and sound to the world
Resident of our homes when we flip a switch
Edison

Choose someone you know, either familiar or famous, and write your own biography poem. You might consider writing about someone you are currently learning about in another school subject you are studying. Add your biography poem to the Journal section of your Writer's Notebook.

EXERCISE: Limerick

Limericks are funny poems that are five lines long. They use an AABBA rhyme scheme, which means that the first, second, and last lines end in rhyming words. The third and fourth lines also rhyme with each other.

The most important part of a limerick is its rhythm. Listen to the rhythm of this limerick. You don't read the "da-Dum" lines as part of the poem. They are included below each accompanying line just to help you hear the repetitive rhythm of a limerick. The "da" syllables are spoken more softly while the "DUM" syllables are emphasized. It may be helpful to say or clap along to the "da-Dum" beats a few times so you get the feel for a limerick's rhythm before you write your own.

> *A clumsy young lady named Kim*
> *(da DUM da da DUM da da DUM)*
>
> *Decided to take a long swim*
> *(da DUM da da DUM da da DUM)*
>
> *She dove off the dock*
> *(da DUM da da DUM)*
>
> *Then she sunk like a rock*
> *(da da DUM da da DUM)*
>
> *The rest of her swim was quite grim.*
> *(da DUM da da DUM da da DUM)*

Go online and read several more examples of limericks so you can get a feel for the rhythm that is common to all of them. Then, write your own limerick. Brainstorm some ideas. Think of a name of a person and something silly that could happen to him or her. The first line usually tells the person's name and then the poem goes on to describe the silly event.

As you compose, there are some important things to consider.

- Keep an AABBA rhyme scheme.
- Make sure lines 1, 2, and 8 have eight or nine syllables.
- Make sure lines 3 and 4 have five or six syllables.

This will create the right rhyme and rhythm in your limerick. Add your finished limerick to the Journal section of your Writer's Notebook.

EXERCISE: Haiku

Haikus are traditional Japanese poems that focus on syllables. There are a total of seventeen syllables in each haiku, separated into three different lines. The first line has exactly five syllables. The second line has exactly seven syllables. The third line has five syllables.

Haikus are usually focused on nature. Go outside into a

☐ Mini-Lesson

When word economy is important in your writing, you need to focus on using precise language. Look at these sentences and choose strong, exact words to shorten each sentence.

The little girl is so very sad.

Ron's shirt was covered in dirt and disgusting.

Bianca said she loved the green fir trees in the forest.

Lucky for him, I saved the day when I drove up in the nick of time.

The ugly little duckling quickly swam from one side of the lake to the other.

The noisy train rumbled as it rolled down the tracks.

That was the worst joke I've ever heard.

Do you want to give me some of your chocolate cookies?

☐ Mini-Lesson

Here's a little poem that uses "Pinch Me" as a name to create a funny punchline.

Adam and Eve and Pinch Me
Went down to the river to
   bathe.
Adam and Eve were
   drowned.
Who do you think was
   saved?

When we write proper nouns, like names, we capitalize them. Can you write a poem that turns something that is not normally a name into a proper noun by capitalizing it?

☐ Mini-Lesson

Free verse is a modern kind of poetry that is very conversational. It often just sounds like someone is talking to you or just thinking out loud. Free verse poetry doesn't follow the rules of any formulas. It doesn't worry about rhyme schemes or meters or patterns. It doesn't require any specific word play or counting of syllables or worry over stressed and unstressed words. But although it doesn't require it, these are all still tools a poet can use to create a singsong rhythm, an expectation, a mood, or meaning. Alliteration, onomatopoeia, rhyme, repetition, and other poetry devices can all be used. Free verse poetry is free. The poet is free to write any poem he or she wishes.

☐ Mini-Lesson

Read the poem *My Shadow* by Robert Louis Stevenson. The poem is about shadows, so have someone trace your silhouette on dark paper using a lamp. Attach a copy of the poem to your shadow art.

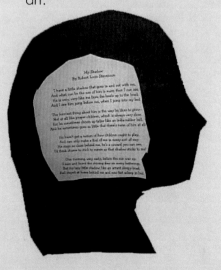

natural setting to feel more inspired as you write your haiku. You can also take pictures or keep a nature journal to record what you see.

Write down three lines of things you observed.

> *Chickens are pecking around the grass in the yard.*
> *They claw and crawl over each other to get to the food.*
> *Their feathers are flying around everywhere.*

Now pare down your description so you have three lines, each one with the right amount of syllables - five, seven, then five.

Chickens pecking grass

Clawing and crawling for food

Feathers are flying

Write your own nature-based haiku and add it to the Journal section of your Writer's Notebook.

EXERCISE: Roll-A-Poem

You'll need a single die and the "Roll-A-Poem" printable from the Printable Pack for this exercise that helps you review some of the basic elements that are used by poets. You will roll a die three times, marking which elements you roll. Write your own poem that incorporates each of the three elements you rolled.

Free Verse Poems

EXERCISE: Shrink The Sentences

One of the beautiful gifts of poets is their ability to distill words down to their very most poignant meanings. It's easy to be wordy, but to pack meaning into just a very few words is much harder.

Use the sentences from the passage on the "Shrink the Sentences" printable from the Printable Pack as a guide, but shrink them, keeping only the most powerful words. Cross out, rearrange, or change the words of the passage to turn it into a poem. It doesn't need to rhyme or have any special rhythm or pattern. You don't need to worry about complete sentences or grammar. Condense the passage from 200 words to just 50 or less.

Poetry

EXERCISE: Memoir Poem

The word memoir means memory. Choose one of your memories to make into a poem. It might be a vacation, a special holiday memory, a big recital, or sporting event you were a part of. Maybe it's the first memory of meeting your new little brother or sister. Try to capture the moments of your memory so others can experience what you did. Remember, it doesn't need to rhyme or be in complete sentences. You can begin a new line whenever you feel it's time. There aren't any rules to free verse poetry.

Draw a picture of yourself in the bottom corner of your page, then create a large thought bubble to write the words of your memoir poem in.

EXERCISE: Persona Poem

As we write stories, we often consider the voice we are using. In other words, there is someone in the story who is being the narrator. The person speaking in a poem is called the poem's "persona" and the words and tone you choose will change depending on who is speaking in the poem.

Here is a little poem called *Mom's Gone*. It is clearly from the point of view of a child who misses Mom very much.

> *There's a waking up in the morning*
> *Where Mom ought to be.*
> *There's a combing my hair and getting dressed*
> *Where Mom ought to be.*
> *There's a breakfast, lunch, and dinner*
> *Where Mom ought to be*
> *There's a going to dance class*
> *Where Mom ought to be.*
> *There's a story time*
> *Where Mom ought to be,*
> *There's a tucking into bed*
> *Where Mom ought to be.*

How would the poem be different if it were about the same situation, but from a different point of view? The poem doesn't specify whether Mom passed away, is missing, if she is too sick to be there, if she's on vacation for a bit, or whether she just left for good because she wanted to, but clearly she is gone.

Writer's Workshop

☐ Mini-Lesson

Read this poem, Dream Deferred by Langston Hughes.

Listen for the conversational tone he used.

Can you add one line to it that would fit right into his poem? Think of another question he could have asked to create another line.

What happens to a dream deferred?

Does it dry up

Like a raisin in the sun?

Or fester like a sore -

And then run?

Does it stink like rotten meat?

Or crust and sugar over -

Like a syrupy sweet?

Maybe it just sags

Like a heavy load.

Or does it explode?

☐ Mini-Lesson

Organization is one of the six traits of writing. The organization of a poem is very different from an essay or a story. Poetry organization is based on lines, line breaks, and stanzas. It has more to do with the effect of your choices than on correctness.

Open the page of a book of poetry and a page of a novel side by side. Discuss what the two pages have in common and some differences you see.

Choose one of those scenarios and a character within it. Perhaps Mom is so sick that she's in the hospital. Tell the story from the point of view of the doctor who is treating her. Maybe Mom died. Tell the story from the point of view of Dad, who also misses her. Or maybe Mom is on vacation because after years and years of housework and kids, she needed a week to find herself again. You could tell that one from the point of view of Mom herself.

Whichever persona you choose, write a poem from that point of view and think about how that changes the words and tone. Will you use the same repeating line? Will the lines be short like these, or longer and more lyrical? Will it be full of hurt or full of hope?

EXERCISE: Poetry For Two Voices
A poem for two voices is like a conversation between two people. It is usually written in columns - one for each person reading the poem. Sometimes a portion of the poem is right in the center, which indicates that both readers speak that part out loud together. Have two people read this example.

In the sky

                On the ground

I fly high

                I stay planted.

Barrel rolls

                Fixing Lunch

Climbs

                Laundry

Stalls

                Story time

My airplane is my happy place

                My home is my happy place

HERE I AM HOME

Use the "Poetry For Two Voices" printable from the Printable Pack to write a poem for two voices. Begin by thinking of two points of view to base your poem around. It might be a fish and a fisherman, a tree and a lumberjack, or Rudolph the Red-Nosed Reindeer and Santa Claus. In the Voice #1 column, write the lines from your first point of view. In the Voice #2 column, write the lines from your second point of view. The center column is for lines that will be spoken together.

EXERCISE: Upside Down Poem

Poetry

Free verse poetry allows you to be completely creative with how you arrange your words. You can group your lines and stanzas any way you want to. You can also make your words climb up the page or fall down the page.

Or you can write an upside down poem like this one:

Everything looks different
When I'm standing on my head.
Shoes and knees
As far as I can see.
The doors are flying way up high;
The chimneys touch the ground.
The sun shines below my feet,
And the sky is grass green.

Try your own upside down poem. Think of a situation that would cause you to be upside down and write a little poem about it. Make sure to draw a picture right side up, but then turn your paper upside down as you write so your words are upside down on the page.

EXERCISE: Sights, Smells, and Sounds

Imagine you were going to pack up some sights, smells, or sounds in a bag to take them along with you.

I'm going on a trip today,
But I can't bear to leave them.
Into my magic bag they'll go
My favorite smells, I'll take some.
The grass, fresh clipped
The rosebuds, just opening
My dog, wagging hello
The muffins from the oven
Popcorn, dripping with butter
Pine trees, deep in woods
Oranges, just peeled

What sights, smells, or sounds would you take along? Choose one of the senses - sight, smell, or sound. Write a free verse poem about what you would take in your magic bag.

EXERCISE: One Word Stands Out

In free verse poetry, one fun technique poets use is putting just one word on a line. If there is only one word on a line, that word can't help but be noticed.

Rain rushing down,
Engulfing me,
Soaking me,
Worries wash away.

☐ Mini-Lesson

Voice is one of the six traits of writing. Often writers want their own authentic voice to come through their writing. Other times they want to sound like someone else entirely. Write a short free verse poem from the point of view of this owl. What can you include in your poem so it sounds like it's written from the owl's point of view instead of your own?

☐ Mini-Lesson

When you are in the editing stage of writing a poem, go through these steps:

- Read it out loud. Listen for any rhythms, rhymes, alliteration, or other language you hear and make adjustments as needed.
- Look at it on the page. Part of poetry is visual, so take a look at the overall view of the poem and make adjustments. Consider line breaks, spacing, and illustrations.
- Have someone else read it and make suggestions.
- Add illustrations, a title, and your name as the poet.

Mini-Lesson

Refrains are often used in poems and songs. A refrain is a line, verse, or group of lines that is repeated over and over again throughout the poem.

Write down this passage from Shakespeare's *Twelfth Night* and then highlight the refrain.

When that I was and a little
*   tiny boy,*
With hey, ho, the wind and
*   the rain,*
A foolish thing was but a toy,
For the rain it raineth every
*   day.*
But when I came to man's
*   estate,*
With hey, ho, the wind and
*   the rain,*
'Gainst knaves and thieves
*   men shut their gate,*
For the rain it raineth every
*   day.*

Mini-Lesson

Poets often use sensory language in their poems. Take turns describing these scenes out loud with sensory language - what you see, taste, smell, hear, and touch.

- Sitting on a bridge overlooking a river.
- Speeding in a car.
- Eating cotton candy at the fair.
- Holding a sleeping baby.
- Riding your bike down a hill.
- Dribbling a basketball.
- Waking up in the morning.
- Visiting the zoo.
- Walking on a beach near the ocean.
- Jumping into a cold lake.

Lightning flashes,
Nature's fireworks.
Thunder rumbles,
Grounding my troubles.
Peace
In a storm.

The word "peace" stands all alone on its line. Think about how different the whole poem would be if that one word said "Fear" instead of "Peace." The one word gave the poem direction. It shaped what it was about. Write a free verse poem of your own that includes at least one line that only has a single word on it.

EXERCISE: Doodle Poem
A doodle poem lets words and pictures work together. It works best if it's some kind of story and scene that involves action. Let your words participate in the action as you write and doodle your poem. Take a look at this doodle poem, and then write one of your own.

EXERCISE: Build-A-Poem
Using at least twenty-five index cards, write one word on each card. Make sure to include nouns, verbs, adjectives, and adverbs. Also include some poetry cliché words like love, night, and beauty. You can add unusual words too, like sled, quirk, serendipity, tadpole, marshmallow, squirming, brunch, and squishy. Once you have your word deck, add ten extra cards with phrases written on them - looking for, always wanted, it reminded me of, you were there when, and other similar phrases.

Put all of your cards into a hat and draw out several. See what kinds of combinations you can make into a poem. Add extra words and phrases as needed.

EXERCISE: My Spirit Animal Poem
In many cultures and spiritual traditions, a spirit animal refers to a spirit who helps guide a person through life. The spirit animal shares many characteristics in common with the person. To write this poem, you will need to decide on an animal that you share characteristics with.

Write a free verse poem about your spirit animal. As you do,

think about all the things that make you YOU! What made you connect with the animal you chose? What do you share in common? Make some notes about your animal and yourself. Use the list below to spark some ideas.

- Your appearance
- Your attitude
- An experience
- Your habits
- Your creative side
- Your taste
- Your hobbies
- Your goals and dreams

There is no single path to follow.
So always choose the outrageous road.
Be colorful.
Be bold.
Be playful.
When your stunning self shines, others follow.
Expectations rarely achieve dreams.
Spread your plumes and bloom.

EXERCISE: Ode

An ode is a poem that celebrates something that might normally be considered ordinary. To write one:

- Choose something ordinary. It might be a yo-yo, or an apple, or a sidewalk - anything you want.
- Write the first line by filling in the blank with the item you chose: Oh, _____.
- Add any lines you would like in which you are speaking directly to the object. Make sure to include wonderful descriptions of the object and how special it is.
- Choose a few of the lines to repeat several times throughout the poem.

Ode To Paper Towels
Oh, paper towels,
I see you with all your soft surfaces cleaning up my spills
and messes day after day.
Oh, paper towels,
Thank you for wiping, for washing, and for absorbing.
Oh, paper towels,
My table is sparkling clean because you are there.

EXERCISE: I Looked Out The Window

Sit at a window with a piece of blank paper and drawing materials. Draw the windowpane and a light sketch of the things you see through the window. Just as you can draw a picture with art supplies, you can also draw a picture with words. Write phrases on top of your window drawing that describe the things you see in concise ways. Imagine that you are describing it to someone far away who has never seen this sight and use your words to paint them a picture.

☐ **Mini-Lesson**

A ballad is a kind of narrative poem that is like a song.

Use a familiar melody you know, like *Twinkle, Twinkle Little Star*, and write your own miniature ballad about your favorite holiday memory.

☐ **Mini-Lesson**

Adverbs are words that describe verbs. Think of at least three adverbs that you could use to describe each of these verbs:

- Run
- Dance
- Breathe
- Snoop
- Cook
- Trip

☐ **Mini-Lesson**

A sonnet is a 14-line poem that has a rhyme scheme.. The word sonnet means "little song."

There isn't a particular formula for a sonnet. It needs to rhyme, but it doesn't matter if you choose two seven line stanzas that each have an ABBAABB rhyme scheme, one stanza that has an ABABCDCDEFEFGG rhyme scheme, or another variation of your choice.

Go read one or two of Shakespeare's sonnets and try to figure out the rhyme scheme he used. You can easily find Shakespearean sonnets online.

☐ Mini-Lesson

Write a group free verse poem together as a family.

Begin by having everyone call out ideas for at least fifteen themes you could write a poem about. Jot down each idea on a slip of paper and then place them all in a hat. Draw one out. Set a timer for five minutes and have everyone call out words and phrases about the theme you chose. Have someone act as scribe.

When the timer runs out, look over your brainstormed ideas and talk about ways you can create imagery in your poem. Make some comparisons or decide on some vivid language that will help others see your topic the way you do.

Brainstorm some word play, rhymes or near rhymes, alliteration, or other figurative language you can include in your poem.

Now it's time to write your poem. Come up with ideas out loud together and have someone act as the scribe.

☐ Mini-Lesson

Get a blank sheet of paper and draw some quick, light sketches of a tornado, a lightning bolt, fireworks, and a wave. Erase bits of the pictures at a time, replacing those sections with words that describe each of the items. On each sketch, choose one of concepts from the apples on your *Poet-Tree* to incorporate into the shape poem. For example, one may rhyme and the next may repeat.

EXERCISE: Feelings

Make a list together of as many feelings as you can think of - sad, worried, frightened, elated. Now answer each of these questions in writing. As you ask the questions, insert one of the emotions you listed in each blank.

- When do you feel _____?
- How does it feel to be _____?
- Why do you feel _____?

Turn your answers and ideas into a poem. Feel free to adjust it and revise and edit to make it just right to match the emotion you chose.

> *Miserable*
> *I feel miserable when*
> *I am asked to take out the garbage*
> *It stinks.*
> *I have to take care of all of the animals by myself*
> *It's my brother's job.*
> *We run out of gas on the way to the park.*
> *It's a long walk.*

EXERCISE: If All The . . . Poem

Think of a way to fill in these blanks:

If all the _____ were _____.

> If all the seas were one sea,
> What a great sea that would be!
> If all the trees were one tree,
> What a great tree that would be!
> If all the axes were one axe,
> What a great axe that would be!
> And if all the men were one man,
> What a great man that would be!
> And if the great man took the great axe,
> And cut down the great tree,
> And let it fall into the great sea,
> What a splish-splash that would be!

It could be if all the cars were flying cars, if all the babies were a hundred years old, if all the bubblegum were replaced by super glue, or if all the amusement parks were free. Use your imagination and be creative with your phrase. Your phrase will become the first line of your poem. Continue imagining what it would be like if your statement were true and write a free verse poem about it. Illustrate your poem.

EXERCISE: Narrative Poetry

Narrative poetry tells a story in poem form. It includes story elements like character, plot, and setting and also poetry elements like figurative language and word play. It is also in the form of a poem, usually written in a number of stanzas.

Think of a famous story like *Pinocchio, Cinderella,* or *The Three Little Pigs* to tell as a poem. Begin by writing the story just as you would tell it. As you revise, try to eliminate extra words. Put it into stanzas, add line breaks, and focus on using sensory details, imagery, and figurative language.

Step 3: Writing Project

During this unit, you should complete at least one writing project, taking a piece of writing through the entire writing process. By the final week of the unit, if you haven't completed the project already, you should turn your attention to creating one or more poems that use the things you've practiced along the way. You could perfect one poem and create an artistic published version or you could write a collection of multiple poems for your project that you make into a poetry booklet.

Choose at least one poem to write that you will take all of the way through the writing process. This poem belongs in the Writing section of your Writer's Notebook. You can use something you've already started during this unit, your own idea, or something from the following idea banks. Make sure you follow each step of the writing process and keep all of your steps to turn in with your finished writing.

- Step #1: Prewrite
- Step #2: Draft
- Step #3: Revise
- Step #4: Edit
- Step #5: Publish

Begin with a prewriting activity, then compose a draft, revise it, edit it with help from someone else, and then publish it. Publishing it could include making a neat final copy, sharing it with someone, creating a book of several poems, or creating some form of finished project that is neat and done well. You'll turn in all of your work, from prewrite to publish.

Your project will be evaluated based on the six traits of writing, so make sure you look at your poem through each of those lenses - ideas and content, organization, word choice, sentence fluency, conventions, and voice. Try to incorporate things you learned from the mini-lessons and the exercises you worked on as well. Do your best work.

☐ **Mini-Lesson**

As you revise and edit your poems, use this checklist to make sure you've included these important elements.

- A meaningful title
- Bold images you've created with words
- Sensory words
- Figurative language or other poetic elements and word play
- Intentional organization
- A clear message or theme
- Unique ideas
- Your voice as a poet

☐ **Mini-Lesson**

Poetry slams are live events at which poets read their poems out loud in front of judges and a live audience. They are competitions that rely on the poems and the performance of the poet to earn points. Usually no props, costumes, or music are allowed. Go watch a few poetry slams on YouTube to experience it.

Parents, please preview first.

☐ **Mini-Lesson**

Your final project should be creative, colorful, and complete. Read through the poems you've written for your final project and make sure that they include each of these three requirements. Take some time to improve each one in little ways before you are finished with it and move on to your next poem.

- Creative
- Colorful
- Complete

Reminders About Your Writer's Notebook

Besides just the writing project, there should be many small writing samples that are being compiled in the Writer's Notebook from the exercises you worked on over the course of this unit. The Writer's Notebook is a tool for helping writers to grow. Explore it frequently and refer to idea lists and helps as you write.

At least once a week, it would be beneficial for you, the writer, to glance back through the exercises, lists, and mini-lessons to review and make sure that you are on track even though most of this work isn't graded.

Specifically, as you are working on the writing project, utilize your Writer's Notebook. You have anchor charts, exercises, and entries in your Journal - all of these can help you as you complete your project. Take time to review some of the concepts you've been working on during the unit so they can be incorporated into the final writing project. The things you've learned should SHOW in your writing project.

Remember that most of the work in the Writer's Notebook will never be graded, but it is still important. Use what you learned to make your project, which will be graded, the best that you can make it.

Poetry Idea Bank

- Write the word CANDY down your page vertically. Think of a kind of candy that begins with each of those letters as you create a candy acrostic poem.
- Divide a sheet of paper into four boxes. Write and illustrate a cinquain in each box that represents one of the four seasons.
- Choose one of Earth's biomes—ocean, desert, grassland, forest, jungle, prairie, etc.—and write a diamante poem about what it is like.
- Write a haiku that only uses words that begin with a single letter of the alphabet of your choice.
- Create a collection of couplets about each member of your family. You can use your immediate family only, or you can add couplets for your extended family—grandparents, aunts, uncles, and cousins.
- Write an ode to someone you consider a hero to you.
- Craft a paper chain using construction paper strips. On each link, write a simple couplet about a topic. On the neighboring link, write a couplet about something related to the first link. Make sure each link you add links the meanings of each couplet.
- Write a quintet, a five-line verse that tells a story, about five things you might see on a walk.
- Look at any nature photograph and write a free verse poem about the scene.
- Compose a three-line tercet about a three-related word. You may choose tricycle, triceratops, triangle, triple, or tripod.
- Write one quatrain about waking up in the morning and a second about going to sleep at night. Make sure to use four lines and choose a rhyme scheme.
- Choose a mythical figure, like a dragon or fairy, to write a limerick about.
- Go outside and pick up an item from nature—a pine cone, leaf, flower, rock, or something similar. Write a list poem about the item.
- Choose your favorite animal and draw or paint a picture of it. Compose an acrostic poem about the animal you chose and incorporate it into your artwork.
- Write a list poem about an object from your home, but don't give it a title. Have everyone in your family read the poem and try to guess the item you are describing with your list.
- Write a list poem about reasons you should be paid to be a kid.
- Write a poem inspired by your favorite song.
- Get out some spices from the kitchen. Smell one without looking at it. Write a free verse poem about the smell.
- Imagine that you had a packet of magical seeds that

could grow anything in the world that you wanted. Write a rhyming poem about what you would grow.

- Write a poem for a baby that sounds like a lullaby.
- Write a poem about loneliness that includes a metaphor of something you think of as lonely.
- Make a list poem that describes a place you've been and lists the things you saw there.
- Choose your favorite kind of weather—rain, snow, sunshine, wind, or another one you like. Write a free verse poem about it.
- Create an acrostic poem about your day today.
- Brainstorm words that begin with the letter P and write a poem about a parade that includes P alliterations.
- Craft a puppet and write a persona poem that speaks in the voice of the puppet you created.
- Create an upside-down poem about a bat, opossum, sloth, or another animal that hangs upside-down.
- Choose a historical person or event and write an ode to the person.
- Write a number poem inspired by your favorite number.
- Think of a happy memory from your past and write a poem about it.

Step 4: Evaluating Writing

The purpose of this unit is to learn to creatively write a wide variety of poetry forms, including both formula poems and free verse. As you evaluate the project, look for word economy, descriptive and figurative language, and other poetic devices.

As you evaluate the Writing Project, you will be using the "6 Traits of Writing Rubric" from the Printable Pack. In addition, you will be looking for each step of the entire writing process. For example, your child will turn in a prewriting activity, a draft that shows both revisions and edits, as well as a finished, published piece. The publishing step should involve sharing the Project in some way - reading it aloud to family, presenting it at dinner time, video chatting to show it off to grandparents, or sharing a video presentation on the internet of the writer sharing his or her writing. Sharing is a time for positive feedback and celebration.

Creating a positive buzz about the published piece will create a motivating, growth atmosphere in your Writer's Workshop. As you evaluate, remember that the process is just as important as the product, so watch for successes in the process as well. The final score will be out of 50 points - 20 for the process and 30 for the final project. You can write rubric scores as well as comments down on the "Writing Report Card" printable from the Printable Pack.

Breakdown of Possible Points

- 5 points for a complete prewriting activity
- 5 points for a completed draft
- 5 points for revisions
- 5 points for edits
- 30 points for the finished writing project

The 30 points for the finished project is further broken down into each of the six traits of writing as shown on the "6 Traits of Writing Rubric" from the Printable Pack.

6 Traits of Writing Rubric — Poetry

Your comments should be specifically focused on the purposes of this unit and the skills you were working on throughout the unit.

What was done well? Is the writer understanding the writing process? What should be improved on? Are there any repeated mistakes to address?

Point out a clear strength.

Comments mean more than scores, so make sure to give clear feedback.

By the end of this unit your kids should be familiar with these concepts and ideas:

Responsibility to the truth

Subjects

Real settings

Facts versus opinions

Chronological order

Dialogue

Showing Instead of telling

Autobiographies

Personal narratives

Family history

Biographies

Newspaper articles & newscasts

More Mini-Lesson Ideas

Along with the sidebars, try these mini-lesson ideas:

- Writer's Workshop links found in Layers of Learning catalog
- Lessons from any grammar workbook
- Every-Day Edits from Education World website
- Sentence diagramming
- Copying great sentences from master writers
- Mad Libs
- Correcting a repeated error from your writing
- Practicing expanding sentences by adding details
- Combining sentences by making two or three into a single sentence

The mini-lesson sidebars in this unit have check boxes so you can keep track of which ones you have completed.

True Stories

True stories include any stories that portray reality. You may be writing about your own life experiences, biographical accounts of others, or actual events. No matter what real life experiences you are writing about, when you write true stories you have a responsibility. It is your job, above all, to be a truth-teller. It isn't ethical or honest to make things up when you're claiming to be writing the truth. Because of this responsibility, you need to make sure to do your research, report the facts, and be as accurate as you can.

As you write true stories, you can learn to masterfully use many of the skills you use when writing fanciful stories; in addition, you have the added burden of telling the real facts. For example, you can still use vivid descriptions to paint a picture of the setting for your reader, but you can't make up events that didn't actually happen. You have to balance truth with entertainment. As you create that balance, it's important to understand that you still need to think about the elements that make a good story. You could write every single accurate detail of your life, but that would probably bore your reader. Instead, you'll be selective about what you tell. Think of a lesson you learned, an important event, or a series of things that helped you grow; write about them. Just because you're telling true stories doesn't mean you can't be selective and decide which parts to keep and which to leave out.

During this unit we'll learn about how to tell true stories in a variety of interesting ways.

Step 1: Mini-Lesson

After handwriting or typing practice has concluded, begin each day of Writer's Workshop with a mini-lesson. You will find some within the sidebars of this unit. You can also use a worksheet from a grammar workbook or practice editing, copying, or diagramming sentences. During writing time, watch for weak areas or mistakes being made and present a mini-lesson the next day to help correct those and improve writing skills in small, continuous ways.

The mini-lesson should take five to ten minutes and always have a positive happy spin, free from criticism. Not every mini-lesson needs to be kept in your Writer's Notebook. Most are merely for practice.

Step 2: Writing

Now it's time to really begin writing. Most of your time during Writer's Workshop should be spent writing. Practicing

is the key to improving. You can use your writing time to free write your own ideas in your Journal anytime, or use the exercises below to practice writing skills and find inspiration for things to write about. Select as many exercises as you would like to do over the month, making sure you leave time to complete at least one writing project that will go all of the way through the writing process before the month is over. The exercises will also go in your Journal section of your Writer's Notebook. If you decide to take something from your Journal through the writing process and turn it into your writing project, move it from your Journal to the Writing section of your Writer's Notebook.

A few tips and reminders:

- You can repeat the units and the exercises in subsequent years, so don't ever feel pressured to get to all of them, and feel free to repeat ones you enjoy.
- Often a single exercise can be presented to all of your children, no matter their ages or abilities. They will naturally write at the level they are at and, as they practice, will grow as writers.
- As you progress through the exercises, watch for something that sparks interest and could become the writing project. Feel free to jump to the idea bank at the end of the unit anytime as well. If there's spare time after the project is published, return to more exercises.
- Your family may all be in different places in the writing process. That's perfectly fine. Remember, your Writer's Workshop is a garden and everyone is growing their own patch. You can all lend a hand to help each gardener's patch thrive, but you won't all grow the same crop.

It's time to write! Choose some exercises and jump right in!

Writing The Truth

EXERCISE: Writing About Real People

When we write fanciful stories, we refer to the people as characters. When we're writing true stories, they aren't characters; they are people. Because we may write about animals or other things, we can generally refer to the people we write about as subjects. It's important for us to remember that we have a responsibility to every single person we write about. We must tell the truth and we must be careful not to slander or offend those we write about. If possible, it's important to ask the people we are writing about if it's okay for us to tell their story.

For this exercise, choose a person you know that you would like to write about. Write a series of interview questions you

---

☐ **Mini-Lesson**

In a lot of writing, the use of personal pronouns like I, me, my, and we is discouraged. They are perfectly fine to use in personal narratives, autobiographies, and other true stories about yourself though. You are telling the story from your point of view, so you should refer to yourself as "I" or "me."

☐ **Mini-Lesson**

Your memories are the best idea bank you have as a writer. The things that have happened to you are better than writing prompts.

☐ **Mini-Lesson**

The car someone drives can often tell you a lot about the person. Think of the person and then imagine that you are sitting in his or her car. What is it like? What's in the glove compartment? Are there any bumper stickers or decals? Do you see trash on the floor?

Ideas and content, one of the six traits of writing, is improved by details. Get into the details of the person's life and you will come to know the person a lot more deeply. Let your readers in on some of the details and they will come to know the people in your stories too.

Choose a person you know or would like to write about and describe the person's car in a simple paragraph.

Mini-Lesson ☐

Before you arrive at an interview you should have a list of written questions and a voice recorder or note taking supplies. Brainstorm some interview questions you could ask.

Mini-Lesson ☐

If you don't know some of the facts when you're writing a true story, it's okay to leave some parts out. It's better to leave something out than to tell a lie on purpose.

Think of a memory you have from a field trip or vacation you've been on. Are there parts of it that you can't quite remember?

Mini-Lesson ☐

Review the difference between fiction and nonfiction. Create an anchor chart using the "Fiction Nonfiction" printable from the Printable Pack. Under each heading, write down characteristics of each.

can ask him or her. During the interview, if he or she reveals something interesting that you would like to write about, ask more questions and dig into the details so you can write the story accurately and honestly. Remember your responsibility to tell the truth as you tell the story.

Here are a few interview questions to get you started:

1. What is your favorite memory?
2. Where is your favorite place in the world and why?
3. What is the biggest challenge you've overcome?
4. What lesson have you learned that you think is important for other people to know?
5. What's the most interesting place you've ever traveled?
6. How did you meet your best friend?
7. What's the funniest (or most embarrassing) thing that's ever happened to you?

EXERCISE: Writing True Stories

As we write true stories, one of the biggest obstacles that comes up is our own fading memories. Even if we personally lived through an event, we won't actually be able to remember every single detail. Furthermore, we may remember something very differently than someone else does, even if you were both together as the story unfolded. We may vividly remember an event but not be able to recall the exact date, the specific words spoken during a conversation, what the weather was like, or what clothing we were wearing. In your story, you might want to share some of those details, but how can you if you can't quite remember them? Is it lying if I tell a detail I can't exactly recall?

Remember that you are the writer. It's your story. You are going to tell it to the best of your ability with the details you remember. You are going to be true to the people and events even if you fill in some extra details. Allow yourself some creative license so your story can include the vivid and interesting descriptions that help your reader to step into your shoes and become part of the story.

Think of a memory from years ago that you have. Make a list of details you recall and a second list of details you aren't sure about in the same story.

I remember the year I learned to snow ski. My dad gave me a little lesson, then put my skis in between his much bigger skis and we started down the snowy slope together. We gained speed far more quickly than we had planned, Terrified at how fast we were speeding down the slope, I stopped listening to his instructions and just crouched a bit, preparing for the worst. Despite all his efforts, without my

cooperation he couldn't get us to slow down or stop. We ended up plowing directly into two people standing still on the mountain, talking, who didn't even see us coming. CRASH! They went down like bowling pins after a direct impact with the ball.

I don't recall what I was wearing, but it wouldn't be dishonest for me to say that my pink snowsuit stuck out like a beacon of disaster on the pure white slope, but even that wasn't enough warning for those poor, innocent snow bunnies. Although I don't know if I was wearing pink, I know that was my normal color choice in those years. I don't recall the explanation my dad gave those poor people, but I have known my dad all my life, and I know he apologized. I know he felt terrible and never would have left without making sure they were okay. Because I know his character, I can fill in some details and still tell an honest story. I wouldn't add that a deer popped her head out of the forest at that very moment with a disapproving glare because that didn't happen. You can fill in details without adding unnecessary ones that would rob the validity of your story.

Use the two lists you created and write a short account of a story from your own life, including filling in some specifics you may not be able to recall but that would have been true to the character or behaviors of the people you are writing about. Add it to the Journal section of your Writer's Notebook.

EXERCISE: Finding a Plot

When we write fictional stories we plan a plot, but when we write true stories we find a plot. Think back in your mind. Have you had any interesting stories happen to you?

I remember catching crawdads in the river that ran behind our house and how scared I was each time I went down under the water and grabbed one, trying my hardest not to get my fingers near the claws. Despite the fear making my hands shake, I pulled out crawdad after crawdad and deposited them in our bucket. Your stories can start with simple memories. What experiences have you had that could become a story?

Make a list of ten memories and put a star by each one that you think you could turn into a story. Add it to the Lists section of your Writer's Notebook.

☐ **Mini-Lesson**

Some stories lie somewhere between fiction and nonfiction. You can write something that is based on a true story. This means most of the story is true, but there are parts that are embellished or added to the truth. If you write one of these, you must include a disclaimer at the front that explains that it is based on a true story but has some fictional elements. This should be written much like a dedication, centered on the page before you write the story.

☐ **Mini-Lesson**

Even when we write factually, opinions and perspective play a big part in how we tell stories. I once had a friend who was very hurt after she slipped and fell in front of her house. I was standing at my window and she thought I saw her and decided not to come help. She was really angry that I didn't run out and help her. The truth is, I didn't see her at all and didn't realize she had fallen. Had I seen her, I would have run to her aid as fast as I could. Sometimes two people can be part of the same story and experience it differently.

Can you think of a time when you had a disagreement with someone because you saw things differently than one another?

☐ Mini-Lesson

Introspection is thinking about yourself, your thoughts, your memories, and your emotions. Introspection is a valuable tool for a writer. When we can think clearly about something we have experienced, felt, or thought about, we are better able to put those thoughts into words. Quiet moments of introspection can be powerful for a writer.

Take a few minutes to sit quietly and just think through one of your small moments, problems, or experiences. Think about what you were feeling, what was important to you, and what surrounded you. Look around in your own mind for details and thoughts. As you write, make sure to include the details of what you see, feel, and experience in your mind so that your readers can see, feel, and experience it too.

As you practice introspection, it will help you create stories with stronger voice, one of the six traits of writing.

☐ Mini-Lesson

As you write true stories, rather than using illustrations, sometimes you can incorporate photographs right into your stories. Cut and paste photos on to your pages or use a computer to insert photographs into documents. Look for photos you can include in your final drafts.

EXERCISE: Setting Glasses

True story settings you write about often involve places you walk, talk, and live in every single day. Your bedroom, your kitchen table, a nearby park, your yard, or your favorite restaurant - these are the kinds of places where the true stories of your own life happen.

Use the "Setting Glasses" printable from the Printable Pack. Within the box, write about an everyday setting you live in. Once your description is done, go to that setting and take a closer look. Put on a pair of imaginary glasses and begin to notice the details of the real life setting you are sitting in. Imagine that the glasses are like a magnifying glass that lets you see more than you would normally see. Look around. Notice things. Inside each lens of the glasses on the printable, write a detail of the setting you are in that you didn't notice at first. Any time you are writing a true story, remember to put on your imaginary setting glasses and notice small details to include that will paint a fuller picture for your reader.

EXERCISE: Picture Perfect Setting

Look through family photographs and find photos of places you've been, Your photos might be special places you've visited, vacations you've gone on, or activities in your own hometown. When one sparks a memory, set that photo aside.

Once you have your photograph or scene before you, write about your story setting using exact language. Describe the sights, sounds, and smells. Picture yourself walking through it real-time and write about your journey and experiences. If possible, focus on one small memory you can write about from that setting. Add it to your Journal.

EXERCISE: Memory Map

Draw a map of a place you have visited that you love or that is particularly memorable to you. Write captions in different areas of the map that tell about the neat things

you've done in each location. Add your map to your Journal. Can you turn your map into a true story? If you do, make sure to include the map with your finished story.

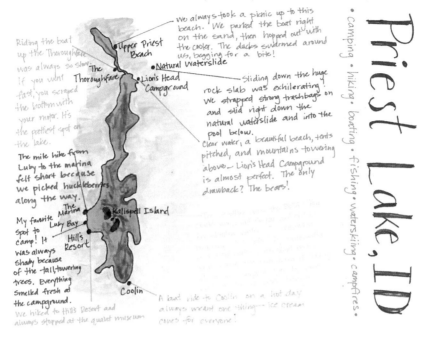

Priest Lake, ID

• Camping • hiking • boating • fishing • waterskiing • campfires •

Riding the boat up the Thoroughfare was always so slow. If you went fast, you scraped the bottom with your motor. It's the prettiest spot on the lake.

• Upper Priest Beach
• Natural Waterslide
The Thoroughfare
Lion's Head Campground

We always took a picnic up to this beach. We parked the boat right on the sand, then hopped out with the cooler. The ducks swarmed around us, begging for a bite!

Sliding down the huge rock slab was exhilerating! We strapped strong trashbags on and slid right down the natural waterslide and into the pool below.

Clear water, a beautiful beach, tents pitched, and mountains towering above — Lion's Head Campground is almost perfect. The only drawback? The bears!

The mile hike from Luby to the marina felt short because we picked huckleberries along the way.

My favorite spot to camp! It was always shady because of the tall, towering trees. Everything smelled fresh at the campground. We hiked to Hill's Resort and always stopped at the quaint museum.

The Marina
Luby Bay
Hill's Resort
• Kalispell Island
• Coolin

A boat ride to Coolin on a hot day always meant one thing — ice cream cones for everyone!

EXERCISE: Historical Settings

When you want to tell a true story you haven't experienced yourself, you need to research to find out about the setting your story happened in. You might look at books, watch a video about the event, or do an internet search. You might even have a chance to visit the modern-day setting of the historical event.

When writing historical stories, it's important to understand not only what the place looked like, but also the customs of the time. You can research foods, dress, daily life, family structure, economics, holidays, and any other historical details that will help you to tell a more accurate story.

This is Joan of Arc, a heroine of the Hundred Years' War which was fought between England and France in the 1400s. She has an amazing story. If you were to tell it well, you would need to understand the time and place she lived in. For example, young French girls in her day were barred from public office or any positions of power. They could not get an education, own property, or fight in the military. They certainly didn't wear suits of

☐ **Mini-Lesson**

Use the "Capitalize with M.I.N.T.S." anchor chart from the Printable Pack to learn about words that need capital letters. Each letter in M.I.N.T.S. reminds you of things to capitalize: months and days of the week, the word I, names of specific people, places, and things, titles, and the first word of any sentence. As you learn about capitalizing, talk about the differences between common nouns that can be any number of things and proper nouns, which refer to one specific person, place, or thing.

☐ **Mini-Lesson**

Brainstorm a list of proper nouns together. Practice writing the proper nouns with capital letters.

☐ **Mini-Lesson**

Along with proper nouns, there are also proper adjectives, or adjectives which are derived from proper nouns. They always begin with a capital letter. They usually end with -ian, -an, -ish, or ese.

English, Canadian, Shakespearean, Italian, Spanish, Christian, African, Hawaiian, Japanese, Columbian

☐ Mini-Lesson

If two people both experienced the very same thing, they would still tell about it differently. Even one person who tells the same story several times tends to vary in the tellings. People might remember new details or have their minds jump to something they had forgotten to tell before.

It is your job to tell true stories from your own point of view. Whether or not your experience exactly matches someone else's doesn't matter. Your story is your own. Tell it in the way you remember it.

☐ Mini-Lesson

If you always show instead of telling, your story will probably be too long. Focus on showing the story during these moments:

- Show the setting
- Show the characters (inside and out)
- Show emotional moments
- Show suspense, excitement, or when an important event is happening.

Instead of telling your reader someone was happy, show the emotion.

"Her shoulders scrunched and she squealed in delight when she turned the corner and saw him."

armor or lead troops, but Joan did. Understanding the time and place she lived will help you tell your story.

Choose a story from history that happened before you were born. Do some research and write down at least ten things you learned from your research about the time and place of the event, including the physical landscape, customs, and cultural norms of the time. If you decide to write a true story from history during this unit, make sure to begin with research and a list of facts about the setting as part of your prewrite.

EXERCISE: Sketch of a Person

Just as you create character sketches as you write fictional stories, you can create sketches about the real people or subjects you are writing about too.

Begin by sketching or printing out a picture of the person you are writing about in the center of a piece of paper. Divide the paper in two halves. On one half, write about what the person is like on the outside - hair color, eye color, stature, build, clothing choices, identifying marks, and other physical characteristics. On the other half, write about what he or she is like on the inside - character traits, habits, talents, personality, preferences, and feelings.

EXERCISE: Interrogate Your Story

As we write stories, we want to do more than just tell our readers about what happened. We want to show them. That means we offer enough details to allow them to picture the people, settings, and events in their minds. Showing someone your true story is much more interesting than just telling it. Interrogating your story is one trick that can help you show your true experiences to a reader. Interrogate is a big word that just means to ask lots of questions. Ask your story all kinds of questions and then give specific detailed answers as you tell the story.

Here's an example of telling:

> *They went to New York to see a musical on Broadway. They enjoyed it a lot. When they tried to get home, their flight was delayed because of a storm so they stayed another night and went back to the show.*

That's a great start, but it just isn't specific enough. Interrogate your story by asking what you saw, who else was there, who spoke, and what was said. The trouble is that you can probably already see it. You lived your story. It's easy to forget that your reader can't see what you can already see in your mind. Pretend that you can't see what

happened and ask yourself all kinds of things about the story. Then show the story in sparkling detail as you write.

Here's an example of showing:

> *Tanya and James flew to New York City in a 747. They got their bags, took a yellow cab to their high rise hotel, and checked into their rooms.*
>
> *"I can't wait to see the show!" Tanya said, "You're going to love it."*
>
> *James shook his head. "I don't get it. It's about Cats who sing and dance? Sounds sorta dumb."*
>
> *"Just trust me," Tanya smiled.*
>
> *Their hotel was just a few blocks from Broadway so they walked. So many people! So many buildings! The foyer of the theater shone like gold and its white marble steps glistened. Hundreds of people were milling about in tuxedos and gowns, all glinting in the light.*

Once you get really specific your story is often a bit longer. You'll have to decide which details are the most important. That was a little better though, right? Instead of "they," we now see Tanya and James. We know Tanya is a bit more enthusiastic while James is wary of the whole experience. We get a little glimpse of the theater and their experience too. We begin to see the people, settings, and events.

Practice changing a telling statement into a showing statement. Begin with this telling statement:

> *The clown was nervous about his first circus. He hoped he would be funny. All of a sudden, the ringmaster gave his signal and the clown went into the big ring.*

Interrogate the story. Ask questions in your mind or to a buddy and come up with more details so you can show more of the people, setting, and events of this simple story. When you're finished, likely you'll have about five to eight sentences instead of the three you started with.

You can also practice interrogating your own true stories from your life. Look through your Journal section of your Writer's Notebook and find a story that you have begun to write. Interrogate your story and revise it to show the story instead of just telling about the event.

EXERCISE: Facts and Opinions
You might think that if you're writing a true story, you need to stick to just the facts, but that isn't always the case. The opinions, perspectives, and experiences of

□ **Mini-Lesson**

Over a series of mini-lessons, use the "Show, Don't Tell" printable from the Printable Pack to create anchor charts for your Writing Helps section. Fill in an emotion, draw the person, then list ways to show the emotion.

Facts are statements that are backed up by evidence. Opinions are based on experiences and emotions. Write two lists together as a group - one of facts and the other of opinions.

Sometimes it can be hard to tell if something is a fact or an opinion. Read these statements and determine if each one is a fact or an opinion.

- There are six people in my family.
- I hate cats.
- Schools should continue through summer.
- Ellen is better at soccer than Matt.
- Giza is not the capital of Egypt.
- The movie grossed over a hundred million dollars.
- Chickens are afraid of everything.
- Bali tigers are extinct.

Answers:

F, O, O, O, F, F, O, F

When listing yourself and another person, it is polite to always list the other person first, then include your personal pronoun - I.

Nan and I rode bikes.

Joaquin and I waited in line for the roller coaster.

Write some of your own.

people are an important part of true stories. I read many books about World War II and could never understand how the German people let Adolph Hitler rise to such power that he killed six million Jews and countless other people. Then I read an account of one German girl's experiences. She lived in the same area as Hitler and grew up learning Nazi propaganda. Her experiences widened my perspective of Nazi Germany. We can tell true stories and still share opinions, but it's important that we recognize the difference. If we're sharing an opinion, we should use opinion language. You can use words like: I believe, I claim, in my view, I suspect, or I argue. If we're sharing facts, we use factual language. We might say things like: there is evidence, research shows, it is true that, it has been discovered, latest findings confirm, or I know that.

For each of these categories, write one statement of fact and one statement of opinion.

- My house
- Summer
- Dogs
- Fruit
- Oceans
- Traffic
- Litter
- Pollution

- My country
- My hometown
- Television
- My friends
- The Eiffel Tower
- Books
- Pigs
- Chores

Both facts and opinions are acceptable in true stories, but you should be mindful not to state an opinion as though it's a fact.

EXERCISE: Truthful Themes

Themes within true stories often come from the life lessons we learn as we experience things. Thomas Edison was a scientist and inventor who has had his life stories told many, many times because of the valuable life lessons he learned along the way. Life lessons often serve as the theme of the story. Here are some anecdotes from Edison's life along with the themes each of the anecdotes shows.

Edison only went to formal school for a few months, but because of his natural curiosity and his mother teaching him to read, he became a brilliant scientist and inventor.

Lesson: Curiosity and reading can pave the way to a wonderful education.

Edison set out with his staff to create a new storage battery. After thousands of attempts, they still hadn't been able to do it. When asked if he was discouraged by so many failures, Edison said, "Why, man, I have gotten a lot of results. I know several thousand things that won't work."

Lesson: Failure is just a learning experience.

When Edison worked on a train selling candy and newspapers, he became determined to grow his business. After doing some research, he tried sending news by wire ahead of time about some of the big headlines in the newspaper and found that it increased his newspaper sales when he arrived. He even started writing his own newspaper featuring stories he witnessed while riding on the trains. He printed the papers in a baggage car.

Lesson: Hard work and ingenuity pay off.

Think of a real person you know of. It could be someone you know personally or someone you have learned or read about. If possible, draw or print out a picture of the person. Write down a short story from his or her life that demonstrates a lesson. At the bottom of the story, write the lesson you learn from the story. Lessons like these serve as the themes of true stories.

EXERCISE: Unique Voices on Voice Mail
Think of several people you know who have strong or distinct personalities. Using a voice recorder, create a voice mail message for each one that reflects his or her personality and interests. Think about the words they use, topics they like to talk about, tone, and mannerisms.

If Bob is a pilot who is adventurous and really friendly, this might be his voice mail message:

Hi there! If I didn't answer your call I might just be cruising at 10,000 feet in my jet right now! Please leave me a message and I'll get back to ya when my feet are on the ground. Over and out!

If Karla is a teacher who is well-mannered and always considerate, her message might say this:

Hello, this is Karla. I'm so sorry that I missed your call. I promise to call right back just as soon as I get these stacks of papers graded. Please leave me an A+ message with your name and phone number after the beep.

☐ **Mini-Lesson**

It's important to stay in the same verb tense throughout your story. Decide ahead of time if you will write in past tense or in present tense and then stay in the same tense throughout.

Can you spot the mistakes in this passage?

I ran to the park as fast as I could yesterday. She's coming after me and I can't seem to get away fast enough. When I got there, I didn't even stop to catch my breath. I run past the slide, go through the tunnel, and dart behind the picnic tables to get away. I thought I would never get away, but I finally escaped.

Choose either past tense or present tense and rewrite the passage in the tense you chose.

☐ **Mini-Lesson**

Can and may are two commonly misused words. Can means to be able to do something. May means to have permission, or be allowed to do something.

Consider the different meanings of these two sentences:

Can I go to the bathroom?

May I go to the bathroom?

Write several of your own sentences that use can and may properly.

☐ Mini-Lesson

Exact word choice is important. Words like cool, awesome, fine, liked, very, and really aren't packed with meaning. Rewrite this passage using more exact language.

I love the log ride. I had to wait in line for a really long time, but it was worth it. It was so cool. It was fun to ride. I went around and around a lot of paths and then went very, very, very high. It was cool to sit at the top just before you go down, down, down the other side of the big hill. The big hill is the most fun part. The log ride makes me happy.

☐ Mini-Lesson

Imagine five people all being told the very same joke. Each one reacts differently. What are some ways each person could react? Sharing reactions of people is an important skill when you're telling true stories.

At the top of a sheet of paper, write down a joke. Divide your paper into four boxes below. Write the names of four people you know, one in each box, and then write down how they would react to hearing the joke. Describe their facial expressions, gestures, body movements, words, and emotions.

As you write about people, your job is to create the stories, messages, and words that reflect each person's personality accurately. It's helpful to think about the everyday things you hear them do and say. As you write, try to reflect each person's unique voice. You may not know the exact words they spoke in a story that happened a long time ago (or even yesterday), but if you can capture their voices, what they sound like, and what they would say, you are writing an accurate depiction of the truth.

EXERCISE: Dialogue and Reactions

You often include dialogue when you tell true stories. As you relate conversations that happened, make sure to include not only what was spoken, but also how the people reacted to it. Here's a conversation between two people in a cancer treatment facility:

> *"How are you?"*
>
> *"I'm okay, I guess. I've been really tired lately."*
>
> *"Me too. I guess cancer will do that to you."*

Here's the same conversation, including actions and reactions of the two people:

> *"How are you?" Jack asked hesitantly, frowning and guessing what the answer would be.*
>
> *"I'm okay, I guess. I've been really tired lately." Tears slipped down Jen's cheek. Putting a gentle arm around her shoulders, Jack drew her in close.*
>
> *"Me too. I guess cancer will do that to you."*

Write a simple dialogue between two people. They could be telling a joke, completing a purchase, giving each other gifts, planning to meet up later, or any other situation you can imagine.

The first time, write only the words they speak. The second time, add in their actions and reactions. You can choose to write about a real conversation you've heard or just practice using a conversation from your imagination.

Autobiographical Stories

EXERCISE: Journaling

Journaling is a wonderful way to begin writing true stories. No one knows you or your story better than you do. Writing stories from your own life experiences can be meaningful. Not only are you recording who you are and what has happened to you, but you get to share your own thoughts,

feelings, and ideas. You are uniquely suited to tell your own true stories. If you've never kept a personal journal or diary before, you can start one by regularly telling what has been happening in your life and what you think about the events. Choose a regular time to journal, whether it's once a day, once a week, or once a month. You will enjoy going back and reading it later, and remembering the experiences and true stories that have happened in your life.

If you've never journaled before, here are a few prompts you can start with to try it out:

- Who do you most admire? What memories do you have with that person?
- What is your favorite song? How do you feel when it's playing?
- What is your best habit?
- What is your worst habit?
- Tell about a time you've helped someone.
- What is your greatest accomplishment?
- What talents do you have?
- What did you do last week?
- What is your earliest memory?
- What special items do you own that mean something important to you? Why are they important to you?
- Who is your best friend? Tell about him or her.
- What do you believe in with your whole self?

EXERCISE: The Pieces of Me
Use the "Pieces of Me" printable from the Printable Pack. Add pictures and words to each piece of the puzzle that show a part of your life that helps make you the person you are. Here are a few ideas to consider:

- Talents you have
- Hobbies you enjoy
- Games or activities that make you happy
- Sports, teams, clubs, or groups you are a part of
- Your place in your family
- Friends you spend time with

Add this to the Journal section of your Writer's Notebook so you can look at it when you need an idea of what to write about. Look back through your Journal often when you are considering a true story to take through the writing process. You have written a lot of things about your own stories and life. You can choose one of them as your writing project when you're ready.

EXERCISE: Lightning Round
Use the "Lightning Round" printable from the Printable

☐ Mini-Lesson

An autobiography is a true story about yourself. It includes the story, important events, and details of your life. It is written in first person point of view (I, my, me). As you write your autobiography, you can share the things that have made you who you are.

Begin by brainstorming main ideas along a timeline of your life. Add in details and examples to build your story. Conclude with a memorable ending that describes you as a unique person.

☐ Mini-Lesson

When you write dialogue in stories, don't be afraid to use slang. Dialogue should sound the way people actually talk. Slang changes really fast, with new generations of people inventing and using new words. Use only the slang that the person in the real situation would use. These words are unlikely to come out of the mouth of a 60-year-old man:

"Hey Bae, don't ghost me."

Used well, slang can let you into someone's reality. Overused or misused slang is confusing though. Practice writing a few lines of natural dialogue that you might say. Then write a few more lines that one of your parents might say.

Mini-Lesson

As you write about yourself, you will have to know when it's appropriate to use "I" and when you should use "me." To decide, split the sentence into two sentences.

Me and my cat snuggled up.

Me snuggled up.

My cat snuggled up.

Hmm, that doesn't sound right. If you fill it in with "I" you will get:

I snuggled up.

My cat snuggled up.

My cat and I snuggled up.

That's better.

Now write some of your own sentences that include me or I and another subject. Determine whether you should use me or I as the pronoun in your sentences.

Mini-Lesson

As you're writing your true story, leave a trail of clues. You know what will happen in the end. Leave two or three clues for your reader along the way. Don't give away the ending, but give hints about what might happen to engage your reader.

Leaving clues is a simple way to create foreshadowing. Readers like to decipher and work out in their minds what might happen in a story. It is engaging to read a story when it has foreshadowing and hints about what's to come. This also improves organization in your story, one of the six traits of writing.

Pack to answer a series of quick questions about yourself, your likes and dislikes, and other choices you would make. Choose at least one of them that strikes a memory. Write a short story about the memory. Add the "Lightning Round" printable and your short story draft to the Journal section of your Writer's Notebook.

EXERCISE: All About Me
Use the "All About Me" book from the Printable Pack. Fill out the sections, add illustrations, and make the book neat and colorful so you can keep it as a keepsake or add it to the library of books you have authored. Older kids can use these ideas to craft their own *All About Me* scrapbook using any information and pictures that reflect who they are.

EXERCISE: Personal Coat of Arms
Draw details on your own personal coat of arms using the "Coat of Arms" printable from the Printable Pack. In each of the six boxes, draw a combination of illustrations and words that answer these six questions.

1. What makes you happy?
2. What makes you sad?
3. What is your best personality trait?
4. Who is important to you?
5. What is one thing you hope to do in your life?
6. What one word best represents who you are?

After you've drawn your answers, choose at least one of them to write a little more about.

EXERCISE: When I Eat . . .
Write a description of what you do when you eat or drink something that you really love. At the top, write "When I eat (and fill in your favorite food)". Explain the food you love so much and also describe yourself and your reactions to it. Cut out your description.

Use card stock to create a background that shows your favorite food or drink, then glue your description to the design. Add it to your Journal.

EXERCISE: The Real Me
Use "The Real Me" printable from the Printable Pack to

help you think about some things that define you in simple ways. Illustrate the boxes. Add it to your Journal and use it as you're looking for ideas of true stories to write about yourself.

EXERCISE: Logo

Design a logo that represents you. Think about the specific things that define who you are as a person and capture that with simple words or symbols in a single logo. Surround your logo with a brainstorm of ideas about things that have happened to you that have helped you know who you are.

EXERCISE: All Dressed Up

Often we dress up in special clothing for special occasions like holidays, dances, funerals, parties, outings, recitals, or concerts. Think of some times you have dressed up. Begin with a description of what you were wearing, then write the story of the event. Did your clothing make you feel any particular way, either positive or negative? Add this to your Journal.

EXERCISE: My House

Count the number of rooms you have in your house. Make a booklet that has the same number of pages as the number of rooms in your house. On each page, draw a picture of one of the rooms as a background image, then write a story, memory, or tradition that happened in that room on top of the picture. You can turn this into a finished project by creating your own illustrated book or you can add the draft to your Journal.

EXERCISE: My Tick Tock Clock Story

Use the "My Tick Tock Clock Story" printable from the Printable Pack. Think of a day in your life. You can choose a special day, like Christmas or your birthday or a day you spent on vacation. You could also choose an average day, even this very day. In each hour segment of the clock, write or draw what you did at that time of the day. Use the clock as a story planner to help you put your story into sequential order. Once you've finished putting the events of your day in order, write about them in the same order. Make sure to add transition words like first, later, afterward, and next to help your story stay organized and lead from one event of your day to the next.

EXERCISE: Growing and Changing

Gather pictures of yourself from each year of your life. Paste each picture to a page, leaving room to write around it.

☐ Mini-Lesson

Draw an upward curve on a sheet of paper. Think of a story from your life. Along the curve, write some ways you grew as a person from that story. Based on what you wrote, what's your story's theme?

☐ Mini-Lesson

When you end true stories about people, you can link it back to where you started. Coming full circle feels like a satisfying ending to readers. For example, if you tell about a lonely day in your life, you may begin by describing what loneliness feels like and end by helping someone else who is lonely.

Think of any story that has happened to you and share with someone how you could take it full circle.

☐ Mini-Lesson

A euphemism is a nice way to say something harsh.

Instead of dead, you might say passed away. Instead of vomiting, you might say feeling ill. Instead of saying euthanize, you might say put to sleep.

As the writer, it's up to you to decide when to soften your message with a euphemism. This is part of word choice, one of the six traits of writing.

How could you soften these adjectives?

overweight, ugly, poor, drunk, lying, unemployed

☐ Mini-Lesson

Writing sentences of varying lengths is an important part of sentence fluency. Roll a die and practice writing a sentence with the number of words that matches your roll. With practice you can get better at being intentional as you choose your sentence lengths.

☐ Mini-Lesson

When you write an introductory phrase in a sentence, you set the phrase apart with a comma.

Yes, I would love some dessert.

To avoid being late, we left fifteen minutes early.

After the movie, would you like to get ice cream?

Write some of your own sentences with introductory phrases and set apart the phrase with a comma.

☐ Mini-Lesson

Avoid filler words as you write in first person point of view. Instead of saying, 'I saw that a forest fire was coming,' say 'A forest fire was coming.'

Extra words create distance between you and your reader. Eliminate them.

Look at something you've written in your Journal and see if you can cross out extra filler words.

Alternately, you could add the pictures to a word processing document and add words surrounding each picture using your computer and then print the pages.

Write about yourself at each age, sharing the things you liked, what you did, things you said, or memories from that year. Your pages can become a scrapbook of your life and how you have changed and grown over the years. Do one for each year of your life and put the pages together to create a book showing how you've grown.

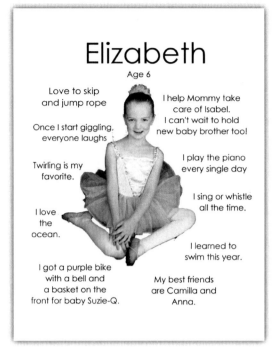

EXERCISE: Numbers

Think of at least one number that means something to you. Draw the number in large block letters, filling a page. Inside of the number, write the story of what that number means to you and why it has significance. You can add illustrations as well.

EXERCISE: Story Quilt

Create a story quilt that showcases your best memories on a series of quilt squares. You can create a paper quilt or sew it into an actual lap quilt. Begin with nine squares of paper or white fabric. Choose an appropriate size depending on how large you want your finished quilt to be. Create a center square by drawing a picture of yourself. Write your name on it, as well as any other information you'd like to show. You could include the place you call home, your birthday, your favorite quote, or words that describe you. On each of the other eight squares, draw a memory from your life.

Put the nine squares together to form your quilt. If you made paper squares, you can hang them on a wall to display them. If you made fabric squares you can sew them together, add a backing, and create a small lap quilt.

A simple way to create the squares on fabric is to use 100% cotton fabric and draw your designs on using fabric markers and crayons. To make the designs washable, you can set them with an iron set to the cotton setting. Put each fabric square between two paper towels as you iron over it to make sure the crayon doesn't melt on to the iron or other surfaces. You can iron each square several times, each time with a clean set of paper towels, to ensure the design has set fully. Your quilt will be washable after this process.

You can write down each of the full stories that you chose to include on your story quilt to have a record of these stories that showcase your life.

EXERCISE: Time Capsule

As a family, create a time capsule that includes items that represent you. Add photographs, awards, or memorabilia. You can each write down memories and favorite family stories too. Seal them all inside of a protected, weatherproof box. You can either bury the box or put it into a safe location. Write down a date in the future in which you will open it together and take a walk down memory lane. Make sure the opening date is at least a few years beyond when you create the time capsule.

EXERCISE: Ups and Downs

Life is full of ups and downs, highs and lows. During this exercise you'll be writing about some of yours. Use the "Ups and Downs" printable from the Printable Pack to help you organize your ideas. Above the mountains, write things that have been highs in your life - exciting or happy moments. Near the valleys, write about low points or hard times in your life. In the clouds, write the things you hope to do someday.

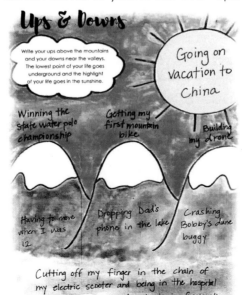

Turn your ideas into a story about the ups and downs of your life.

☐ **Mini-Lesson**

Brainstorm ideas for a story quilt by creating a prewrite on a piece of card stock using paper squares. You can rearrange the papers, sketch your ideas, and decide on your design before committing to it on your finished quilt.

☐ **Mini-Lesson**

Anytime you address someone directly in a sentence, set apart their name with a comma. If the name is written first, it is followed by a comma. If it is in the middle, commas surround it. If it is written last, a comma comes right before it.

Trey, will you go first?

It is important, Mary, to drink your water.

Thanks so much, Mom.

Use sentence imitation to create your own direct address sentences patterned after these.

☐ **Mini-Lesson**

Questions always end with a question mark. Write some "Would you rather . . .?" questions on note cards and take turns answering them out loud.

Writer's Workshop

Mini-Lesson

John Greenleaf Whittier wrote this poem:

When things go wrong, as they sometimes will,

When the road you're trudging seems all uphill,

When the funds are low and the debts are high,

And you want to smile, but you have to sigh,

When care is pressing you down a bit,

Rest! if you must - but never quit.

Discuss some things that have gone wrong in your family or personal life. Talk about ways you can keep going and lessons you can learn from not quitting. Tough events can become stories and the lessons we learn can become themes.

Mini-Lesson

Compound sentences have more than one main clause. The clauses can be joined by a comma and a conjunction or by a semi-colon.

Leslie bakes wedding cakes, and she also arranges flowers.

Leslie bakes wedding cakes; she also arranges flowers.

Semi-colons show a close relationship between the two clauses.

Imitate those sentences and write some examples of your own.

EXERCISE: Tagebuch

In German, a tagebuch is like a day book, or combination diary and planner. It is a working journal in which to keep calendars, lists, thoughts, sleep logs, recipes, prices of things, exercise logs, and any other day-to-day items. For at least one week, keep your own tagebuch, writing down all sorts of little things you do each day. Include many small details (like the price of the gallon of milk your mom just bought) even if they don't seem important.

EXERCISE: Small Moments

Make a list of small moments from your life. Small moments are memories you have of simple experiences. You aren't telling a whole story. You are simply telling about a memorable minute or two. It might be the first time you held your puppy, when you learned something new, or when you had to miss something important because you were sick. Anything that stands out in your mind is an important small moment in your life. I vividly remember sitting on a huge boulder on the beach and watching the waves during a family camping trip when I was eight years old. Nothing exciting happened at that moment, but it was a small moment that I have always remembered.

Once you've made your list of small moments, choose one of them to write about. Describe it completely. Make sure to include each of these elements in your description:

- A metaphor or simile
- Personification
- Adjectives
- Adverbs
- A preposition
- A strong verb
- Sensory details
- A writer's voice that sounds like yourself
- Sentences with a variety of lengths

EXERCISE: Explode a Moment

Choose a memorable moment in your life. Try to find one that only lasted a few seconds, one minute at the most. Describe everything you can about that moment. What was around you? What were you thinking? How did you feel? Did you or anyone else say anything? What were you doing? Use as many details as you can to help your reader become a part of that moment.

As you write true stories, you won't explode every moment. You will carefully choose important moments within your story to explode, or richly describe. These moments help your reader connect emotionally to the story.

EXERCISE: Musical Story

Sometimes certain songs transport our minds to memorable events or important people in our lives. Do you have a song that always makes you think of a certain person or event? Write about the song and its connection to your life. Share the memories it elicits in detail.

EXERCISE: Strong Emotions

Strong emotions can create interesting stories. Think of a time you felt fear. Use the "Fears" printable from the Printable Pack to help you generate ideas. After you've filled it out, choose one moment when you experienced fear and write about it. Begin by describing what fear felt like in every part of your body without revealing what triggered it. Once you've described your response, go on to explain what happened to you that caused such a strong emotion.

You can repeat this exercise using these strong emotions: surprise, pain, joy, alarm, love, disgust, anger, or sadness.

EXERCISE: Family Recipes

Use the "Family Recipe" printable from the Printable Pack to write down a recipe your family makes. Record a story that goes with the recipe. It could be the story of how you learned to cook it, or a special holiday party where it's always served, or maybe the time it went terribly wrong.

Once my sister and I made a pumpkin pie and left the sugar out because each of us thought the other had added it. That story has been told in our family for years. I've made dozens of perfect pies since then, but every time we eat pumpkin pie, someone brings up that one unfortunate pie.

EXERCISE: Travel Scrapbook

If you go on an outing or trip, take a small blank book along. Write your experiences as you go. Insert photographs, postcards, and small memorabilia in your book.

EXERCISE: My Life Categories Game

Make enough copies of the "My Life Categories" game from the Printable Pack for each person who will be playing. Choose a letter from the alphabet for the first round. Set a timer. Try to write a unique answer that begins with the selected letter of the alphabet for each category on the list. When the timer ends, read each category and give each player a chance to share their answers.

☐ **Mini-Lesson**

Fewer and less are two commonly misused words. Use fewer when the things can be counted and less for things that can't be counted.

I received fewer awards than Tom.

I have less to do than Sheila.

Can you write some of your own sentences using fewer and less?

☐ **Mini-Lesson**

Repetition is a fun literary technique to use in stories. Much like a song has a chorus, a story can repeat a phrase that the reader can latch on to.

Think of a story from your own life and write a phrase that you could repeat about the story again and again as you tell it.

☐ **Mini-Lesson**

In particular, when you're writing family stories, it can be helpful to ask the other members of your family what they remember. You are the only person on the whole planet who sees things through your eyes. Ask for other people's perspectives too. They can fill in details you've forgotten or tell about how they saw the same thing in a different way.

☐ Mini-Lesson

You can decide on the order you wish to write your true stories in. Some stories can be told according to straight chronological order. Chronological means that you tell about the events in the exact order they happened. You can also include flash backs or flash forwards. A flashback is when the writer inserts part of the story that happened previously into the writing. Similarly, a flash forward involves telling about an event that hasn't happened yet at an earlier point in the story.

Often true stories begin with the end (usually at the crux of the problem) and then rewind back to the beginning to see how the subjects got into the mess in the first place.

Do a quick write of a short story that includes either a flashback or a flash forward. Always plan your story's organization ahead of time to help your story flow.

☐ Mini-Lesson

Each time you write a story, you have to decide on the point of view you will write from.

You can tell it from first-person point of view, which is the I/we perspective. Second-person point of view is the you perspective. Third-person point of view is the he/she/it/they perspective. It is often told from the point of view of a narrator who is uninvolved in the story.

If the answer begins with the letter and is unique (no one else said the same thing), that player scores one point. After you've finished scoring the game and determined a winner, play the second round. After both rounds, everyone can choose at least one of their unique answers from the categories to do a 5-minute quick write about.

EXERCISE: A Problem and The Heart of the Problem

Think of a time you had a problem in your life. It could be anything from a bee sting or an illness to losing your dog or experiencing the death of a loved one. Write about the problem in the following format, writing each paragraph on its own index card:

- Paragraph 1: Events leading up to the problem.
- Paragraph 2: The problem.
- Paragraph 3: Something that made the problem even worse.
- Paragraph 4: The breaking point, where you didn't know how you were going to get past the problem.
- Paragraph 5: The conclusion, including how you overcame and solved or dealt with the problem.

Make sure each paragraph is descriptive, clear, and organized. When you're finished with this draft on index cards, revise your story. Rearrange the note cards in a new order to see how it feels to tell the story another way.

Sometimes instead of telling a story in chronological order, it's more effective to plunge right into the heart of the problem. Paint the scene of the hardest part of a problem you faced first. After that, you might go back and explain the events that led up to it. Just when the situation seems hopeless, reveal how you were able to overcome and rise up to meet the challenge. You may need to change some of the wording to fit your new organization.

EXERCISE: The Best Thing I Do

Write a personal reflection story about the best thing you do. It could be an activity, sport, talent, or personality trait you have. Include examples that show how you are great at the thing you chose.

EXERCISE: Personal Narrative

A personal narrative is a story about one specific event in the writer's life. It is not an entire life history. Instead, it is a very detailed story about one particular event. You will include where the story took place, who was involved, what happened, what was said, how it ended, and sometimes a lesson you learned or favorite memory you

have from it. Personal narratives usually involve emotional and sensory descriptions so the readers can feel like they are there experiencing the story too.

You can look back over your journal entries, lists, or some of the exercises you've completed during this unit for ideas, or look through this list for more ideas.

Tell about a time you:

- Went to the dentist or doctor
- Fought with a friend
- Helped someone
- Realized you had a hero
- Celebrated a special holiday
- Had a happy day
- Developed a new talent
- Went on a memorable vacation
- Got hurt
- Were really embarrassed
- Were positively miserable
- Had a first experience (like your first airplane ride)

Jot down the main events of the narrative in chronological order using the "Timeline" chart from the Printable Pack. Make more than one copy, if needed. Decide if you wish to use a flashback, flash forward, or straight chronology.

Draft the narrative, writing in the first-person point of view. Show, don't tell, the story. Provide your readers with specific details and images that paint the scene and help the reader experience the story with his or her senses and emotions. If you take it through the writing process, consider the following steps.

As you revise your personal narrative, include:

- Figures of speech sprinkled into the story
- Sensory details
- Engaging dialogue that uses actions as well as words
- A clear focus (theme)

As you edit, check for:

- Spelling and grammar mistakes
- A title and heading
- Consistent first-person point of view

EXERCISE: Memoir

A memoir is very similar to a personal narrative. The key difference is that the focus of a personal narrative is on an event while the focus of a memoir is on a person.

To begin writing a memoir, think of a quality you possess,

☐ Mini-Lesson

Write down a list of at least ten words that you like to use as you speak. We all have words that we use often, and using them when we write our own true stories will help our writing to have our own authentic voice. Sometimes speaking parts of your story out loud before you write them will help you to write in your own voice.

☐ Mini-Lesson

Do you have any personal possessions that mean more to you than they would mean to someone else? I have a tiny locket that I got from my parents when I was a little girl. On its own, it probably has no significant value, but it is invaluable to me. It is a symbol of their unconditional love, my happy childhood memories, and my place in my family. My heart glows when I hold it and my mind fills with fond memories.

You can include symbolic possessions in your personal stories as symbols of bigger emotions and events.

Draw a picture or gather some items that have sentimental value to you. Tell or write about what they symbolize to you. Include at least one symbol in a story you are writing.

☐ **Mini-Lesson**

Carol Tavris said, "History is written by the victors, but it's victims who write the memoirs."

What do you think she meant?

☐ **Mini-Lesson**

Both personal narratives and memoirs involve written personal experiences. The two are closely related. A key difference is that a narrative focuses on an event while a memoir centers on an individual.

☐ **Mini-Lesson**

As you're drafting, it may be helpful to type your stories on a computer if you know how to type. Some computers even have voice typing. This will allow you to revise the stories without rewriting the whole thing. If you highlight words, phrases, or sentences and right click on them, you can select cut. You move your cursor to the new place you want to insert them in, right click again, and select paste. You can quickly make lots of changes without any rewriting.

Try adding a flashback, flash forward, or another form of foreshadowing into a story you've already typed. It's easy when you can move your cursor to the spot without having to rewrite the rest of your story.

either good or bad. Next, think of at least three stories from your life that caused you to develop that quality. Within the memoir you will tell all three stories, but each will tie back to how the story shaped you and helped you gain the quality you possess. The focus is on you, the individual. The stories are just an illustration of how you came to be you.

The order the stories happened in isn't important. You might have learned courage when you successfully went rock climbing at age twelve and also learned courage when you were eight and had to own up to stealing a candy bar and apologized to the store clerk. Maybe you developed courage when you got the lead in the community play and went on stage to perform. It doesn't matter which of those happened first, just that they happened and that each one of them showed you ways you could develop courage.

Write a memoir by choosing a quality you possess and sharing anecdotes (or short stories) about how you came to have that quality.

EXERCISE: Life History
A life history is different from a personal narrative or a memoir. To write your life history, you will tell as many of your important life events as you can remember. You will tell the events in order, beginning with your birth and continuing up until today.

Here are some events to include:

- Details of your birth (time, place, circumstances)
- Details of your family members (names, places, ages)
- Moves to new houses or new places
- Births and deaths of family members
- Important events, travels, awards, and honors
- Difficulties you've faced
- Triumphs you've had

To share your life history, read it out loud and record the reading so you will have it preserved in your own voice. Keep it so future generations of your family can hear your own voice telling your own story.

Biographical Stories

EXERCISE: Family Interview
Interview a member of your family. Write some questions down before the interview. Take notes or ask if you can record the interview using a voice recorder. Choose something interesting the person shared and write a short story about him or her based on the interview.

EXERCISE: Family Tree

Create a lift-the-flap family tree. Begin by drawing a tree on a large sheet of paper or poster board. Add little doors made of card stock for each member of your extended family. Draw or paste a picture and write each name on the door, then on the inside, write something interesting about the person.

EXERCISE: Family Member Memories

With everyone joining in, create stick puppets for each member of your family. Take turns holding each stick puppet and telling out loud a favorite memory about that person. Each person can choose one of the shared memories to write down in story form.

EXERCISE: Family Biography Picture Book

Create an illustrated picture book that tells a story about a member of your family. You may need to ask parents, grandparents, aunts, uncles, or other family members to

share their stories so you can choose one that would make an interesting picture book. Write a few lines of the story on each page and then illustrate all of the pages and bind it into your own family keepsake picture book.

EXERCISE: Family History

The stories in your family go much further back than the people who are still living can remember. Try to do a little research about some of the deceased members of your family. Visit a website that helps you trace your family history and type in any information you know. Ancestry.com is the biggest website and has an extensive database to search. They also have an app that helps you search and record information about your family. See if you can find information or stories about someone from your family

---

☐ Mini-Lesson

A biography is a written story about a person other than the author. Biographies include details, facts, and stories. Look at the "Biography" anchor chart from the Printable Pack and add it to the Writing Helps section of your Writer's Notebook.

Read at least one biography before you begin writing one.

☐ Mini-Lesson

Unless you're the only person in your story, you need to be considerate of the other people you write about. Remember the Golden Rule: treat others as you wish to be treated.

☐ Mini-Lesson

As you describe real people, you will reveal their traits. Traits are qualities a person has. Someone could be honest, kind, loyal, evil, jealous, or ambitious. As you write about traits, you can show they are true traits by giving examples instead of relying on your opinion only.

Use the "True Traits" printable from the Printable Pack and think of a person you know. Write three traits you see in that person. Below each one, write evidence from the person's life that shows him or her displaying that trait.

Writer's Workshop

☐ Mini-Lesson

Sometimes we can get too carried away with telling all of the details of a person's life story. Much of life isn't actually interesting. As you watch characters on television or in the movies, do they ever show the parts where they clean their house or mow the lawn for hours or use the restroom? No, instead they show the events that matter in the story. As you write about a person, include the events that matter in the story you are telling.

☐ Mini-Lesson

Hyphens are used when you connect verbs together to create a noun.

The date was an eye-opener.

You can always count on the gift-giver to show up.

We are going to the restaurant to break the burger-buster record.

Make a list of your own verb phrases with hyphens that act as nouns.

☐ Mini-Lesson

If you are writing true stories that might be of a sensitive nature, you can alter some details to protect the people you're writing about. Just add this disclaimer: Some names and details have been changed to protect identities.

history who might otherwise be forgotten. Record their story by writing it down and include any dates, names, places, or other information you find out. You can also record stories about your grandparents or others you know on the Ancestry.com site so those people will not be forgotten.

EXERCISE: Zenith & Nadir

Talk with someone who is much older than you. Ask him or her to think of the very highest, happiest point and the very lowest, saddest point in life. Find out the stories behind that high and low. A zenith is the very highest point, the best, or the top. It is a word used by astronomers to describe the highest point a celestial body, like a star or planet, can go. The nadir is just the opposite, it represents the lowest low.

Ask the person you are talking with to tell you his or her zenith and nadir stories and experiences. Does s/he have regrets or great delights about the zenith and nadir of life? Make sure you have permission to write the stories.

Once you've learned all you can and asked lots of questions, write the story of these two moments in the person's life. Did you find a common thread between the two experiences? If possible, tie the two together into one theme.

EXERCISE: Hero

Write about a hero of yours. It might be an Olympic athlete, historical figure, or someone you know personally. Draw a sketch of the person and surround the sketch with qualities or admirable acts that you have seen.

Write a one-pager. A one-pager is a story that is limited to only a single page. You have to think carefully about your words so you can adequately describe the heroism of the person without going over a page.

EXERCISE: Animal Story

Research a famous animal or tell the story of one of your pets. Because this is a true story, if you imagine what the animal is thinking or saying, it's important to be clear that you are imagining those thoughts. Write a few lines of the story on each page of a short booklet and then illustrate the pages to create a picture book.

EXERCISE: Biography Notebooking

Choose a subject and use "The Life and Times of _____" printable from the Printable Pack to help you craft a biography notebooking page about any noteworthy person. Arrange the elements on the page. The printable

includes a title; a map area; a timeline with spots for eight significant events; a portrait, childhood, education, and family flip book; and a major achievements interlocking booklet.

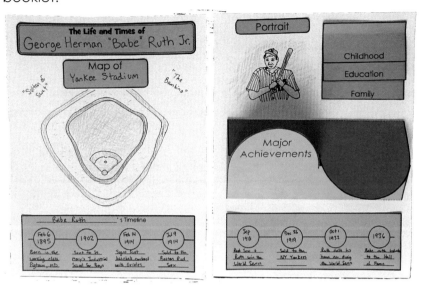

EXERCISE: Biography Project

Use the "Biography of _____" printable from the Printable Pack. Little ones might begin and end with the form, but older kids can use it as a graphic organizer to begin their writing process for a biography. Research an important historical person and create a biography project about his or her life: make a poster, digital slide show, oral presentation (dress up like the person for added impact), puppet, wax museum poster with a cutout for your face, or a biography bottle in which you craft the person using a two-liter bottle with a foam head.

If you can't think of who you might like to write about, here are a few fascinating people from history:

- Jane Goodall
- Pablo Picasso

☐ **Mini-Lesson**

Look back through your Journal and find a piece to revise. Add each of these figurative language story elements to your draft:

- Understatement
- Alliteration
- Personification
- Simile

If you lack space on your page, you can insert them using sticky notes.

☐ **Mini-Lesson**

When you are writing out fractions or any numbers from twenty-one to ninety-nine, use hyphens between the number words.

two-thirds

seventy-two

forty-nine

Practice writing fractions and numbers with hyphens.

☐ **Mini-Lesson**

Idioms are phrases that mean something other than their literal meaning. Practice using idioms by including all of these idioms in one quick-write that is a description of at least one person or animal you know.

a sight for sore eyes

sharp as a tack

Achilles' heel

weak at the knees

hands are tied

pain in the neck

bag of tricks

Writer's Workshop

- Wilbur and Orville Wright
- Thomas Edison
- Florence Nightingale
- Alexander Graham Bell
- Joan of Arc
- John Muir
- Marie Curie
- Isaac Newton
- Albert Einstein
- William Shakespeare
- Georgia O'Keefe
- Claude Monet
- Michelangelo
- Mary Cassatt
- Norman Rockwell
- Rosa Parks
- Harriet Tubman
- Martin Luther King, Jr.
- Nelson Mandela
- Mahatma Gandhi

☐ **Mini-Lesson**

Go visit www.thefamouspeople.com for ideas about people you would like to write about. Make a list of people you see that interest you. Add your list to the Ideas section of your Writer's Notebook.

☐ **Mini-Lesson**

Formal biographies are less casual than autobiographies or personal narratives. They are typically told from third-person point of view. The language is less personal. Typically, you avoid using contractions like can't and won't, personal pronouns like "me" and "I," and colloquialisms or slang language.

☐ **Mini-Lesson**

Any time you aren't telling your own true story, you must be careful not to plagiarize. Plagiarism is stealing someone else's words or work. As you research, take notes about the person in your own words. Use your notes to write the story in your own words again. If you have a book about the person open as you write, there's a lot more chance that you will accidentally plagiarize. Read it, but then close it to take notes and write your story. Your telling of the story should come from you, not the book you read.

EXERCISE: Formal Biography
Use the "Step-By-Step Biography" printable from the Printable Pack to help you write a formal biography.

EXERCISE: Biographical Impact Essay
Rather than writing a biography that begins with birth and ends with death, make your focus about the impact the person had. Center your paragraphs and structure around the idea of the person's legacy and the difference they made rather than a chronological timeline of events. Include at least three ways the person had an impact on the world and discuss each one in a paragraph. Include an introduction and a conclusion to round out your five-paragraph essay.

More True Stories

EXERCISE: Newspaper Article
Newspaper articles typically begin with a single sentence that tells about the big moment, or the overall result of the story. In one line it reveals who, what, where, when, why, and how. Then the author jumps backwards and fills in the details from the beginning.

Local authorities arrested John Jones after he allegedly robbed the Big Gem Jewelry Store in Big Rock City last night using only a rock. Jones had been spotted casing the store over the past few days. He reportedly broke the front glass windows with the rock and entered the store around 10:30 P.M., loaded a single bag with jewels from a single display case, and then exited within five minutes, escaping on foot. Police officers arrived on the scene minutes later and pursued Jones. They captured him almost immediately and placed him under arrest. The rock was found at the scene. The Big Gem Jewelry Company has indicated that they plan to press charges.

Now it's your turn to practice writing some news stories. Write an article about the event below following the pattern of newspaper articles.

Passersby called police when they noticed green slime coming out of the second story windows of the office building.

Once you've practiced on this imaginary story, choose a true story to write an article about. You can get information about current events from the newspaper, internet news, or a television newscast.

EXERCISE: Family News

Think back to a funny memory that your family has shared. Write a newspaper article about the humorous event. Record it on the "Newspaper Template" (with the big ribbon banner at the top of the page) from the Printable Pack. Make sure to include an eye-catching headline.

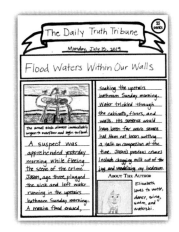

EXERCISE: Newscaster

Write a newscast about an event. Write it in the same voice you would use to tell the story to your friend. Newscasts should be simple and get right to the facts. Make sure to tell the story of the event in order.

- Write your script.
- Practice delivering the newscast.
- Record your news segment on camera.

After the script is written, practice delivering the newscast. When you're prepared, deliver it for a camera. Make sure to dress the part, plan your background, and speak clearly. It might help if you watch several news anchors before you record yourself on camera.

EXERCISE: Obituary

Write an obituary for a famous person who died long ago. In an obituary, you tell about the most important events, people, and places of the person's life. Write one following this formula:

1. Death Announcement - A brief description of how, when, and where the person passed away and any important details.
2. Life Sketch - A brief recounting of the person's life, including important events and experiences with

---

☐ **Mini-Lesson**

Use a newspaper and separate a photograph from its article. Without reading the article at all, practice writing an article about what you think happened based only on the photograph. Have everyone read the article draft out loud, then read the real article out loud.

☐ **Mini-Lesson**

Practice writing a newspaper article about a true event that happened historically. For example, write a short article about building the Great Wall of China, discovering Penicillin, Mt. Vesuvius burying Pompeii, or the bombing of Pearl Harbor during World War II. Choose any event you know about and practice writing a brief newspaper article about it by opening with the big moment and then going back and sharing some details.

☐ **Mini-Lesson**

When you write out words you will be speaking, as in a speech or a newscast, you can use informal language. It is even okay to write fragments rather than complete sentences, especially if you are having a conversation with another person. Write the way you naturally speak if you will be presenting it orally.

☐ **Mini-Lesson**

Sometimes you listen to the stories of others while they are in the revising stage and sometimes you listen while they are in the publishing stage.

While you are listening to others share their stories in the revising stage, think about questions you have for the writer. What things do you wonder? Who do you wish you knew more about? Could you picture the setting in your mind? Ask at least one thoughtful question that will help them as they are revising.

While you are listening to others share their published stories, think about the things you are enjoying about the story. Offer compliments, kudos, and congratulations. Publishing is a time for celebrating and finding the good in the writer. Don't offer suggestions at that point in the writing process.

☐ **Mini-Lesson**

Ask someone older and more experienced than you to help you edit. Sit together and read through your story out loud. Discuss any grammar, spelling, or usage mistakes you can find. Use editing marks and then go back and fix the mistakes you found together. Ask questions and learn from the mistakes to improve for the next time.

family members or friends. You can also include accomplishments or things the person is remembered for.

3. Surviving Family - List of the surviving family members (In your historical obituary this might include people who have since died, but you are imagining that you are writing it at the time of death, so you would list any family members who outlived the subject).

4. Funeral Service Information - This part of the obituary serves as an invitation to the funeral for anyone who wants to pay their respects.

5. Message of Thanks - Often obituaries end with a message of thanks to supporters, friends, neighbors, or anyone who has helped the loved ones of the subject. In addition, sometimes a poem, song lyrics, a scripture, a meaningful quote, or a prayer is penned at the end as part of the message of thanks.

EXERCISE: Historical Story

Research is the key to writing a historical story. If you are going to write a story about a time and place you've never lived in from history, you must do a lot of research to understand what it would have been like to be there. Once you've done your research, most of it stays hidden. Famous author, Ernest Hemingway, described this like an iceberg. The readers only sees what's on the top, but underneath the surface there's a lot of research supporting the story.

Research one story from history and write about the event in story form, with a clear beginning, middle, and end. Include a conflict that must be solved, rising action, and a conclusion.

Step 3: Writing Project

During this unit, you should complete at least one writing project, taking a piece of writing through the entire writing process. By the final week of the unit, if you haven't completed the project already, you should turn your attention to creating one polished piece of writing that uses the things you've practiced along the way.

Choose one topic to write about that you will take all of the way through the writing process. This piece of writing belongs in the Writing section of your Writer's Notebook. You can use something you've already started during this unit, your own idea, or something from the following idea banks. Make sure that you follow each step of the writing process and keep all of your steps to turn in with your finished writing.

- Step #1: Prewrite

- Step #2: Draft
- Step #3: Revise
- Step #4: Edit
- Step #5: Publish

Begin with a prewriting activity, then compose a draft, revise it, edit it with help from someone else, and then publish it. Publishing it could include making a polished final copy, sharing it with someone, creating a book, or creating some form of finished project that is neat and done well. You'll turn in all of your work, from prewrite to publish.

Your project will be evaluated based on the six traits of writing, so make sure you look at your composition through each of those lenses - ideas and content, organization, word choice, sentence fluency, conventions, and voice. Try to incorporate things you learned from the mini-lessons and the exercises you worked on as well. Do your best work.

True Stories Idea Bank

- I have never been more frightened than when . . .
- Write about a time in your life when you struggled with a choice and made the right one.
- What do you consider your greatest accomplishment to date and why?
- Write one characteristic or habit about yourself that you like and describe it. Or write about one thing you don't like about yourself. Incorporate a story that includes the characteristic or habit.
- What is your hobby? Why do you enjoy it?
- Did you ever stick up for someone?
- Describe a bully you've encountered and how you handled it.
- Write about a babysitting experience (either with you as the kid or you as the babysitter).
- Describe a great fort you built for a great game you played as a child.
- Write about an enemy who eventually became your friend.
- Write about a time you cheated and got caught.
- Write about a privilege you earned.
- Tell the story of a stray animal you brought home.
- Did you ever order something that turned out to be a disappointment?
- What is it like to go shopping with your mother?
- Write about a time you performed in front of an audience.
- Write about a difficult decision you had to make.
- Write about learning to skate, ride a bike, climb a tree, turn a cartwheel, or do a trick on a trampoline.

☐ **Mini-Lesson**

As you prepare your piece for publishing, make sure to make it visually appealing as well as correct. In general, published works are colorful, tidy, and correct. They include enough white space to rest your eyes, but not so much that it's distracting. They include illustrations or other visual elements and are pleasant to look at.

Look at something you're working on publishing and discuss together how to make it more visually pleasing.

☐ **Mini-Lesson**

As you are sharing your true story with an audience, make sure to read with feeling. In particular, if it's your own personal story, your sharing voice should sound like you as you speak with your friends and family. Practice reading it enough times that you can speak it naturally and smoothly.

☐ **Mini-Lesson**

For the publishing stage, give your story a title that will catch your reader's eye. Which of these titles would you choose for a story about a frog?

Hopper

Under the Lily Pad

Frogs

Write three possible titles for a story you're working on.

Reminders About Your Writer's Notebook

Besides just the writing project, there should be many small writing samples that are being compiled in the Writer's Notebook from the exercises you worked on over the course of this unit. The Writer's Notebook is a tool for helping writers to grow. Explore it frequently and refer to idea lists and helps as you write.

At least once a week, it would be beneficial for you, the writer, to glance back through the exercises, lists, and mini-lessons to review and make sure that you are on track even though most of this work isn't graded.

Specifically, as you are working on the writing project, utilize your Writer's Notebook. You have anchor charts, exercises, and entries in your Journal - all of these can help you as you complete your project. Take time to review some of the concepts you've been working on during the unit so they can be incorporated into the final writing project. The things you've learned should SHOW in your writing project.

Remember that most of the work in the Writer's Notebook will never be graded, but it is still important. Use what you learned to make your Project, which will be graded, the best that you can make it.

- Did you ever get lost?
- Were you ever locked in or out? What did you do?
- What was it like to spend your first night away from home?
- What was it like to come back home after a long vacation?
- Write about a disappointment you've experienced.
- Write about something minor that turned into a big deal.
- Did you ever win or lose a contest? Tell the story about what happened.
- Write about the time as a child you played in one of the following: tree house, a cornfield, a construction site, a junkyard, an abandoned house or barn, a stream, a cemetery, a swamp, a pasture, or on railroad tracks.
- Did your mom or dad ever make you wear something you hated?
- Write about a time you were talked into something and you regretted it.
- Were you ever in a helicopter, airplane, limousine, race car, hot-air balloon, submarine, or horse-drawn carriage?
- Did you ever forget something really important? What happened as a result?
- Write about an experience in a hospital.
- Were you ever accused of something that you didn't do?
- Write about a disastrous trip or vacation.
- Were you ever given a responsibility that you couldn't handle?
- Were you ever in a fire, flood, tornado, hurricane, blizzard, or another natural disaster?
- Write about a window or something else valuable you broke or lost.
- Did you ever catch fireflies? Crickets? Frogs? Snakes?
- Write about a time you tried to help and ended up making things worse.
- Did you ever break an important promise?
- Write about moving to another city or neighborhood.
- Write about building sandcastles or mud pies.
- Did you ever meet a famous person?
- Write about mowing the lawn, burning leaves, or weeding the garden.
- Write about a day spent in another country.
- Describe a painful experience you had.
- Share the story of a time you've felt totally alone.
- Write about one of your possessions and a story related to it.
- Write a biography of your mother, father, or one of your grandparents.
- Visualize a time when your mother was laughing or you two shared a good laugh and write about it.

- What's the most fun or meaningful memory you have with your father?
- Describe a happy memory of your family.
- Tell the story of a family heirloom.
- Write a story from the life of one of your grandparents.
- Choose a famous person and write a short story that really happened in his or her life.
- Relate the story of a single battle from a real war.
- Tell the story of a real-life celebration that has occurred.
- Tell a true story about one of the holidays you celebrate that happened long before you were born or that you weren't there personally to witness.
- Think of a time that fascinates you from history and research someone who lived at that time. Write their biography.
- Write a short story from the life of someone who inspires you.

Step 4: Evaluating Writing

The purpose of this unit is to write true stories in an interesting way. Finding a plot, describing real settings, and introducing real people are the tasks. As you evaluate the project, look for those three things. You can also look for interesting descriptions, figurative language, and story elements like foreshadowing and flashbacks. The writer should have also chosen some emotional or impactful moments to show, not tell.

As you evaluate the writing project, you will be using the "6 Traits of Writing Rubric" from the Printable Pack. In addition, you will be looking for each step of the entire writing process. For example, your child will turn in a prewriting activity, a draft that shows both revisions and edits, as well as a finished, published piece. The publishing step should involve sharing the project in some way - reading it aloud to family, presenting it at dinner time, video chatting to show it off to grandparents, or sharing a video presentation on the internet of the writer sharing his or her writing. Sharing is a time for positive feedback and celebration.

Creating a positive buzz about the published piece will create a motivating, growth atmosphere in your Writer's Workshop. As you evaluate, remember that the process is just as important as the product, so watch for successes in the process as well. The final score will be out of 50 points - 20 for the process and 30 for the final project. You can write rubric scores as well as comments down on the "Writing Report Card" printable from the Printable Pack.

Breakdown of Possible Points

- 5 points for a complete prewriting activity
- 5 points for a completed draft
- 5 points for revisions
- 5 points for edits
- 30 points for the finished writing project

The 30 points for the finished project is further broken down into each of the six traits of writing as shown on the "6 Traits of Writing Rubric" from the Printable Pack.

6 Traits of Writing Rubric - True Stories

Your comments should be specifically focused on the purposes of this unit and the skills you were working on throughout the unit.

What was done well? Is the writer understanding the writing process? What should be improved on? Are there any repeated mistakes to address?

Point out a clear strength.

Comments mean more than scores, so make sure to give clear feedback.

Key Concepts

By the end of this unit your kids should be familiar with these concepts and ideas:

Researching, evaluating, and citing sources

Primary versus secondary sources

Taking notes

Organizing information into webs, outlines, and report categories

Thesis statements

Evidence

Comparing and contrasting

Writing a basic report

Writing a basic essay

More Mini-Lesson Ideas

Along with the sidebars, try these mini-lesson ideas:

- Writer's Workshop links found in Layers of Learning catalog
- Lessons from any grammar workbook
- Every-Day Edits from Education World website
- Sentence diagramming
- Copying great sentences from master writers
- Mad Libs
- Correcting a repeated error from your writing
- Practicing expanding sentences by adding details
- Combining sentences by making two or three into a single sentence

The mini-lesson sidebars in this unit have check boxes so you can keep track of which ones you have completed.

Reports & Essays

Reports and essays involve expository writing. Expository means writing that is intended to explain something. During this unit, you will be explaining true things. Expository writing is usually filled with facts and figures and it has a very logical, organized order. Reports and essays are a specific kind of expository writing that allow you to choose any true topic at all, learn about it, then record what you know.

A report is a written way to organize information about a topic, whether it's a person, an animal, a place, an event, a book or movie, a concept, or anything else you're interested in. Reports are usually divided into sections, with each section covering a topic. For example, a report on an animal might include sections about its habitat, diet, reproduction, lifespan, and behavior. Because of the way they are broken into sections, reports typically include elements like headers, boxes of information, graphics or charts, and categories. A report can be created on a simple sheet of paper, a word processor, a poster, a brochure, or a variety of other projects and 3-D displays.

Unlike reports, essays usually don't involve visual displays or separate boxes, sections, and headers. An essay is composed in organized paragraphs, usually on a word processor. Essays are considered more formal pieces of writing. They include an underlying thesis statement at the end of the first paragraph to direct the purpose and organization of the essay. They often give credit to sources and show where information was gathered by including a bibliography or works cited page.

As you choose exercises from this unit, be aware that you can mix and match ideas you come across. You might really like the way the animal report is organized in a folder with envelope pockets, but you would prefer to write about a country you've been studying in geography. Go for it! You are the writer. Perhaps you would prefer to write a formal essay about a book you've read instead of a creating a report. If you have something you're interested in writing about and can choose a format you enjoy, all the better. The ideas within this guide can be used for many topics, so as you write, just choose a topic and a format and start writing.

Choose several exercises from this unit, and then go on and select a writing project that you will take all of the way through the writing process. We recommend working on some exercises from each section - Expository Writing Skills, Reports, and Essays - before beginning your writing project. Younger kids may have a greater focus on reports while

more advanced writers can delve into the realm of essays.

Step 1: Mini-Lesson

After handwriting or typing practice has concluded, begin each day of Writer's Workshop with a mini-lesson. You will find some within the sidebars of this unit. You can also use a worksheet from a grammar workbook or practice editing, copying, or diagramming sentences. During writing time, watch for weak areas or mistakes being made and present a mini-lesson the next day to help correct those and improve writing skills in small, continuous ways.

The mini-lesson should take five to ten minutes and always have a positive happy spin, free from criticism. Not every mini-lesson needs to be kept in your Writer's Notebook. Most are merely for practice.

Step 2: Writing

Now it's time to really begin writing. Most of your time during Writer's Workshop should be spent writing. Practicing is the key to improving. You can use your writing time to free write your own ideas in your Journal anytime, or use the exercises below to practice writing skills and find inspiration for things to write about. Select as many exercises as you would like to do over the month, making sure you leave time to complete at least one writing project that will go all of the way through the writing process before the month is over. The exercises will also go in your Journal section of your Writer's Notebook. If you decide to take something from your Journal through the writing process and turn it into your writing project, move it from your Journal to the Writing section of your Writer's Notebook.

A few tips and reminders:

- You can repeat the units and the exercises in subsequent years, so don't ever feel pressured to get to all of them, and feel free to repeat ones you enjoy.
- Often a single exercise can be presented to all of your children, no matter their ages or abilities. They will naturally write at the level they are at and, as they practice, will grow as writers.
- As you progress through the exercises, watch for something that sparks interest and could become the writing project. Feel free to jump to the idea bank at the end of the unit anytime as well. If there's spare time after the project is published, return to more exercises.
- Your family may all be in different places in the writing process. That's perfectly fine. Remember, your Writer's Workshop is a garden and everyone is growing their own patch. You can all lend a hand to help each gardener's

☐ Mini-Lesson

Reports and essays are both expository writing - pieces that explain true subjects. The formats are a little different though.

A report is broken down into sections. Each section has its own header followed by information about the topic of that section. For example, a country report may have sections about geography, economy, and culture. Reports often include illustrations, diagrams, charts, maps, and other visuals.

Essays use paragraphs instead of sections. Every essay begins with an introductory paragraph and ends with a concluding paragraph. In between, there are body paragraphs that discuss parts of the essay topic. All of the paragraphs relate directly back to the overall topic of the essay. Transition sentences are used between the paragraphs to connect the ideas. There are a variety of formats for essays, but they generally include typed documents with paragraphs.

☐ Mini-Lesson

Unlike stories, poetry, and journaling, reports and essays stem from research more than imagination. Add a page to your Ideas section of your Writer's Notebook and begin a list of true topics you might want to write a report or essay about. Add to your list as often as you get an idea.

Imitate this sentence:

Although many people believe dolphins are fish, they are actually water-dwelling mammals.

Write your own version of the sentence following the pattern:

Although *many people believe _____, they are actually _____.*

In the sentence, **although** is a subordinating conjunction. This means that the clause needs a main clause to complete the thought. Notice that a comma separates the two clauses. When you place a subordinating clause before the main clause, you must separate them with a comma.

If you reverse the order of the two clauses, placing the main clause first, you do not need the comma.

Dolphins are water-dwelling mammals although many people believe they are fish.

Can you write a version of your sentence that doesn't need a comma?

Mini-Lesson

Go back and review the "Fiction/Nonfiction" anchor chart from Writer's Workshop Jump Start.

patch thrive, but you won't all grow the same crop.

It's time to write! Choose some exercises and jump right in!

Expository Writing Skills

EXERCISE: Explore Your Library
Go visit your local library. Take a tour if possible. In particular, learn where each of the sections in the library is located and the kinds of resources you will find in each. After you are familiar with your library, use the "Explore Your Library" printable from the Printable Pack to get to know your way around your library.

EXERCISE: Fact and Fiction Pairs
Read two books about the same topic, one that is factual and one that is fictional. For example, you could read a nonfictional book about caterpillars and then read *The Very Hungry Caterpillar* by Eric Carle or a book about frogs and toads and then read *Frog and Toad are Friends* by Arnold Lobel.

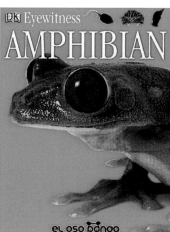

Write two paragraphs (young children could just write two sentences). The first paragraph will describe similarities within the two books and the second paragraph will describe differences. You may notice similarities or differences between the subjects, the writing styles, the presentations, or the truthfulness of each book. Have a discussion about what you found, pointing out differences you noticed about fictional versus nonfictional writing.

EXERCISE: Brainstorm
Brainstorming is a really excellent prewriting tool for any nonfiction writing. Write any topic that interests you at the top of the "Brainstorm About" printable from the Printable

Reports & Essays

Pack. Now write down all the things you know about the topic all over the page. Anything that comes to your mind should go on the page. This creates an idea bank and can help you see patterns, find sub-topics, and see areas you might need to research further to fill in. Add the printable to the Writing Helps section of your Writer's Notebook so you can use it again and again.

EXERCISE: Web

Choose from one of the two "Web" charts from the Printable Pack. Write your topic in the center and the big ideas about the topic you will write about surrounding it. You may have to do some research to fill in the web.

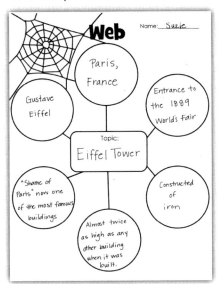 

Notice that you can add extra lines for details you come across in your research.

The web for beginners contains only a topic box and circles surrounding it for big ideas about your topic. You can fill them in with interesting facts you find out. If you're using the more advanced web that shows squares surrounding each big idea circle, you'll fill in details about that big idea in the boxes adjacent to it. These branches of the web will later become paragraphs or sections if you decide to use this prewrite to draft an essay or report.

EXERCISE: K-W-L

K-W-L stands for Know, Wonder, Learned. Use the "K-W-L Chart" from the Printable Pack for this exercise. As you begin to research, think about what you already know about your subject. Write as many things as you can in the Know column. Then write down the things you wonder, or want to find out as you research. While you're reading, add the things you learn to the Learned column. Your chart can give you ideas of what to include in your report or essay.

☐ Mini-Lesson

Topic knowledge may be the most important contributor to writing successful essays and reports. If we know about something inside and out, have ideas about it, and are interested in it, writing about it becomes easy. If we feel we have little to say or contribute, writing feels impossible. If you're stuck, go do some research. Watch a video or read a book about your subject. Talk through it with someone. Learn as much as you can before you try to write about it. Research is the most important prewriting you will do in expository writing.

Can you brainstorm at least ten ways to learn about something?

☐ Mini-Lesson

Together, discuss the rules of your home for researching online. What can you do to be safe online and find good information? Discuss what to do if you come across something inappropriate online.

☐ Mini-Lesson

Verbs are action words that describe what a person or thing is doing or being. Every single sentence requires a verb.

Write some true sentences that use strong verbs. Underline each verb. Circle the person or object that is performing the action.

☐ Mini-Lesson

Create an anchor chart about how to annotate texts. Add it to the Writing Helps section of your Writer's Notebook.

☐ Mini-Lesson

Reports and essays are usually written in past tense. Why do you think that is?

Divide a sheet of paper in half. On one side, write a list of present tense verbs. On the other side, rewrite each of them in past tense.

On the back of your paper, practice writing sentences in past tense using some of the verbs you wrote.

Make sure that as you write your reports and essays you stay in past tense to avoid confusion by switching tenses.

EXERCISE: Highlighting and Annotating

Reading an article, highlighting the important points, and annotating it, are all important skills you need for expository writing. As you highlight, make sure not to highlight more than about 30% of the words. If everything is highlighted it doesn't accurately draw your eye to the most important points. As you highlight, annotate the article. Annotating simply means adding notes. You will read what is written and add notes about it in your own words. You might note things you wonder, connect it with prior knowledge you have, or just write some of your own thoughts about the article.

Practice highlighting and annotating "Frog Hunters" from the Printable Pack. It's an article about frog tongues and saliva. Aim to highlight the most important points, which should include no more than 30% of the article. Add notes around the margins, on note cards, or on a separate sheet of paper. Try to think of what information you would want to include if you were writing your own report on frogs.

EXERCISE: Finding Facts

Choose any children's nonfiction book about a topic that interests you. Gather paint chips and writing utensils. As you read the book, write down facts you find in your reading on the colorful squares of the paint chips. Read through the facts out loud together, then have each person offer an opinion about the topic instead of a fact.

Discuss the differences between facts and opinions. Facts provide evidence in reports and essays. Opinions should only be expressed sparingly. They are usually reserved for persuasive writing or opinion essays. When you state an

opinion in expository writing, you must be clear that you aren't stating it as a fact.

EXERCISE: Inferring

Inferring, or making an inference, means to deduce or conclude. Imagine putting together a puzzle. Each piece shows just a bit of the picture. It isn't until we put the pieces together that we can really see what the puzzle is about. As you write about topics, it's your job to learn about the topic through the research others have done and then make your own inferences. You will read books and articles, watch movies, or listen to speakers. Think about what you have learned and add your own ideas to it.

Use the "Making Inferences" printable from the Printable Pack. Write things you researched about your topic on the puzzle pieces, then make inferences and fill in the border with your own conclusions about the topic.

EXERCISE: Labeling

Draw or print a picture or diagram. Write labels showing the different parts or features of the picture. This can be a stand-alone project for younger learners or an element added to a larger report for older learners. Plants, animals, cells, architectural details, insects, the human body, parts of a castle, areas of the brain, parts of a camera, landmarks within a country, or the planets within the solar system are all good labeling pictures to begin with.

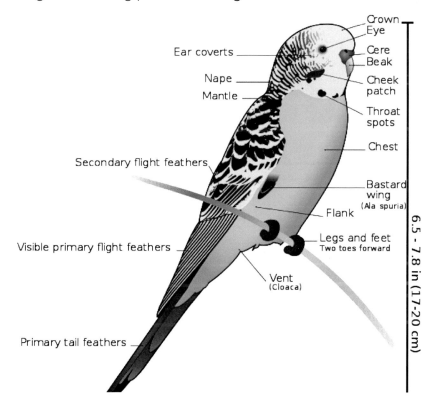

☐ **Mini-Lesson**

As you research, you need to be aware of what kinds of sources you are reading.

Most high school and college papers require sources that are scholarly journals or are peer-reviewed, meaning that other experts have also read and written about them.

One of the most important habits good researchers have is finding out about the author that created the source they are using.

Pick up a book, article, movie, or another source and find out who is behind it. Besides just knowing the name of the author, you should find out what the person's background and expertise is. Learn what else they have written or accomplished.

☐ **Mini-Lesson**

The infinitive form of a verb is its simplest form. It is usually preceded by the word to.

*The woman needed **to buy** groceries.*

*Cars honked and angry drivers tried **to yell** even louder than the horn chorus.*

Can you brainstorm ten infinitive forms of verbs?

Just think of to _____ and fill in the blank with a verb.

☐ Mini-Lesson

The verbs *was* and *were* tell about something that happened. Use *was* if the sentence tells about one person and *were* if the sentence tells about two or more people.

Practice writing some sentences that tell about real people. When you write about one person, use *was*. When you write about more than one, use *were*.

Which form would you use with *children* as the subject? Write one more sentence using *children* with its correct form.

☐ Mini-Lesson

There is no hard and fast rule for how many sources you should use to write a report or essay. A good rule of thumb is to use as many sources as you have pages in your essay. A simple report may have one to three sources, but a ten-page essay should have at least eight to ten sources.

☐ Mini-Lesson

The entries in a bibliography are always listed in alphabetical order by the author's last name. In bibliographic entries, list the author's last name followed by a comma, and then the author's first name. Practice writing the author's names from some of the books you own.

Whitman, Walt

EXERCISE: Researching

Researching is finding out information from a variety of sources. Choose a topic and find one of each of these that discusses your topic.

- An article
- A video
- A book
- A website
- A quote
- A diagram, illustration, visual, or map

Gather each of the resources you found and read about your topic, making notes about interesting things you learn as you conduct your research.

EXERCISE: Bibliography

Not all reports and essays require a bibliography, but if you are doing formal writing or want to quote a source, you can include a bibliography with your report or essay. A bibliography is a list of the sources you used to research. Any book, movie, article, poem, interview, website, or other source will have its own entry in your bibliography.

There are lots of different formats for reference pages. If you are writing for a teacher or company, they will tell you which format to use. You might be asked to use MLA (if you're writing a literature, English, history, or art paper), APA (if you're writing about a science or math topic), Chicago, or another format. Some teachers will ask you to use a Works Cited and a Works Consulted page, which is a bibliography that separates works you directly used and others you read but didn't cite directly. There are lots of formats and the exact requirements for each one changes over time, so it's always best to look up a current style guide online to help you format your bibliography in the most current way.

Use the "Bibliography" and "Bibliography Helps" printables from the Printable Pack to practice writing a basic bibliography. You can also add the "Bibliography Helps" anchor chart to the Writing Helps section of your Writer's Notebook and refer to it whenever you are creating a bibliography.

EXERCISE: Research Note Cards

Note cards are a perfect way to record the things you learn about in your research. You can write facts, quotes, and data on the note cards and label each one with the source and page number it came from. Then you can physically sort the note cards by topic or paragraph and still know

where the information came from. Physically sorting the note cards can even help you see what your paragraphs might be about as you look for common threads across all the sources you read.

> Long Ago in a Castle.   Source. #3
>
> Castles were built by lords so the people in nearby villages could shelter there in case there was danger.
>
>   Pg. 7

At the top of each note card, write the title of the book and assign it a source number that corresponds with your bibliography, a list of your sources. At the bottom, write the page number where you got the information from. In the center of the card, write the information you learned. For each source you could have one or more note cards, depending on what you learned from the source. If you quote directly from the source, add quotation marks around the quote on the note card so you will know it is a direct quote and can give the author credit for it.

EXERCISE: Making Connections

An important skill you need to develop to write strong reports and essays is making connections as you research. There are three kinds of connections you're looking for as you research. The first kind is connecting text to text. This means that you will read a variety of sources about the same topic and compare the information. If you read two articles on a subject, they may or may not agree on the information they present. Here are two quotes about the former leader of China, Emperor Mao Zedong, each one from a different article.

> *"Mao is the George Washington figure, the founder of the People's Republic of China, the great unifier of his ancient, far-flung and multifarious people."*
>
> *-Mao Zedong Remembered: China's Multifaceted Deep-Thinking Leader by BBC News, 25 December 2013*

> *"In an attempt to re-assert his authority, Mao launched the 'Cultural Revolution' in 1966, aiming to purge the country of 'impure' elements and revive the revolutionary spirit. One-and-a-half million people died and much of the country's cultural heritage was destroyed. In September 1967, with many cities on the verge of anarchy, Mao sent in the army to restore order."*
>
> *- Mao Zedong (1893 - 1976), Historic Figures, bbc.co.uk, 2014*

So who was Mao Zedong? A great leader and unifier or a

☐ **Mini-Lesson**

Read an article about an animal together and practice taking notes on note cards with each person responsible for making several cards. Assign a different color for each topic:

- Appearance and characteristics
- Life cycle and other biological information
- Habitat and diet
- Enemies and threats

Discuss together how the note cards' color stacks can become sections in a report or paragraphs in an essay.

☐ **Mini-Lesson**

In addition to periods at the ends of sentences, periods are also used in other places. For example, websites use periods to separate the parts of a website.

www.layers-of-learning.com

If you use a website at the end of a sentence, you also put a period after it.

☐ **Mini-Lesson**

The correct order to research for a report or essay:

- Choose a topic
- Gather sources
- Make a bibliography
- Read sources and make note cards with information
- Organize information

☐ **Mini-Lesson**

Avoid plagiarism when you write about true topics by always giving credit to your sources. If you find information from a book or another source, just make sure you give the author credit and tell your readers where they can find it by creating a bibliography and using quotes or citations to show where the information came from. In general, if you use more than five words directly from a source, they should be surrounded by quotation marks.

☐ **Mini-Lesson**

The prewriting step of a report or essay is the most important step and often requires the most time.

Don't begin drafting until you have finished your research and made an outline or plan for your essay.

Choose a topic you're already learning about in history, geography, science, or art. Gather some sources and practice researching and organizing the information. Even if you don't write a complete essay about every topic you research, you'll learn a lot just by doing this important prewriting step.

Create a note sheet or note cards about the topic you chose that you're learning about to show your research.

man who murdered his own people and destroyed their heritage? If you are reading both of these articles, you might need to dig a little deeper. Even less controversial topics will contain information that needs to be sorted through and evaluated as you do research. As you connect texts, find similarities and differences.

The second connection you'll be looking for is text to self. This is where you read something and make a connection to your own life or experiences.

This is an excerpt from an article about black bears:

> *"American black bears are omnivores, with their diets varying greatly depending on season and location. They typically live in largely forested areas, but do leave forests in search of food. Sometimes they become attracted to human communities because of the immediate availability of food."*
>
> *-American Black Bear, Ursus Americanus, Nature, PBS. org*

Instantly, I made a connection to an experience I had while camping. When we brought our trash to the garbage dump near the campground we stayed at, we discovered a number of black bears that had wandered away from the forest and were sitting on the garbage piles, eating the scraps they could find from the dump. I had actually witnessed first-hand what the article was talking about.

The third connection you need to make is text to world. This is when you read information and spot a way that it relates on a larger scale - to your community, your nation, or the world.

Here's an excerpt from a book about medieval castles:

> *"From the mid 13th century, castles were built with rings of stone walls, one inside the other. These are called concentric castles. The outer wall was fairly close to and lower than the inner, sometimes so low that it seemed no more than a barrier against siege machines (such as catapults). But it meant that archers on the inner walls could shoot over the heads of those on the outer, bringing twice the fire power to bear on an enemy. If attackers broke through the outer wall, they would still be faced with the inner wall."*
>
> *-Castle, by Christopher Gravett, Dorling Kindersley Publishers, 1994*

Although we don't use a lot of castles these days, I can connect the ideas of lines of defense to the modern world. Beyond physical protections like locks, gated communities,

and security systems, in the modern world we also fortify ourselves electronically. We use protected networks, passwords, and firewalls as safety and security.

Read a book or an article about something that interests you. While you are reading, find ways to connect the text to another text, to yourself, and to the world. Write down your connections on the "Making Connections" printable from the Printable Pack. Little ones may enjoy writing their connections on paper chain links instead of on the printable to show how they can connect ideas together.

EXERCISE: Evaluating Sources - Little Learners

As you read books and look at websites, it's important to know who wrote them and why they were written. Anyone can write a book or make a website, and you can't believe information just because you see it printed somewhere.

Before you trust a book or website, you should always find out who wrote it and why. Look for an About the Author page in a nonfiction book you are reading. With help from a parent, search online for more information about the author. Find out who he or she is, what other books s/he has written, and what life experiences have made the person qualified to write about the topic.

Use the "Who Wrote This?" printable from the Printable Pack to write down some information about the author of the book you read.

EXERCISE: Evaluating Sources - Older Learners

An important research skill includes evaluating your sources. There are millions of published books in the world and even more websites. That number continues to grow day by day. When we are so inundated by information, an important skill becomes sifting through it and evaluating it to determine how valuable and accurate it is.

Use the C.R.A.A.P. test to help you evaluate a source. C.R.A.A.P. is an acronym for currency, relevance, authority, accuracy, and purpose. As you read a book, article, or website, consider each of those aspects and answer the questions on the test to help you evaluate your source.

Currency - Look at the date the resource was produced and think about the impact that has on the information. If you are learning about Russia, you probably don't want a source that was made more than twenty years ago because that country has changed a lot since then. However, some of the most interesting books I've read about World War II were written during and shortly after the

---

☐ **Mini-Lesson**

Be really careful as you research online. Anyone can create a website. Anyone can write anything. Just because you read something online does not make it true.

Go visit a website and use these questions to help you evaluate it:

Author:

- Is there an author listed?
- Is there an "About" page?
- What else has the author written?

Domain:

- Do you recognize the site name?
- Is the website littered with advertisements?
- How does the url end? (.com, .net, .edu, .gov, .org) What does the ending tell you about the website?

Purpose:

- Do the stories from the site seems shocking or sensational?
- Are they selling something?

Triangle of Proof:

- Can you find at least two other reputable sources that say the same thing? (three total)
- Are the images original or were they taken from another source?

☐ Mini-Lesson

While evaluating web sources, watch for these red flags:

- Websites with lots of ads and pop-ups.
- Ending urls with odd suffixes (.com.co).
- Lots of spelling and grammatical errors within the articles.
- Sites that use ALL CAPS a lot.
- Sites that use lots of exclamation points in a row!!!!!!!!!
- Sites that act like they are giving information but entice you to click on links or advertisements that take you elsewhere.
- Sites that do not divulge who wrote the information.
- Articles that include pictures that are unrelated to the article.

☐ Mini-Lesson

Use "two" to mean the number. Use "too" to mean more than enough. Use "to" to mean toward or to do something.

Amy had two puppies.

There are too many cookies for me to eat.

Let's go to the beach.

Can you write your own sentences that include two, too, and to?

war. First person accounts of people who experienced the topic are very valuable.

- What date was it published or produced?
- Has it been updated or revised?
- Does your topic require current information?

Relevance - The questions about relevance examine how much your source applies to your specific topic. Imagine you are writing about echolocation. You might read a really interesting book about bats that briefly mentions echolocation. You can use that source, but it won't be enough on its own to cover your topic.

- Does the source relate to your topic?
- Who is the intended audience?
- Have you compared it with other sources about your topic and found it to be valuable?
- Does it include quotes or information you can include in your report or essay?

Authority - This is a look at who actually wrote your source.

- Who is the author?
- What credentials does he or she have? This doesn't necessarily mean someone needs a college doctorate in your topic, but if I check out a book about welding, I would want to know it was written by someone who has actually welded.
- Who is the publisher, source, or sponsor?
- If it's a website, is there clear contact information? Does the URL (.com, .edu, .gov, .org, .net) reveal anything about the source?

Accuracy - Does the information seem reliable, truthful, and correct?

- Is there evidence?
- What sources did the author use?
- Does the language feel overly emotional or biased?
- Do other sources back up the information?

Purpose - Why does this source exist? For what purpose was it published?

- Does the source sell, persuade, teach, inform, or entertain?
- Are there underlying political, ideological, cultural, religious, personal, or institutional biases?
- Are the purposes of the author clear?

Look at some books about a topic and go through the questions on the C.R.A.A.P. test. Evaluate a source of your choice using the "C.R.A.A.P. Test" printable from the

Printable Pack. Add it to the Writing Helps section of your Writer's Notebook so you can refer to it as you evaluate other sources. Use the C.R.A.A.P. test for each source you use when you write a report or essay for your writing project this month and turn it in along with your prewrite, draft, revisions, and final draft.

EXERCISE: Primary and Secondary Sources

All sources are either primary sources or secondary sources. A primary source is one that was created by someone who experienced the topic or event first-hand. They represent original thinking. Primary sources can include:

- Autobiographies
- Newspaper articles written by people who witnessed an event
- Journal entries
- Speeches, letters, and interviews by people who were involved
- Original research or data
- Photographs, audio recordings, or videos of an event
- Original artwork, poetry, literature

Secondary sources are a step removed from the event. If I were to write a book on World War II, no matter how much research I did or how expert I was on the topic, it would be a secondary source because I was not alive during World War II and didn't witness the events that took place. Secondary sources include:

- Most books about a topic
- Newspaper articles written by people who didn't actually witness the event
- Scholarly articles
- Documentaries
- Analysis of research or data
- Textbooks
- Biographies

Write the words "Primary Sources" and "Secondary Sources" on sheets of paper, one per sheet. Each player holds a flyswatter or another swatting tool (like a spatula or paper fan) Read aloud a source from the bulleted list above. Each kid tries to quickly swat the correct option - primary or secondary source. Score a point for each correct swat as you practice classifying sources.

EXERCISE: Outlining

Writing outlines is a way to organize your information. Once you have written an outline, you'll find that writing an essay is easy. The outline is a detailed plan of what will go within

---

☐ Mini-Lesson

Make a primary and secondary source anchor chart. Divide a sheet of card stock into two columns and write down a list of primary sources on one side and a list of secondary sources on the other side. Use the lists in the Primary and Secondary Sources exercise to help you with ideas of kinds of sources to add to each list.

☐ Mini-Lesson

Outlining is an essential prewriting step for an essay. Once you have a strong outline, the writing is easy. You can write simple phrases or complete sentences in your outline. Whichever you choose, be consistent throughout the outline.

There are five steps to writing a strong outline.

1. Define your topic and your purpose. Make sure everything you add in your outline meets the topic and purpose.

2. Create a list of main ideas and then let those main ideas become your highest-level topics.

3. Organize the main ideas in an order that makes sense.

4. Flush out your main ideas with quotes, facts, examples, and other research.

5. Look over the outline and make sure you covered your topic well. Use the outline as you draft your essay.

Writer's Workshop

☐ Mini-Lesson

The standard order of an outline is:

I. Roman numerals (I, II, III, IV, V, etc.)
  A. Capital letters (A, B, C, etc.)
    1. Arabic numerals (1, 2, 3, etc.)
      a. Small letters (a, b, c, etc.)
        i. Small Roman numerals (i, ii, iii, iv, v, etc.)

☐ Mini-Lesson

As you write reports and essays, your evidence will back up what you write. These are some evidence based terms you can include:

- For instance . . .
- One reason why . . .
- Because . . .
- For example . . .
- The author said . . .
- On page ___ . . .
- A study showed . . .

☐ Mini-Lesson

Days of the week, months of the year, and holidays are special days that are capitalized because they are proper nouns. Write sentences about your favorite day, month, and holiday. Make sure you use capital letters on each proper noun.

each paragraph of your report or essay.

Each Roman numeral represents a paragraph and is aligned left on the page. Each capital letter represents a topic you will include within the paragraph. Under the letters are details that are written next to numerals that are even further indented. You continue to break down the information with further numbering, indenting each level further than the previous one. You may add or omit any of the example or detail hierarchy levels on your outline, depending on the information you want to include. Everything listed under any level must relate to the big topics above it.

Here's the basic format for an outline:

I. Introduction - Include a hook to get readers interested
  A. Introduction to topic #1
  B. Introduction to topic #2
  C. Introduction to topic #3
  D. Thesis statement

II. 1st Topic
  A. Evidence #1
    1. Examples or details
    2. Examples or details
  B. Evidence #2
  C. Evidence #3
    1. Examples or details
      a. Even more details
      b. Even more details
    2. Examples or details

III. 2nd Topic
  A. Evidence #1
    1. Examples or details
    2. Examples or details
  B. Evidence #2
  C. Evidence #3
    1. Examples or details
      a. Even more details
        i. More specifics
        ii. More specifics
      b. Even more details
      c. Even more details
    2. Examples or details
  D. Evidence #4

IV. 3rd Topic
  A. Evidence #1
  B. Evidence #2
  C. Evidence #3
    1. Examples or details

2. Examples or details

V. Conclusion - Restate your main points
   A. Sum up your conclusions
   B. Apply what you wrote or explain why it matters
   C. Tie it back into the introduction

An outline isn't a prison; it's a map to guide you in organizing your ideas in a format your reader can follow. As you create an outline it will help you structure your essay with clarity and focus. Outlines also help you write more efficiently.

Use two printables: the "Basic Outline Format" and the "Essay Outline" from the Printable Pack. The first one is a reference for you to add to the Writing Helps section of your Writer's Notebook. The second one is a blank outline form to practice creating an outline.

Choose a topic that interests you and write an outline. Add or eliminate levels of details, examples, and specifics as needed to fit your topic. For some topics, you may use all of the levels of hierarchy down to the lowercase Roman numerals and on others you may not go beyond the capital letters or plain numerals listed. You may even make assertions without any supporting evidence at all, but you will come to know through practice that the more you include specifics and examples, the more compelling your essays will be.

EXERCISE: Thesis Statements

Thesis statements sum up the central message of your essay. If you had to tell someone using only a single sentence what an entire essay is about, that is a thesis statement. They should be direct, clear, and detailed. They often touch on the main points of each essay paragraph. In the revised thesis statements below, can you spot what each body paragraph of each essay will be about?

Avoid:

Being too general

- Original: Europe is a cool continent.
- Revised: Europe has an interesting history, varied landscapes, and many unique cultures.

Pronouncing your topic without saying much else.

- Original: I will talk about fairy tales.
- Revised: Fairy tales provide insights into cultural beliefs, societal values, and individual psychology.

Trying to cover too many topics.

☐ **Mini-Lesson**

Here are some more tips for thesis statements:

Avoid merely announcing the topic as your thesis statement. Instead, tell about your topic from your specific angle.

Original: In this paper, I will discuss the relationship between fairy tales and early childhood.

Revised: More than just empty stories for kids, fairy tales shed light on the psychology of young children.

Avoid making universal judgments that oversimplify complex issues.

Original: We must save the whales.

Revised: Because our planet's health may depend upon biological diversity, we should save the whales.

Avoid merely reporting a fact. Say more than what is already proven fact.

Original: Hoover's administration was rocked by scandal.

Revised: The many scandals of Hoover's administration revealed basic problems with the Republican party's nominating process.

Take turns throwing out a topic and having everyone write a thesis statement about each topic. Read each aloud and make suggestions about how to improve each one.

☐ Mini-Lesson

One of the six traits of writing is organization. Part of organization in reports and essays includes supporting all of your claims with evidence. You need to have facts, specific examples, statistics, descriptions, or anecdotes.

Practice gathering evidence. Pretend you are writing an essay about careers at NASA and this is your thesis statement: Beyond just astronauts, NASA hires people from many fields in all kinds of careers.

Go visit NASA's Featured Careers website and find evidence to back up your thesis. Find some facts, examples, quotes, and more. Write a paragraph that includes the thesis statement and incorporates the evidence you found.

☐ Mini-Lesson

To show the evidence you found, include some of these phrases and fill in the author's name or source title in each blank:

- According to _____ . . .
- _____ shows it is evident that . . .
- For instance, _____ says . . .
- _____ offered proof that . . .
- _____ demonstrated . . .
- _____ claims that . . .
- _____ concludes that . . .

- Original: The Hunger Games includes lots of themes like revolution, survival, love, identity, power, and materialism.
- Revised: The Hunger Games showcases the basic ingredients needed for a successful revolution - a common cause, a unifying figure, and individuals who are willing to sacrifice themselves for the benefit of all.

Trying to cover too few topics.

- Original: People should stop smoking because cigarettes are expensive.
- Revised: Smoking is expensive, addictive, and can cause cancer and other illnesses.

Practice writing five clear, direct, focused thesis statements about these topics:

- The theme of a book you enjoy.
- A social cause you believe would benefit the world or your community.
- Character traits you think are essential for success
- An interesting place in the world.
- A person, animal, holiday, or event that is important to your family, society, or culture.

EXERCISE: Evidence

Presenting evidence is an important part of expository writing. If you are going to write something and claim it is true, you need evidence to back it up. Here are some kinds of evidence you might include:

- Examples and anecdotes
- Quotations or information from experts or other writers
- Facts, statistics, or objective information
- Information from sources like books, websites, articles, and movies

As you write a report or essay, you will need to use evidence. The best reports and essays incorporate several kinds of evidence. Think of yourself like a detective. You need to find evidence for what you are saying in your report or essay.

Write the word EVIDENCE on a file folder. Just like a detective, gather evidence to put in your folder as you prepare to write about a topic. Search for evidence in books, articles, and other sources and write down facts, statistics, quotes, examples, and other information about your topic. You can staple the pages in or hole punch them and attach them with brads. Make sure to note where each bit of evidence came from. You will get better and better at searching for evidence as you practice this skill

using lots of topics, each one in its own evidence folder.

Once you've found a topic that really interests you and you have been able to gather plenty of evidence about it, that's a good indication that it would make a good report or essay to use as your writing project for the month.

EXERCISE: Incorporating Evidence

Once you've read information about your topic and gathered evidence, you need to include that evidence in your report or essay. There are a few ways to do this, and often using a combination is the best way to write a rounded, complete essay.

Read "Kangaroos" from the Printable Pack, then read the examples of incorporating evidence below.

- Use a direct quote. Make sure to attribute it to the author or source and put his or her exact words in quotation marks.

  According to kangaroo expert, Ken G. Roo, "They can leap up to 30 feet in a single bound, which is about as far as a bus is long or twice as far as a giraffe is tall."

- Paraphrase or summarize the information given.

  Kangaroos protect and defend themselves in lots of ways. Working and living together in large groups, they fight, kick, bite, and pound on the ground to scare off any predator who is threatening them.

Choose your own quote from the "Kangaroos" printable. Introduce the quote and make sure to surround the exact words with quotation marks. Also, write your own sentences

---

☐ **Mini-Lesson**

An important job you have as a writer is making inferences. An inference is a conclusion based on evidence and reasoning. Think of yourself as a detective. Just as a detective must find clues and put them together to solve a case, we can take the clues from books we read and videos we watch and put them together to understand things. Sometimes the sources we explore will not always agree with each other. Books and articles and movies are created by people who have opinions, their own experiences and ideas, and biases. We read a variety of ideas and add our own to them, then come to conclusions.

Read several articles about the same topic and make some inferences. Draw conclusions about the topic.

☐ **Mini-Lesson**

Practice writing quotes. Introduce each one by stating who is speaking, inserting a comma, and then including the quote within quotation marks. Place the end punctuation mark within the quotes.

Albert Einstein claimed, "Imagination is more important than knowledge. Knowledge is limited. Imagination encircles the world."

☐ Mini-Lesson

Writing doesn't have to be dull just because it's true. The same interesting descriptions you used in other writing can be incorporated into expository writing.

If I were writing about World War I, I could use personification to describe death, by using the word grasped, something that is normally done by a person:

Death grasped the soldiers one by one as the bullets whizzed near the trenches.

Can you write three examples of personification about these three topics?

- Fish
- Forests
- Volcanoes

☐ Mini-Lesson

Similes and metaphors are powerful tools to use in reports and essays.

Write a sentence about computers that includes a simile, a comparison using the words like or as.

Like an unending library, computers began solving seemingly impossible problems.

Now write a sentence about rocket ships that includes a metaphor, a direct comparison.

The moon was a slingshot for the rocket.

Middle and high schoolers should include at least two similes or metaphors in any essay or report they write.

to paraphrase some of the article in your own words. Add it to the Journal section of your Writer's Notebook.

EXERCISE: Comparing and Contrasting

Gather two items that are very similar to each other, like two leaves from different trees. Although it's very obvious that they are similar, can you also list their differences? Divide a sheet of paper in half and write "Compare" at the top of the first column and "Contrast" at the top of the second. Write the similarities you observe within the first column and the differences within the second. Turn your lists into a paragraph that acknowledges their similarities, but points out their many differences as well.

Here are a few more things you can compare and contrast:

- Dogs and cats
- Apples and oranges
- Babies and toddlers
- Rain and snow
- Movies and books
- Bicycles and tricycles
- Pens and pencils

EXERCISE: Describing True Things

We often talk about using descriptive words in stories and fictional writing, but it's also important to be able to describe true things. Set a piece of fruit out on the table. Try to describe the fruit in as many ways as possible. Share sensory details, facts you know, or related true stories or connections you have with the fruit. See how many descriptors you can come up with together as you describe the fruit. Create a word bank about the fruit by writing down the descriptive words you come up with together on note cards, a white board, or a sheet of paper.

Practice writing a factual paragraph about the fruit using vivid descriptions. Include a topic sentence, several descriptive facts, and a concluding sentence. Use your word bank as a reference for ideas and to help you spell the words properly. Add your factual paragraph to the Journal section of your Writer's Notebook.

EXERCISE: Truthful Metaphors

At times we describe abstract ideas that are true. Metaphors can be a powerful tool for describing abstract ideas. Try this metaphor activity to practice writing metaphors about truthful ideas.

Begin with an abstract idea - *bravery*

Think of an animal that exhibits that trait - *a lioness*

Describe attributes, descriptions, actions, and phrases

about the animal - *large, golden, determined, majestic, focused, pounce, roar, hunt, prowl, pride, unity, leader, unafraid.*

Now, use the word bank you created to draw a comparison and write a metaphor.

> *Elizabeth Cady Stanton was a lioness in the women's rights movement, majestically leading the pride of women to roar until their voices were heard.*

Choose one of these abstract ideas and try creating a metaphor of your own about a true person from history that possessed that attribute. Add your description to the Journal section of your Writer's Notebook.

- Determination
- Wisdom
- Courage
- Love
- Unselfishness
- Cruelty
- Fear
- Pride
- Patriotism
- Faith
- Hope
- Intelligence

EXERCISE: Paragraphs in Reports and Essays

A paragraph in a report or essay is quite different from a paragraph in a story. As you write a report or essay, you will write expository paragraphs. An expository paragraph is one that explains a topic or idea. Each expository paragraph has its own topic and is organized with a topic sentence, supporting sentences, and a concluding sentence. Use the printable "TREES" anchor chart from the Printable Pack to learn about writing expository paragraphs.

Choose one of the topics below and try writing an expository paragraph about it using the "TREES" printable as your guide. You'll need to come up with a main idea; look up some reasons, evidence, and examples; make some connections; and write a creative conclusion. Add it to the Journal section of your Writer's Notebook.

- Different kinds of teeth
- The importance of sleep
- The benefits of exercise
- The life cycle of a butterfly
- Ways to reduce stress
- Your favorite sport or hobby
- What makes a great leader
- Animal homes
- The importance of families
- Why honesty is important
- The best way to cook eggs

☐ Mini-Lesson

When writing a report or essay about a person, you generally write in past tense. Whether or not they are still living, you are telling about things they have already done. Which of these is correctly written in past tense?

> *Copernicus suspected that the planets orbited the sun and discovered that each planet rotates on its own axis.*

> *Copernicus is my hero because he explains the planets and their orbits.*

Can you write your own past tense sentence about a famous person?

☐ Mini-Lesson

Because past tense is commonly used in reports and essays, you will generally use a lot of verbs that end in -ed. Make a word bank to add to the Writing Helps section of your Writer's Notebooks that lists a lot of -ed verbs.

> *walked, talked, shopped, washed, watched, waited, explored, wanted*

☐ Mini-Lesson

Can you think of any past tense verbs that do not end in -ed? Make a word bank of these as well.

> *slept, caught, forgot, hit, hid, laid, brought, took, lay*

☐ Mini-Lesson

Strong verbs are as important in reports and essays as they are in the stories you write.

Change each of the underlined verbs in the sentences below to make them stronger or more descriptive.

Neil Armstrong _went_ to the moon.

Koala bears _like_ eucalyptus leaves.

Sailboats _sit_ on the water.

Vincent Van Gogh _has_ 200 paintings in Amsterdam's Van Gogh Museum.

☐ Mini-Lesson

Animal groups often have special names that are fun to learn. Make your own matching game by writing a list of the animals in one column and a scrambled list of their group names in a second column. Trade papers and solve each other's matching games. Here are a few fun examples to get you started.

- Elephants - parade
- Parrots - pandemonium
- Cobras - quiver
- Jellyfish - smack
- Bats - colony
- Camels - caravan
- Toads - knot
- Crows - murder
- Porcupines - prickle
- Leopards - leap
- Wild cats - destruction
- Flamingos - stand

EXERCISE: Nonfiction Text Features

Gather a variety of nonfiction books and also the "Nonfiction Text Features" printable from the Printable Pack. See if you can find each of the features in at least one of the books you have. Some will be within the body pages of the book itself - graphics, photographs, labels, maps, captions, comparisons, subtitles, and special print. Others will be kept in their own section, either at the front or at the back of the book - table of contents, glossary, and index.

Choose one or more of these text features to add to one of your reports or essays during this unit. You might draw some graphics or maps and add labels or captions. You could create a table of contents. Perhaps you'll add headings or subtitles. Practice creating a few of these nonfiction text features right now. When it's time to complete your project, make sure you've incorporated some of these nonfiction text features.

Reports

EXERCISE: 4-Square Report

To learn to write a basic report, use the "4-Square Report" printable from the Printable Pack. Write your topic at the top. Write a topic sentence in the center - a single sentence that explains what your report is about. Then add details about your topic in each box, also written in complete sentence form. Finally, write a concluding sentence that summarizes your topic on the last line.

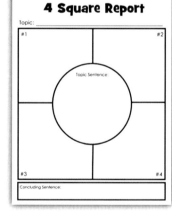

As your reports get bigger and include more information, you can keep using this basic format. As they grow, add another "4-Square Report" printable. For example, you could use two printables to write a report about the moon. One could explain basic information about the moon and a second could explain the first voyage astronauts took there.

The next time you draft a report, you can include three "4-Square Report" printables. Perhaps you will write a country report about Spain. The first grid could be about the geography of Spain, the second about the history and government of the country, and the third about the people and culture.

As you practice writing reports, they can grow and include

more and more interesting information, always grouped by topics. Each topic within the subject gets its own grid that serves as a section of your report. Use as many sections, or "4-Square Report" printables, as you need to create an interesting overview of your topic.

EXERCISE: Mobile

Choose a topic. Create a mobile about it by drawing pictures with caption boxes, finding pictures online or in a book to print, and creating word strips. Print your word strips on card stock or attach them to poster paper or thin cardboard. Write a paragraph on the back side of each piece to record what you learned about the topic.

Each part of your mobile will be about a different subtopic of your overall topic. Cut out each piece, hole punch the top, and tie a loop of yarn or string on the piece. Tie the tops to an embroidery hoop, piece of thick wire, or a metal clothes hanger to create a hanging display of pictures and words.

When you are done displaying your mobile, remove the pieces by cutting the string. Add them to the Journal section of your Writer's Notebook by gluing an envelope to a piece of card stock and inserting the pieces into it.

EXERCISE: Poster

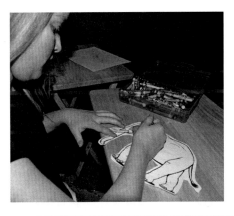

Create a poster based on a topic that interests you. You can choose anything at all that you can find information about. If you aren't sure what to write about, sometimes it helps to consider interesting things you have learned. Think about a science

☐ Mini-Lesson

Inserting voice into essays is difficult. In most expository writing, rather than trying to sound like yourself, you are trying to sound like an expert. You want your reader to trust you and your message. In order to be trustworthy, you must have an organized and accurate message.

Read a passage in a nonfiction book and try to point out something that is written like an expert.

☐ Mini-Lesson

Word choice is one of the six traits of writing. An essential part of word choice in reports and essays is avoiding redundancy. You will feel tempted to repeat your topic over and over, but using the same words a lot is boring. Find several ways to say your topic so you can avoid repetition. Using precise, novel words will create a more interesting paper for your reader.

For example, if you are writing about a submarine, you might also call it a submersible, an underwater craft, a vehicle of the deep, or an exploration vessel.

Make some lists of other ways to say these topics:

- Airplane
- Biologist
- France
- Doctor
- Bear

topic like stars, sea creatures, or volcanoes. Maybe there's a historical event you find fascinating, like the invention of the computer or the fall of the Berlin Wall, or maybe something from long ago, like the ancient Olympic Games. You might even choose an interesting place you've traveled to or wish you could go visit. Whatever topic you choose, find some information about it in books or online. You'll use the information to create a poster highlighting your topic.

You'll need to consider your information and your design as you make your poster. These are some elements to include:

- A clear title
- A color scheme
- Even spacing and a full (but not overly crowded) design
- Neat boxes of organized information
- Images, charts, graphs, or other visual elements
- Caption boxes to describe the visual elements

Make your poster neat, tidy, and visually appealing. Use a ruler or another straight edge to create straight lines. You can choose to type or write your information, but make sure you have someone help you revise and edit it before you add it to your poster if this will be your writing project. It helps if you create the elements of the poster individually and check each one before gluing it down.

EXERCISE: Country Report
Use the "Country Report" printable from the Printable Pack to research a country. Find out information about each topic and fill in the boxes of the report. Add it to the Journal section of your Writer's Notebook. Use the information you gathered to help you draft any type of report or essay if you are interested in continuing the writing process.

EXERCISE: Illustrated Fact Sheet

Use a single sheet of card stock and colored pens and pencils as you do this exercise. You may want to use clip art, how to draw tutorials, or reference pictures from books as you complete your illustrated fact sheet.

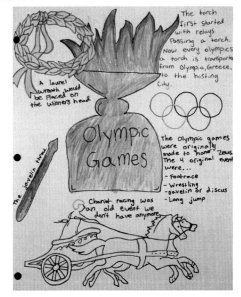

Write your topic on your paper in bold lettering. Draw or paste pictures about your topic all over the page. Create a caption to write next to each picture that explains the picture and tells about your topic. Add it to the Journal section of your Writer's Notebook.

EXERCISE: Animal Report

Choose an animal you would like to learn more about. Gather some books or other sources about your animal, a two pocket folder, five letter-sized envelopes, and some 3" x 5" note cards.

Interesting information about nests would go within the "Habitat & Diet" envelope on my folder about swallows.

Glue an envelope on to each pocket on the inside of the folder, and two more envelopes on the interior of the folder above the pockets. Label the envelopes, one for each

Mini-Lesson

There and their and they're are three words that are often confused.

There means "in that place."

Their means "belonging to them."

They're is a contraction for "they are."

Write sentences that properly use each of these words.

Mini-Lesson

Possessive pronouns show ownership. Think of some possessions people might own and speak or write a sentence for each of these possessive pronouns: his, hers, mine, yours, its, our, theirs.

Mini-Lesson

Interrogative pronouns are used to ask questions about unknown subjects. Speak or write a sentence for each of these interrogative pronouns: who, whom, what, which, whose.

Mini-Lesson

As you are in the revising stage of the writing process, ask yourself if you taught your reader anything new. Eliminate statements that are too general or that are common knowledge. Instead, fill your reports and essays with interesting information that teaches your reader something.

section of your animal report, as follows:

- Appearance and characteristics
- Life cycle and other biological information
- Habitat and diet
- Enemies and threats

You'll also make one more envelope labeled "Sources" and stick it to the back of the folder. Create a note card for each source that includes the title, author, publisher, date, and place of publication. Place those note cards in the envelope on the back of the folder.

As you read through your sources, write specific details on the note cards, one detail per card, and place it in the proper envelope based on the topic. Make sure to also write which source it came from. You can use a simple numbering system so you don't have to rewrite the source titles over and over. Write some details in your own words, and write others using quotation marks.

Use the information from your note cards to write a report about your animal that includes an introduction, a section with a header for each of your envelope topics and includes the information from that envelope, and a conclusion.

When you're finished, put your report in the pocket of your folder. Keep your rough draft in the left pocket and your final report in the right pocket. Add a picture of your animal, a title, and your name to the front cover of your folder.

EXERCISE: Technology and Inventions

Technology has come a really long way in recent decades. Write a report on a specific recent invention or technology that has had a big impact on the world and how we live.

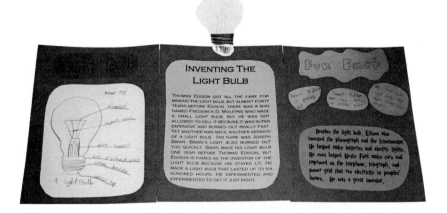

You can format it as a typed paper or choose to highlight

the invention by creating a visual triptych. Draw or print a picture of your invention, cut it out, and back it with poster paper or card stock, cutting around the border. Tape three additional sheets of card stock together, then attach the picture of your invention to the top. With the two outside doors and the three inner sheets, you will have five sections to write on.

- Tell the story of the inventor.
- Describe how and when the discovery or invention came about. You can include earlier inventions that led up to it as well.
- Tell about what the invention does and how it is used or create a labeled diagram that shows its parts.
- Outline the impact the invention has had on the world. Why is it important?
- Discuss at least three significant changes that have occurred as a result.

EXERCISE: Cereal Box Report
Design a cereal box that showcases a topic you have researched. Give it a fitting name and include pictures, labels, caption boxes, and even an ingredients list. You can size the project to an actual cereal box from your pantry and then tape or glue your report right on to the box.

EXERCISE: Informational Brochure
Informational brochures are another kind of expository writing. They typically involve sheets of paper that are folded into thirds and include pictures, captions, and short blurbs of information about people, animals, places, or events.

  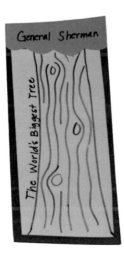

Select either a famous person, an important landmark, a historical event, or another true topic and make a brochure that includes both pictures and words. Keep everything

☐ **Mini-Lesson**

Colloquialisms and slang are informal words and phrases. They are often specific to a certain region or group of people. It is normal to hear them spoken, but they should not be used in formal writing like reports and essays.

Formal writing demands a more formal tone, It also requires that it can stand the test of time and span larger geographical regions. Most informal language changes quickly with the trends in an area.

For example, your friend might tell you that your back flip on the trampoline is "Sick!" She doesn't mean that it is ill.

Avoid informal language like that as you write reports and essays to avoid confusion and strike the proper tone.

☐ **Mini-Lesson**

As you write each section of a report, stick to the exact topic of that section. For example, if you are writing a report about five life cycles of different animals, make sure you dedicate each section to one specific animal without overlapping. You want to provide a clear description that informs your reader about your topic.

In a story, twists and turns are fun, but in a report they are confusing. Choose a topic and make a list of five clear subtopics you could write about.

Mini-Lesson

Pronouns replace nouns so you can avoid being too repetitious as you are writing about a specific person or subject. Be careful though! If you aren't clear, you might confuse your reader.

The fish on her plate made her stomach upset. It twisted and turned.

In this case, I'm not sure whether the fish was twisting and turning or whether her stomach was.

Can you rewrite these two sentences to clarify?

Mini-Lesson

Pronouns must always agree in number and in person to the noun it is referring to.

*Incorrect: **Each** of the girls remembered **their** food.*

*Correct: **Each** of the girls remembered **her** food.*

In the first example, **each** is singular, so it isn't correct to use **their**, which is plural.

*Incorrect: When **a patient** is late to an appointment, **you** should apologize.*

*Correct: When **a patient** is late to an appointment, **he or she** should apologize.*

In this example, a patient is referring to someone in the third person, so the pronoun should match.

Imitate the sentences above to write your own.

factual. Brochures are descriptive, but brief. They are usually organized by subtopics, and only the most important information or interesting facts are shared.

EXERCISE: Report in the Round

Choose a topic and create a round report using the printable "Report in the Round" from the Printable Pack. Cut out the circle on the printable and cut another circle to match it using another sheet of paper. Attach the two with a brad at the center. As you spin the top circle, write facts about your topic in each blank spot on the lower circle. Little ones can end with this activity and older kids can use this as a prewrite to develop ideas for a longer report. Each fact could become a paragraph topic in a longer report.

EXERCISE: Five-Page Tabbed Booklet

Use the "Five-Page Tabbed Booklet" pages from the Printable Pack to write about five related items. You can choose from the blank version or the lined version. Here are a few to consider:

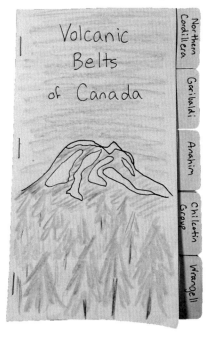

- Five greatest mapmakers of all time
- Five famous rivers
- Five classical composers
- Five types of landscape
- Five types of magnets
- Five life cycles
- Where I live (my house, my town, my state or province, my country, my continent)
- Five ancient pyramids around the world

Create your booklet using a combination of colorful pictures and writing. Look up information from books, movies, and websites to learn about five components of your topic. Fill in the five sections in an organized way. This exercise will go into the Journal section of your Writer's Notebook.

EXERCISE: All About Book

Make a booklet about any topic - a person, country, landmark, animal, plant, science concept, natural disaster, holiday, tradition, or any other topic of interest. Use the six pages from the Printable Pack that begin with the "All About" cover. Write things about your topic on each page

of your book, illustrating it as you go. Each page should have at least one sentence and include interesting facts you didn't know before. Include headlines in the book that divide your information into sections. Make sure your book is colorful, tidy, and complete. Don't leave any blank pages or huge areas with whitespace. Add it to your family library or to the Journal section of your Writer's Notebook.

EXERCISE: Book Report
A book report gives information about a book you've read. Young kids can use the "Book Report" printables from the Printable Pack to write a simple book report. Middle grades and up can write a book report using the "Book Report Outline" from the Printable Pack as a prewrite and then draft a book report. Add these to the Journal section of your Writer's Notebook.

EXERCISE: Book Report Card
After reading a book, evaluate your book using the "Book Report Card" printable from the Printable Pack. You will be evaluating the book and giving it a grade based on the elements within the story. Include textual evidence to back up your claims. For example, if you complain that the characters weren't very interesting, make sure to include at least one quote from the story that demonstrates the blandness of the characters. Add your page to the Journal section of your Writer's Notebook.

EXERCISE: Nonfiction Book Report
Use the "Nonfiction Book Report" printable from the Printable Pack for this exercise. You'll need a nonfiction book of your choice as well. Write your name, the title, and the author's name on the spine. On the cover, write interesting things from the book as you read. If you need to, you can turn the page over and continue on the back. At the end, write your opinion of the book in the thought bubble at the bottom. Present your book, the things you learned, and your evaluation of it out loud to an audience. Add it to the Journal section of your Writer's Notebook.

EXERCISE: Book Projects
Instead of a book report, you might enjoy a book project. Choose a book project idea from the "Book Project Ideas" printables from the Printable Pack, which you

☐ Mini-Lesson
Seven Golden Rules for Writing a Strong Essay:

1. Have a clear point that is explained in your thesis statement.

2. Present compelling topics in each body paragraph that all relate directly back to your thesis statement.

3. Include evidence from sources.

4. Don't use first person pronouns like "I" or "me" and avoid casual language like contractions or slang.

5. Link each of your ideas with transition words.

6. Stick to your topic.

7. Sandwich your body paragraphs with an interest-catching introduction and a compelling conclusion.

☐ Mini-Lesson
Typically, essays are typed and use a specific format. Use a standard font and size, such as Times New Roman, 12-point. Your page margins should be one inch. Also, use a double-spaced format. Do not insert extra spaces between paragraphs or between the title of your essay and the body paragraphs. Finally, include a header with the author's last name and page number at the top of each page and a heading with the author's name, course, date, and teacher, if needed. Practice formatting an essay using a computer.

☐ Mini-Lesson

Organize the introduction of your essay by starting with broad details and then narrowing down to one specific thesis statement. The details can include interesting facts, quotes, statistics, examples, or anecdotes to draw your reader in. Your thesis statement should be the final sentence of your introductory paragraph and should clearly state your point.

☐ Mini-Lesson

Not every five-paragraph essay is identical. Some merely present information, like an essay about an animal species, while some have a strong thesis and are trying to convince the readers of an argument.

No matter what the purpose of the essay is though, the common thing five-paragraph essays share is their strong organization.

Look over the "1-3-5 Paragraph Essay" anchor chart from the Printable Pack.

Discuss the structure and why you think this order is important.

Together, choose a possible topic (you can use the Reports and Essays Idea Bank if you would like to) and discuss things that could go in each box of the anchor chart if you were writing the essay.

Share how you think the structure creates a strong, organized overview of your topic.

can also add to the Ideas section of your Writer's Notebook to refer to whenever you need a book project idea.

Once you've read a book, look through the list and decide on a project you'd like to complete. Regardless of which project you choose, make sure to add a written component. For example, if you make a puppet show, you will write a script. If you create a setting box, also craft a paragraph about the setting of the story. Present your book project to your family or another audience out loud.

Essays

EXERCISE: Examining Example Essays
Within the Writer's Workshop links in the Layers of Learning catalog, you will find some example essays you can read together. They are all written by real kids. They aren't perfect, but they will guide you as you learn about each essay format.

As you read, look for each essay's organization. Search for thesis statements, transition words, reasons, and hooks. Look for ways the essay tied in the introduction with the conclusion to create a full circle. Evaluate the writing using the six traits of writing and the rubric. Look for mistakes, suggest edits and revisions, and suggest ways you would strengthen the essay.

Unlike most exercises in Writer's Workshop, this is one we suggest you do in parts. For example, when you are writing a one-paragraph essay, use an example one-paragraph essay. Read through it out loud together and evaluate it as described above. Use it as an example while you write your own one-paragraph essay. When you move on to a response essay, use the example response essay and repeat this exercise again. The example essays can guide you in the style of each format.

EXERCISE: 1-3-5 Paragraph Essay
Essays can be any length and can be written in many formats, but understanding a basic one, three, or five-paragraph essay is a helpful starting place.

A one-paragraph essay is for beginners. It is composed by writing a topic sentence, three supporting details, and then a concluding sentence about the topic.

A three-paragraph essay is similar, but with a little added length. Once you've mastered a one-paragraph essay, you are ready to move on to this format. The first paragraph is an introduction, the second paragraph houses the

supporting ideas, and the third paragraph is the conclusion.

Five-paragraph essays are a basic format you will use for most of the academic writing you do. This one format, if mastered well, will prepare you for all kinds of expository writing. Regardless of the specific topic or kind of essay, a five-paragraph format is the most commonly used. It expands on the format of the three-paragraph essay.

The reason five-paragraph essays are so useful is because of their high level of structure. The specific structure specifies exactly what information goes where and in which order to put it. It is true that before you can break the rules you have to understand them well and that is what the five-paragraph essay does – it gives a great foundation for the rules so that you become comfortable with the rules and feel confident in your writing.

Basically, there are five paragraphs and each paragraph has four to five sentences. Choose a topic to write about. Then make an outline following the structure below.

I. Introduction
    A. The main theme of the paper (often told through an interesting hook)
    B. Background information #1
    C. Background information #2
    D. Background information #3
    E. Thesis statement that states your main idea and outlines your three supporting points.

II. Point #1
    A. Supporting detail
    B. Supporting detail
    C. Supporting detail
    D. Transition sentence

III. Point #2
    A. Supporting detail
    B. Supporting detail
    C. Supporting detail
    D. Transition sentence

IV. Point #3
    A. Supporting detail
    B. Supporting detail
    C. Supporting detail
    D. Transition sentence

V. Conclusion
    A. Why your ideas about the subject are correct
    B. What you proved in the previous paragraphs
    C. A summary of your conclusions that ties back to your introduction.

☐ Mini-Lesson

Sentence fluency, one of the six traits of writing, includes creating balanced pacing. Pacing means how slowly or quickly you move through the points you are making. If you spend two pages on the first point and only two sentences on the second point, your pacing needs to improve.

Each point you make should carry similar weight in your essay. That means each of your paragraphs should be similar in length.

☐ Mini-Lesson

The difference between middle school essays and high school essays is that in high school, writers should be including their evaluations about topics.

Young kids share some interesting facts. Middle grade kids present a topic fully, with sources. High schoolers present the topic fully and also evaluate the information and the sources. They inject their own ideas and claims. They present a unique slant in some way.

For example, if I am writing about dogs, I might make claims about the personal, social, and psychological benefits of dog ownership. Another possible slant would be evaluating the domestication of animals and sharing whether or not I believe people should keep domesticated animals.

☐ Mini-Lesson

Organization is one of the six traits of writing. Your task is to travel from point to point in a logical way, with connected ideas. Transition words help you show connections between your ideas. They can be used within sentences and should definitely be used to bridge the ideas between paragraphs.

Make an anchor chart of transition words to add to the Writing Helps section of your Writer's Notebook.

☐ Mini-Lesson

Practice writing a thesis statement for an essay that would feature this statistic presented by David Walsh in its introduction: "79% of American children now play computer or video games on a regular basis. Children between the ages of seven and 17 play for an average of eight hours a week."

Depending on your writing level, choose a one, three, or five paragraph essay to write. You'll find a "1-3-5 Paragraph Essay" anchor chart in the Printable Pack to add to the Writing Helps section of your notebook and to guide you as you write. A one-paragraph essay will only use one main idea box. A three-paragraph essay will use the introduction, main idea, and conclusion boxes. All of the boxes from the anchor chart will be used in a five-paragraph essay.

No matter what length you choose, begin by making an outline. Use your outline to help you draft your essay. If you decide to take your essay through the writing process, make sure to apply some of the tools you learned during this unit. Add transition words, metaphors, and lots of evidence to make sure you cover your topic in a thorough and interesting way.

EXERCISE: Breaking Down A Topic

One of the most important skills in writing a five-paragraph essay is to break down your topic into parts. Commonly, you'll look for three parts within your overall topic. Take a look at these examples:

Topic: Why basketball is a popular sport.

> Sub-topic 1: Players can creatively combine moves both individually and as a team.

> Sub-topic 2: It incorporates strength, flexibility, agility, and a bigger range of skills than most sports.

> Sub-topic 3: Because of the small court, spectators get to sit closely and be involved in the game.

Topic: Education is important to life satisfaction.

> Subtopic 1: Getting an education prepares you for a job that can provide for you financially.

> Subtopic 2: Hobbies, interests, and passions can be pursued through learning.

> Subtopic 3: Being educated feeds your understanding about the world and helps you interact with people, ideas, and issues you will encounter.

Choose your own essay topic, then break it down into three sub-topics. Use the "Breaking Down A 5-Paragraph Essay" printable from the Printable Pack to record your ideas. Once you have your three basic parts, keep taking notes on the sheet about more ideas that fall within those three areas. Assign each of the sub-topics to a body paragraph in your essay. Use your ideas to draft an essay.

EXERCISE: Five-Paragraph Essays With A Thesis Statement

The strongest five-paragraph essays include a thesis statement that sums up what the essay is about in one sentence. You might want to combine this exercise with the "Thesis Statement" exercise from the beginning of this unit. Choose one of the thesis statements you wrote during that exercise to use for your five-paragraph essay.

Use the "5-Paragraph Essay Plan" printable from the Printable Pack. Write your thesis statement within the introduction box. Write each of the main points in each paragraph box, then add some notes about your ideas for each of those paragraphs. Finally, write a new way to state your thesis within the conclusion box. Use your plan to help you draft your essay. Make sure to begin your essay with an interesting hook and place your thesis statement as the last sentence in your introductory paragraph. Finally, try to think of a way to come full circle by referring to your hook one more time in your conclusion.

EXERCISE: Response Essays

Response essays ask you to respond to something you've experienced. They can take the same form as a 1-3-5 paragraph essay. Whether you are responding to a book you just read or a movie you just saw, articulating how you came to a conclusion on your math problem, or giving your opinion on a current issue in the news, there are a few things that all response writing should include. When writing a thoughtful response you should:

- Write from your own unique perspective. It should sound like you!
- Give not only your first impressions but also some thoughtful reasons to back up how you feel or think.
- Include your own opinions. Explain them but don't apologize for them. It's fine to state what opposing people believe, but don't get caught up in an argument. This is your personal response.
- Keep your message simple and straightforward. No tangents.
- Keep it positive. People rarely learn or see topics from other perspectives when they are presented negatively.
- Be thoughtful. Worry more about your ideas and content than about perfection in your writing.

You will find a "Rules for Response Writing" printable in the Printable Pack to add to the Writing Helps section of your Writer's Notebook. Keep it handy as you write a short response to one of these:

- Read a fictional book and write about which character you most connected with. Include specific things from

---

☐ **Mini-Lesson**

Contractions are words that are formed by shortening and combining two words.

can't = can not

don't = do not

won't = will not

I'll = I will

I've = I have

isn't = is not

I'm = I am

we'd = we would

There are over seventy common contractions that are used in speaking and informal writing. We use them so frequently that often we don't even notice.

However, because essays are considered formal writing, you should never use contractions in them. It's like wearing a swimsuit to a fancy wedding in a cathedral; it just doesn't strike the right tone.

Re-write the paragraph below and eliminate the contractions to give it a more formal tone.

College is becoming more and more expensive by the year, which means a lot of students can't afford it anymore. It wasn't long ago that it was an affordable option for young adults, but it isn't any longer. Tuition, books, housing, fees, parking, and other costs add up to an unaffordable level for students who aren't wealthy.

☐ Mini-Lesson

Read a picture book out loud together and analyze it. *Where The Wild Things Are* by Maurice Sendak or *The Cat in the Hat* by Dr. Seuss are good options.

Discuss the books according to the topics in the "Literary Analysis" exercise to practice analyzing.

For example, you might discuss the setting within *Where the Wild Things Are*. The story has a setting within a setting. The boy has an entire adventure in his imagination while he is within his very own bedroom. The more involved he becomes in his imagined setting, the larger the illustrations grow on the page. This shows the significance of his imagination in providing an escape from a difficult situation. How does the setting reflect the boy's mood as the story progresses?

If you read *The Cat in the Hat*, discuss the relationships between the characters, dialogue, and tone. How do the dialogue and tone of the children differ from the cat's? Can you tell a little about the mood of each character as the story unfolds? The author, Dr. Seuss, is known for his playful word choice. Can you find words that reflect the cat's playful tone?

the text that provide evidence of your point of view.

- Watch a movie and respond to what you believe the theme of the movie was. What parts of the story demonstrated the theme?
- Read a fairy tale and write about one lesson you learned from it. Draw parallels between the story and real life experiences.
- Watch a music video and write about the tone of the song and what it made you feel.
- Read a poem and write about how the words had an effect on you or discuss the tools or techniques the poet used to help convey a message.
- Watch a TV show and choose at least two characters that were featured. Write a response about their relationship or connection.
- Research a recent news story and write about what you feel should follow it. For example, if a crime occurred, write about what punishment the criminal should face or what should be done to deter similar crimes. If it's about a natural disaster, respond with what aid should be given and describe how help could best be administered. If it's about a political issue, respond with your viewpoint of the issue.
- Look at a painting, picture, or photograph of a landscape or seascape. Write a response about what it would be like to be there. Tie in emotions and experiences with physical elements of the picture.
- Look at a painting, picture, or photograph of people or animals. Imagine the thoughts of one of the figures and respond in writing about what they are thinking and why. Use evidence from the picture.

EXERCISE: Reading Response

Reading response essays fall somewhere in between a journal entry and a book report. As you write one, you will include information about the plot, characters, and setting, much like you would if you were writing a book report. In addition, you will also include quotes or summarize parts of the story that stood out to you. You will then insert your own ideas, opinions, or thoughts about the quotes or instances you discussed. The difference between a book report and a reading response is that you are responding to what you read, not just reporting on it. The majority of what you write should be about how the book affected you.

Here are a few ways you can respond to something you've read:

- Keep a quote log. As you read a quote you like (or dislike), write it down. Then write your thoughts about it.
- Make a list of characters with descriptions that include

how they relate to people you know or have witnessed.
- Write down a list of questions you would ask the author if you had the opportunity.
- Describe a good alternate ending to the story that you would have enjoyed.
- Choose one character you related to and make ties between the two of you with examples from the story and from your own life.
- Describe one event from the story and write about what you would have done in the same situation.

EXERCISE: Literary Analysis

A literary analysis is more than just a summary of a book. It is an essay that clearly expresses your perspective, interpretation, opinion, or evaluation of a book. As you write, you will be examining why the author used specific literary devices, formats, and ideas. You will examine how things like word choice made a difference in what the author wrote. You may also examine themes, characters, settings, and other choices the author made.

Begin by reading the text closely. Take notes and think about the author's writing techniques. Make notes about things you find interesting, important, unusual, or otherwise noteworthy. Think about what the author's purpose is, and how his or her choices drive the purpose.

Choose one or more of these topics to analyze:

- Characters - Are the characters static or dynamic as the book goes on? Are any of the characters symbolic? Are any of the characters archetypes? Can you compare and contrast several characters?
- Setting - Can you see a relationship between the setting and the mood? Does the setting impact the characters in some way? Is the setting key to the conflict?
- Plot - How is suspense built as the plot goes on? Were there any techniques like foreshadowing or flashbacks used? What things contribute to the conflict?
- Theme - What is the major idea? Are there any repeating patterns or symbols? How do the characters showcase the theme? What does the title have to do with the theme?
- Dialogue - What does the dialogue reveal about the characters? How does the author use dialogue to show mood or to reveal the theme or the main conflict?
- Imagery - What images or scenes were important to the theme? What images impacted the characters or the plot? Were there symbolic elements?
- Figures of Speech - Identify similes, metaphors, hyperboles, and other figures of speech and how each

☐ **Mini-Lesson**

As you write essays, you will find that you need to compare and contrast things frequently. Being able to articulate the similarities and differences you see between things is an important analysis skill.

Create a word bank for the Writing Helps section of your Writer's Notebook that lists these words that will help you explain the similarities and differences you identify.

Words to use as you are comparing:

- Like
- Likewise
- Both
- As well
- In common
- Same
- Similar or similarly

Words to use as you are contrasting:

- Instead
- On the other hand
- Meanwhile
- Although
- Yet
- Whereas
- In contrast
- Nonetheless

Look over one of your essay drafts and see if you can add two or three statements that use these words to help you make comparisons.

was important to the text.

- Tone - Identify the tone of the author (serious, casual, playful, somber, angry, careful) Does it match the plot, setting, and characters?
- Word Choice - Identify powerful or descriptive words and the impact they had on the overall text. Watch for alliteration, rhyme, rhythm, and more word play.
- Point of View - Did the author write in first, second, or third person point of view? What effect did this have?

A literary analysis paper needs a strong thesis statement that explains the text through the lens of several of the topics listed above. Once you have a thesis statement, make a list of evidence from the text that supports your thesis. Organize your points and group them into paragraphs. You might do this by writing an outline, making a web, or writing your evidence on note cards and then putting the note cards into groups. Like many other essays, a five-paragraph format is a strong choice of organization for a literary analysis.

Once your organization is in place, you can begin writing a rough draft. As you write your rough draft, make sure you include your own point of view and your opinions alongside the evidence you found.

Have someone read over your analysis with you and together, revise your draft. Finish by proofreading the paper and making final edits.

EXERCISE: Critical Essay

A critical essay analyzes and evaluates something. Often it analyzes a book, poem, play, movie, speech, painting, or another piece of art.

When you write a critical essay, you will discuss the theme and explain evidence from the piece that shows the theme you are presenting. It is always helpful for you to have background information about the author or artist in order to understand his or her work. You can use the 1-3-5 paragraph format for a critical essay.

Every critical essay must make a claim. For example, you might claim that Van Gogh's *Starry Night* painting is about death. You would then use background information, quotes by Van Gogh, and things within the painting to prove your claim. For example, the cypress tree in the foreground was associated with mourning and was often found in cemeteries. Similarly, the church spire pointing to heaven signifies spirituality and the artist's concern with the afterlife. Van Gogh also once said, "Why, I ask myself, shouldn't the shining dots of the sky be as accessible as the black dots

on the map of France? Just as we take the train to get to Tarascon or Rouen, we take death to reach a star."

Besides making your own arguments, a good critical essay also expresses potential counterarguments and then uses evidence to dispute them. For example, some argue that *Starry Night* is about mental illness because Van Gogh painted it from an asylum, but just because a person suffers from mental illness does not mean that his or her condition is the only thing the person thinks about, or paints about, for that matter.

Make sure to include these ingredients within a critical essay:

- An introduction with background information
- A claim at the end of your first paragraph
- Evidence to back up your claim
- At least one counterargument and why you dispute it
- A conclusion that sums up your point of view

To practice, write an essay about a painting or another piece of art. Research the artist, the painting, and the time period. Find out the story behind its creation. Write about its theme and point out specific parts of the painting that show the theme.

Here are a few suggestions of paintings to write about:

- Van Gogh's *Starry Night*
- Munch's *The Scream*
- *The Lenin Bust* in Antarctica
- Giotto's *Adoration of the Magi*

☐ Mini-Lesson

The concluding paragraph in an essay is like a funnel. It restates the main ideas and wraps them up, drawing them into a tidy conclusion. The end of the funnel, at the narrowest point, is your concluding sentence.
Here are some options for gracefully exiting your essay:

- A profound thought
- A surprise
- A powerful quote
- A tie-up
- A question
- A summary
- A laugh
- A call to action

☐ Mini-Lesson

Use a thesaurus and a dictionary to help you improve your word choice within an essay you have written. Find a draft of an essay in your Writer's Notebook and read through it. Circle a few words you believe could be stronger.

Look each of those words up in the dictionary and in the thesaurus. Use the entries you read to give you ideas for stronger words you could use instead, and make the changes.

You may want to try using both book and computer or online versions of a dictionary and thesaurus. All of them can be fantastic tools for helping you to improve word choice in your writing.

☐ Mini-Lesson

Every essay needs a bibliography or works cited page. You will learn to create works cited pages in the Research Paper unit, but you can practice for that by including a bibliography, or list of your sources.

Gather the books you used to write one of your essays and create a bibliography to include. A bibliography is always included as a separate page at the end of your essay. It should be typed and in the same format, font, and size as the rest of your essay.

☐ Mini-Lesson

While revising your essay, make sure that each paragraph is properly supported. Imagine that your paragraph is a little table. The main point is the tabletop. Each bit of evidence you provide is another leg. Do you have enough legs to support the table? If not, make sure to add enough evidence to make each paragraph strong.

- Michelangelo's Sistine Chapel artwork
- Grant Wood's *American Gothic*
- *Netherlandish Proverbs* by Pieter Bruegel the Elder

EXERCISE: Compare & Contrast Essay

To write a compare and contrast essay, think of two things that are different but share commonalities. Begin with the "Venn Diagram" printable from the Printable Pack. Label each circle with one of the items and write things that are specific to each item in the outside section of each circle. Where the circles intersect, list things they have in common.

- Books and movies
- Night and day
- Being poor and being rich
- Sadness and loneliness
- WWI and WWII
- Email and letters
- Love and jealousy

Use the "Venn Diagram" to help you compose your essay. Write an introduction that will hook your reader, then write a paragraph comparing the two that showcases their similarities. Paragraph three will contrast the two, describing their differences. The fourth and final paragraph will be an evaluation of the similarities and differences along with a concluding sentence. Add your essay to the Journal section of your Writer's Notebook.

EXERCISE: Exemplification Essay

Use a story or personal experience from your own life to prove a point in an exemplification essay.

Some topics for exemplification essays:

- The best job I ever had.
- The best way to spend your time.
- Things strong families do.
- A true friend.
- What it means to be a good citizen.
- The worst vacation.
- How hard things can make you strong.
- What real success looks like.

Like other essays, you will discuss your topic by breaking it down into subtopics which will form each of your paragraphs. The difference in this essay is that the support you provide will come from examples from your own life experiences.

EXERCISE: Definition Essay

A definition essay is like a dictionary entry that is expanded on in a big way. You will delve into the subject to promote understanding, explain a concept deeply, and tell about

how people perceive the subject or the effects that it has on people. Use one of the words below and write an extensive definition of what the word means. You will need to offer examples and evidence for your ideas. Try to create the entire essay in only 250 words. You will need to use vivid, powerful, and descriptive language and eliminate words that do not clearly explain the definition.

- Liberty
- Death
- Destruction
- Force
- Love

- Popularity
- Fame
- Wealth
- Industry
- Wisdom

Step 3: Writing Project

During this unit, you should complete at least one writing project, taking a piece of writing through the entire writing process. By the final week of the unit, if you haven't completed the project already, you should turn your attention to creating one polished piece of writing that uses the things you've practiced along the way.

Choose one topic to write about that you will take all of the way through the writing process. This piece of writing belongs in the Writing section of your Writer's Notebook. You can use something you've already started during this unit, your own idea, or something from the following idea banks. Make sure that you follow each step of the writing process and keep all of your steps to turn in with your finished writing.

- Step #1: Prewrite
- Step #2: Draft
- Step #3: Revise
- Step #4: Edit
- Step #5: Publish

Begin with a prewriting activity, then compose a draft, revise it, edit it with help from someone else, and then publish it. Publishing it could include making a polished final copy, sharing it with someone, creating a book, or creating some form of finished project that is neat and done well. You'll turn in all of your work, from prewrite to publish.

Your project will be evaluated based on the six traits of writing, so make sure you look at your composition through each of those lenses - ideas and content, organization, word choice, sentence fluency, conventions, and voice. Try to incorporate things you learned from the mini-lessons and the exercises you worked on as well. Do your best work.

☐ **Mini-Lesson**

Organization is one of the most important traits of writing when it comes to reports and essays. Read each section or paragraph in a piece you are taking through the writing process. Make sure that everything in the section or paragraph relates to the main idea. Also check for transition words that link your ideas together.

☐ **Mini-Lesson**

Can you spot the mistakes in this sentence and correct them?

my sister the one with the black hare tunes pianoes and violins fir a living

Answer:

My sister, the one with the black hair, tunes pianos and violins for a living.

☐ **Mini-Lesson**

Look over the essay or report you are taking through the writing process. Do a final check for voice to make sure it is formal and you sound like an expert. Make sure you avoided:

- Contractions
- Personal pronouns (I, me, we)
- Present tense verbs
- Slang
- A casual, personal tone

☐ Mini-Lesson

Your Writer's Notebook is your best tool for helping you grow as a writer. Take a few minutes to peruse your journal and look for something you might like to take through the writing process. Spend a few more minutes reviewing concepts by looking through the Writing Helps section.

☐ Mini-Lesson

An allusion is a reference to a well-known figure or event. As you draft or revise your report or essay, add an allusion within it. For example, if you are writing about The Pig War, a historical border conflict between the United Kingdom and the United States in the San Juan Islands, you might also allude to the Hatfields and the McCoys, two feuding families who were featured in a movie because of their own border dispute.

The Pig War turned out to be just another Hatfield-McCoy incident, but this one involved pigs and potatoes.

☐ Mini-Lesson

Anytime you are doing research as part of your writing, be careful not to plagiarize. Never copy someone else's words and claim them as your own. Instead, read and take notes, then write from your own perspective. You can quote your sources if needed, but always give credit.

Reports Idea Bank

- Choose an extinct species of animal to write a report on. Paste each finished section of your report to a hand-drawn silhouette of the animal.
- Research a planet, moon, satellite, solar system, galaxy, or celestial body. Make an All About _____ book.
- Choose a famous explorer and write a report that includes these sections: childhood and family, travels and explorations, legacy.
- Write a leader biography report. Select a world leader, historical or modern, and write about the person's life, family, policies, accomplishments, and legacy.
- Choose any science topic that interests you and write a report about it - why we have seasons, the function of cells, the laws of motion, chemical reactions, ecological impact, or another science topic that interests you.
- Select any significant historical event and write a report about the people, places, and events surrounding it.
- Create a heroes report that includes various heroes, their heroic acts, and the impact each hero had.
- Write a report about someone you know who is brave. For each section, highlight something that shows the person's bravery.
- Compose a report about a landmark, location, or event within your community.
- Choose a holiday and write a report about the traditions that surround it.
- Write a brochure about one of these topics: sea animals, ancient Rome, Stonehenge, manatees, classic cars, the Titanic, fast food, pollution, Antarctica, or water slides.
- Write a report about higher education and what its purpose is.
- Research a career you think you might like to do when you grow up. Include information about it on a report that includes a job description, required education or training, job satisfaction and pay, and also skills it takes to do the job well.
- Choose a particular kind of natural disaster. Research it and write a report about it.
- Create a poster-style report about an invention.
- Write a report about the different biomes on the earth.
- Choose a microscopic animal and create a report about it.
- Find a product in a grocery store and do some research about it. Write a report about your findings.
- Make a book report about your favorite book.
- Write a report about some of the wonders of the world. You can choose the ancient wonders, the natural wonders, or another list.
- Create a visual report on a poster about one of the

continents. Include sections about people and daily life, plants and animals, government, landmarks, and industry.

- Choose a famous historical figure and write a report about the person's life, accomplishments, and legacy.
- Write a talents or hobbies report. Include information about a talent or hobby you are pursuing.
- Choose a culture to highlight in a report about somewhere in the world that is very different than the place you live.
- Write a report about an animal species that is native to your area.
- Choose a drug and write a report about it and its effects.
- Select a technology-based topic to research and write a report about.
- Write a biographical report about an Olympic athlete.

Essays Idea Bank

- Write an essay about what freedom means to you.
- Craft a 1-3-5 paragraph essay about ways that troubled teens can be helped.
- Compare and contrast how people can be different in some ways and yet still be best friends.
- Compare and contrast Mondays and Fridays.
- Explain some causes and effects of racism in an essay.
- Imagine that your house were going to burn down in a wildfire, and you had to evacuate within thirty minutes. In essay form, write about what items you would take with you and why.
- Write an essay about control and whether you think control is a positive or negative thing and why.
- In an exemplification essay, tell about your three most profound learning experiences.
- Write a 1-3-5 essay about your biggest failure and what you learned from it.
- Using specific examples, write an essay about whether or not you believe social media represents truth and reality.
- Write an essay about insecurity. Discuss the physical, mental, and social effects being insecure has on people your age.
- Write a prediction essay about how the world would change if the internet crashed tomorrow and could never be restored. What would the immediate, mid-range, and long-term effects be?
- Is ethnicity an important part of identity? Why or why not? Choose a side and describe why you believe that way in an essay. Back up your claims.
- Write a compare and contrast essay about yourself and a friend of yours.

☐ Mini-Lesson

The subject is what a sentence is about. The predicate tells what the subject does. Identify the subject and predicate within this sentence:

The heroic Ahab dropped a tear into the sea.

Answer:

(SUBJECT) The heroic Ahab (PREDICATE) dropped a tear into the sea.

☐ Mini-Lesson

Ideas and content is one of the six traits of writing. To help you include enough ideas and content as you are writing a report or essay, it helps to gather information and then make sure you add your own personal perspective to your research. It is the combination of reputable information and your own analysis that makes a report or essay strong.

☐ Mini-Lesson

Parallel structure is an important part of sentence fluency. Each part of the sentence needs to share the same grammatical structure.

Correct this sentence so it has parallel structure:

He realized he would need to skip lunch, running to his car, and be driving straight there to make it on time.

Answer:

He realized he would need to skip lunch, run to his car, and drive straight there to make it on time.

Writer's Workshop

Besides just the writing project, there should be many small writing samples that are being compiled in the Writer's Notebook from the exercises you worked on over the course of this unit. The Writer's Notebook is a tool for helping writers to grow. Explore it frequently and refer to idea lists and helps as you write.

At least once a week, it would be beneficial for you, the writer, to glance back through the exercises, lists, and mini-lessons to review and make sure that you are on track even though most of this work isn't graded.

Specifically, as you are working on the writing project, utilize your Writer's Notebook. You have anchor charts, exercises, and entries in your Journal - all of these can help you as you complete your project. Take time to review some of the concepts you've been working on during the unit so they can be incorporated into the final writing project. The things you've learned should SHOW in your writing project.

Remember that most of the work in the Writer's Notebook will never be graded, but it is still important. Use what you learned to make your project, which will be graded, the best that you can make it.

- Write a compare and contrast essay about yourself and someone you admire.
- Compose a four-paragraph problem and solution essay about bullying.
- In a literary analysis essay, examine the theme, setting, and literary devices within a children's book.
- What role does failure play in life? Write a five-paragraph essay about three people who had huge failures before succeeding.
- Write an exemplification essay about fear using examples from your life of times you've been afraid and how you handled it.
- Write a compare and contrast essay about needs versus wants.
- Compare and contrast a small business with a large corporation. You can write from the point of view of a business owner, an employee, or a customer.
- Write an essay that explains the contributions and drawbacks of the internet.
- Watch a movie and write a response essay that includes your opinion about what you saw.
- Compose an essay about a problem your generation faces and propose some solutions.
- Write an essay about a historical person who inspires you.
- Compare and contrast living in the country with living in the city.
- Write an exemplification essay about why you believe getting an education is important.
- What is your philosophy of life? Write an essay about it.
- Compose an essay about your personality and highlight stories from your life that showcase who you are.
- What is the biggest conflict you have ever been a part of? How did you resolve it? Write about ways to resolve conflict and use your own experiences for inspiration.
- Choose a health topic, like immunizations or blood pressure, that interests you and write about it in essay form.
- Describe a sport, hobby, or other interest and what it contributes to the people who participate in it.
- Explain the problems of obesity from a personal and a societal perspective.
- Write an essay about the positives and negatives the internet has brought to society.
- Examine how communication has changed in the past several decades.
- Describe how your culture differs significantly from another culture of your choice.
- Explain pet ownership in an essay.
- Compare a book with its movie version and write an analysis of the two.

Step 4: Evaluating Writing

The purpose of this unit is to learn the basic skills you need to write reports and essays. Expository writing requires gathering facts and information from good sources, using an organized style, and writing about true topics in interesting ways. Writers should have clear topics with adequate evidence. In this unit, you will also be looking for a bibliography or works cited page. Little learners should use at least one to two sources. Middle grades should use three to five sources for their final project. High school writers should use five to ten sources. You may ask for a C.R.A.A.P. test or specific nonfiction text features, like images, diagrams, or charts to be included as well, depending on the writing project chosen.

As you evaluate the writing project, you will be using the "6 Traits of Writing Rubric" from the Printable Pack. In addition, you will be looking for each step of the entire writing process. For example, your child will turn in a prewriting activity, a draft that shows both revisions and edits, as well as a finished, published piece. The publishing step should involve sharing the project in some way - reading it aloud to family, presenting it at dinner time, video chatting to show it off to grandparents, or sharing a video presentation on the internet of the writer sharing his or her writing. Sharing is a time for positive feedback and celebration.

Creating a positive buzz about the published piece will create a motivating, growth atmosphere in your Writer's Workshop. As you evaluate, remember that the process is just as important as the product, so watch for successes in the process as well. The final score will be out of 50 points - 20 for the process and 30 for the final project. You can write rubric scores as well as comments down on the "Writing Report Card" printable from the Printable Pack.

Breakdown of Possible Points

- 5 points for a complete prewriting activity
- 5 points for a completed draft
- 5 points for revisions
- 5 points for edits
- 30 points for the finished writing project

The 30 points for the finished project is further broken down into each of the six traits of writing as shown on the rubric from the Printable Pack.

Your comments should be specifically focused on the purposes of this unit and the skills you were working on throughout the unit.

What was done well? Is the writer understanding the writing process? What should be improved on? Are there any repeated mistakes to address?

Point out a clear strength.

Comments mean more than scores, so make sure to give clear feedback.

Key Concepts

By the end of this unit your kids should be familiar with these ideas:

The five parts of a friendly letter

The seven parts of a formal letter

The difference in tone between friendly and formal letters

How to type a letter

How to send an email

How to fill out basic forms in ink and follow the given instructions

The standard way names, dates, and locations are written in your area (There is no universal global standard, so look up the formatting for your location.)

More Mini-Lesson Ideas

Along with the sidebars, try these mini-lesson ideas:

- Writer's Workshop links found in Layers of Learning catalog
- Lessons from any grammar workbook
- Every-Day Edits from Education World website
- Sentence diagramming
- Copying great sentences from master writers
- Mad Libs
- Correcting a repeated error from your writing
- Practicing expanding sentences by adding details
- Combining sentences by making two or three into a single sentence

The mini-lesson sidebars in this unit have check boxes so you can keep track of which ones you have completed.

Letters

Writing letters is very different from much of the other writing we do. When we correspond with people through letters, we know specifically who our audience is. Usually, it's just one person we are writing to, so the writing becomes a lot like a conversation. You will think of your specific audience and use clear language to communicate a specific message.

You will likely spend your whole life writing letters in lots of different formats, from a friendly greeting card to the cover letter you include with your resume as you apply for a job. In this world of e-mail, instant messaging, and video chat, you might feel like you don't need to write letters anymore, but there are a lot of times when you will be corresponding with people through writing. Many of the letter writing conventions you learn apply to the messages you write to people whether it's on a sheet of stationary or sent from your smart phone. During this unit we'll learn about both friendly letters and more formal letters. We'll also learn a few other ways of corresponding, including skills like filling out forms and writing checks.

The skills you practice during this unit will help you in your day-to-day written communication with the people you interact with. Take the opportunity to actually put these skills into practice. Send a friendly letter to your grandma in the mail. Fill out your own forms when you go in for your dentist appointment. Write a letter to the editor and send it to your local newspaper. Buy a postcard and send it to someone you know. Create a real resume for yourself that you can use when you're ready to apply for a job. Some of these exercises will be added to your Writer's Notebook, but hopefully many of them will actually be sent off in the mail to the people you are writing to.

Step I: Mini-Lesson

Begin each day of Writer's Workshop with a mini-lesson. You will find some within the sidebars of this unit. You can also use a worksheet from a grammar workbook or practice editing, copying, or diagramming sentences. During writing

time, watch for weak areas or mistakes being made and present a mini-lesson the next day to help kids correct mistakes and improve their writing skills in small, continuous ways.

The mini-lesson should take five to ten minutes and always have a positive happy spin, free from criticism.

Step 2: Writing

Now it's time to really begin writing. Most of your time during Writer's Workshop should be spent writing. Practicing is the key to improving. You can use your writing time to free write your own ideas in your Journal anytime, or use the exercises below to practice writing skills and find inspiration for things to write about. Select as many exercises as you would like to do over the month, making sure you leave time to complete at least one writing project that will go all of the way through the writing process before the month is over. The exercises will also go in your Journal section of your Writer's Notebook. If you decide to take something from your Journal through the writing process and turn it into your writing project, move it from your Journal to the Writing section of your Writer's Notebook.

A few tips and reminders:

- You can repeat the units and the exercises in subsequent years, so don't ever feel pressured to get to all of them, and feel free to repeat ones you enjoy.
- Often a single exercise can be presented to all of your children, no matter their ages or abilities. They will naturally write at the level they are at and, as they practice, will grow as writers.
- As you progress through the exercises, watch for something that sparks interest and could become the writing project. Feel free to jump to the idea bank at the end of the unit anytime as well. If there's spare time after the project is published, return to more exercises.
- Your family may all be in different places in the writing process. That's perfectly fine. Remember, your Writer's Workshop is a garden and everyone is growing their own patch. You can all lend a hand to help each gardener's patch thrive, but you won't all grow the same crop.

It's time to write! Choose some exercises and jump right in!

Parts of a Friendly Letter

During the exercises in this section we will be working on a series of three letters you will be sending to friends. You can choose kids you know, someone in your neighborhood,

☐ Mini-Lesson

During this unit, set up a mail system in your home to send lots of letters back and forth between the members of your family. Everyone in the family can get involved in writing notes, cards, and letters and leaving them in each family member's mailbox.

You can use small mailboxes, baskets, or just set letters on the pillow, dresser, or mirror of the person it is for. Have each member of the family leave at least one note or letter each day. If possible, also arrange for family members from far away to mail letters to the kids during this unit.

☐ Mini-Lesson

In the Printable Pack you will find an example of "A Friendly Letter" written to June. Read through it and talk about each part of a friendly letter, labeled in red. In addition, you'll see more formatting notes labeled in blue. Add the printable to the Writing Helps section of your Writer's Notebook so you can refer to it as you write your own friendly letters.

Writer's Workshop

Sometimes years are written using two digits and sometimes four digits.

16

2016

The months can be expressed in one or two digits or can be written out using the full month's name or a three-letter abbreviation.

8

08

August

Aug.

Likewise, a single-digit date can be expressed in either one or two digits.

9

09

When writing the dates in numerical formats, you can choose to separate the day, month, and year with a hyphen (-), a slash (/), or a period (.).

8-9-16

08/09/2016

08.09.16

Practice writing the birth dates of people you know in a few formats.

☐ **Mini-Lesson**

The words *deer* and *dear* are homophones. They sound alike but have different meanings. Look up each word in a dictionary to more fully understand its definition. Write a short note to an imaginary deer that is a friend of yours.

Dear Deer,

members of your family, your piano teacher, or anyone else you are friends with. You will keep the letters, adding to them a bit at a time as you learn more about how to write friendly letters. At the end, you will have three complete letters you can stamp and send off in the mail to your friends. If you are new to writing letters, this could be your writing project for this unit. Alternately, you can choose a different project based on the skills and ideas from the other sections of the unit. You will find stationary printables in the Printable Pack - one with bears, one with a bee, and one with a bird to write your three letters on. You can also use your own stationary or another format if you'd like.

EXERCISE: Parts of a Friendly Letter

A friendly letter has five basic parts - a heading, a greeting, the body, the closing, and your signature. Look at the "Parts of a Friendly Letter" printable from the Printable Pack to help you understand each of these parts. Remembering the bear can help you remember each part of a letter. His head reminds you of the heading. His mouth reminds you of the greeting, because when we greet someone with a hello we are using our mouths to speak it. His body reminds you of the body of the letter. His feet remind you of the closing. His paw print reminds you of the signature.

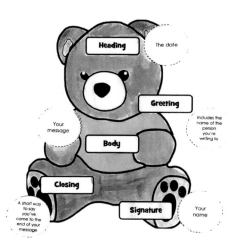

The circles at the bottom of the printable contain a short description of each part. Cut out each circle and glue it on to the bear near the matching part. Add the printable to the Writing Helps section of your Writer's Notebook.

EXERCISE: Friendly Headings

The heading of a friendly letter usually just includes the date you are writing the letter. It is positioned at the top of the letter, usually off to the right hand side of the page. You can write the date in a variety of formats, and the most common way to write it depends on where you live in the world. Here are a few ways to write the exact same date:

- Year/Month/Day (used in Canada and many other countries, and is becoming the International Standard Format):
  2020/05/02

Letters

- Month/Day/Year Formats (used in the United States):
  - 05/02/2020
  - 05/02/20
- Day/Month/Year Formats (used in the U.K., Australia):
  - 02/05/20
  - 02/05/2020
- Single-Digit Day/Month/Year Formats (used in many Hispanic countries):
  - 2/5/20
  - 2/5/2020
- Written Word Options:
  - May 2, 2020
  - 2 May 2020
  - 2020 May 2

Write your date of birth in each of these formats to learn about each one. Then, depending on where you live, practice writing today's date in the most accepted norm for your country three times, once on each of the three letters you are preparing.

EXERCISE: Friendly Greetings

The greeting of a letter is placed on the left-hand side of the page with one extra space left after the heading. Your greeting in a friendly letter says "Dear _____," and then you fill in the person's name in the blank.

Notice that the letter d on "Dear" is capitalized. You will also capitalize the person's name since names are proper nouns. After the name you always include a comma and then skip a line before beginning the next part - the body of the letter. The greeting phrase is the only one that belongs on that line of the letter.

Just for fun, imagine you are writing a letter to ten of your favorite things and practice writing a proper greeting to each one. Whether or not the things have an actual name, we will treat their names as though they are proper and capitalize each one. Remember to capitalize the d in "Dear" as well as the name. Make sure to include a comma after each name as well.

☐ Mini-Lesson

Whenever we write anything, we should always think about our purpose. A friendly letter could have several purposes. Here are a few:

- Express appreciation
- Say hello
- Persuade
- Invite
- Connect
- Inform
- Show love
- Preserve memories
- Apologize
- Ask questions
- Inform
- Share
- Surprise
- Communicate
- Sell
- Make a change
- Speak to the future
- Encourage
- Ask for help
- Give sympathy
- Get a job

Each time you begin to write a letter, think of what your purpose is. Your tone, word choice, length, and style should all change depending on your purpose for writing.

☐ Mini-Lesson

The voice you use in letters depends on who your audience is. Write the first three lines of the body of a letter to your grandma about pollution and our planet.

Now write the first three lines to your senator about the same topic.

How did your voice change depending on your audience?

Mini-Lesson

Voice is one of the six traits of writing. As you write letters, the primary voice you want to reflect is your own. If you didn't sign your letter at all, would your family and close friends be able to read it and know it was written by you?

Look through a few parts of letters you've written and see if your letters sound like you. What do you notice about them that captures your personality?

Mini-Lesson

Beyond just capturing your own voice, you should also consider the tone you are using in letters you write. Gather a variety of greeting cards and read through them, identifying the tone of each one. Greeting card tones can be funny, sarcastic, romantic, spiritual, sentimental, formal, casual, cute, and much more.

As you write letters, consider the tone that fits your message. Your letters communicate more than merely the words you speak through their tone.

Mini-Lesson

Days of the week are proper nouns and are capitalized.

Write each of the days of the week, making sure you capitalize and spell each correctly.

Next to the name, write the abbreviation for each day.

Dear Chocolate Muffin,

Dear Sunshine,

Dear Paintbrush,

Dear Basketball,

Dear Ladybug,

Dear Skittles,

Dear Kindle,

Dear Fluffy Sweater,

Dear Bicycle,

Now that you're a pro at writing greetings, add a greeting to each of the three letters you wrote a heading for using the names of the three friends you plan to send letters to. Choose people you really want to write to because you will be sending the letters in the mail later.

EXERCISE: Body of a Friendly Letter

The body of your letter is your message. After the greeting, you skip a line, indent, and then begin writing your message. You can write just a few sentences, several paragraphs, or a few pages if you have a lot to say.

Consider your audience as you compose the body of your letter. Writing a letter to your best friend will sound very different than a letter to your boss. A love letter will not sound like a cover letter for a job application. A birthday invitation will sound very different than a letter of complaint to a company. Even among friendly letters, a letter to your grandfather may sound quite different from a letter to your best friend who lives next door.

> May 2, 2020
>
> Dear Ryder,
>
> I've missed you so much the past few weeks! I can't wait until you get back so I can hear all about your adventures in Florida. What was your favorite part? Did you see any alligators like you hoped?
>
> I've been keeping pretty busy lately. We went on a cool hike in the canyon—ouch! sore muscles the next day! I also learned how to make homemade popsicles. We cleaned up litter in the park last week too. I can't wait to tell you about my crash in the pond! See you soon!

You might write this to your buddy:

Hey! Wondering if you want to hang out? I'd be cool with catching a movie this weekend. You buy the tickets and dinner in the food court is on me.

The same tone might not go over so well if you're inquiring about a job:

Hey! Wondering if you're hiring? I'd be cool with working for you. I'll start next week. You hire me and I'll

bring the celebration snacks.

You might write this to a company you need a refund from:

I regret to inform you that the earbuds I purchased from you are not working. I request a complete refund and I will happily send them back to you. Please reply with instructions for completing the return and refund.

If you used that same tone to propose marriage to your girlfriend or boyfriend, chances are it wouldn't go over well.

I am pleased to inform you that the recent purchase of your ring was a success and request that you place it on your finger. I require your company and will provide you with the aforementioned ring. Please reply with instructions for completing the transfer of the ring.

Practice writing short bodies of friendly letters with various tones in each of the scenarios below. Include a proper heading and greeting on each one as well.

- Write a letter to your friend, Jane, inviting her to go camping with your family. Now, using the same tone, try writing to your boss, Mrs. Hanks, asking for a raise.
- Write a letter to your friend, Bill, telling him about your bike ride to the park and how you wished he had been there. Now, using the same tone, write a happy birthday letter to your great-grandma for her ninetieth birthday.
- Write a letter to your friend, Javier, inviting him to go to an amusement park. Now, using the same tone, write to your neighbors, Mr. and Mrs. Morales, asking if they would hire you to mow their lawn this summer.

See how the audience matters? Use the three letters you have begun and write the bodies of each of your letters to your friends.

EXERCISE: Friendly Closings

The closing of a friendly letter is a signal phrase that lets your friend know the letter is ending. After the body, you skip a line and then write the closing just to the right hand side of the center of the page, There are lots of phrases you can close a friendly letter with. Use the "Closing Cloud" printable from the Printable Pack and choose some closing phrases to add to the letters you've been writing to your three friends.

May 2, 2020

Dear Ryder,

I've missed you so much the past few weeks! I can't wait until you get back so I can hear all about your adventures in Florida. What was your favorite part? Did you see any alligators like you hoped?

I've been keeping pretty busy lately. We went on a cool hike in the canyon—ouch! Sore muscles the next day! I also learned how to make homemade popsicles. We cleaned up litter in the park last week too. I can't wait to tell you about my crash in the pond! See you soon!

Yours truly,
Karen

☐ Mini-Lesson

Formatting the closing and signature of a friendly letter is easy. Once you have chosen a word or phrase to use as a closing, follow it with a comma. Skip down to the next line and then add your signature below the closing.

If you are sending a typed letter, leave four lines of space between the closing and your typed name. After you print the letter, use the space where you skipped four lines to add your signature in ink.

☐ Mini-Lesson

Capitalize only the first word of your closing in a letter. If you use two words, like "Yours truly," as your closing, only the first word is capitalized. Write ten examples of closings using the correct capitalization.

☐ Mini-Lesson

Use the "Proper Heading, Greeting, & Closing" printable from the Printable Pack for this mini-lesson.

In the first column, look at all three examples of each of the headings, greetings, and closings. Find the one that is written correctly and circle it.

In the second column, spot the mistake in each example and use your pencil to correct it.

In the third column, write your own example of a heading, greeting, and closing that is written in the proper format without any mistakes.

Writer's Workshop

Mini-Lesson

Use the "Bits and Pieces of Letters" printable from the Printable Pack to help you review the parts of friendly letters. Read the words in each box and identify which part of a letter it is. Color the headings yellow, the greetings green, the bodies blue, and the closings red. Which part of a friendly letter was not included in any of the boxes? **(signature)** Write yours on the line at the bottom of the printable.

Mini-Lesson

Cities, states, provinces, countries, and other specific locations are all proper nouns and are capitalized.

Practice writing place names you are familiar with using capital letters.

Mini-Lesson

Place a comma in between the name of a city and state when you write both together, whether you are using the full name or an abbreviation.

Richland, Washington

Richland, WA

Mini-Lesson

Some postal services request that you use all capital letters, no punctuation, and a flush left margin as you address envelopes. This allows computers to more easily read and sort the mail. Look up the guidelines for your postal carrier.

EXERCISE: Signature

Your signature is more than just your name. It is your identifier. It's almost like a password, and you are the only one who can write it in just your style. Throughout your life you will use it to sign official paperwork, sign for packages, and write checks and other financial agreements. When you sign something, it is a symbolic agreement.

Each person has a unique signature not just because of the letters they write to spell out their name, but also because of the style of starting and stopping the letters, the pen lifts between letters, the speed and pressure, and the details and styles of the cursive letters used. It can take a long time, usually years, for people to develop their unique signature. Start practicing yours now. The very same name can look unique depending on how you write it.

Write your name in cursive a number of times. You might want to try various styles and slants until you are happy with it. In a friendly letter, you can use just your first name or both your first and last. Unlike a contract, a letter is casual; you probably aren't agreeing to anything. Still, it's good to practice your signature now so you'll be prepared when you are asked to sign something.

Add your signature to the three friendly letters you've been writing.

EXERCISE: Addressing an Envelope

Sometimes letters can be hand-delivered in person, but often you will need to address an envelope that will be sent a greater distance by a postal carrier. An envelope includes two different addresses on it - the send to address, which is the address of the person you are sending the letter to, and the return address, which is your own address.

Learn to write your home address correctly. Practice on a blank sheet of paper first. It is important to write addresses perfectly and neatly because the postal service needs to be able to quickly and accurately read the address, sort it by location, and then deliver it. If you write the wrong number or the person can't read your handwriting, chances are, your letter will never make it.

Practice writing addresses neatly on the "Addressing Envelopes" printable from the Printable Pack. Include your own address in the top left-hand corner of each envelope and addresses of people you could send mail to in the

centers of the envelopes. Cut out the three stamps and attach each one to the top right-hand corner of each envelope.

Gather three real stamps and three envelopes. Write your return address on each envelope. Write the addresses of your three friends you wrote letters to as well. Insert each of your letters, add a stamp to each one, and send them off in the mail to your three friends.

More Friendly Letters

EXERCISE: Responding To A Friendly Letter

You will need several copies of the "Dear _____" printable from the Printable Pack and at least one buddy for this exercise. The printable is a letter template. Your job is to each take on a persona and write a letter to one of your buddies, to whom you may also assign a persona. You may be asking your friend to go to a dance with you, inviting someone to your birthday party, reconnecting with a friend you haven't seen in a long time, writing to your neighbor to report that her dog damaged your property, or any other topic you can think of. Write a letter on the template that fits with the persona and letter topic you decided on. When you and your buddy have both written a letter, deliver it to each other, read the letters, then use another copy of the printable to respond to the letter you received. Read each letter carefully to decide who your audience is and what tone you should respond with.

EXERCISE: A Letter To Me

Write a letter to your future self. Write about what you're doing with your life right now and what is important to you. Include some goals, hopes, and dreams you have for yourself. Also, mention a few things you would like to

---

☐ Mini-Lesson

Write the names of each of these places correctly, using proper capitalization and commas between the cities and states, provinces, or regions. Here is an example of an original with it re-written correctly on the next line:

salt lake city utah

Salt Lake City, Utah

Each word of the names should begin with a capital letter. A comma should be placed between the city and state or region. Here are some for you to try:

hilo hawaii

brisbane queensland

memphis tennessee

banff alberta

johannesburg gauteng

munich bavaria

bekasi west java

seoul gyeonggi-do

☐ Mini-Lesson

Many locations, like cities, states, provinces, regions, and countries use abbreviations for their names. Use a globe or map to find some interesting locations. Look up each one and find out if it has an abbreviation for that location. Add any you find to a word cloud that shows locations and their abbreviations.

Word choice, one of the six traits of writing, has a different role in letters than in descriptions and stories. Extra words and details are usually out of place in letters. Your message should be direct, concise, and understandable. You can still play with language and use powerful and descriptive words, but you should also edit your letter and not be too wordy.

Read through this example:

Too many words: My new, fuzzy puppy couldn't be any cuter! He is a sweet, adorable bundle of joy. I can't stop hugging him!

Too few words: My new puppy is cute.

Just right: My new puppy is a ball of white fuzz with the sweetest blue eyes I have ever seen.

Can you write your own example of a passage that has too many words, then too few words, and then just the right amount of words?

☐ **Mini-Lesson**

Months of the year are proper nouns and should always be capitalized. Write and illustrate each month of the year on a sheet of paper to practice writing the names of the months. Add your illustrated months to the Writing Helps section of your Writer's Notebook.

do differently or be better at between now and when you open the letter later. Put it in an envelope, seal it up, and write the date you intend to open it on the outside of the envelope. You could choose to open it at the end of the school year, on your next birthday, in five years, when you graduate from high school, or any other date you set.

EXERCISE: Time Capsule
A time capsule is a weather-proof container that you bury or hide away for a number of years. It is meant to capture a moment in time.

Create a time capsule in a waterproof container with a sealing lid. Metal tins, plastic dishes with sealing lids, paint cans, and even large mason jars work well for this. Fill the container with a few mementos. You can include pictures, a current magazine or newspaper, ribbons or certificates from a competition you participated in, a favorite book with a note in it, a list of prices of common items, a family heirloom, an old cell phone, an artifact from your area, and a zip drive of popular music or movies from this year.

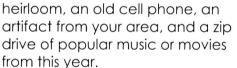

In addition, write a letter to yourself to include in the time capsule. It might include a description of the time you live in, a list of your favorite things, an accounting of people who are important to you, or a description of your hopes or goals for the future, Tuck the letter into an envelope and place it in the time capsule with the other items you chose to include.

Write the date you intend to open it on the outside of the box, then hide or bury the time capsule. Resist the urge to dig it up early! Make sure to set yourself a calendar reminder for the date when you intend to open it. It could be one year, five years, ten years, or even longer.

EXERCISE: Pen Pal Letter
Writing friendly letters is extra fun when you have a pen pal. A pen pal is someone you regularly write and send letters to through the mail. It's neat to learn about what life is like for someone who lives in a different place and circumstance than you do. However, because you are writing to a stranger, always be careful not to share too much personal

information, be open with your parents about each correspondence, and be aware of any inappropriate questions or remarks. You are looking for a pen pal like you - a kid about your age who enjoys writing to other kids to learn and have an interesting mail exchange. You can usually find these through pen pal websites, social media groups, or people you both know. For example, maybe your cousin has a friend who wants a pen pal.

To get you started, use the "To My Pen Pal" printable from the Printable Pack. Fill in the boxes and send your letter.

Here are some ideas of things you can include in a pen pal letter:

- Introduce yourself.
- Tell something interesting or surprising about you.
- Tell about your family, including the names and basic ages of your siblings (no full names, birth dates, or specifics) and something interesting about your parents or others who live in your household.
- Tell about the area you live.
- Share what you've been learning about lately.
- Discuss your favorite things - sports, color, foods, activities, books, and movies.
- Share a memory you've had, like a vacation, a new pet, an outing, or your favorite holiday.
- Ask your pen pal some questions about his or her life.

EXERCISE: Post Card

Post cards are like miniature friendly letters. A post card typically has a picture of a place you have visited on the front and a short message you write on the back. You can get post cards to send to your friends and family any time you go on a trip somewhere or you can even get one from your hometown to send to friends who are far away. They are inexpensive to buy and use a postage stamp that costs less than a regular letter.

Write a message on the left-hand side of the back of the post card. Include the date, a short message, and your name, but don't include any confidential information since the message will be visible to anyone who comes across it. Make sure your message doesn't spill over to the right-hand side of the card. On the right, you will

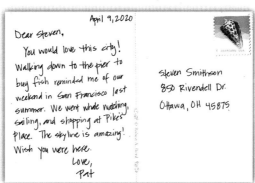

Mini-Lesson

Acronyms are words that are formed from the initial letters of a longer name or phrase. For example, EU is an acronym for European Union. Acronyms are commonly used in everyday speech, informal writing, and in text messages and similar correspondence. There are so many acronyms that you couldn't possibly memorize them all, but you should know what acronyms are so you can look one up if it's unfamiliar to you.

Play a game where you come up with what these acronyms could stand for. Perhaps if the acronym were DIET I might say it stands for "Did I Eat Today?"

Afterwards, look up the actual phrases they represent.

- BRB
- SEAL
- TASER
- DOB
- DIY
- AKA
- IMO
- ROFL
- FO
- ASAP
- UFO

Mini-Lesson

You will need the "People I Could Send Letters To" printable from the Printable Pack. Use the page to brainstorm ideas of all kinds of people you could write to - friends, teammates, family, people in your community, and more. Add the page to the Writing Helps section of your Writer's Notebook.

A post script is an afterthought on a letter. It is abbreviated P.S. and means post scriptum, which is Latin for "written after."

If you forgot to say something while writing the letter, it's acceptable to add a post script after your signature.

P.S. Dad said he would talk to your parents about coming to see us this summer!

Sometimes, there are even two afterthoughts, with the second one called a post post script.

P.P.S. If you come, please bring your new kitten!

Together, think of a friend you know who needs some encouragement right now. Brainstorm several ideas of things you could say in a letter to cheer and uplift your friend. Share the pen to collectively write a letter to the person you chose. Here are a few ideas you can include:

- Share some favorite admirable qualities your friend possesses.
- Remind him or her of a successful accomplishment.
- Thank your friend for being there for you when things were tough.
- Express belief in him or her.

neatly write the name and mailing address of the person you are sending it to. Attach a post card stamp to the top right-hand corner of the back side and drop it in a mailbox.

EXERCISE: Invitations

Invitations are a special kind of letter that conveys information about an upcoming event - often a party, gathering, group activity, or another celebration. As you write invitations, it's important to be clear and informative. The person receiving it should be able to clearly know the event, date, time, location, and any extra information.

Use the "You're Invited" printable invitation from the Printable Pack to practice creating your own invitation. Decide on an imaginary event and details to fill out. Make sure to include extra details in the box, as needed. For example, if it's a costume party or a formal event, you may need to include a dress code. If it's a potluck party, you may need to include a food assignment. Include an R.S.V.P. at the bottom with your own name and phone number. R.S.V.P. comes from the French expression *répondez s'il vous plaît*, meaning "please respond." If RSVP is written on an invitation, it means the host has requested that the guest respond to say if they plan to attend.

If you'd like, you can decide on an actual event you would like to host and send out real invitations to your family or friends. It could be as simple as inviting your family to a pizza night for dinner or inviting your best friend to a play date at a park.

EXERCISE: Greeting Card

Greeting cards are short, thoughtful versions of a friendly letter. You can make your own greeting cards or purchase cards from a store. Some cards are for special events, like a birthday or holiday card, and some are just to say hello. Some greeting cards are even blank, allowing you to put in any message you would like.

Select a person you would like to send a greeting card to. Choose a card that fits his or her personality or celebrates an upcoming event or holiday. Write a short, thoughtful

message inside of the card. Follow the format of any friendly letter, making sure to include personal elements. Incorporate all five parts of a friendly letter. Neatly address an envelope, attach a stamp, and mail your letter off.

EXERCISE: Thank You Card

Learning to write thoughtful thank you cards is an important life skill. Think of something kind someone has done for you and write a message thanking him or her for it. Begin by writing the date as your heading and your friend's name and a greeting. Skip a line to begin the body of your letter.

There are three key things that will help your message communicate your gratitude. First, thank the person for the gift or kind thing he or she did. Second, tell what difference it made to you or explain how you enjoy the gift or gesture. Third, express something about the person that you admire, respect, or love. Of course, after you have written the body of the letter, add your closing and signature.

August 20, 2018

Dear Gertie,

Thank you so much for the neat art set you got me for my birthday. I love it! I have already made two paintings and started to fill my sketch book with lots of colorful new drawings. You are a generous, thoughtful friend. Being with you always makes me smile.

Love,

Savannah

Purchase or craft a thank you card and transfer your message to the card to send to your friend.

EXERCISE: Gift Tags

Gift tags are miniature versions of friendly letters. If you give someone a gift, make sure it is clear who the gift is to and from by attaching a gift tag.

Craft your own gift tag. Write "To:_____" and fill in the recipient's name. Write a brief, single sentence message below. Go down another line and write your closing and signature. You don't need to include a

---

Mini-Lesson

Review compound words by creating a compound word flip book. Each part of the word goes on the outside doors. When you open both, you see the compound word that is created by the two words together.

Mini-Lesson

As you write letters, avoid clichés. You can still write vivid and original sentences without overusing clichés.

Clichéd: My trip got canceled after I paid the deposit for it and it made my blood boil.

Original: My trip got canceled after I paid the deposit for it and it makes me want to go to the gym and punch the bag for a few hours.

Change the following cliché into something more original.

I've never seen such a huge storm! It's raining cats and dogs out there.

date or a body paragraph. Attach your gift tag to a small gift and give it to someone. It could be as simple a baking a batch of cookies and delivering them to a neighbor or painting a picture for your parents. Wrap the gift, attach your tag, and give the gift to the person.

EXERCISE: Notes

Notes are one of the most informal of all the writing forms. You can leave a note for anyone, anytime. You can leave a note on your mom's pillow telling her you love her, or a note on the kitchen counter as a reminder that your family needs milk from the grocery store. You can put a note on the steering wheel of someone's car with a compliment on it to start their day out right. You can leave a note for your dad to remind him to pick you up from hockey practice.

Notes are tiny messages that remind us of things. There is no proper format or requirements for writing notes. Write some notes to people in your family and post them around your house in places they will be found.

EXERCISE: Simulated Letter

A simulated letter is a letter that lets you imaginatively assume the role of another person and write from that person's point of view. You might enjoy choosing a historical person you are learning about right now. Research the person's life, family, and notable events. Imagine what it would be like to live in that time and place. Write a letter to someone that details a major life event the person experienced. Here are a few ideas of people you could assume the role of as you write a simulated letter:

- Queen Nefertiti right after her husband, a pharaoh of Egypt, passed away and she assumed the role of co-regent.
- Archimedes, the Greek scientist, after discovering an approximation of pi that helped us solve for the circumference of circles.
- Ti Ying, the Chinese girl, who bravely challenged Emperor Wen of Han to abolish the Five Punishments.
- Edvard Munch, the famous Scandinavian expressionist painter, while painting *The Scream*.
- Harriet Tubman, heroic Underground Railroad conductor in early America during her first escape from slavery.
- A Nazi guard at a German World War II concentration camp after releasing poison gas into the gas chamber full of Jews.
- Sir Joseph Banks, a naturalist and scientist, after his first day exploring Botany Bay, Australia and discovering and collecting numerous new plants.

- The Wright Brothers, right after their first successful flight.
- Margaret Knight, inventor of the flat-bottomed paper bag that has changed many shopping experiences, when she decided to make her own bag company.
- Anna Filosofova, Russian women's rights activist, after discovering how mistreated female serfs were in her society.

EXERCISE: Letter to an Author

Choose your favorite author to write a letter to. Many authors share either their address or email address on their websites and enjoy receiving letters from their readers. Before you begin your letter, make sure your author is still living and that you can find contact information for the author from one of his or her books or online. Your letter will include all five parts of a friendly letter.

In the body of the letter, write about the book or series by the author. Here are a few topic ideas:

- My favorite part of the book was . . .
- I predict that . . .
- One part that was hard for me to understand was . . .
- The character I liked best was . . .
- What surprised me most was . . .
- The book reminded me of . . .
- If I had written the story, I would've . . .
- While reading, I figured out . . .
- A question I have is . . .
- I think you chose the title because . . .

You can also tell a little about yourself. When you finish writing your letter, send it to the author by mail or email.

EXERCISE: Sending A Friendly Email

Not all friendly letters are written out on paper. You can use a computer or another device with internet to send an email. Email, or electronic mail, is a lot like a normal friendly letter, but there are a few key differences.

You don't normally include a date because email is automatically dated by the email service provider. Before

> June 6, 2020
>
> Dear Mrs. George,
>
> I am a huge fan of your books. I have read the Tuesdays at the Castle series more times than I can count! When I come to the end of a chapter, I can't put it down even though I've read the story before. My favorite character is Celie. I'm making my own atlas just like she did, but mine includes my house, my neighborhood, and the beach and park in my town.
>
> I like to write stories just like you. I even wrote one about Celie and Rufus. It has griffins and unicorns and lots of magic. Thank you for giving me so many cool ideas. When I'm finished I would like to send you my collection of stories. In the meantime, I'm also going to be reading the Dragon Slippers series. I can't wait! I hope you have a great day and never stop writing!
>
> From,
> Anna Johnson

☐ Mini-Lesson

The words lie and lay are often confused with each other and misused.

Lay means to place an object down. Lie means to recline your body.

Fill in these sentences with the proper word:

My hen can _____ an egg a day.

I am tired and can't wait to _____ on my bed.

When I'm cold, I _____ a blanket across my lap.

(lay, lie, lay)

☐ Mini-Lesson

If you don't have one, set up your own email account. You can get a free Google account with an email address. Add your profile information and photo. Adjust the settings so the account looks and functions the way you prefer. Also, create a signature that will automatically be placed at the end of each email you send.

☐ Mini-Lesson

Learn to create an address book in your email account. Each email service has its own specific process, but they are pretty simple to learn. Add the email addresses and contact information for your friends and family so you can always have the contacts on hand that you may be writing to, no matter which of your devices you write from.

Mini-Lesson

Some email guidelines:

Do:

- Reread your email once to revise it and a second time to edit it before hitting send.
- Feel free to attach appropriate images or files as needed.
- Add emojis or extras with your friendly messages.
- Send messages to family and friends you know.

Don't:

- Ever send or open junk mail or SPAM.
- Click on a link or download an attachment you don't recognize.
- Correspond with or give personal information to strangers online.
- Log into your account on other people's devices and forget to log out.
- Be afraid to get a parent if something inappropriate shows up.

Mini-Lesson

Practice conventions. Type an email that is full of mistakes and have someone else edit it. Meanwhile, they can type an email that's full of mistakes for you to edit.

Mini-Lesson

If your computer is equipped with Microsoft Office, the Letter Wizard can be used to take the guesswork out of formatting business letters. Explore what your word processing software offers.

you begin typing out the main body, you will type the email address of the person you are sending it to and also choose a subject line so the recipient can immediately see what the email is about. The subject line can be as simple as "Hello!" or be more specific. When you have filled in the applicable fields at the top, move your cursor to the main field of the email screen.

Begin with a greeting that includes the person's name, just as you would in any friendly letter. You will also be writing the body, called the "message" in an email, just as you would in any friendly letter. The message is typed using complete sentences and paragraphs, though you don't need to worry about indenting paragraphs. Just hit enter to go the next line and begin your new paragraph.

At the end of the message, you should include a closing and a signature. You won't be physically writing or signing your name, but it is perfectly acceptable to simply type your signature in an email. Some people adjust the settings in their email service to automatically add a signature to each email they send.

Always read over your email before sending and revise it as you go. Since you are using a computer, you can use spellcheck and grammar check to help you edit your email. When your message is complete and you have finished revising and editing, just hit send and it will arrive within seconds.

Formal Letters

Formal letters are used for more official purposes than friendly letters. If you are writing to business contacts,

companies, authorities, dignitaries, or politicians, you will use a formal letter. Because these aren't people you speak to casually, there are specific conventions you use when writing formal letters.

EXERCISE: Basic Format for a Formal Letter

You will need the "Formal Letter" printable from the Printable Pack for this exercise. Look at and discuss each part of a formal letter and practice writing your own as you go. You will need the parts of a formal letter labeled in green and extra formatting notes shown in blue on the printable.

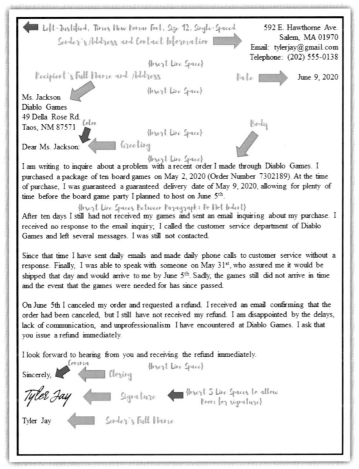

First, you'll need to choose a business contact and sit at a computer to write your own formal letter as you learn about each part. Formal letters are typed, not hand-written. Use Times New Roman font in size 12 or another standard font and size. The entire letter will be left-justified and single-spaced, Here is the basic format for a formal letter:

#1 - Sender's Address and Contact Information

Include the sender's address (your address) at the top of the letter, above the date. Do not write the sender's name or title, as it is included in the letter's closing. Include only

You will need the "Formal Farewells" printable from the Printable Pack.

To close a formal letter, you need to use an appropriate closing. Business and employment-related letters just don't have the right professional tone if they use closings like "Love," or "Yours truly," or other familiar phrases. Write your favorite ways to say farewell in a formal closing inside each speech bubble on the printable. Here are a few ideas you can choose from:

- Sincerely,
- Regards,
- Yours sincerely,
- Cordially,
- Yours respectfully,
- Warm regards,
- Best wishes,
- With appreciation,
- Best,
- Cordially yours,
- Fond regards,
- In appreciation,
- Many thanks,
- Respectfully,
- Thank you,
- Warmly,
- With appreciation,

Add the completed printable to the Writing Helps section of your Writer's Notebook so you can refer to it as you write formal letters.

Remember, even among formal letters, there are different audiences and purposes in your letters. Always consider who you are writing to and why you are writing, and choose a fitting closing.

☐ Mini-Lesson

The final sentence in the body of a formal letter usually refers to future contact. You might use one of these phrases:

- I look forward to your reply.
- I hope we can speak in person soon.
- Thank you for clearing this up and getting back to me.

☐ Mini-Lesson

The tone you use in letters depends entirely on how formal the letter is. To adapt your writing to a more formal voice in formal letters.

- Avoid colloquial words
- Avoid slang
- Avoid clichés
- Use "such as" instead of "like"
- Avoid contractions

Read through this list of kinds of letters and determine whether or not it is formal or friendly. Each time it is formal, read through the bullet points above to learn how to adapt to a more formal tone.

College applications

A letter to your best friend

A note to your dad

Your resume

Your journal

A letter to your boss

A text message to your aunt

A form at the doctor's office

A letter to a pet store in town

A social media post about your latest vacation

the street address, city, and zip code.

#2 - Date

Skip one space after the sender's address and write the date in the proper date format for the country you live in.

#3 - Recipient's Address

The recipient's address is placed on the left hand side after skipping one space. The first line includes the recipient's full name with a title (Ms., Mrs., Mr., Dr., etc.). On the next line, write the street address. The line after that will contain the city, state, and zip code. For international addresses, type the name of the country in all-capital letters on the last line.

#4 - Greeting

Use the same name you wrote on the inside address, including the personal title and last name followed by a colon. Leave one line blank after the greeting.

If you are writing to a business or professional group and don't know the specific name of the person who will be reading your letter, you can write "To Whom it May Concern:" in place of a name and title.

#5 - Body

Single space each paragraph within the body of the letter. Leave a blank line between each paragraph. Unlike other writing, paragraphs in a formal letter are not indented. Be concise in your message. You can include a friendly opening, a statement of the main point, any necessary details and background information, and then a clear statement or request of the action you are hoping will be taken.

#6 - Closing

The closing begins one line after the last body paragraph. Capitalize the first word only, place a comma after it, and leave four lines between the closing and the sender's name. That area is for you to write your signature after you have printed your letter.

#7 - Signature

Your signature is the only part of a formal letter that is handwritten instead of typed. Leave four spaces as you type the letter. After you've printed it out, sign your full name in cursive using a pen with black ink.

You may send it in the mail if you wrote it for a real purpose to a real contact. Otherwise, add it to the Journal section of your Writer's Notebook if you wrote the letter just for

practice. Add the "Formal Letter" printable to the Writing Helps section of your Writer's Notebook.

EXERCISE: Business Letter

Choose a business in your local community that has impressed you that you could write to. Perhaps you want to thank them for the good they do in your area or call attention to a positive experience you had there. Maybe you had an excellent time at a movie theater or another entertainment-based business. Possibly you really enjoyed your meal at a restaurant in your town. Did you notice an employee going above and beyond in a store or see a business that was really clean and well-kept? You can write a letter to give a kudos and thank the company for doing an excellent job.

Using the format of a formal letter, type a letter to the company. Make sure you have included all seven parts of a formal letter. Revise your letter and edit it with someone else's help. Print the letter out and sign your name in the signature area. Address and stamp the envelope before mailing your letter.

EXERCISE: Political Letter

Politicians work for the people they help to govern, so it's important that those people tell the politicians their thoughts, ideas, and opinions about political decisions and policies. Choose one of the politicians who governs either locally or nationally and write a formal letter sharing your ideas or opinions about a current issue. Mail the letter.

EXERCISE: Letter To The Editor

A letter to the editor is not really intended to be for the editor of a newspaper. It is an opinion letter that is published in the newspaper so that anyone can read it. Typically, letters to the editor are focused on specific current events or issues. You may need to get a copy of the newspaper, either in print or online, and read about some current news stories and events. As you read, ask yourself what your opinion is. What should be done? How should the issue be handled or viewed?

Type a letter to the editor using the format of a formal letter. Make sure to be clear and organized as you write your ideas. Include any evidence you can. Have someone else read your letter and help you revise it. Finally, do a careful edit to make sure there are no mistakes in the conventions. Print it, sign it, and mail it to the newspaper office. Your letter might even get published in the newspaper.

☐ Mini-Lesson

Review punctuation marks by playing *Name That Punctuation Mark*. Speak a sentence out loud and have the kids shout out what kind of punctuation mark should be placed at the end.

☐ Mini-Lesson

If you have enclosed any documents along with the letter, such as a resume, you indicate this simply by typing the word Enclosures below the closing. As an option, you may list the name of each document you are including in the email or envelope. For instance, if you have included many documents and need to ensure that the recipient is aware of each document, it may be a good idea to list the names of each item you included.

☐ Mini-Lesson

When writing formally, avoid informal language. Here are a few characteristics of informal language you should avoid:

- Slang words
- Contractions
- Extra punctuation (Hooray!!!)
- Jokes and attempts at humor
- Casual phrases

Together, brainstorm a few examples of informal language that could fall into these categories. Can you come up with more formal ways to say the same phrases?

☐ Mini-Lesson

You will need the "Strong Words To Use On A Resume" printable from the Printable Pack for this mini-lesson.

Look over the words and find some that you especially think describe you.

At the bottom of the page, write at least five descriptions of yourself that you could include on a resume. Use some of the strong words you suggested.

Your descriptions can include interpersonal skills, leadership skills, communication skills, analytical skills, and organizational skills.

Descriptions on resumes are often phrases, not complete sentences. Here is an example of someone who had been an assistant manager at his last job:

Demonstrated strong leadership skills by delegating tasks, evaluating job performances, and motivating staff.

☐ Mini-Lesson

Often hitting the proper tone in a letter, either friendly or formal, comes from being able to come up with another way to say the same thing. Use the "Other Ways To Say It" printable from the Printable Pack.

Write a letter that includes a message with each of these phrases. Rewrite the same message using other ways to say it. Did it change the tone? When you're finished, add the printable to the Writing Helps section of your Writer's Notebook.

EXERCISE: Sending A Formal Email

Sending a formal email is a lot like sending a friendly email. Make sure you always use a subject line, a short, concise message, and professional language. The only real difference between friendly and formal email is the tone you use. The casual or formal feel to writing is called the "tone" of the letter.

In a friendly email you might say, "Hi, I'm Rene." However, in a formal email you would more likely say, "Allow me to introduce myself. My name is Renee Prim." In a friendly email, you might say, "Do you get it?" In a formal email, a better phrase would be: "Let me know if you have any questions."

Use the "Writing Tones" printable from the Printable Pack. Look at the phrases in the casual column and in the formal column and come up with a companion phrase that matches the meaning but uses the opposite tone.

When you have finished filling out the printable, use the ideas from it to help you compose a formal email to someone. Get on your computer and write to a company or another formal contact. Use a professional tone that is appropriate for a formal email.

EXERCISE: Resume

A resume is a one-page document that tells prospective employers about you. There isn't one specific format, but all resumes seek to be an organized, clear, and attractive one-page document that describes your objective, education, experience, and other skills, volunteer experiences, activities, and awards that showcase who you are. At the bottom, a resume typically lists references as well - people who know you well and can attest to your character and qualifications.

You will need two printables for this exercise - the example "Bridget Cameron" resume and the blank resume template that matches this example.

First, read through the entire example resume. Use the blank template to create a handwritten version of your own to practice on. Use real information from your life. When you have finished drafting your resume, use a computer to type your own version. You can use any word processing software or can search for a free resume builder online.

BRIDGET CAMERON

BCAMERON@GMAIL.COM - (256) 749-1902 – 1143 PEN LANE COLUMBUS, AL 31901

OBJECTIVE
To obtain a position in the restaurant management field.

EDUCATION

Layers of Learning Academy	Columbus, Alabama
Expected Graduation Date	June 2021
Grade Point Average	3.8

EXPERIENCE

Subway Restaurant · Columbus, Alabama · Sept 2019 – present

Provided excellent and efficient customer service. Given outstanding employee bonus. Exceeded all required training and management courses and was promoted to assistant manager. Trained, scheduled, and supervised other employees.

VOLUNTEER WORK

Little Dancers Mentor · Jan 2019 – present

Instructed and mentored young dancers at Little Dancers Studio. Helped sew recital costumes, choreograph dances, and track monthly tuition payments.

Adopt-A-Highway Volunteer · Sept 2019 – present

Adopted four miles of the main stretch of highway running through Columbus, Alabama. Coordinate clean-up efforts twice a year to pick up and dispose of all of litter, branches, and debris to keep the city clean. Coordinated clean-up efforts with the city.

ACTIVITIES & AWARDS

State Speech Competition Winner	June 2019
Robotics Club President	Sept. 2019 – present
Swim & Water Polo Teams	July 2017 – present
National Honor Society Member	2020

REFERENCES

James Vernon	Swim Coach	(256) 555- 7410
Mary Ricci	Subway Manager	(256) 555-9090

When you have finished your resume, make sure to proofread it carefully and check for these things:

- Is it one page long? Most resumes should fit on a single page and include only the most important information about you.
- Is your resume easy to read? It should have a neat and organized layout, adequate white space to feel restful to the eye, and include a simple, consistent layout.
- Did you carefully edit? Make sure there are no spelling, grammar, or punctuation mistakes.
- Does your resume describe you clearly and positively? You should have included strong verbs, accurate information, and things that are unique to you and your skills, traits, and experiences.

EXERCISE: Cover Letter

A cover letter is a letter you include with your resume to help the company understand who you are, your qualifications, and the goals you have within the company you are applying to. Cover letters are friendly, but still professional and formal in tone.

☐ Mini-Lesson

Some tips for writing successful cover letters:

- Send a customized cover letter to each company you are applying to.
- Always include the name of the person hiring if possible. Taking the time to show that you know the person instead of just writing, "To Whom It May Concern:" will make a positive impression.
- Read through the description of the position and learn a bit about the company so you can include the reasons you would be a good fit for their position.
- Connect your skills and strengths with what the company is specifically looking for.
- Don't duplicate your resume. Complement it.
- Don't be afraid to describe your accomplishments and positive character traits
- Feel free to tell a very brief story that explains who you are or what you have been successful at.

☐ Mini-Lesson

Resumes and cover letters are usually printed on quality, white paper. They are not overly cluttered with color or distracting pictures or layouts.

Your resume and cover letter design may change depending on the job you are seeking. An aspiring illustrator will likely have a more artistic resume and cover letter than an aspiring accountant.

Often a thesaurus can help you change informal language into a more formal tone. For example, instead of using the word cheap, I could say inexpensive.

Look up each of these words in a thesaurus and find a more formal way to say it.

- Live
- Job
- Get
- Mad
- Tell
- Give
- Want
- Think

Be careful. A thesaurus is a valuable tool, but you should always know the meanings of the words you choose. Stalwart and stubborn are together in the thesaurus, but they actually have very different connotations.

☐ **Mini-Lesson**

Titles of respect are commonly used in formal letters. If you write to someone other than a friend or family member, you should use a title of respect. They are commonly abbreviated. Always capitalize the beginning of a title and the names since they are proper nouns. Write formal letter greetings that uses each of these titles:

- Mr.
- Mrs.
- Miss
- Ms.
- Dr.

Read through the example "Cover Letter" from the Printable Pack, then write your own. Think of a company you would like to either work for or have an internship with. Use your real experiences, traits, and skills to describe why you would be a good fit for the company.

If you've already written a resume for yourself, look at the resume while composing your cover letter. Make sure you don't repeat what you wrote on your resume, but instead, tell more deeply about the things you stated. For example, if your resume describes you as organized, tell a brief example of a time you arranged or categorized something.

Print your letter and put it with your resume in your Writer's Notebook. They can be added to your Journal, or to the Writing section of your Writer's Notebook if you took the resume and cover letter through the entire writing process.

EXERCISE: Letter of Recommendation

A letter of recommendation is a letter written about someone you know to a person or company who is looking into the person. For example, a coworker of yours may be looking for a new promotion and has asked you to write a letter to a company on his or her behalf. Write letters of recommendation in the format of all formal letters, using the seven parts.

Sit down at your computer and type an imaginary letter of recommendation about an imaginary friend. You'll write the body of the letter in three paragraphs.

In paragraph one, explain how you know the person. Tell how you met, how long you have been acquainted, and describe what kind of relationship you have. If you are a next door neighbor that will be different than if you are the person's boss, for example.

In paragraph two, positively explain the person's skills, traits, and experiences that show he or she would be an asset to the person you are writing to. Focus on three to five specific qualities that showcase the person individually. Give several examples and use strong, positive, exact verbs to describe your friend.

In paragraph three, share your own recommendation and contact information. Let the person know why you are recommending your friend and how they can reach you if they want to discuss more about the person.

When you are finished with the body, go back through the seven parts of a formal letter and make sure you included each part correctly. Print your letter and add it to the Journal section of your Writer's Notebook.

EXERCISE: Resignation Letter

You will need the "Letter of Resignation" printable from the Printable Pack for this exercise. When it's time for you to quit working for a company, you may need to write a letter of resignation. Writing one can be an uncomfortable task. It is important to be gracious and professional even as you are resigning. After all, your current boss just may get a call from your future one asking about what kind of employee and person you are.

As you write your letter of resignation, follow all of the standard professional letter rules. In addition, make sure you graciously thank your employer for what you gained by working for him or her. Also, be positive as much as you can.

Read through the letter from the printable. First, spot each of the parts of a formal letter. Next, use a highlighter pen to highlight each positive phrase that was used to write the letter. This resignation letter is just for practice. You don't need to keep it in your Writer's Notebook.

More Correspondence Skills

EXERCISE: Writing Reviews

Reviews give us a chance to share our opinions with others about the books, products, and places we have tried out. In addition, we get the benefit of reading other reviews before we buy things to help us make decisions about what to buy and where to spend our money. It's rare that I buy anything online without first reading some of the reviews.

Reviews are usually fairly friendly in style, but because we are writing to a variety of people we've never met, it's best to use a more formal tone as we write reviews.

Choose a book you've read, a product you've purchased and used, or a restaurant you've eaten at. Go online and write an honest review about the book, product, or restaurant. Searching for the item and the word review will usually lead you right to a place you can leave a review. Make sure to be honest, respectful, and formal in tone. People will trust your review more if you are detailed with the things you like or dislike about the item and if you are thorough and respectful in your description.

EXERCISE: Writing Checks

Checks aren't nearly as common as they used to be, but it's still really important to know how to write them for those occasions when a check is required. Writing a check is

---

☐ Mini-Lesson

There are many purposes for writing business letters. Here are a few:

- Inquiring about information.
- Requesting that someone do something.
- Apologizing.
- Complaining.
- Thanking or expressing gratitude.
- Asking for a job, a pay raise, a title, or another professional assignment.

Can you think of any specific formal letters you could send and then state the purpose for that letter?

☐ Mini-Lesson

In formal letters, we avoid using contractions. Change each of these contractions into their more formal version.

- couldn't
- we'll
- shouldn't
- didn't
- who'd
- what's
- he'd
- isn't
- she'll

☐ Mini-Lesson

As you begin to fill out applications, forms, and any official documents, you should always use blue or black ink unless instructed otherwise. Some forms specifically require black ink.

☐ **Mini-Lesson**

☐ **Mini-Lesson**

Actual checkbooks usually have duplicate checks. The first one is the copy you write on, and the check underneath creates a carbon copy of what you wrote for your own records. You tear off the top check and give it to the person you are paying. The copy gets retained for your own records so you record what you spent from your checking account.

If you have one available, try writing in an actual checkbook and watch the carbon copy be created. Make sure to use the tab on the checkbook cover so the writing doesn't press through to other carbon copies.

Once you've written the check, make sure to cross it out and write VOID across it so it can't be used.

☐ **Mini-Lesson**

Tips for check security:

- Always use a pen when you write a check. Anyone with an eraser could change the amount if you use pencil.
- Never sign a check until you've filled out everything else. Signing a blank check is like giving someone unlimited access to the money in your checking account.
- Keep track of your checkbook. If someone finds your checkbook, they can pretend to be you and forge checks, paying for things from your account.

really easy once you've practiced once or twice. You'll need the "Writing Checks" printable from the Printable Pack for this exercise. Fill out each part of the first check as we go through it, step by step. Then cover the first check and see if you can fill out the second one all by yourself.

Before you begin the steps, there are a few things you need to write on the checks first. Checks you receive from the bank will have your name and contact information printed directly on them. Fill in your name and address in the upper left corner. You may include your phone number as well if you would like. In addition, real checks have the name of the bank listed below the account holder's information. Optionally, you can add the name of your bank, Now let's get on with the steps of writing a check.

Step 1: Write today's date in the top right-hand corner. Use the standard way dates are written in your location.

Step 2: Go down to the "Pay To The Order Of" line and clearly write the name of the person or business you are paying.

Step 3: Using numerals, write the amount of payment in the box with the $ sign in front of it. Typically, the dollar numerals are written larger and are followed by a decimal point, then the cents are written smaller, often above a fraction bar.

Step 4: On the line below, write the payment amount again, this time using words. This is a safety feature of checks so people can't just change the amount before cashing it. The numerals and words must match. Write out the dollars followed by the word "and," then write the cents in fraction form with 100 as the denominator. Always draw a line across the remainder of the space so it can't be altered.

Step 5: The line that says "for" is simply a memo for yourself. It gives you a chance to write a note to yourself about what the payment was for. It isn't required, but it can come

in handy. Certain payments need to have an account number or another identifying feature listed, and this line is also a good place to do that.

Step 6: Add your signature in cursive to the line in the right-hand corner at the bottom of the check. Until you sign it, the check isn't valid. Your signature should be the same each time you write it. You can keep practicing signatures until you are happy with yours and the way it looks.

EXERCISE: Job Application

Use the "Application For Employment" printables from the Printable Pack for this exercise. There are two pages for you to fill out on the application. If possible, print the two pages on one sheet of paper - front and back.

Practice filling it out all by yourself. You use a pen to fill out an application, and you typically only get one copy of it, so you have to think about what you are writing before you just begin to fill it in. Use your best handwriting so it is easy to read.

Once you've finished, share your application with someone and get their feedback about what you can improve. It may be helpful to practice a few times so when you are really filling out job applications, you'll be prepared. Application forms aren't all identical, so you need to read every single one completely and fill it out carefully when you're really applying for jobs.

This application is for practice. You don't need to keep it in your Writer's Notebook.

EXERCISE: College Application

Most college applications are now filled out completely online. Every school has its own application and requirements. If you know what colleges, universities, or trade schools you might be interested in applying to, go visit their websites and see if you can access the applications. You may need to create an account. Most college applications are not filled out in a single day. You will log in to your account to work on your application. Often there will be essays in addition to the basic information you will be required to fill out.

The application will not actually be sent to the school until you complete everything, officially submit it, and usually pay a fee. The wonderful part about that is that you can practice your application without submitting it at all. Go do some research on the websites of one or two schools you may be interested in attending. If possible, practice

---

☐ **Mini-Lesson**

Use the "Filling out Forms" printable from the Printable Pack for this Mini-Lesson. The printable shows several ways forms ask you to fill in basic information about yourself.

Look at each of the four boxes and practice filling out the forms using a pen. Make sure to follow all of the directions. Some tell you to use all capital letters. Some specify how the date should be written. Anytime it requires a signature, that must be done in cursive. Some allow space to write above the lines while others expect you to write below the lines.

Look over the variety of fields and talk together about some of the similarities and differences you may come across as you fill out forms.

☐ **Mini-Lesson**

Your full name includes your first, middle, and last names. Some people have more than one. For example, my grandmother had two middle names, so her full name would have included her first name, both middle names, and her last name.

Furthermore, each person who gets married can choose whether or not to keep, change, or add to their last name. Women who change their last name must often use their maiden name (their last name before they took their husband's surname at marriage) for certain official forms and documents.

☐ **Mini-Lesson**

In the revising stage of the writing process, we listen for mistakes. In the editing stage, we look for mistakes.

Use the acronym CUPS to help you remember what to look for as you edit.

Capitalization - of sentences, proper nouns, titles, and anywhere else a capital belongs.

Usage - Complete sentences, proper formatting, verb tenses, subject-verb agreement

Punctuation- correct punctuation throughout the letter, including within the date, after the greeting and closing, throughout the body of the letter, and in abbreviations you used.

Spelling - look up words you aren't sure about and make sure everything is spelled correctly.

☐ **Mini-Lesson**

Instead of using your middle name, many forms ask for your middle initial. This is the first letter of your middle name, capitalized and followed by a period to show you are abbreviating it.

filling out the applications. College applications are a cross between a resume and a job application. Use a formal tone and be exact and descriptive about why you deserve a place at their school. Practicing ahead of time will help you be more successful when it is time to actually begin applying.

EXERCISE: Community Forms

Many places you go frequently ask you to fill out forms, so you need to know how to do that ahead of time.

Before you ever write on a form, it's important to read over the whole thing first. Often there are specific requirements, like using only black ink or writing in all capital letters. If you skip over the instructions, you may make a mistake and have to start over. Also note that on a lot of forms, there are sections that aren't supposed to be filled out. For example, when I applied for a library card, I wrote in my personal information, but the librarian was the one who had to write in the library's information and my new card number. There was a box with those parts inside that said, "Library use only." Those words told me that the box was not a place for me to write.

Also, make sure whenever you sign a form that you understand what you're agreeing to. Your signature is your agreement, so make sure you know what you're signing and ask any questions you have ahead of time. Gather some of these forms from around town and practice filling them out.

- Medical information at a doctor's or dentist's office.
- Library card applications.
- Store rewards card applications.
- Change of address form from the post office.
- Magazine subscription cards (you can find these right inside of magazines you may have at home).
- Order forms from catalogs.

EXERCISE: Vehicle Collision Report

When you get into a traffic accident, the police will ask you to fill out a vehicle collision report. Use the "Vehicle Collision Report" printable from the Printable Pack to practice. This printable only includes some of the most basic information. On the back side, you will need to write a detailed narrative of what happened and the events that led to the accident, occurred during it, and followed. Include all of the important events and the injuries that occurred. The police also usually ask you to draw a diagram of the crash.

You may need to go out to your family vehicle and write

down the important information from it. Find the license plate number, the VIN number, the registration and insurance information, and anything else you need in order to fill out the report.

This form is for practice. You don't need to keep it in your Writer's Notebook.

Step 3: Writing Project

During this unit, you should complete at least one writing project, taking a piece of writing through the entire writing process. By the final week of the unit, if you haven't completed the project already, you should turn your attention to creating one polished piece of writing that uses the things you've practiced along the way.

Choose one topic to write about that you will take all of the way through the writing process. This piece of writing belongs in the Writing section of your Writer's Notebook. You can use something you've already started during this unit, your own idea, or something from the following idea banks. Make sure that you follow each step of the writing process and keep all of your steps to turn in with your finished writing.

- Step #1: Prewrite
- Step #2: Draft
- Step #3: Revise
- Step #4: Edit
- Step #5: Publish

Begin with a prewriting activity, then compose a draft, revise it, edit it with help from someone else, and then publish it. Publishing it could include making a polished final copy, sharing it with someone, creating a book, or creating some form of finished project that is neat and done well. You'll turn in all of your work, from prewrite to publish.

Your project will be evaluated based on the six traits of writing, so make sure you look at your composition through each of those lenses - ideas and content, organization, word choice, sentence fluency, conventions, and voice. Try to incorporate things you learned from the mini-lessons and the exercises you worked on as well. Do your best work.

Letters Idea Bank

- Make a handmade card for the next holiday that's coming up and write a letter in it to someone you know. Send it in the mail.
- Send a thank you card to a hero who has served well in your community - a soldier, a paramedic, a firefighter, a

---

☐ **Mini-Lesson**

There's a Chinese proverb that says:

Never write a letter while you are angry.

The letters and other pieces of correspondence you write are a reflection on you, so remember to present the best version of yourself. Even if you are angry, you can choose to present yourself kindly and intelligently.

☐ **Mini-Lesson**

Words like mom, dad, grandma, and grandpa, are capitalized only when they are used as names.

I miss you so much, Mom!

Notice the capital M because I was calling her by that name. However, if I am speaking about her without referencing it as her name, I don't need a capital.

I am going to ask my mom if I can go to the movies.

A good check is to fill in the person's actual name and see if the sentence would still make sense.

I miss you so much, Harriet!

I am going to ask my Harriet if I can go to the movies.

That second one didn't make sense, so I can tell I didn't use "mom" as a name and shouldn't capitalize it. Write several sentences about your relatives - parents, grandparents, aunts, or uncles, and decide whether or not each one should have a capital letter as you write the sentence.

Reminders About Your Writer's Notebook

Besides just the writing project, there should be many small writing samples that are being compiled in the Writer's Notebook from the exercises you worked on over the course of this unit. The Writer's Notebook is a tool for helping writers to grow. Explore it frequently and refer to idea lists and helps as you write.

At least once a week, it would be beneficial for you, the writer, to glance back through the exercises, lists, and mini-lessons to review and make sure that you are on track even though most of this work isn't graded.

Specifically, as you are working on the writing project, utilize your Writer's Notebook. You have anchor charts, exercises, and entries in your Journal - all of these can help you as you complete your project. Take time to review some of the concepts you've been working on during the unit so they can be incorporated into the final writing project. The things you've learned should SHOW in your writing project.

Remember that most of the work in the Writer's Notebook will never be graded, but it is still important. Use what you learned to make your project, which will be graded, the best that you can make it.

police officer, or another hero you know of.

- Write a humorous thank you note to a friend who gave you onion and garlic-flavored chewing gum.
- Pretend you have a long lost relative you've never met. In a letter, describe yourself, including what you look like, your personality, and your interests so your relative can get to know you before you meet. Be sure to ask questions so you can get better acquainted.
- Write to someone who has a birthday coming up.
- Put a few stickers, a bookmark, or another small item into an envelope along with a little note for one of your friends and send the miniature gift as a surprise.
- Write a letter to a relative that includes a recipe you really love and let the person know you thought they might like it.
- Write a letter to your postal carrier and thank him or her for delivering your mail and packages. You don't even need to include a stamp. Just tape it to the mailbox.
- Send a joke in a letter to one of your friends with a good sense of humor.
- Write to someone who is in the military or living overseas.
- Write a friendly letter to a friend who has accomplished something. Maybe he or she won a game or ran a race. Congratulate him or her.
- Send a post card that is from your city or town to someone you know who used to live there but has since moved away.
- Write a thank you note to one of the people you have had an appointment with, like your doctor or dentist.
- Write to a neighbor and leave the note on the doorstep instead of mailing it.
- Write a note to yourself that includes some of the goals you have. On the outside of the envelope, write: "Open on New Year's Eve" and seal up the envelope. Put it away somewhere safe and write a reminder on your calendar to open it on the next New Year's Eve.
- Create a collection of Christmas gift tags to attach to your gifts this year.
- Write a "remember when" letter to a friend. Share a favorite memory you have with that friend.
- Choose someone in your family and write a letter that describes the top ten things you love about him or her.
- Pen a letter of advice to someone you know who is struggling with something.
- Write letters to each of your grandparents that describes what you've been doing lately.
- Compose a simulated letter from a character in a television show or movie that you enjoy. Imagine what it would be like to be that character. Have the character write to another character in the show.
- Write a simulated letter from an important historical figure

who died a long time ago. You will have to put yourself in another time and place in your mind to imagine what the person may have had to say in a letter.
- Write to a local business in your area about something you appreciate about the company.
- Write a formal letter to a congressman or another government official about a local issue.
- Create a complete resume and cover letter for a future job you hope to have when you grow up.
- Write a letter to the whole entire world about your ideal future world.

Step 4: Evaluating Writing

The purpose of this unit is to learn to write a variety of kinds of letters, including friendly letters and formal ones.

As you evaluate the writing project, you will be using the "6 Traits of Writing Rubric" from the Printable Pack. In addition, you will be looking for each step of the entire writing process. For example, your child will turn in a prewriting activity, a draft that shows both revisions and edits, as well as a finished, published piece. The publishing step should involve sharing the project in some way - reading it aloud to family, presenting it at dinner time, video chatting to show it off to grandparents, or sharing a video presentation on the internet of the writer sharing his or her writing. The most authentic way to share a letter is to send it. Sharing is a time for positive feedback and celebration.

Creating a positive buzz about the published piece will create a motivating, growth atmosphere in your Writer's Workshop. As you evaluate, remember that the process is just as important as the product, so watch for successes in the process as well. The final score will be out of 50 points - 20 for the process and 30 for the final project. You can write rubric scores as well as comments down on the "Writing Report Card" printable from the Printable Pack.

In addition to evaluating the project, continue to write letters to the members of your family even after this unit ends. Leave them in fun places around the house and keep sending letters to each other. If you've begun the tradition of mailing letters to distant friends and family, keep it up! Letters are one of the most authentic, ongoing styles of writing we will all do throughout our lives, so begin that habit now in your family.

Breakdown of Possible Points

- 5 points for a complete prewriting activity
- 5 points for a completed draft
- 5 points for revisions
- 5 points for edits
- 30 points for the finished writing project

The 30 points for the finished project is further broken down into each of the six traits of writing as shown on the rubric from the Printable Pack.

6 Traits of Writing Rubric
Letters

Your comments should be specifically focused on the purposes of this unit and the skills you were working on throughout the unit.

What was done well? Is the writer understanding the writing process? What should be improved on? Are there any repeated mistakes to address?

Point out a clear strength.

Comments mean more than scores, so make sure to give clear feedback.

Key Concepts

By the end of this unit your kids should be familiar with these concepts and ideas:

What persuasion Is

Hooks

Facts and opinions

Evidence, examples, and experts

The Rule of Threes

The rhetorical triangle - ethos, pathos, logos

Rhetorical questions

Hyperbole

Inclusive language

Absolute versus qualified statements

Introductions and conclusions

Transitions

Formats of various persuasive essays (problem/solution, opinion, persuasive essay, argumentative essay)

More Mini-Lesson Ideas

Along with the sidebars, try these mini-lesson ideas:

- Writer's Workshop links found in Layers of Learning catalog
- Lessons from any grammar workbook
- Every-Day Edits from Education World website
- Sentence diagramming
- Copying great sentences from master writers
- Mad Libs
- Correcting a repeated error from your kids' writing

The mini-lesson sidebars in this unit have check boxes so you can keep track of which ones you have completed.

Persuasive Writing

To persuade means to convince by explaining or reasoning. The purpose of persuasive writing is to change someone's mind or convince them to learn more about a topic, believe a certain way, or act on something. Throughout this unit you will learn how to use reason, data, research, convincing language, and other means to persuade your reader to listen to your message.

Often people misunderstand persuasion. We call the points we make arguments, and that can sound like we are trying to pick a fight. Persuasive arguments are not fights though. The goal of a fight is to come out on top - to dominate. The goal of a persuasive argument is to bring people together. As you write persuasively, you will be trying to change the hearts and minds of your readers in a positive way.

In this unit, you will be practicing various skills and ways of crafting and organizing your arguments in the Persuasive Writing Tools section. After you have practiced the tools, you will be writing a variety of persuasive pieces. The Simple Persuasion section is for kids of all ages. The Advanced Persuasion section is intended for teens.

Step 1: Mini-Lesson

Begin each day of Writer's Workshop with a mini-lesson. You will find some within the sidebars of this unit. You can also use a worksheet from a grammar workbook or practice editing, copying, or diagramming sentences. During writing time, watch for weak areas or mistakes being made and present a mini-lesson the next day to help kids correct mistakes and improve their writing skills in small, continuous ways.

The mini-lesson should take five to ten minutes and always have a positive happy spin, free from criticism. Once you've practiced the skills, you can begin writing a variety of persuasive writing forms, both short and long.

Step 2: Writing

Now it's time to really begin writing. Most of your time during Writer's Workshop should be spent writing. Practicing is the key to improving. You can use your writing time to free write your own ideas in your Journal anytime, or use the exercises below to practice writing skills and find inspiration for things to write about. Select as many exercises as you would like to do over the month, making sure you leave time to complete at least one writing project that will go all of the way through the writing process before the month is over. The exercises will also go in your Journal section of your Writer's Notebook. If you decide to take something from your Journal through the writing process and turn it into your writing project, move it from your Journal to the Writing section of your Writer's Notebook.

A few tips and reminders:

- You can repeat the units and the exercises in subsequent years, so don't ever feel pressured to get to all of them, and feel free to repeat ones you enjoy.
- Often a single exercise can be presented to all of your children, no matter their ages or abilities. They will naturally write at the level they are at and, as they practice, will grow as writers.
- As you progress through the exercises, watch for something that sparks interest and could become the writing project. Feel free to jump to the idea bank at the end of the unit anytime as well. If there's spare time after the project is published, return to more exercises.
- Your family may all be in different places in the writing process. That's perfectly fine. Remember, your Writer's Workshop is a garden and everyone is growing their own patch. You can all lend a hand to help each gardener's patch thrive, but you won't all grow the same crop.

It's time to write! Choose some exercises and jump right in!

Persuasive Writing Tools

EXERCISE: Choosing a Topic
You'll need the "Persuasive Topics" printable from the Printable Pack for this exercise. Before you can begin to write persuasively, you need to decide on a topic you have an opinion about. It can be anything from government,

---

☐ **Mini-Lesson**

Write about things that matter to you. Some people are actively involved in promoting and supporting a cause, such as the release of international political prisoners or protecting the environment. Is there a cause you actively support? Draft a paragraph convincing readers to support your cause.

☐ **Mini-Lesson**

Prewriting is the first stage in the writing process. Before you begin a persuasive piece, you can brainstorm a list of things you have an opinion about, create a jar with slips of paper that describe what you believe in, or use a printable world map and add captions of things you believe would make the world a better place. These, as well as other prewriting activities, will get you started thinking about things you could persuade others to believe in the way you do.

Choose a prewriting activity and gather any supplies you need to complete it. Set a timer for five minutes and get as many ideas down as you can until the timer goes off. During a quick write, you never let your pen stop.

Mini-Lesson

Before you can write persuasively you need to understand what it means to persuade. To persuade is to convince someone of something.

Think of some examples of when you've tried to change someone's mind. Have you ever asked someone to buy you something or tried to talk them into watching the show that you wanted? What did you say to convince them? What would you say to convince your parents to make the dinner you want to eat tonight? Talk about the ways you persuade people.

Mini-Lesson

Have a discussion together about this issue:

Is it okay to squish bugs?

As you discuss, notice opinions and facts that are shared and point out the difference between the two.

Mini-Lesson

A colon can be used to introduce a list. The part of the sentence that comes before the colon should be able to stand on its own as a complete sentence. Commas are used between each item on the list.

At the store, I need to buy these items: milk, eggs, celery, apples, and cheese.

Write your own list using a colon and commas.

---

animal testing, and human rights to the best place to shop for shoes, the most delicious flavor of ice cream, or your favorite book and why everyone should read it.

Begin to brainstorm topics on the printable. Think of something you want to change. Do you wish your bedtime were later? Do you have a better idea for how to stop people from driving while intoxicated? Do you have something you love that you wish others would try too? Choose ideas that you care about.

It can be helpful to think of the different parts of your life as you consider things you want to change. What do you want to change in your home or family? Is there anything you wish you could change in your group of friends? What about in the teams or clubs you are a part of? Is there anything you wish you could change in your community? Your nation? The world?

As you think of topics, remember that it will be much more effective if it's something you have experience in or knowledge about. If not, you will need to research before you begin writing. If you are planning to persuade someone of something, it is your responsibility to be an expert on the topic.

Add the list of ideas you've created to the Ideas section of your Writer's Notebook.

EXERCISE: Hook Your Reader
A hook is a statement that immediately gets the attention of your reader. A good persuasive writer is like a fisherman. First, you hook your reader, then you reel in bit by bit with each bit of evidence you present, until you've caught him!

Use the "Hooks" printable from the Printable Pack to help you learn about some ways to hook your reader. You can use strong statements, statistics, fun facts, quotes, unusual details, or empathetic questions. In the left-hand column of the printable, you will see each of these kinds of hooks listed. On the right-hand side, you will see examples of each kind of hook that could be used to convince

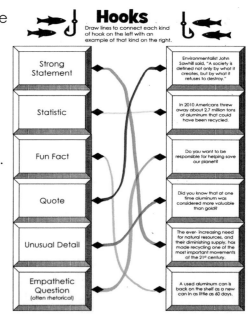

Hooks

Draw lines to connect each kind of hook on the left with an example of that kind on the right.

Strong Statement	Environmentalist John Sawhill said, "A society is defined not only by what it creates, but by what it refuses to destroy."
Statistic	In 2010 Americans threw away about 2.7 million tons of aluminum that could have been recycled.
Fun Fact	Do you want to be responsible for helping save our planet?
Quote	Did you know that at one time aluminum was considered more valuable than gold?
Unusual Detail	The ever-increasing need for natural resources, and their diminishing supply, has made recycling one of the most important movements of the 21st century.
Empathetic Question (often rhetorical)	A used aluminum can is back on the shelf as a new can in as little as 60 days.

someone of the importance of recycling aluminum cans. Match each kind of hook with its example. The answers are shown here. Add the printable to the Writing Helps section of your Writer's Notebook.

Now, pretend you are writing a persuasive essay about the importance of drinking water every day. Write six different possible hooks you could use at the beginning, one for each kind you just learned about on the "Hooks" printable. Once you've written all six, draw a little fish next to the one that would best capture the interest of your reader if you were to write about the importance of drinking water daily. Even though you created six hooks, you would only use one of them in a persuasive essay, so choose the best one. The hook would become the very first sentence in your essay.

EXERCISE: Would You Rather . . .

For this exercise you will need the three "Would You Rather . . ." printables from the Printable Pack. Print them on card stock, cut them apart, and place them in a jar. Along with the preprinted cards, you will also find a page of blank cards you can use to write your own "Would You Rather . . ." questions. Take turns pulling one out and reading it aloud. Answer which one you would prefer, telling why you feel that way. Afterward, choose one or more of the questions to write about in a brief journal entry, listing your reasons for your choice.

Thinking about reasons for our opinions helps us think more deeply and we begin to develop our mindset. Talk about how we make decisions by thinking through things and reasoning them out in our minds.

EXERCISE: Fact Versus Opinion

Facts are statements that can be proven by objective evidence. Opinions are beliefs and are typically based on the values of the person who expressed the opinion. If I say that ice cream is better than pie, that is an opinion. There is no evidence that can say which is better. I must value ice cream more than pie since I declared that opinion.

☐ Mini-Lesson

One of the six traits of writing is ideas and content. Having enough content sometimes requires you to extend your ideas. Think of it as writing the long version instead of writing the short version:

Here's an example of short writing:

Joel should mow the lawn.

Here's an example of longer writing:

Joel should mow the lawn this afternoon because it's supposed to be rainy the rest of the week. The lawn always looks so well kept after he mows. He creates the prettiest spot in the neighborhood each time. Plus, he gets paid $20 each time he mows, and he will miss out on it if he skips this week.

Writing long includes offering compelling reasons for the statement you are making. Practice writing this short statement as a longer argument:

We should all go for a bike ride this afternoon.

☐ Mini-Lesson

Word choice is one of the six traits of writing. As you try to persuade others, choose exact words to convince your reader that you are knowledgeable and can be trusted.

Write a sentence about how dogs need enough food, space, and attention. Use strong verbs, exact nouns, and descriptive adjectives. Underline your best word choices.

Mini-Lesson

Bullet points are used by writers to create lists. They are commonly found in presentations, on websites, and in documents that show steps or procedures. They can also be used to emphasize or outline important points in an essay. As you are outlining the arguments you want to include as you persuade your audience, you can create a bulleted list as a prewriting activity. Each of those bullet points could then be turned into paragraphs within your persuasive essay. Here's an example:

There are several reasons pets should be allowed on the beach:

- *It's a family beach and many pets are considered members of the family.*
- *Pets like to run and swim just like people do.*
- *There are pet waste bags and garbage cans already available near the tables, benches, and walkways of the beach.*
- *Pets have a healing and soothing effect on many pet owners.*

Now create your own bulleted list of reasons pets shouldn't be allowed on *the beach.*

Mini-Lesson

Add the "Persuasive Word Bank" printable from the Printable Pack to the Writing Helps section of your Writer's Notebook. Use it to help you incorporate persuasive language in your writing.

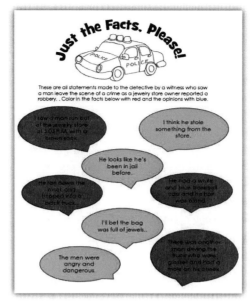

Use the "Just the Facts, Please" printable from the Printable Pack. Use a red pen to show the facts and a blue pen to show the opinions. You can see the answers on the image. When a police detective investigates a crime, he or she does not write down the opinions of the witnesses on the report. Instead, the detective wants to gather facts. Each fact is recorded and evidence is gathered and presented to the jury.

Even though they are secondary to facts, opinions still have value. Sometimes there are certain opinions presented, even in court cases. Experts, witnesses, and other knowledgeable people can share their opinions about the evidence. They are especially valuable if the person can be trusted. For example, if my mechanic tells me she believes I should replace my brakes, I will likely trust her opinion as an expert on my car. I can seek out both facts and opinions, deciding for myself whose opinions I will trust.

As you write persuasively, you will be using both facts and opinions. It is important, however, to recognize the difference between the two. Facts are stronger motivators than opinions, but if you are a reliable, trustworthy person, your opinions can be persuasive too.

EXERCISE: Evidence, Facts, & Statistics

A big part of convincing people is presenting them with the truth. Before you even form an opinion about something, you need to do some research yourself. Learn about your topic by reading books, articles, websites, or asking experts.

Using true and researched information will go a long way toward backing up your point of view. As you read from any source, it's important for you to write down where you got the information.

You'll need two different colors of note cards for this exercise, as well as the internet to conduct your research. Choose one of these topics to research:

- Setting goals
- Crying

- Smoking
- Pets
- Bullying
- Screen time
- Exercise
- Sleep or dreams
- Social media
- Music
- Cheating in school
- A topic you are interested in

As you read articles, watch videos, and conduct your research, notice the source you are reading. Is it a trustworthy, expert source? Can you identify facts or expert opinions? Can you find real evidence? For each fact, statistic, bit of evidence, or expert opinion, make a note card that records what you learned. Record the opinions on one color and the facts on the other color of note card.

EXERCISE: The Rule of Threes

In persuasion, we rely on the Rule of Threes. Anytime you want to convince someone of your point of view, it's helpful if you have at least three reasons.

In this exercise, you will decide whether you think dogs or cats make better pets. Your job is to convince someone of your opinion. Remember the Rule of Threes. Come up with three reasons why your choice is clearly the best. Write a clear statement of what you believe. Below it, write your three reasons. Add this to the Journal section of your Writer's Notebook.

EXERCISE: Convince Me in 1, 2, 3

The first step to learning to persuade is to practice the three basic steps to convincing people.

Step 1: State your opinion.

We should bake some cookies this afternoon.

Step 2: Give reasons for your opinion. Keep the Rule of Threes in mind. Make sure you have at least three reasons in this step.

We haven't had cookies in a long time. We could make your favorite kind - peanut butter and chocolate chip, because we all know those make you happy. We could deliver some to the neighbors and spread more happiness. We'll all pitch in to make them and clean up afterwards too.

☐ **Mini-Lesson**

Write example sentences for these commonly mistaken words.

There
"there" refers to a location

Their
"their" shows ownership

They're
apostrophe

"they're" is a contraction for they are

☐ **Mini-Lesson**

Often people will create arguments that sound logical, but have fallacies within them.

Premise: All whales are mammals.

Premise: Humans are mammals.

Conclusion: Humans are whales.

The trouble is, humans aren't whales. The mistake was that there wasn't anywhere in the premises that said all mammals are whales, but the conclusion assumed that. Instead, the conclusion could have said that whales and humans are both mammals.

To learn more about creating logical arguments, you can learn about the mistakes people make as they form them. Those mistakes are called logical fallacies.

Mini-Lesson

As you begin coming up with arguments, it can be helpful to make a web before you begin writing. Prewriting helps you keep track of and organize your ideas and makes the drafting process easier. Make a web about something you have an opinion on.

Mini-Lesson

Aristotle described the three persuasive appeals: ethos, pathos, and logos.

He was an ancient Greek philosopher and teacher. His ideas about logic and reasoning still shape how we form arguments and logical statements today. Watch a biography about Aristotle on YouTube.

Step 3: Explain by giving an example or two.

When we made those cookies last month and delivered them, it was one of our favorite family memories because it was amazing to share our yummy treats and spread so much happiness. We used to make cookies every Sunday; it was a fun tradition.

Think of something you would like to convince someone of. Write down each of the three steps - your opinion, your reasons, and some examples. Add it to your Journal.

EXERCISE: Ethos Argument

An ethos argument is a persuasive technique that relies on your character and reputation. Using ethos in an argument means that you sound like an expert, have done your research, and are sharing expert advice.

You can provide:

• Personal experiences.
• Expert advice from someone who knows your topic well.
• Strong, intelligent word choice.

If you wanted to convince me to take vitamins daily, you might say you started taking vitamins last year after your doctor encouraged you to, and that it has energized you and boosted your immune system. In that argument you used your own experience as well as relying on your doctor, an expert. "Energized" and "boosted your immune system" are powerful word choices to help you sound informed.

How could you convince me to do these things using ethos?

• Never leave delivery packages on the doorstep overnight.
• Floss teeth daily.
• Always look both ways before crossing the street.

Write your ethos arguments on a sheet of paper and then present it out loud to your family. Give each member of your family a piece of paper with a star drawn on it. Each person who felt you gave an expert opinion will hold up a star. See how many stars you can earn.

EXERCISE: Pathos Argument

A pathos argument is a persuasive technique that uses feelings and personal connection. You will use words that draw in your readers' emotions. If they feel angry, shocked, surprised, sad, guilty, or empathetic as they read your words, chances are, you will convince them.

You will use:

- Emotional language.
- Arguments that sound like they would benefit your audience - a way to be happier, safer, healthier, or better off or provide a way to avoid negative emotions like sadness, anger, loneliness, or guilt.
- Personal stories about experiences.

If you wanted to convince your parents to let you sign up for soccer, you might say, "It will mean the world to me to get to play on a real team. I can already imagine running up and down the field and looking over at you smiling at me when I make my first goal." You are hoping to tug at the heartstrings of your reader to make them tie emotions to your point of view.

How could you convince me to do these three things using pathos?

- Adopt a pet from the pet shelter.
- Wash hands before eating.
- Buy you a milkshake.

Write a pathos arguments on a sheet of paper and then try them out on your family. Give each person a paper plate and have them draw the face of an emotion they felt because of your pathos presentation.

EXERCISE: Logos Argument

Logos uses reasons and evidence in your persuasive statements. Let's say you are writing about how quickly the population of the planet has grown and is taxing the earth's resources.

You could say:

There are a lot more people walking, biking, and driving around my city these days, so the population is clearly skyrocketing. We should probably do something to save the planet from all those extra people.

Mini-Lesson

Fill in the blank to complete this logical argument:

All mammals are warm-blooded.

Whales are mammals.

Therefore, _____.

Now, use sentence imitation to write your own example of a logical argument.

Answer: Therefore, whales are warm-blooded.

Mini-Lesson

Discuss this use of logos from Sojourner's Truth's speech in support of women's rights:

"That man over there says that women need to be helped into carriages, and lifted over ditches, and to have the best place everywhere. Nobody ever helps me into carriages, or over mud-puddles, or gives me any best place! And ain't I a woman? Look at me! Look at my arm! I have ploughed and planted, and gathered into barns, and no man could head me! And ain't I a woman?"

Can you identify the logically linked points of her argument?

However, it is far more persuasive to say:

According to the United Nations, the world population has gone from 2.6 billion in 1950 to over seven billion today and is expected to increase by two billion more people in the next 30 years. On average, each one of those people drives 627,000 miles, uses over 700,000 gallons of water, and lives in ten homes, which equals more that 64 trees being cut down. If one person creates that kind of environmental impact, imagine the impact of billions of people.

The second statement appealed to logic by linking little pieces of evidence together to make a claim.

You can provide:

- True premises that lead to a conclusion.
- Evidence.
- Straightforward, logical language.

How could you convince me of these things using logos?

- Keep a first aid kit in the car.
- Buy you a cell phone.
- Stop worrying about making the beds every day.

Cut a sheet of paper into strips and write each of the pieces of your logos argument on one strip. Attach the strips together in a logical order so they create a chain that proves your point. Make sure to write compelling statements that are presented in a logical order. This chain says, "All men are mortal. Socrates is a man. Socrates is mortal." Present your linked argument out loud to your family.

EXERCISE: The Rhetorical Triangle

Use "The Rhetorical Triangle" printable from the Printable Pack for this exercise. Rhetoric is the art of spoken and written communication. By using pathos, ethos, and logos together, you can create one solid argument. All three together are known as the rhetorical triangle.

Use the printable and write down at least one claim on

each corner of the triangle. On the pathos corner, you will appeal to emotions. On the ethos corner you will appeal to character, and logos corner you will appeal to logic.

If I wanted to convince you that kids should wear helmets when riding motorcycles, I could approach it from each point of the rhetorical triangle. Combining all three of these will help to more fully persuade people.

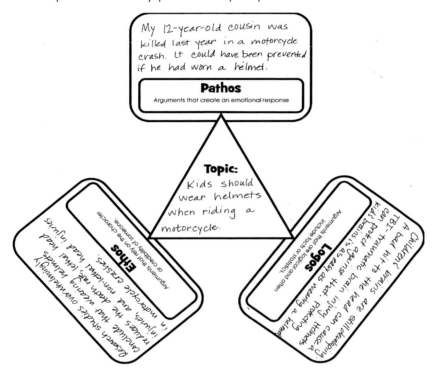

My 12-year-old cousin was killed last year in a motorcycle crash. It could have been prevented if he had worn a helmet.

Pathos
Arguments that create an emotional response

Topic:
Kids should wear helmets when riding a motorcycle.

Ethos
Arguments that rely on the character or credibility of someone.

Research studies overwhelmingly conclude that wearing helmets reduces the death rate, lethal head injuries and non-lethal crashes.

Logos
Arguments that are logical and often include facts or statistics.

Children's brains are still developing. A blow to the head can cause a TBI-traumatic brain injury. Practicing kids' brains is as easy as wearing a helmet.

EXERCISE: Rhetorical Questions

A rhetorical question is one that does not require an answer. It assumes that anyone who hears the question would automatically agree. Asking a well-placed rhetorical question can be a powerful motivational tool because it causes people to feel they want to jump on the bandwagon and join your viewpoint.

After writing about how every kid in your family should have a membership to the local swimming pool this summer to participate in swimming lessons, you might ask,"Do you want your children to drown?" You don't require an answer to that. It's rhetorical. You are saying that obviously you don't want your children to drown, so you should get on down to the pool and buy a family membership right away.

Write "Rhetorical questions don't need to be answered" at the top of a sheet of paper. Think of three things you would like to convince someone of and write a rhetorical question for each one of them. Add your page to the Writing Helps section of your Writer's Notebook.

☐ **Mini-Lesson**

Word choice, one of the six traits of writing, is important to consider as you summarize. Summarizing means repeating the same point again. Be careful not to repeat what you already said in the exact same way though. Choose new words. Don't just copy sentences word for word from your writing over again.

Look through the Journal section of your Writer's Notebook and find something persuasive you've written. Practice using new words to summarize an argument or opinion you wrote.

☐ **Mini-Lesson**

When you write about another person and yourself, always name yourself last and use the word I. Remember to capitalize proper nouns.

Tammy and I enjoy karate more than dance.

Change these sentences into the proper format, then write more examples on your own.

I and Cary jumped off the diving board.

Me and Al rode scooters across the bridge.

Me and him love burritos.

Answers:

Cary and I jumped off the diving board.

Al and I rode scooters across the bridge.

He and I love burritos.

☐ Mini-Lesson

A thesis statement is the main idea of your essay. It is the point you are arguing in persuasive writing. It is usually a one-sentence explanation of your opinion or claim. You place it as the last sentence of your introduction and everything that comes after it should support the thesis.

Practice writing thesis statements about a few of the topics listed in the Idea Banks from the end of this unit.

☐ Mini-Lesson

You'll need the "3 Wishes" printable from the Printable Pack for this mini-lesson. Within each wish cloud, draw a picture and write a description of three realistic things you wish for. They could be things you wish for immediately or that you hope to have or achieve at some point during your life.

I wish I could sleep in on Saturdays.

When we sleep in and get adequate sleep, we have less stress, healthier hearts, and improved memories.

Write a sentence for each wish that uses inclusive language - you, we, our, us - to help your reader visualize receiving your wish too. Inclusive language draws your audience in and helps them see things your way.

EXERCISE: Hyperbole

Hyperbole is just a big word that means exaggeration. If you exaggerate, you are making something seem more extreme than it actually is. Perhaps you want to convince your friend to come help you fold your laundry because you have to get it done before you're allowed to go outside and play. You might tell him to come help you because you have a *mountain of laundry* and it will take you *forever* to fold by yourself. Your laundry pile likely isn't as big as an actual mountain and it's probably not going to take forever, in reality, but hyperbole can be very convincing.

Practice writing your own hyperboles on a sheet of paper by finishing these sentences:

- I'm so hungry I could . . .
- He was angrier than . . .
- She walked so far . . .
- The toys in the playroom were . . .
- They sing so well . . .
- She is stronger than . . .
- Being tired makes people . . .
- He cried so long that he . . .

Write "Hyperboles are Exaggerations" at the top of the page and add it to the Writing Helps section of your Writer's Notebook.

EXERCISE: Inclusive Language

As you write, use language that includes your readers. Use words like we, you, our, and us to draw each reader in and help him or her feel that you care and that each of them should be invested personally.

For example, if you've written a brochure trying to convince your neighbors that the park needs to be cleaned up this weekend, you might say, "Together, we can make a difference in our neighborhood!"

Write your own persuasive argument that uses inclusive words like we, you, our, and us. Imagine that you need to convince the people in your city to come participate in an upcoming city event. Write and illustrate a convincing, inclusive message that will get them involved. Add it to the Journal section of your Writer's Notebook.

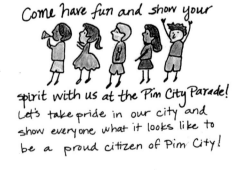

Come have fun and show your spirit with us at the Pim City Parade! Let's take pride in our city and show everyone what it looks like to be a proud citizen of Pim City!

EXERCISE: Absolute and Qualified Statements

Often people believe that in order to convince their reader, they must make an absolute statement about their opinion.

Absolute Statement: Animals are happier in the wild.

Anytime you make an absolute statement, immediately your reader's mind will look for exceptions.

"What about my hamster? He would die if I set him free in the yard, but he loves his home! I play with him and take care of him every day. We need each other!"

A qualified statement is more accurate and allows your reader's mind to look for examples that prove it rather than looking for exceptions.

Qualified Statement: For many animals, living in their normal habitats in the wild is preferable to living a caged, domesticated life.

Immediately my mind looks for examples instead of exceptions.

"I'm pretty sure the gorillas living in the Congo are a lot happier than the ones in tiny cages at the zoo."

Qualified statements use words that make their statements less certain. Notice that in the example above, it says, "many animals" rather than "all animals." This qualifier admits that it may not be true one hundred percent of the time.

Use the "Absolutely Qualified" printable from the Printable Pack to practice transforming absolute statements into qualified ones.

EXERCISE: OREO Arguments

To really make this exercise memorable, you'll need a Double Stuf Oreo cookie snack as well as the "OREO" printable from the Printable Pack. The word OREO can help you remember how a persuasive argument is sandwiched by your opinions on each end. First, you state your opinion. Write your opinion about something on the first O cookie layer on the printable. Next, fill your argument. The R in OREO stands for reasons and the E stands for examples. Add reasons and examples for your opinion in the filling of the cookie on the printable. Finally, you will end with your opinion again. This time, you are summarizing, so make sure to clearly state your opinion using new word choice in the final layer of the cookie. A summary uses sentences that are similar to what you already said but are expressed in a new way.

☐ **Mini-Lesson**

When you use an absolute statement, your reader's mind will often look for exceptions. Absolute statements claim that 100% of the time something is true. On the other hand, qualified statements acknowledge that there are exceptions, even to true statements. When you make a qualified statement, your reader's mind will often look for examples. For this reason, qualified statements are usually more convincing. Look over the "Absolute and Qualified Anchor Chart" for some examples. Use it to help you with the "Absolute and Qualified Statements" Exercise, then add it to the Writing Helps section of your Writer's Notebook.

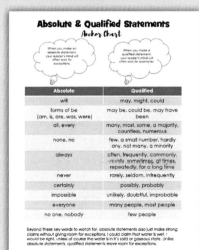

☐ **Mini-Lesson**

Using qualifiers strengthens your arguments. Practice writing a claim about whether or not video games should be considered a sport. Use qualifiers like appears, seems, indicates, and suggests.

☐ Mini-Lesson

If you were forced to spend the rest of your life in a library, a zoo, or a museum, which would you choose?

Draw a quick sketch of the one you prefer and surround it with caption boxes that explain your choice.

☐ Mini-Lesson

While writing persuasively you will likely be using some statements and some claims as your evidence. There is a difference between the two, and you need to be able to recognize the difference.

A statement is a declaration of something that is factual.

A claim is a sentence that can be argued because there isn't enough evidence to prove or disprove it. Often a claim is more of an opinion than a fact.

It's perfectly fine to use claims in your persuasive writing, but if that's all you have, chances are you won't convince anyone.

Statement: Apples contain Vitamin C, Potassium, and Vitamin K and have been linked to lower risk of diabetes, heart disease, and cancer.

Claim: Apples taste better than bananas, oranges, berries, or melons.

Write some examples of statements and claims about one of these topics: water, zoos, bicycles, stoplights, chocolate, or mice.

Inside each section of the cookie on the printable, write each part of your argument about one of your opinions.

EXERCISE: PEEL - Point, Evidence, Explanation, Link
You will need the "PEEL" printable from the Printable Pack to help you complete this exercise. Add it to the Writing Helps section of your Writer's Notebook.

Beyond just giving reasons for your opinions, there is a pattern you can use to make your points more effectively as you write arguments, and the acronym PEEL can help you remember the steps.

Point

Your position on this issue, written briefly and directly. This is usually the topic sentence of each body paragraph in a persuasive essay.

I believe that . . . In my opinion . . . It is clear that . . . The fact is . . . I know that . . .

Evidence

A fact, statistic, example, or expert opinion about your topic.

For example . . . Experts agree . . . Evidence shows that . . . One reason . . . For instance . . .

Explanation

Your personal commentary about why the evidence you presented matters.

This demonstrates . . . This reveals . . . This suggests . . . This confirms . . . This shows . . .

Link

Link, or connect, the point you just made to your next point. Usually this is the concluding sentence of a paragraph in persuasive writing.

In addition . . . Consequently . . . Likewise . . . On top of that . . . Furthermore . . .

Try writing your own persuasive paragraph using the PEEL acronym to guide your writing. The issue you will address is: Is chocolate healthy?

Compose a paragraph that includes a topic sentence with your point, one or two evidence sentences, one or two explanation sentences, and finally, a concluding sentence that links to what would be your next point. You may need to do a bit of research before you decide on your opinion and the point of your paragraph.

EXERCISE: Thinking Tug of War

Sometimes it can be difficult to decide how you feel about an issue. Not every topic is simple or clear. When you are considering both sides of an issue, it can be helpful to create a thinking tug of war. Write your issue on a card and place it in the center of your workspace. Next, write facts, observations, expert opinions, and other evidence on sticky notes, placing them on either one side or the other of the issue. As you weigh the evidence, it can help you make thoughtful, educated decisions about issues.

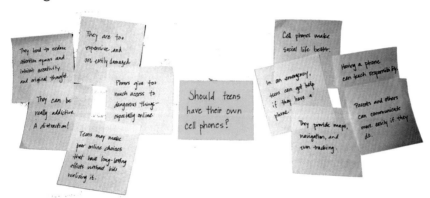

Choose an issue from your own mind or from the Idea Bank at the end of this unit that you don't feel certain about and create your own thinking tug of war. Weigh your evidence and make a decision about what you believe.

Simple Persuasion

EXERCISE: This or That?

You will need the "This or That?" printable from the Printable Pack and some note cards for this exercise. Choose two things that are similar, but not exactly the same. You could pick something like cream-filled donuts versus glazed donuts or singing versus playing an instrument. Choose any two things that you can compare. Draw each thing in a box and then write the two things in the blanks of the first sentence.

Write a paragraph explaining which of the two you prefer. When you're finished, add your paragraph to the Journal section of your Writer's Notebook.

EXERCISE: My Opinion About . . .

You will need the "My Opinion About . . ." printable from the Printable Pack for this exercise. Choose something you have an opinion about, specifically something that you either like or dislike. Fill in the blanks on the printable with your subject, your name, whether you like or dislike it, and

---

☐ Mini-Lesson

Write some sentences that use dashes or parenthesis to add information.

Darius loved fruit (especially grapes and strawberries) and was heading to the fruit stand before it closed.

She couldn't remember his name - John, Joe, Jess - something with a J seemed to ring a bell.

Parenthesis and dashes allow you to include additional information without creating an interruption that could otherwise make your sentence unclear.

☐ Mini-Lesson

Do a quick write. Set a timer for five minutes and don't stop writing the entire time. Imagine that you are an ant. In five minutes, try to convince an anteater not to eat you.

☐ Mini-Lesson

Your personal opinion alone is valid, but it is not a reason. Facts, examples, and evidence are needed if you want others to share your opinions. Whenever possible, back up your opinions with more substance. Write down evidence convincing a friend not to take drugs.

Verbs can be action words or state of being words.

*The kitty **ran** to her water bowl.*

This sentence's verb is ran, which is an action.

*The kitty **was** thirsty.*

This sentence's verb is was, which is a state of being.

Verbs that show a state of being are called linking verbs. Can you identify which of these verbs show action and which are linking verbs that show a state of being?

- Dance
- Am
- Was
- Sleep
- Wore
- Are
- Cook
- Were

Write some sentences using action verbs and some sentences using linking verbs.

Answers: The action verbs above are dance, sleep, wore, and cook. The linking verbs are am, was, are, and were.

Linking verbs get their name because they link the subject of the sentence to an adjective that describes the subject. Imitate this sentence's structure to write some of your own sentences that link the subject and adjective with a linking verb.

The kitchen floor is filthy.

the topic you chose. Fill in the boxes with three reasons that explain your opinion. At the end, write a concluding sentence that sums up your reasons and your opinion.

Here are a few ideas for things you may have an opinion about:

- Chores
- Vegetables
- Playgrounds
- Pets

- Shopping
- Litter
- Candy
- Allowance

EXERCISE: Paragraph of Persuasion

For this exercise you'll need the "Paragraph of Persuasion" printable, a stapler, scissors, and a colorful sheet of paper to create your own persuasive booklet. Copy the printable on the colorful paper and attach it to a sheet of white paper using a stapler along the left edge. Use a pair of scissors to cut around the outside edge and along the dotted lines on the printable. Make sure not to cut the white background at the same time.

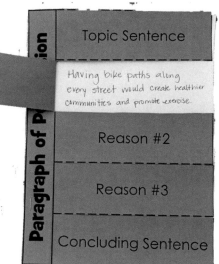

Decide on a topic you have an opinion about and want to persuade others of. If you need ideas, read through the idea banks from the end of this unit. Open each door and write one sentence behind it that explains your opinion in a topic sentence, each of your three reasons, and then a concluding sentence that sums up your viewpoint.

EXERCISE: Persuasive Paragraph

Think of something you feel strongly about. It could be something personal . . .

- What should your family have for dinner tonight?
- Should your family get a pet?
- Where should you go on vacation this summer?
- How much screen time should you get each day?
- What is the best season of the year?

Or a more social, national, or global issue . . .

- Should it be illegal to travel in a vehicle without a

seatbelt?
- Is war a good thing or a bad thing?
- Should the internet be free and available to everyone on the globe?

First, choose a topic. Then use the "Persuasive Paragraph" printable from the Printable Pack to help you plan and organize your thoughts and information.

After you've thought through your reasons and filled out the printable, write a single paragraph on a sheet of paper that convinces your reader to agree with your point of view. Add it to the Journal section of your Writer's Notebook.

EXERCISE: My Own Diary

Often in diaries or journals people express their strongest opinions. This is because it's writing that no one will ever read except the writer. We can be completely ourselves in a diary.

Write at least one journal entry about anything at all. This won't be graded and it isn't for anyone else to read. Many people start with one journal entry and then keep writing throughout their lives. Diaries and journals can be a place to work out our thoughts and feelings without worries about who might judge us for feeling the way we do. Write anything you want about your life, your feelings, or your thoughts. Express them honestly and be completely yourself. No one else has to read it. You can add it to the Journal section of your Writer's Notebook or you can begin your own journaling book that you write in regularly and keep only for your own eyes.

EXERCISE: Advice Column

Read a few articles from the advice column of the newspaper together. Begin by just reading the question and asking everyone to share what their advice would be. Then read the columnist's opinion. The columnist may be right or wrong, but either way, he or she is writing to persuade. You can offer up your own opinions about things when you are writing.

Try writing your own advice column. Read one of the questions below out loud and have everyone write a response. Share your responses out loud and talk about the advice and opinions you offered. You may have to back up your ideas with examples and other evidence, so make sure you've written thoughtful responses.

I'm about to have a baby, but my other kids are already feeling ignored with how busy I've been. What

Mini-Lesson

Sometimes action verbs can function as linking verbs.

Your lotion smells delightful.

Smells can be a action, but in this case, the lotion isn't actually smelling anything.

Write a sentence that uses looks as a linking verb instead of an action.

Mini-Lesson

Imagine you were asked to write a persuasive article convincing someone they needed to clean out their dirty aquarium. Either draw a picture of the aquarium or picture it vividly in your mind. Create a word cloud that includes strong and exact nouns, adjectives, verbs, and adverbs that could help you create a strong argument.

Mini-Lesson

Use the word does to tell about one person and the word do to tell about more than one. Fill in the sentences below with do or does, then write some of your own examples.

We _____ a lot during the holidays. **(do)**

My grandpa _____ the dishes after dinner. **(does)**

Mini-Lesson

Write one topic sentence about whether you prefer to watch TV shows or movies. Follow it up with three more sentences that include your reasons. After you've written the sentences, add transition words like "first," "furthermore," "additionally," or "finally" to make your argument organized and fluent. Organization and sentence fluency are two of the six traits of writing. To finish your paragraph, add a concluding sentence that sums up your opinion by restating it in a new way.

Mini-Lesson

As you make posters, brochures, or other visual projects, make sure to add color for visual interest.

Mini-Lesson

Adjectives that compare things can be valuable tools to use when you are writing persuasively.

Add -er to certain adjectives to compare two people and -est to compare more than two.

bright - brighter - brightest

tall - taller - tallest

strong - stronger - strongest

Write some sentences that compare two items you may discuss in a persuasive essay and include adjectives that can end in -er or -est.

*Dentists agree that flossing your teeth gets them **cleaner** than brushing alone.*

can I do so they love their new little sister instead of feeling resentful?

-WORRIED MOM

My extended family all wants to come to my house for the holidays this year because I live in a central location everyone can travel to easily. I'm not a great cook or housekeeper though, and even though I love my family, it's stressing me out! What should I do?

-HOLIDAY AMATEUR

My kids constantly have messy bedrooms! Toys, clothes, books, and garbage are just everywhere! I've tried talking to them about it and I've even grounded them, but nothing changes. Should I just clean it for them? Help! I can't find the floor!

-BURIED IN TOYS

Add your advice column to the Journal section of your Writer's Notebook.

EXERCISE: Book Review

What is your favorite book? Write up a short review of the book, persuading others to read it. As you write, make sure to include logic and emotions. Avoid making absolute statements, choosing qualified ones instead. Also, use at least one rhetorical question as you provide convincing reasons to read the book. You can add your book review to the Journal section of your Writer's Notebook or publish it on a book website online.

EXERCISE: Fundraiser Poster

Think of something that could benefit your community in some way. It could be benefiting a single individual or family, a small group of people, a charity group, the entire community, your whole country, or even the whole world. Make a colorful poster that both illustrates your opinion and has written explanations of your arguments. Explain your cause, the benefits, and

also asks for funds to be raised to make it happen. Help your viewers feel that they will be part of something big and important if they join your cause.

EXERCISE: Brochure

Imagine that you have been asked to create a brochure to attract visitors to your hometown. Craft a tri-fold brochure that highlights the things to see and do there and convinces people to come visit your city. Make sure to use persuasive language and techniques to be convincing. You can take some pictures to print and include or get some from the internet that showcase where you live.

EXERCISE: Advertisement

Think of a product you think is amazing. It can be an actual product you love, like your favorite candy bar, video game, electric scooter, or robot vacuum. It can also be an invention from your own imagination, like a brand new hover snowboard or a phone with an infinite battery that never needs to be charged.

This commercial used a catchy jingle and slogan and some humor to sell "Bottomless Baggies . . .the baggies that never get full."

Decide on a sales tactic that will successfully sell the product you chose. Use one or more of these approaches:

- Using a catchy slogan, logo, or jingle.
- Creating a color scheme or an eye catching scene to capture attention.
- Offering a deal or a sale.
- Asking rhetorical questions to get your audience thinking.
- Making them laugh to create a memorable ad.
- Using the bandwagon approach - everyone is doing it.
- Making purchasing the product seem patriotic.
- Using testimonials of other satisfied customers.

☐ **Mini-Lesson**

Advertisers use propaganda techniques to persuade people. Watch some TV commercials together and try to identify the techniques the advertiser is using to convince you.

☐ **Mini-Lesson**

Advertisers often use figurative language; research shows that it sells.

Here are a few examples:

Metaphor: A diamond is forever.

Simile: Ride like the wind.

Personification: What does your lipstick say about you?

Alliteration: All you need is a dollar and a dream.

The goal of figurative language in advertising is to create a positive and memorable impression of a product or service. The company who produces Red Bull, an energy drink, had to change its famous slogan, "Red Bull gives you wings," because a consumer sued for false advertising. He argued that after ten years of drinking Red Bull, he did not have wings or any enhanced athleticism. The company had to pay out millions when they lost the huge class action lawsuit.

☐ **Mini-Lesson**

Which dessert is the best? Write your favorite dessert down the page vertically and turn it into an acrostic poem that describes what you love about it.

A semi-colon looks like a dot over a comma. It is a punctuation mark you use to show that two independent clauses of a sentence are closely related. Anywhere a semi-colon can go, you could put a period, because on both sides of the semi-colon you must have what could be a complete sentence. The semi-colon is just a tool you are using to show how close each part is to the other.

Pam and I had a fight. I'm not speaking to her.

Pam and I had a fight; I'm not speaking to her.

The second one emphasizes that you aren't speaking to her because of your fight.

Write your own sentences that include a semi-colon to show the relationship between the two parts.

☐ **Mini-Lesson**

Colons are used to connect the main clause of a sentence with an explanation, list, or quote that relates to the clause. Read the examples below and then write your own.

Henry knows my secret: I'm afraid of the dark.

Billie Jean has a lot to do before bedtime: wash her sheets, fold her laundry, do the dishes, and take out the garbage.

Six-year-old Jezebel was quoted in the newsletter: "Halloween is my favorite holiday! I'm going to dress up as a dinosaur this year!"

- Using fear if they don't purchase.
- Exaggerating to make it seem even better than it is.
- Making your company or product sound trustworthy.
- Including facts, studies, or statistics.
- Using a celebrity endorsement to make it seem cool.
- Using repetition to make the message stick in their minds.

When you have worked out your sales approach, choose to either design a printed advertisement or create a commercial that you star in. When you are finished, show off your finished advertisement or the video you created of your commercial, then explain the sales techniques you used to persuade people to buy it.

EXERCISE: Writing To Inspire
Some writing persuades gently, by using inspiration rather than direct persuasion. For example, when I read accounts of Jane Goodall's excursions with apes, I am inspired to care for animals a little more. When I read about survivors of the Holocaust, I feel a little more determined to overcome the hard things that happen in my life.

Write a story of something positive you have done in your life. Share your honest feelings and tell how the experience shaped you. Maybe your account of picking up your neighborhood litter will inspire others to take care of the planet. Perhaps your experience of helping someone who was being bullied will give someone else courage. Writing about working hard to learn something new could empower someone else to give it their all. Write an inspirational story from your life to add to the Journal section of your Writer's Notebook.

EXERCISE: Writing a Speech
The speeches or talks people give are often persuasive. As a speaker, you use many of the same tools to convince people as persuasive authors do. You can use logic, emotion, your character, rhetorical questions, inclusive language, and other persuasive techniques you've learned in this unit to help you craft your speech. Choose one of the topics below to write about, then deliver your speech out loud to your family or another audience.

- If you could choose for everything in the world to be turned the same color, what color would you choose? Convince us of your choice.
- Convince us that a smart person is not necessarily wise.
- Decide which came first, the chicken or the egg and convince us that you're right.
- You are a shirt salesman and have to convince everyone to buy the shirt you're wearing.

- What are the three things your family should begin doing right now to be a happier family?
- Should sodas and candy be sold in vending machines at hospitals?

Advanced Persuasion

EXERCISE: A Change for the Better
Think of a time in your life when you've made a change or created a new habit that changed your life for the better. It may be something related to your social, physical, emotional, mental, or spiritual health. Write it in story form and then add paragraphs that explain how the experience changed you. Detail the steps you took to make the change and then list the benefits you've enjoyed as a result. Write with the purpose of persuading someone else to improve their lives by making the same positive change. Use logic, convincing points, and personal examples.

EXERCISE: Social Issue
People often write passionately about social issues because they believe that the success of our society hinges on enough people believing in the right things and doing things the right way. The problem is, there aren't always definitively right answers. We have to examine our beliefs and decide for ourselves what we think is right.

Consider this issue, examine your beliefs, and then write about it:

Some argue that children have greater chances for success and happiness when their mothers stay at home full time while others challenge that there is no negative impact on kids whose moms work outside the home.

What do you think? Write a five-paragraph essay that explains your beliefs and reasons.

EXERCISE: Legal Issue
One of the important rights of citizens is helping to create laws that benefit society. We select political representatives, vote, and voice our opinions on issues that are often legislated as a result. Many laws are born from peoples' opinions. When enough people in a society begin to believe a certain way collectively, those mores eventually become laws.

Recently, more and more governments have made laws prohibiting drivers from using cell phones while driving a

☐ **Mini-Lesson**

When you are writing any type of persuasive essay, there are steps you will take within the writing process.

Prewriting:
- Choose a topic and decide on your viewpoint.
- Write your claim or thesis.
- Brainstorm at least three strong reasons to support your claim.
- Identify a counterclaim if needed.

Drafting:
- Craft an introduction that begins with a hook, briefly introduces your reasons, and ends with a thesis statement or claim.
- Write three paragraphs with strong topic sentences, persuasive language, and concluding sentences.
- Create a conclusion paragraph that summarizes your claim and ends with a call to action.

Revising:
- Add more details, examples, persuasive language, and authoritative wording.
- Delete or improve ineffective words and sentences.
- Move sentences around, beginning and ending with your strongest reasons.

Editing
- Check your spelling, grammar, and formatting.

Publish
- Prepare a finished version.
- Share it!

Discuss this issue: Should we have pizza for dinner? Have everyone write three arguments to support their opinion - each one on its own note card. Practice putting them in a persuasive order. The strongest arguments should be first and last. If you place the very strongest argument at the end, it can often erase any doubts your reader may have.

Read the arguments in order together and have everyone give their opinion on whether or not the presenter had strong arguments and placed them in the proper order.

Try this prewriting activity for a problem-solution essay: Carpooling, recycling, and planting trees are all activities that are good for the environment. Draw a quick sketch of the earth with the outlines of all seven continents on it. On each continent, write down one tiny thing that you can personally do for our planet. Think of something beyond the standard answers. Everyone on this earth is quick to point out problems, but very few people actually come up with real solutions. We often search for single solutions to a problem, but more often than not, problems are solved when a number of solutions are all implemented together.

vehicle. Often this includes texting, talking on the phone, and using it to navigate. Do you agree or disagree with these laws? Are they too harsh or are they a benefit to drivers and passengers? Argue your point of view using facts, persuasive claims, and the rhetorical triangle of arguments.

EXERCISE: Satirical Essay

Some writers use satire to make a point. Satire is using humor, irony, or exaggeration to demonstrate shortcomings in people's thought patterns. For example, I once wrote a persuasive essay about how to end world hunger entitled, "Cannibalism: A Sure Solution." My satirical solution to world hunger was promoting cannibalism. After all, if people were cannibals, they would not only curb starvation with an abundant food source, but there would be fewer mouths to feed. Obviously, I don't actually believe in cannibalism nor would I promote it as a virtuous solution to overpopulation and hunger. The essay was actually making the point that there is no single, simple solution to these complex problems and that those who were promoting singular solutions could never solve complex problems.

Choose an enormous problem like crime, hunger, drugs, overpopulation, or war. Write a satirical and oversimplified solution to the problem. In the end, make a valid point about the complex nature of the problem you discussed.

EXERCISE: Problem-Solution Essay

You'll need the "Common Formats for Problem-Solution Essays" printable from the Printable Pack for this exercise. Look over the printable and compare the formats shown. This is just a sample of the possibilities. Unlike a basic five-paragraph essay, there is not one right way to organize a problem-solution essay. Look at the information you want to present and construct an outline that will show each of your paragraphs and what you intend to say within each one.

The format of a problem-solution essay depends largely on the problem you are solving and the solutions you are proposing. If there is one clear problem and one proposed solution, you will choose a different format than if you are describing a complex problem with several potential solutions. Choose your format after you have brainstormed the problems and solutions you plan to discuss. There is not one right way to do it, so choose the number and function for the paragraphs that fits your message.

In a problem-solution essay you will examine a problem and then propose a solution. Think of a real-world problem like school shootings, discrimination, pollution, overpopulation,

suicide, drugs, child labor, endangered animals, social media addiction, obesity, stress, bullying, or any other problem you are aware of. Research your topic. Choose at least one specific problem within your topic to address. For example, if you researched discrimination, you may choose to write about pregnant women being discriminated against in the workplace. On the other hand, you may choose to highlight a number of different groups of people that face discrimination. You will describe the problem and then propose solutions that will help solve the problem.

EXERCISE: Opinion Paper

You'll need the four-page "Opinion Paper Packet" printable from the Printable Pack for this exercise. An opinion paper is unique among essays because you are encouraged to write from your own perspective and use personal pronouns. It's perfectly okay to say, "I believe anyone who wants to own a firearm should be required to take firearm safety classes before purchasing one." It is acceptable to use "I," "my," and other personal language when you are writing about your own opinion.

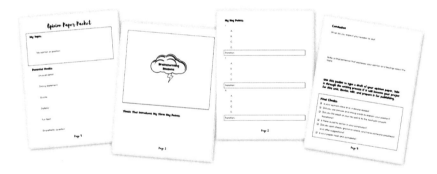

First, your task is to think of something that you have an opinion about. Write your topic as well as your specific opinion about the topic in the box on the first sheet of your packet. The more you write in complete sentences in the packet, the easier it will become to draft your opinion paper later.

Use the bottom of the first page to come up with some potential hooks you could use at the beginning of your opinion paper. Put a star by the strongest one that you intend to use.

Next, ask yourself why you feel the way you do about your topic. Brainstorm your reasons in the box on the second page of the packet. Look over your reasons and make some notes. You may circle the strongest three, draw a line that connects two that could be combined, draw a question mark next to something you need to spend a little time researching, or even cross some out if you don't find

☐ Mini-Lesson

As you practice persuasion, remember that just because you have an opinion about something, you aren't necessarily right. It can be enlightening to see things from other perspectives.

Write down an argument and three reasons why prayer should be allowed in schools.

Once you're finished, write down an argument and three reasons why prayer should not be allowed in schools.

As you learn to look at issues fully from more than one perspective, you will automatically become more informed and thoughtful. You may still keep the opinion you began with, but you will have increased the level of thoughtful communication you can engage in.

☐ Mini-Lesson

Read these sentences and then write another sentence on your own that uses the same punctuation marks.

We had to postpone the game; rain dumped on us and destroyed the fields.

Gamers spend too much time in front of screens: televisions, computers, and phones.

I bought macaroni and cheese; two large, ripe bananas; and a can of lemonade for my yellow-themed meal.

The beach is beautiful— wish you were here!

It was Juliet who asked: "What's in a name?"

them convincing. The strongest three will be become your key points.

At the bottom of page two, compose a thesis statement that tells your opinion and briefly mentions the three key points you will be using to back up your opinion.

On page three of the packet, write each of your key points in complete sentences. Use the letters below to make notes about facts, statistics, quotes, examples, or other evidence you can use to explain each key point. Write transition sentences in the boxes between each key point that lead from each point to the next.

Finally, on the fourth page of the packet, make notes about your conclusion and how you can sum up your main points in a new way. You might also include a call to action if it is appropriate to your opinion.

Use the packet to help you draft an opinion paper. Type the paper using your packet as an outline of ideas to guide you. If you decide to take this through the writing process the rest of the way, revise your paper, have someone help you edit it, and make sure it is properly formatted and uses correct conventions for publishing.

EXERCISE: Persuasive Essay

Remember, persuasive writing is like fishing. You have to hook your reader, then reel him or her in steadily with your arguments, and finally pull the reader right into the boat with you, hopefully sharing your viewpoint by the end.

To write a persuasive essay, you need to decide on a topic you have an opinion about. You will be convincing your readers of your opinion, so make it something you care about. Use the "Persuasive Writing Idea Bank" from the Printable Pack or the end of this unit to help you decide on a topic if you don't already have one in mind.

There are three basic parts to persuasive writing:

1. An introduction with a great hook, some background information, and a clear thesis.

2. A body, usually three or four paragraphs, that includes your arguments written using persuasive language. Each body paragraph will highlight one of your arguments. Every single one should tie directly back to your thesis.

Your opinions are valuable, but if you can add facts, statistics, anecdotes, and examples you will be even more likely to convince your reader. Typically, the strongest arguments are placed first and last, with the weaker arguments residing in the middle. Between each paragraph you will include transitions that lead from one argument to the next.

3. A conclusion that restates your arguments clearly, brings home your point, and encourages your reader to do something about it. This is called the call to action, and it's often the final sentence in your persuasive essay. Ask your readers to join you in your point of view. They are now in the same boat as you.

Use the "Persuasive Essay Checklist" from the Printable Pack to guide you as you begin writing.

EXERCISE: Argumentative Essay

An argumentative essay is very similar to a persuasive essay. You will create an argument and give reasons that back up the argument you are making. Each reason will reside in its own paragraph with transition words that link the paragraphs together. You will include evidence, facts, data, and persuasive language, just as in all the persuasive writing you do.

There are just two additional parts you will add to make it argumentative - a counterclaim and a rebuttal. A counterclaim is your explanation of what people who don't agree with you would say. There are at least two sides to every argument and you are presenting both sides.

Argument: A traffic light needs to be installed at the intersection of Main St. and Sullivan to help the flow of traffic, aid pedestrians in crossing, and minimize accidents.

Counterclaim: Some might argue that signal installation is costly and unnecessary given the small population of Centerville.

Rebuttal: However, the cost of a signal can never outweigh the cost of human lives. Furthermore, the rapid rate of population growth in Centerville demands improvement in our roadways, and it's better to prepare now than to be overwhelmed by crippling problems of rapid population increases.

Choose an issue you want to convince someone of. It could be a personal issue, like why you should have a car; a local issue, like why a new recreation center is needed in your town; or even a national or global issue, like pushing for a prestigious Nobel-like prize to be awarded to innovative

☐ Mini-Lesson

The types of topics between persuasive and argumentative essays are the same. The only difference between the two is that in argumentative essays you include a paragraph that explains the counterclaim and your rebuttal.

☐ Mini-Lesson

As you are in the editing stage of the writing process, make sure to check for capitalization, punctuation, spelling, indenting paragraphs, using transitions between paragraphs, proper page formatting and page numbers, and correct font style and size. Add a title if you haven't already.

Also, make sure your essay includes a heading with your name, the date, the assignment. Editing is a time to check for conventions.

☐ Mini-Lesson

Pronouns take the place of nouns. Change each bold word below into a pronoun.

*Mrs. Simmons did not like pigs. When **Mrs. Simmons'** neighbor, Mrs. Miegs, brought home six piglets **Mrs. Simmons** was angry. Pigs were smelly. **Pigs** were dirty animals and **Mrs. Simmons** was determined to rid the neighborhood of **pigs**. **Mrs. Simmons** put up signs, sent out fliers, and begged the neighbors to get rid of **the pigs** or get rid of Mrs. Miegs!*

Mini-Lesson

Read the "Sample Persuasive Essay" from the Printable Pack.

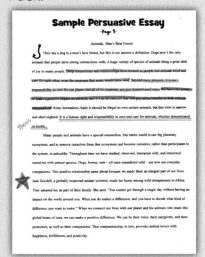

Highlight the fourth, fifth, and sixth sentences within the introduction, each with a different color.

Read the body paragraphs and put a star in the coordinating color by each paragraph that matches the topic of that sentence from the introduction.

Draw a hook by the first sentence and then underline the thesis statement.

As you read, feel free to make notes about other persuasive techniques you notice.

Re-read the introduction and conclusion, noting how they have the same message with different wording.

Now that you have read the sample essay, come up with a rebuttal. Do you believe that people should be allowed to own any animals they want to or should that be regulated? What reasons could you give in response to support laws that limit what pets people can own?

inventors. You can also use the Persuasive Essays Idea Bank for ideas. Use the "Argumentative Essay Planner" from the Printable Pack to organize your thoughts.

Step 3: Writing Project

During this unit, you should complete at least one writing project, taking a piece of writing through the entire writing process. By the final week of the unit, if you haven't completed the project already, you should turn your attention to creating one polished piece of writing that uses the things you've practiced along the way.

Choose one topic to write about that you will take all of the way through the writing process. This piece of writing belongs in the Writing section of your Writer's Notebook. You can use something you've already started during this unit, your own idea, or something from the following idea banks. Make sure that you follow each step of the writing process and keep all of your steps to turn in with your finished writing.

- Step #1: Prewrite
- Step #2: Draft
- Step #3: Revise
- Step #4: Edit
- Step #5: Publish

Begin with a prewriting activity, then compose a draft, revise it, edit it with help from someone else, and then publish it. Publishing it could include making a polished final copy, sharing it with someone, creating a book, or creating some form of finished project that is neat and done well. You'll turn in all of your work, from prewrite to publish.

Your project will be evaluated based on the six traits of writing, so make sure you look at your composition through each of those lenses - ideas and content, organization, word choice, sentence fluency, conventions, and voice. Try to incorporate things you learned from the mini-lessons and the exercises you worked on as well. Do your best work.

Persuasive Writing Idea Bank

- Is it better to live in the country or city?
- What book should everyone read?
- Would you want to be able to live forever if you could?
- Should every child be given their own computer for school?
- What should be done about bullying?
- Is there a limit to how much television kids should be able to watch?

Persuasive Writing

- Is it ever okay to lie?
- What should happen to people who litter?
- What would you improve your neighborhood or city?
- What makes a good friend?
- Should children be given an allowance? If so, should it be earned or based on behavior, or should it just be automatic in order to teach kids how to handle money and be responsible?
- At what age should teens be able to get a driver's license and have the responsibility of being allowed to drive?
- Choose a specific health habit to promote and persuade your reader to adopt. It could be physical, emotional, or mental.
- Should everyone have a garden to grow food?
- Should daily exercise be a requirement?
- What is the perfect playground?
- How many sweets should people eat?
- What should your bedtime be?
- What is the best flavor of donut (or fill in another treat)?
- Should animals be allowed in stores, schools, libraries, and other businesses?
- What is the best way to celebrate a birthday?
- What is the best part of the day - morning, afternoon, evening, or nighttime?
- What magic power would you have if you could choose? Convince me I should want the same one.
- Should we devote time and money to building a space station on the moon or Mars?
- Which character from a book would you most like to meet and why?
- Which would you rather read: A funny book that makes you laugh or a mystery novel that is really scary and suspenseful?
- Who is the person from history that you would most like to meet and talk to? Why? What would you like to ask?
- What is the best book you have ever read? Why did you like it? Did reading the book change you in any way? What way?
- What law would you like to see enacted which would help people? How would it help?
- What current fashion in clothing do you particularly like or dislike? Explain.
- Convince someone why music or art or computers are important in your life. Make them appreciate your viewpoint.
- Imagine you have the task of telling a person from a distant planet or from another era what pollution is. Make that person understand what causes it and what you believe should be done about it.
- Do you think girls are raised differently from boys? If so,

---

☐ **Mini-Lesson**

Verbs tell what a person, place, or thing does. Brainstorm fifty action verbs on a sheet of paper.

☐ **Mini-Lesson**

Present tense verbs tell about something happening now. Past tense verbs tell about something that already happened. Future tense verbs tell about something that will happen.

Write some sentences that tell about yesterday, today, and tomorrow and include all three tenses of verbs. Mark which verbs are past, which are present, and which are future.

*Yesterday I **jogged** three miles.* **(past)**

*Today I am **swimming** down at the beach.* **(present)**

*Tomorrow I **will cook** dinner for my family.* **(future)**

☐ **Mini-Lesson**

Persuasive writing should be confident but not aggressive in tone. You won't win people over by sounding angry or judgmental.

Always be kind. The world is changed by your example more than your opinion.

Reminders About Your Writer's Notebook

Besides just the writing project, there should be many small writing samples that are being compiled in the Writer's Notebook from the exercises you worked on over the course of this unit. The Writer's Notebook is a tool for helping writers to grow. Explore it frequently and refer to idea lists and helps as you write.

At least once a week, it would be beneficial for you, the writer, to glance back through the exercises, lists, and mini-lessons to review and make sure that you are on track even though most of this work isn't graded.

Specifically, as you are working on the writing project, utilize your Writer's Notebook. You have anchor charts, exercises, and entries in your Journal - all of these can help you as you complete your project. Take time to review some of the concepts you've been working on during the unit so they can be incorporated into the final writing project. The things you've learned should SHOW in your writing project.

Remember that most of the work in the Writer's Notebook will never be graded, but it is still important. Use what you learned to make your project, which will be graded, the best that you can make it.

in what ways? Do you think you are treated differently because you are a boy or girl?

- Do you think men and women are equal in today's society? Why or why not? Do men or women have it easier in our culture? If so, why do you think so?
- Do you think women should take men's last names when they marry? Why or why not?
- Write about the pros/cons of year-round school or a four-day school week.
- Who should be paid more, professional athletes or teachers?
- The saying goes, "Money cannot buy happiness." Do you agree or disagree? Why?
- What do you think about gambling? Vandalism? Drugs? Smoking? Alcohol? Choose one of these topics and write an opinion paper about it.
- What is your opinion on studying history? Is it valuable or a waste of time?
- In this technological era, can you foresee a time when paper and pencils and books will become obsolete?
- Is graffiti vandalism or street art? Detail your position on this issue and why you believe the way you do.
- Do you believe there is life on other planets?
- What makes a better leader - someone who is loved or someone who is feared?
- Should all students be required to learn a foreign language?
- Does technology distract us too much?
- Should kids have cell phones?
- What do you think about doctor's offices giving out candy?
- Should there be bike and walking paths along all streets?
- Many parents give their children certain chores or tasks to do at home. Should children have to do chores?
- Famous people sometimes get the privilege of having their picture put on a postage stamp. Who, living or dead, do you think deserves to have a portrait on a postage stamp?
- Do you believe television violence has a negative effect on society?
- Medical researchers, cosmetic companies, and others often perform experiments on animals. Many people feel that experimentation on animals is wrong and should be stopped immediately. What do you think?
- Since the cloning of the sheep, Dolly, there has been much debate over whether or not human beings should be cloned. What do you think?
- Does online and long-distance communication hinder our ability to develop in person communication skills or allow us to be even better communicators with more opportunities to build relationships and stay in touch?
- Lots of farmers plant genetically modified crops to decrease diseases, improve flavor, and increase

production. Do you think genetically modifying food is a good idea?

- Many cities suffer from serious air and noise pollution and overcrowded streets. Some people feel that cities with extensive public transportation systems should ban passenger cars and require people to walk, bike, or use public transportation. What do you think?
- The internet includes many websites with images and content that are dangerous or inappropriate. Should websites like these be censored? Why or why not?
- Today's top professional athletes often have salaries and bonuses in the tens of millions of dollars. Do you think these athletes deserve such high compensation?
- Many parents do not allow their children to play with toy guns. In your opinion, is this a wise decision?
- Many science fiction stories deal with the possibility of being able to "design" our children by choosing the specific physical and personality traits we would like them to have. Do you think this is a good idea?

Step 4: Evaluating Writing

The purpose of this unit is to learn to write persuasively and be convincing. You will be using facts, opinions, evidence, and persuasive language and techniques.

As you evaluate the writing project, you will be using the "6 Traits of Writing Rubric" from the Printable Pack. In addition, you will be looking for each step of the entire writing process. For example, your child will turn in a prewriting activity, a draft that shows both revisions and edits, as well as a finished, published piece. The publishing step should involve sharing the project in some way - reading it aloud to family, presenting it at dinner time, video chatting to show it off to grandparents, or sharing a video presentation on the internet of the writer sharing his or her writing. Sharing is a time for positive feedback and celebration.

Creating a positive buzz about the published piece will create a motivating, growth atmosphere in your Writer's Workshop. As you evaluate, remember that the process is just as important as the product, so watch for successes in the process as well. The final score will be out of 50 points - 20 for the process and 30 for the final project. You can write rubric scores as well as comments down on the "Writing Report Card" printable from the Printable Pack.

Breakdown of Possible Points

- 5 points for a complete prewriting activity
- 5 points for a completed draft
- 5 points for revisions
- 5 points for edits
- 30 points for the finished writing project

The 30 points for the finished project is further broken down into each of the six traits of writing as shown on the rubric from the Printable Pack.

6 Traits of Writing Rubric — Persuasive Writing

Your comments should be specifically focused on the purposes of this unit and the skills you were working on throughout the unit.

What was done well? Is the writer understanding the writing process? What should be improved on? Are there any repeated mistakes to address?

Point out a clear strength.

Comments mean more than scores, so make sure to give clear feedback.

Mini-Lesson Index

We recommend teaching grammar and writing skills daily, utilizing one short lesson each day. Within the sidebars of each Writer's Workshop unit you will find a variety of mini-lesson ideas. Many of the mini-lessons apply to the focus genre of the unit, but the grammar, punctuation, Writer's Workshop procedures, six traits of writing, literary devices, and writing skills lessons that can be applied to any unit are indexed topically here.

At the beginning of each unit there is a sidebar list with "More Mini-Lessons Ideas" including:

- Writer's Workshop links found in the Layers of Learning catalog
- Lessons from any grammar workbook
- Every-Day Edits from Education World website
- Sentence diagramming
- Copying great sentences from master writers
- Mad Libs
- Correcting a repeated error from your writing
- Practicing expanding sentences by adding details
- Combining sentences by making two or three into a single sentence

In addition to the mini-lessons found within units, you may supplement with any grammar workbook or spine, especially if you don't feel confident teaching grammar concepts yourself. We recommend choosing from these spine books to accompany Writer's Workshop if you want an extra teaching resource for grammar:

- *Spectrum Language Arts Workbooks.* These are straightforward workbooks that are available across the grade levels. You can either purchase one for each child or you can teach the concepts from within the workbook and then ask your kids of all ages to craft sentences that demonstrate the concept they learned from the mini-lesson. Often crafting their own sentences instead of merely filling out a workbook helps kids to internalize the lesson.
- *Help Your Kids With Language Arts: A Step-By-Step Visual Guide to Grammar, Punctuation, and Writing* by DK Publishers. This guide walks you through the basics of writing and grammar. We recommend that you read a snippet from the book with your kids and then ask them to write sentences that showcase the skill you read together as a mini-lesson as needed.
- *A Sentence a Day* by Samantha Prust. This small guide gives you a sentence each day that includes errors. You will spot and correct the errors. This is similar to the *Everyday-Edits* passages that are recommended as a regular mini-lesson within the units. If you would prefer a printed guide rather than retrieving sentences from the online source, this simple book is a good resource.
- *Grammar and Composition Handbook, Grade 7*, part of the Glencoe Language Arts series. There are a variety of grade levels, but the 7th grade version is a terrific one for utilizing with your whole family if you have several ages of kids and are all doing mini-lessons together as a family. It is adaptable to younger kids but can provide the skills needed up through high school as well. It includes a complete grammar and punctuation course and includes exercises. The writing mentor can guide the lesson out loud and then lead kids in the provided exercises.

Genre Skills

You will find mini-lessons within each Writer's Workshop unit that teach genre skills within the unit. As you progress through each day, the mini-lessons will take you on a step-by-step journey for improving your skills as a writer and teaching you specific skills for the unit's genre. For example, both the *Fanciful Stories* and *True Stories* units include mini-lessons about plot, characters, and setting. You will learn about proper greetings for friendly letters within the Letters unit. Reports and Essays includes mini-lessons about introductions, conclusions, sources, and bibliographies. Look for genre-specific mini-lessons within each corresponding unit.

Grammar

Parts of Speech	15, 21, 26, 64, 65, 85, 126, 136
Nouns	13, 21, 26, 65, 85, 93, 107, 157, 174, 206, 265
Proper Nouns	27, 97, 141, 157, 194, 226, 228, 229, 230, 233, 242, 247, 259
Plural & Collective Nouns	26, 85, 93, 100, 206
Verbs	13, 21, 29, 65, 67, 70, 73, 80, 85, 94, 96, 99, 174, 185, 187, 188, 200, 264, 265, 275
Verb Tenses	94, 96, 161, 186, 199, 246, 275
Pronouns	9, 13, 21, 85, 153, 157, 160, 164, 204, 206, 259, 273
Adjectives & Adjective Modifiers	13, 21, 41, 63, 65, 66, 68, 69, 73, 75, 77, 78, 79, 81, 82, 84, 85, 138, 165, 264, 265, 266
Adverbs & Adverb Modifiers	14, 21, 29, 63, 65, 68, 73, 77, 78, 79, 80, 81, 82, 84, 85, 147, 265
Prepositions	14, 21, 46, 77, 85
Conjunctions	14, 43, 168, 184
Interjections	28, 110
Articles & Determiners	20, 21, 85
Sentences & Fragments	11, 21, 23, 26, 33, 34, 35, 36, 37, 38, 39, 40, 41, 42, 43, 44, 45, 47, 51, 56, 57, 85, 157, 168, 177, 219, 246, 268
Clauses	33, 34, 35, 48, 168, 184, 268
Capitalizing Letters	11, 27, 35, 45, 47, 57, 97, 157, 194, 226, 227, 233, 246, 247
Sentence Order/Subject-Verb-Object Order	35, 45, 85
Subjects & Predicates	33, 34, 36, 219
Sentence Combining or Expanding	29, 42, 43, 48, 66, 72
Compound Sentences	11, 29, 43, 44, 168
Paragraphs	49, 50, 51, 57, 101, 271

Punctuation

End Marks	38, 45, 239, 268, 272
Periods	79, 83, 102, 189, 202, 246, 268, 272
Ellipses	56
Exclamation Points	28, 38, 102, 110, 118, 239
Question Marks	28, 40, 102, 167
Colons & Semi-colons	47, 168, 252, 268, 272
Commas	48, 66, 79, 80, 86, 102, 110, 115, 166, 167, 184, 228, 229, 252, 272
Parenthesis	29, 263
Apostrophes & Contractions	10, 69, 176, 211, 238, 239, 243
Hyphens & Dashes	174, 175, 263, 272
Quotation Marks & Dialogue	76, 101, 102, 103, 163, 197, 272
Bullets	254, 272
Numbers, Days, and Dates	81, 203, 224, 226

Writer's Workshop Procedures

Writer's Notebooks	8, 9, 30, 72, 75, 99, 218
The Writing Process	16, 20, 28, 72, 106, 269
Prewriting	7, 9, 16, 17, 41, 47, 50, 81, 96, 105, 125, 135, 167, 185, 190, 193, 251, 254, 256, 269, 270
Drafting	17, 18, 50, 113, 172, 256, 269
Revising	18, 22, 57, 95, 105, 112, 113, 116, 118, 149, 172, 175, 178, 204, 213, 216, 236, 246, 269
Editing	19, 28, 57, 102, 113, 116, 118, 145, 149, 178, 230, 236, 246, 269, 273
Publishing	19, 21, 22, 51, 53, 81, 83, 106, 114, 116, 118, 119, 178, 179, 269

The Six Traits of Writing

Ideas & Content	22, 53, 87, 153, 219, 253
Organization	22, 23, 51, 52, 87, 105, 144, 164, 170, 196, 208, 210, 217, 256, 266
Word Choice	23, 61, 62, 63, 65, 87, 99, 102, 103, 116, 127, 162, 165, 201, 215, 230, 253, 259
Sentence Fluency	23, 41, 45, 72, 87, 114, 116, 166, 209, 266
Conventions	24, 28, 57, 87, 236, 273
Voice	25, 87, 145, 156, 171, 201, 217, 225, 226

Literary Devices

Descriptive, Figurative, Emotional, or Sensory Language	65, 66, 73, 81, 99, 138, 146, 158, 159, 267
Synonyms & Antonyms	65, 97, 139
Puns, Homonyms, & Homophones	71, 143, 224
Metaphors & Similes	71, 73, 130, 131, 132, 134, 175, 198, 267
Alliteration, Assonance, Consonance, & Repetition	71, 73, 113, 133, 134, 146, 169, 175, 267
Onomatopoeia & Sound Effects	11, 71, 76, 134, 135, 136
Personification & Anthropomorphism	71, 74, 110, 175, 198, 267
Cliché	234, 238
Euphemism	165
Hyperbole	71
Oxymoron	71
Anaphora	71
Irony	71
Idiom	71, 175
Allusion	71, 73, 77, 218
Sarcasm	71
Understatement	71, 175
Imagery	71, 130, 131
Rhyme, Rhyme Scheme, & Rhythm	128, 129, 134, 140
Synecdoche & Metonymy	71

More Writing Skills

Word Economy & Precise Language	62, 114, 141, 201, 230
Symbolism	100, 108, 137
Passive vs. Active Voice	67, 115
Parallel Structure	202, 219
Dictionary, Thesaurus, & Alphabetical Order	12, 23, 62, 64, 65, 125, 135, 137, 139, 188, 215, 242
Formal vs. Informal; Colloquialisms & Slang	12, 103, 163, 176, 177, 205, 211, 217, 238, 239, 242
Fiction vs. Nonfiction	91, 154, 155
Fact vs. Opinion	155, 160, 252
Overused or Commonly Misused Words	63, 66, 67, 74, 83, 114, 161, 169, 192, 204, 224, 233, 235, 255, 265
Compound Words	234
Theme	106, 107
Mood & Tone	130, 226, 238, 240, 257
Point of View	92, 145, 158, 163, 166, 170, 176, 213
Comparing & Contrasting	55, 214
Transitions	51, 80, 109, 217, 266, 271
Abbreviations and Acronyms	79, 83, 202, 226, 229, 231, 232, 242
Standard Fonts, Sizes, Margins, & Spacing; Italics, Underlining	49, 56, 57, 111, 129, 207
Plagiarism; Crediting Sources	176, 190, 216, 218

About the Authors

Michelle and Karen are sisters from Idaho, USA. They grew up playing in the woods and on the lakes of the northern Rockies. Karen is married with four children, two boys and two girls. Michelle is married with six kids, all boys.

Michelle has a BS in biology and Karen has a BA in early childhood education. Since the early 2000s they have been homeschooling their kids and taking them to the lake as often as possible.

In 2008 at a family get together (at the lake of course) they were opining about all the things they wished they could have in a homeschool curriculum. Their mom suggested they write their own curriculum. They looked at each other in doubt, then thought "why not?" And Layers of Learning was born. Thanks, Mom.

Visit **www.Layers-of-Learning.com** for more family-style curriculum, planners, and resources to add to every unit.